THE UNAPPEASABLE HOST
STUDIES IN IRISH IDENTITIES

Robert Tracy, Professor of English and Celtic Studies at the University of California, Berkeley, has been a distinguished literary critic in the field of Irish Studies for four decades. His interests in comparative literature extend also to Russian writing, and he has translated poems of Osip Mandelstam into English. He has been based at the University of California at Berkeley since 1960 and has held visiting appointments at Leeds University, Trinity College Dublin, and Wellesley College, Massachusetts.

THE UNAPPEASABLE HOST

Studies in Irish Identities

ROBERT TRACY

University College Dublin Press
Preas Choláiste Ollscoile Bhaile Átha Cliath

U.S. DISTRIBUTOR
DUFOUR EDITIONS
CHESTER SPRINGS
PA 19425-0007
(610) 458-5005

First published 1998 by University College Dublin Press,
Newman House, St Stephen's Green, Dublin 2, Ireland

© Robert Tracy 1998
ISBN 1 900621 06 1 (hardback)
1 900621 07 X (paperback)

Cataloguing in Publication data available from the British Library

Typeset in Ireland in 10/12 Plantin by
Seton Music Graphics, Bantry, Co. Cork
Printed in Ireland by Betaprint, Dublin

Contents

Acknowledgements

For many good talks about Irish matters over many years, and/or for kind
invitations to lecture that evoked some of this book's content, I am indebted
to those named in the dedication, and also to Stephen Arkin, Angela
Bourke, Terence Brown, Adele Dalsimer, Seamus Deane, John Dillon,
Joris Duytschaever, Audrey Eyler, Richard Finneran, Mary Fitzgerald,
Thomas Flanagan, Robert F. Garratt, Luke Gibbons, Nicholas Grene,
Seamus Heaney, Dillon Johnston, Richard Kearney, Joan Trodden Keefe,
Brendan Kennelly, Declan Kiberd, Benedict Kiely, Hermione Lee, David
Lloyd, Edna and Michael Longley, W.J. McCormack, Brenda Maddox,
Maureen Murphy, David Norris, the late Brendan O Hehir, the late
Thomas Parkinson, Thomas Dillon Redshaw, Anthony Roche, Ronald
Schuchard, Patrick Sheeran, and my son, Dominick O'Donovan Tracy.
I also wish to express my thanks to the many editors and publishers who
have allowed me to reprint previously published material. My greatest debt,
as always, is to my wife, Rebecca Garrison Tracy, shrewd critic and heart-
ening companion on all Irish forays, including those only of the imagination.

Note

I have left these items as they were originally published or delivered, except
that I have occasionally excised repetitious material—for example, a plot
summary of *Castle Rackrent* in my discussion of Maria Edgeworth and
Lady Morgan. In some cases I have revised citations so that they now refer
to generally accessible texts, and revised a few passages that no longer seem
precise or accurate.

IN MEMORY OF
AUGUSTINE 'GUS' MARTIN
WHO SUGGESTED THIS BOOK
AND OF
EILÍS DILLON
VIVIAN MERCIER
AND
SEAN WHITE
THE READERS I IMAGINED

The whole power and property of [Ireland] has been conferred by successive monarchs of England upon an English colony, composed of three sets of English adventurers who poured into this country at the termination of three successive rebellions. Confiscation is their common title; and from their first settlement they have been hemmed in on every side by the old inhabitants of the island, brooding over their discontents in sullen indignation.

John Fitzgibbon, Earl of Clare, urging adoption of the Act of Union,
10 February 1800

Oh ye fair hills of holy Ireland, who dares sustain the strangled calumny that you are not the land of our love? . . . Who is he who ventures to stand between us and your Catholic sons' good-will? . . . We will not suffer two of the finest races of men in the world, the Catholic and Protestant, or the Milesian and Anglo-Irish, to be duped into mutual hatred . . .

Samuel Ferguson, *Dublin University Magazine*, April 1834

I know how barren one side of my life would have been without that poetry of the soil, those words and dreams and cadences of the people that helped me to give some echoed expression to that dragging driving force.

Lady Gregory, *Seventy Years*

Introduction

I

I have borrowed the title of this book from Yeats's early poem about the *sidhe*, that race of mysterious beings traditionally believed to share Ireland with its human inhabitants. The *sidhe*, 'people of the mounds', were menacing because sometimes they enticed children, or young men and women away to their dwelling places underground, in ancient burial mounds. At the same time they were fascinating, attractive. Their underground dwellings were spacious, luxurious, and splendidly illuminated, in contrast to the dark and narrow confines of a peasant cottage. They were handsome, and beautifully dressed. Soulless or pagan, they could never enter Heaven. It was best not to talk of them or their doings, but if they had to be mentioned, they were called 'the good people' or 'the gentry'. In the folk mind they seem to have been a kind of synthesis of the ancient dead and the Anglo-Irish gentry, combining an awareness that the mounds were burial mounds with awed glimpses of the 'Big House' and its splendours, and perhaps memories of women coaxed away to share the master's bed. They represent a view of the Anglo-Irish as irredeemably 'other', a notion Yeats seems to touch on in a preliminary draft of 'Sailing to Byzantium': 'Others, that as the mountain people say/Are in their hunting and their gallantries/Under the hills as in our fathers' day' (Bradford 160, 103).

Elsewhere in his writings, Yeats imagines the unhyphenated Irish as a fascinated but critical audience, avidly watching and judging their Anglo-Irish masters, who respond by acting out 'a play that had for spectators men and women that loved the high wasteful virtues' (*Explorations* 27). Maria Edgeworth's Thady Quirk is an eager audience for his Rackrent masters' extravagant behaviour, urging them on to greater follies. At the same time, he too is playing the role of the amusing but ever faithful servant. Lois, the Anglo-Irish protagonist in Elizabeth Bowen's *The Last September* (1929), thinks of herself as 'rather theatrical', creating a version of carefree impulsive youth; 'She had never refused a role' (*Last September* 35). Bowen notes the mutual role-playing of Irish and Anglo-Irish, each offering the other a version likely to be approved:

> the gentry became more dashing, the lower classes more comic . . . while there is a gallery, we must play to it (*Bowen's Court* 263–4).

I see the Irish as the unappeasable host, resenting the comic role they have accepted as protective colouration, resenting also their prescribed role as admiring audience, and nursing those resentments in secret even as they played their roles. The burning of so many Big Houses in 1919–21 put an end to an already discredited myth, that the Irish loved and admired their Anglo-Irish masters, and felt towards them a feudal loyalty.

The Anglo-Irish varied in their attitudes towards Ireland and the Irish. But, as Yeats pointed out in a 1925 Senate speech, the Anglo-Irish—the Protestant minority—were the source 'of the best of [Ireland's] political intelligence' and 'most of the modern literature of this country' (*Senate Speeches* 99). Parnell amply justifies the first claim, Maria Edgeworth, Samuel Ferguson, Standish O'Grady, Sheridan Le Fanu, Douglas Hyde, Augusta Gregory, John Synge, and Yeats himself the second. They also present an unusual situation, in which a country's major modern writers were members of a minority, separated from the majority of the population by religion, ancestry, and usually by class and education. If they wrote about their own class they were sometimes seen as solipsistic; if they wrote about the Irish they were often seen as patronizing and exploitative. Their right to consider themselves Irish writers has been challenged by some of their contemporaries and by more recent critics.

Accepted as Irish or not, Anglo-Irish writers were uniquely situated to depict Irish life. What Yeats called 'the Anglo-Irish solitude' (*Explorations* 325) imposed a valuable detachment. Their role as outsiders made Irish life at once familiar and fascinatingly other. Their tenacious claim to membership in the Irish community was a powerful commitment to entering Irish life emotionally and imaginatively. Yes, they often romanticized their own class, or simplified the complexities of Irish life. They often condescended. They often failed to *see*. But in their best work their position as outsiders made them acute observers. They made literature out of their sense of their own apartness. The detachment that a writer must have was their complex birthright, coupled with an often unsatisfied wish to feel themselves accepted, even loved. Literature, Yeats reminded us, is made 'out of the quarrel with ourselves'.

II

In July 1996 the International Association for the Study of Anglo-Irish Literature voted to re-name itself the International Association for the Study of Irish Literatures. The change recognized the inadequacy of the term

'Anglo-Irish Literature' as a catchall category for Irish literature written in English rather than in what the 1937 Constitution of Ireland calls 'the first official language'. In doing so, it also evaded those class and sectarian implications which have impeded scholars and critics, offering instead a non-gendered version of Wolfe Tone's 'common name of Irishman'.

In this book I am using the term 'Anglo-Irish' specifically to indicate members of the Protestant minority who wrote about Ireland from their ambiguous position as at once insiders and outsiders. The writers I discuss are all in fact Irish writers, as most critics have come to recognize. But as Anglo-Irish by class, ancestry, and religion, they were particularly interested in issues of identity and identification, inclusion and exclusion. In England they were considered Irish, in Ireland English. Maria Edgeworth becomes Thady Quirk to study her own class. The arguable Anglo-Irish family in Sheridan Le Fanu's *Carmilla* live in great isolation, and carefully preserve their English identity. Yeats broods over his separation from the Catholic schoolchildren in 'Among School Children'. Synge is an observant outsider on Inishmaan. Even Joyce, who was neither of English ancestry nor Protestant, imitates Anglo-Irish writers in focusing on those separated or excluded from the Irish life around them—the narrator in 'An Encounter', Mr Duffy in 'A Painful Case', Gabriel Conroy in 'The Dead', Stephen Dedalus and Leopold Bloom in *Ulysses*. Identities, whether present as a fear of miscegenation or as an anxiety about belonging, is for Anglo-Irish writers a major theme.

III

The essays and lectures in this book have been written over a period of some thirty years' interest in the peculiar tension I perceive in the Anglo-Irish writer's struggle to define his or her own identity. Irish-American myself, of unhyphenated Irish ancestry so far as I have been able to discover, I suspect that my continued preoccupation with issues of Irish identities has its origins in the similarities between Anglo-Irish and Irish-American ambiguities. Hyphens both unite and divide. 'Yanks' in Ireland, 'Irish' in America, Irish-Americans have traditionally pirouetted on that hyphen, at once proud and ashamed of their origin, eager like other immigrant groups to assimilate, a little unsure if they could. One moment they might be stagily 'Oirish', the next insistently American—especially if they happened to be visiting Ireland.

When I was growing up near Boston in the 1930s, Ireland was a constant but rarely acknowledged presence. Three of my grandparents had been born there, but they never talked about Ireland. My maternal grandparents were Irish speakers, but I never heard them speak Irish, nor did I know they could do so until they were long dead. Many emigrants from the Aran Islands, including one of Synge's Irish teachers, had settled in my home town, but they were seen as clannish and secretive by the rest of the Irish population. There was an instinctive, even deliberate distancing from an Irish identity, surviving from the fairly recent era when 'No Irish Need Apply' had often appeared in advertisements for employees. My aunts successfully concealed my grandmother's Irish birth on her death certificate, choosing New York as more respectable. Many Irish-Americans simultaneously came to consider themselves fully accepted as American and to value their Irish ancestry only after John Kennedy became President. Rich, Harvard-educated, sophisticated, he was a model of successful assimilation who paradoxically chose to emphasize his Irish background.

The tentative Irish identity of my childhood was therefore an unplanned and unconscious preparation for studying the ambiguities of Irish identities, with their role-playing, anxieties, and evasions. The essays collected here will indicate whether that preparation has served me well or badly.

IV

Oddly enough—or perhaps not—it was when I entered graduate school at Harvard in the early 1950s that I first found Ireland taken seriously. Harry Levin had written his early and still valuable study of Joyce, and bracketed him with Proust and Mann in a popular course. Jack Sweeney, Curator of the Poetry Room at Lamont Library, visited Ireland every summer, always returning with new books, recordings, and news of the latest literary developments there. His wife, Máire MacNeill, was at work on her magisterial *The Festival of Lughnasa* (1962). Though concerned relatives warned me that any calling of attention to myself by showing an interest in Irish matters might be undesirable, I enrolled in the only Irish literature class I have ever taken, John Kelleher's Yeats seminar. Kelleher recognized the individuality of Yeats and his importance as a modernist, but he also emphasized his place in an Irish literary tradition that stretched back more than a millennium, and included even earlier material, oral poetry from a heroic age.

At that time, Kelleher's attention to Yeats's biography, to Irish history, and to the legendary source material that underlay many of Yeats's plays and poems, seemed a little out of date to some. The New Criticism, with its exclusive focus on the text, was in the ascendancy. John Crowe Ransom had defined the critic's task as the study of literary technique, including a text's 'tropes, its fictions, or inventions, by which it secures "aesthetic distance" and removes itself from history . . .' (Ransom 347).

Irish literature, like Irish politics, never removes itself from history. We are not sure who Wordsworth's Lucy was, nor does her identity much matter; we are little the wiser in identifying an original for Arnold's Marguerite. But Yeats, for example, made the political identity and activities of Maud Gonne a central theme, intimately connected with contemporary cultural issues and with those tensions between artist and man of action that obsessed him, shaping both the life and the work. The career of Parnell is a sustained subtext in Joyce's work.

I was once told of a classroom discussion of 'An Irish Airman Foresees his Death' in the late 1960s, at a reputable college. The class decided that the lines 'Those that I fight I do not hate,/Those that I guard I do not love' indicated existential indifference and despair, because the instructor had failed to notice that the airman is Robert Gregory, flying a British plane against the Austrians on the Italian front during the First World War, and that his true allegiance is to Ireland rather than the British cause. The poem also reflects Yeats's anxiety about the government's plan to extend conscription to Ireland, forcing Irishmen to fight for Britain and 'the rights of small nations' after the 1916 Rising had been brutally suppressed. New Critical methods helped us in many ways to understand Yeats's work, but usually failed to address the political and social preoccupations shaping it.

Nevertheless, the study of Yeats in his time and place was already under way. Important studies by Richard Ellmann, who knew Ireland well, and A. Norman Jeffares, who shared Yeats's Anglo-Irish background, appeared at the end of the 1940s, soon to be followed by T.R. Henn's *The Lonely Tower* (1950) and Thomas Parkinson's *W.B. Yeats, Self-Critic* (1951). Hugh Kenner's *Dublin's Joyce* (1956) placed Joyce in context, to be crowned by Ellmann's monumental biography (1959)—the book I bought to celebrate completing my PhD. Also in 1959, Thomas Flanagan published *The Irish Novelists 1800–1850*, examining some of the writers who preceded and to some extent influenced the Irish Literary Movement of the 1890s. It was later my good fortune to have Parkinson and Flanagan as colleagues and friends.

The political, social, and intellectual ferment of the 1960s made context important again, so that Yeats and Joyce were recognized as *Irish* writers rather than unique phenomena or self-engendered modernists. The very eminence and complexity of Yeats, Joyce, and later Beckett, had deflected critical attention from their Irish preoccupations. Did Joyce create his own language in *Finnegans Wake*, for example? Did Beckett decide to write in French, in response to nationalist rhetoric about the need to free Ireland of the English language? Joyce had made the daily life of Dublin universal, but at the same time intensely local. When a small group of historians and literary scholars founded the American Committee (later Conference) for Irish Studies in 1962, their then unusual alliance made Irish Studies less exclusively literary, and anticipated, perhaps unconsciously, how political and cultural issues would come to affect so many academic disciplines in the 1960s. For Irish studies, such seminal books as William Irwin Thompson's *The Imagination of an Insurrection: Dublin, Easter 1916* (1967), and Malcolm Brown's *The Politics of Irish Literature* (1972) represent this combined approach.

Thompson described his book as 'not precisely a work of literary criticism, and not precisely a work of history, but a cultural study' (Thompson vii); Brown declared that 'Modern Ireland provides us with the classic case of an impressive literature brought to birth by politics' (Brown vii). During the 1960s, American literary scholars began to recognize racial, feminist, and colonialist issues, fuelled by controversy over the Vietnam War. In Ireland as in America, scholars of Irish literature brought new concerns and newly awakened sensibilities to their work, especially after the highly visible suppression of civil rights and beginnings of the troubles in Northern Ireland. Eavan Boland has eloquently described the kinds of quizzical non-acceptance a woman poet could encounter in 1960s Ireland. Theories of colonialism, neo-colonialism, and post-colonialism began to shape critical discourse about Irish writing, especially as similar themes were discerned in the work of the poets who emerged in the sixties: Richard Murphy, John Montague, Derek Mahon, Seamus Heaney, to name only the most prominent.

Ireland and Irish life began to change drastically in the 1960s, as the first generation of national leaders passed from the scene. '*Puritan Ireland's dead and gone,/A myth of O'Connor and Ó Faoláin*', declared Montague in 1967, a little prematurely, as it turned out, but he rightly sensed that change was coming. Inevitably the study of Irish literature has reflected those changes. Still firmly local, Irish writers since the 1970s are much more likely than their British counterparts to think of themselves as European. Europe has responded, with distinguished critics of Irish writing emerging in France, Germany, Austria, Belgium, the Netherlands, Spain, Italy, Sweden, Russia, and further afield in Brazil, Egypt, Japan—a kind of literary version of the European Union.

Discussions of Ireland as still to some extent affected by her former status as a colony, and of Irish literature as emerging from a kind of cultural colonialism, have evoked new questions and new answers. An equally exciting area of exploration has been the continuity of Irish literature from the earliest times, despite the change of language. Here Vivian Mercier's *The Irish Comic Tradition* (1962) has been for me the determining book, connecting, as it does, Swift and Joyce with the satire and fantasy of Gaelic Ireland. Mercier's recognition of a sustained comic tradition suggested a general continuity in Irish literature, overt when Yeats wrote plays about Cuchulain, implicit when he celebrated Coole Park and Lady Gregory as a traditional bard celebrated the power and hospitality of his chieftain.

In 1974, my colleague Brendan O Hehir and I developed and taught together a two part course in Irish literature at Berkeley. We began with the *Táin* and *Lebor Gabála* and proceeded through Ossianic material, *immrama*, *Castle Rackrent*, poems by Mangan and Davis, works by Synge, Yeats, and Joyce, John Montague's *The Rough Field* and the poems of Seamus Heaney. O Hehir, who had learned his Irish as a boy in Dublin, was responsible for Part I, which ended around 1800 (or, if you like, at the end of the Winter term). I began with Maria Edgeworth. Apart from examining selected works from each period, we stressed the continuity of Irish literature despite the shift in language from Irish to English. O Hehir had already published his *Gaelic Lexicon for Finnegans Wake* (1967), which demolished the myth that Joyce had little interest in or knowledge of the Irish language. Joyce's use of Irish, and of the Ossianic legend, was for us a striking instance of this continuity, as were Yeats's mythological plays, the learned fooling of Flann O'Brien, real or parodic celebrations of patrons by Yeats and Maria Edgeworth's Thady Quirk, translations from the Irish by Mangan, Thomas Kinsella, John Montague, and Seamus Heaney, the *immrama* of Paul Muldoon. We were also inspired—better, infuriated—because, not long before, the Irish section of the Modern Language Association of America had voted to split itself in two, creating a foolish *apartheid* between Irish literature in Irish and Irish literature in English. We taught the class together a number of times before Brendan's death in 1991, and it still survives, offered now in Berkeley's Celtic Studies Program. A great deal of my own thinking about Irish literature has come out of teaching that course.

My own work, as I have already suggested, tends to combine literary criticism with political and cultural history. At the present time, especially among younger critics, there is a wide variety of critical methods which are being applied to Irish literature as to other literatures: Formalism, Structuralism, Psychoanalytic Criticism, Reader Response Theory, Marxist Criticism, Deconstruction, the New Historicism. Even committed Homeric scholars have been known to nod over his catalogue of ships, but I want to name a few of those who have impressed me by employing some of these methods while not being confined by them: Karen Lawrence as a Formalist; Hélène Cixous, Stephen Heath, and Colin McCabe among Psychoanalytic critics; Margot Norris as a Deconstructionist. Terence Brown, Luke Gibbons, Cheryl Herr, Richard Kearney, Joep Leerssen, David Lloyd, Emer Nolan, and Kevin Whelan have contributed brilliantly as cultural critics, while Margaret Kelleher, Bonnie Kime Scott, and Clair Wills have worked profitably as Feminist critics. Robert Garratt and Dillon Johnston have given us lively overviews of Irish poetry since Yeats and Joyce, and Anthony Roche has done the same for contemporary drama. R.F. Foster's *Modern Ireland 1600–1972* (1988) presents literature as very much a part of history, while his *W.B. Yeats: The Apprentice Mage* (1997), the first part of a two volume biography, gives full attention to Yeats's politics, whether national or occult.

There are two major synthesizers who have both contributed to and drawn on this body of work and much else, Seamus Deane and, more recently, Declan Kiberd, whose *Inventing Ireland* (1995) is full of provocative ideas that set a kind of agenda for future work. Deane edited the controversial *Field Day Anthology of Irish Writing* (1991), which presents a canon to be welcomed, attacked, or endured. The earlier Field Day pamphlets, also edited by Deane, have presented essays by Terry Eagleton, Fredric Jameson, and Edward Said, critics not primarily associated with Irish studies.

It is said that Gandhi, in his campaign for Indian independence, modelled some of his tactics on those of the Home Rulers and Sinn Féin, while his hunger strikes owed something to the example of Terence MacSwiney— who may in turn have remembered Yeats's play *The King's Threshold* (1904). Menachem Begin, General Giap, and Che Guevara are all rumoured to have studied the guerrilla tactics of Commandant Tom Barry's West Cork Brigade in the War of Independence. In a similar way, it may be that Irish studies have implications for the study of other literatures, especially minority literatures and the literatures of nations that were once colonies. There are already signs that such intellectual cross-fertilization is taking place.

V

'Who thought Cuchulain till it seemed/He stood where they had stood?' asked Yeats in his last play. He was suggesting that the Cuchulain of his own work had 'stood in the Post Office/With Pearse and Connolly' to inspire their aesthetic heroism. By implication, the images of heroism he had created had played their part in the political developments that were the ultimate legacy of 1916. 'A nation is the heroic theme we follow', he proclaimed in 'First Principles' (*Samhain* 1904; *Explorations* 142). Yeats imagined a splendid fiction called *Ireland*, a romantic fantasy of lords and ladies, fairies and peasants, at once beautiful and heroic.

Yeats mastered a less sinister version of that aestheticization of politics which Walter Benjamin connected to Fascism (Benjamin 241–2). For Yeats and for his fellow writers of Anglo-Irish origin, Ireland was the fiction they invented to examine an identity that was at once blurred and all too clearly defined. Maria Edgeworth exposes the game with her loyal/manipulative Thady, who masks his cunning with deference, while Edgeworth masks herself as Thady to study her own class and their servants. Yeats's assertions, Le Fanu's anxieties, Elizabeth Bowen's hesitancies are workings out of problems of identity through elaborate role-playing.

The effort to discover what role their class was to play became the Anglo-Irish writers' theme in the nineteenth and twentieth centuries. They developed out of their uncertainties a literature of interrogation, culminating perhaps in *Waiting for Godot*. Their achievement is the articulation of a search for an identity—a confused search, hesitating between a claim to leadership, cultural if no longer political or economic, and a petition for acceptance. 'Confusion', as Hugh reminds us in Brian Friel's play *Translations*, 'is not an ignoble condition'.

Berkeley, California, 6 May 1997

1

The Cracked Lookingglass of a Servant

Inventing the Colonial Novel

It is the spectator, and not life, that art really mirrors.
                    Oscar Wilde, *The Picture of Dorian Gray*

I seriously believe that you will retard the course of civilization in Ireland by
preventing the Irish people from having one good look at themselves in my
nicely polished looking-glass.
    Joyce to Grant Richards, 23 June 1906, urging the publication of *Dubliners*

When 'Stately, plump Buck Mulligan' climbs to the parapet of the
Martello tower, he carries among his shaving implements a mirror
'cleft by a crooked crack'. He has 'pinched it out of the skivvy's room'. For
Mulligan the mirror is simply a practical aid in shaving, but for Stephen
Dedalus it becomes a symbol for the flawed art of a people and country
subject to an external imperial power. Stephen studies his own image in
the glass, provoking Mulligan's sardonic comment:

—The rage of Caliban at not seeing his face in a mirror, he said . . .
    Drawing back and pointing, Stephen said with bitterness:
—It is a symbol of Irish art. The cracked lookingglass of a servant
                    (*Ulysses* 3–6).

A colony is usually a backwater, its art at once imitative and flawed, dimly
reflecting the art produced at the imperial capital. The colonized may
seem docile, even loyal. But often they chafe under alien rule and plot to
subvert it.
    Joyce is scratching at the running sore that has troubled so many Irish
writers who write in English, as they ponder Ireland's colonial or post-
colonial status. Decisions and judgements, political or artistic, were always
being made somewhere else, and even the English language had been
imposed by English rule. 'The language in which we are speaking is his
before it is mine', Stephen muses, fencing with the English-born Dean of
Studies in *Portrait*:

How different are the words *home, Christ, ale, master,* on his lips and on mine! I cannot speak or write these words without unrest of spirit. His language, so familiar and so foreign, will always be for me an acquired speech. I have not made or accepted its words. My voice holds them at bay. My soul frets in the shadow of his language   (*Portrait* 189).

As for political domination, Stephen describes himself to the Englishman Haines as 'a servant of two masters . . . The imperial British state . . . and the holy Roman catholic and apostolic church' (*Ulysses* 17).

Joyce—or Stephen—has borrowed the looking-glass image from the preface to *The Picture of Dorian Gray*, where Wilde described 'The nineteenth-century dislike of Realism' as 'the rage of Caliban seeing his own face in a glass. The nineteenth-century dislike of Romanticism is the rage of Caliban not seeing his face in a glass' (*Picture* 3). Wilde was well aware of the tensions—political, social, linguistic—between an Irish artist and an English audience. Son, like Joyce, of an ardent Irish nationalist, he was determined to conquer the English literary world by becoming 'a lord of language' (*De Profundis* 66). He used that status to challenge English convention with mockery and the English language with epigram, as Shaw was to challenge it by synthesizing a perfect English speaker in *Pygmalion*, as Joyce was to challenge it by subverting it with multi-lingual puns in *Finnegans Wake*. Wilde's terrible punishment was that of a rebel, a subject challenging his masters. It is foreshadowed in his 'The Birthday of the Infanta', when the dwarf, captured and brought to court, believes that his art has made him the Infanta's equal. He dies heartbroken when he sees his misshapen self in a mirror, seeing himself as the Infanta and courtiers see him.

Joyce in his way, Wilde and Shaw in theirs, proved that the colonized could challenge the colonizer artistically, that the imitative and flawed nature of the subject people's art could become a strength rather than a weakness. Joyce's parody/imitation of the *Odyssey* re-invents the novel by subverting its form and technique, a more profound challenge than the comments on British misrule scattered through his work. Shaw and Wilde use their 'servant' status as inferiors, outsiders who are also insiders, to mock the complacencies of English society. The servant of two masters can become master of both.

These devices, subverting conventional narrative form and letting the servant/colonized subject speak to subvert the master, appear in one of the first Irish novels, Maria Edgeworth's *Castle Rackrent* (1800). *Castle Rackrent, An Hibernian Tale Taken from Facts, and from the Manners of the Irish Squires, before the Year 1782*, to give it its full title, is a consistently ambiguous novel, both in subject and in technique. It relies on the ambiguities of spoken narrative and on the ambiguities of the master/servant relationship or dependency—for which read also colonist and colonized. Edgeworth examines the dichotomies of Irish and Anglo-Irish life, each with its own aims and allegiances, and on the dichotomies that can arise between what is said and what is meant. The title itself hints at Maria Edgeworth's purposes and method: in the incompatibility between the pretentious *Castle*, which we learn is a rather shabby place, and the economically dangerous practice of rack-renting, leasing land at an exorbitant rent to short-term tenants who frequently fail and abscond; in the simultaneous similarity and difference of the words *Hibernian* and *Irish*; in the tension between *Tale* and *Facts*; and in the contrast between then—*before the Year 1782*— and now, 1800, a contrast internal evidence denies. That 'The race of the Rackrents has long been extinct in Ireland' (*Castle Rackrent* 4) should not be taken at face value.

Castle Rackrent is a remarkable technical achievement. Thady Quirk, the servant-narrator of the novel, tells a story which we must read simultaneously in two different ways: as the account of a loyal servant, as the account of a servant who is actually master. The reader is initially inclined to take him at face value as a naive but sincere narrator, foolishly impressed by the Rackrents' careless swagger. We recognize his naiveté and smile as the estate deteriorates and Thady continues to praise folly. Then we begin to realize that Thady is the gainer from the foolish behaviour he records and praises. As manipulative servant he controls his masters, as narrator he controls the narrative. His devotion to 'the family' notwithstanding, he shows us what fools the successive masters of Castle Rackrent are. By doing so, he questions their hereditary right to own and rule their estate, a right based on confiscation, as his earliest readers well knew. Wearing the mask of Thady, Maria Edgeworth questions her own class's rule of Ireland by showing how the Anglo-Irish might lose their power. Even more subversively, she raises questions about her own place in the scheme of things, as a woman who could manage the Edgeworth estates but never own them. To approach this text in the light of feminist and post-colonial critical writings is to recognize its explicit and implicit subtleties. Maria Edgeworth has contrived her novel so as to reveal the subversive nature of Thady's loyalty and the manipulative function of his narrative.

Castle Rackrent consistently employs ambiguity, and, in the sense that it is about ambiguity, continually interrogates its own processes. Thady studies his masters from behind a mask of adulation, and cynically plays upon their weaknesses. 'The lower Irish are such acute observers, that there is no deceiving them as to the state of the real feelings of their superiors', Maria Edgeworth remarked in her continuation of her father's *Memoirs* (1820):

They know the signs of what passes within, more perfectly than any physiognomist, who ever studies the human face . . . Combining quickly every circumstance in the manners, gestures, and slightest actions, of those, whom it is their interest to study; the result is, that the ruling, or the reigning passion can scarcely escape their detection (Richard Lovell Edgeworth, *Memoirs* 385).

Ambiguity is at the heart of the colonial situation, and shapes the behaviour of the colonial master and subject. In *Castle Rackrent* and her three other Irish novels—*Ennui* (1809), *The Absentee* (1812), and *Ormond* (1817)—Edgeworth focused on the peculiar circumstances—the peculiar dichotomies—of Ireland, where the Anglo-Irish minority, indifferent to public opinion, ruled a resentful subject people, who dreamed of an invasion or a rising that would vanquish their masters. Meanwhile they adopted the devices of a subject people: a deceptive contentment with their lot, even a deceptive affection for their masters. At the same time, they watched to take advantage of the masters' every weakness. They fashioned for themselves the mask their masters expected to see, that of uncritical, even enthusiastic loyalty. Stephen Dedalus described his weapons as 'silence, exile, and cunning' (*Portrait* 247); the dispossessed Irish chose loquacity, tenacity, and cunning.

The reckless self-destructive behaviour of the Rackrents is based on fact, matched by some of the gentlemen whose activities are chronicled by Sir Jonah Barrington in his *Personal Sketches and Recollections* (1827–32): drinking bouts, duels, gambling for high stakes. We can best imagine eighteenth-century Ireland by remembering the serf-owners of Gogol's Russia, the slave-owners of the *ante-bellum* American South. As in those societies, the bravado of the rulers concealed a lurking fear, that serfs/slaves/peasants would revolt and wreak a terrible revenge on their masters. Maria Edgeworth and her first readers had lived through the rebellion of May–July 1798, when peasants murdered landlords and other Protestants and burned many Big Houses. Though the rising, and the French-supported rebellion in the West that followed were savagely suppressed, fear of a peasant rising haunted the Anglo-Irish until the end of British rule in 1922. It was not an imaginary fear. When Ireland's final rebellion, or War of Independence, broke out in 1919, the Big Houses of the Anglo-Irish gentry were an immediate target. Many were burnt to the ground.

Anglo-Ireland's nightmare of peasant insurrection was closely related to an anxiety about losing their estates to their tenants, and so ceasing to be a ruling class, the 'Ascendancy' they had christened themselves in 1792 (McCormack 1985, 40). Apart from the practical consequences of such a loss, there was also the potential destruction of the myth by which Anglo-Ireland lived, that the peasants loved and trusted 'the family', felt for them a sentimental and feudal loyalty, and were happy to be ruled by them. The myth implied that the Irish themselves were incapable of governance. They allegedly recognized an English and Anglo-Irish right to rule based on a talent for ruling.

In her Preface to *Castle Rackrent*, Maria Edgeworth promises an intimate, anecdotal history. 'We cannot judge either of the feelings or of the characters of men with perfect accuracy from their actions or their appearance in public', she declares;

> it is from their careless conversations, their half finished sentences, that we may hope with the greatest probability of success to discover their real characters . . . After we have beheld splendid characters playing their parts on the great theatre of the world . . . we anxiously beg to be admitted behind the scenes, that we may take a nearer view of the actors and actresses.

Her solution is to rely, not on the professional biographer but rather on a biographer poorly endowed with 'intellectual powers . . . and literary talents . . . When we see that a man has the power, we may naturally suspect that he has the will to deceive us' (*Rackrent* 1–3). Edgeworth assures us that the Rackrents' biographer will take us behind the scenes, as indeed he does. Thady also disingenuously assures us that he will use no art, that we will hear 'A plain unvarnished tale' rather than the complex and deceptive story that follows.

Edgeworth's novel is about servants and masters. It reveals the servant's intimate knowledge of the masters and the masters' weaknesses. As narrator, Thady is a kind of mirror, in which the Rackrents see themselves as they imagine themselves to be, lords of creation. But it is also a cracked and distorting mirror, showing the foolish Rackrents as noble even as it reveals that they are fools.

It is a cliché to speak of fiction as mirroring reality. Maria Edgeworth herself does so in a letter of 1834, when she declines to write a novel about Ireland after Catholic Emancipation (1829). 'It is impossible to draw Ireland as she is now in a book of fiction', she told a kinsman;

> —realities are too strong, party passions too violent to bear to see, or care to look at their faces in the looking-glass. The people would only break the glass and curse the fool who held the mirror up to nature—distorted nature, in a fever. We are in too perilous a case to laugh, humour would be out of season, worse than bad taste (ME to MP Edgeworth, February 1834; Butler 452–3).

If Thady's mirror reflects and distorts, it also enables him to spy. Aware that Sir Condy and his lady are at odds, and that Lady Rackrent has received a long-awaited letter, Thady positions himself outside their chamber to eavesdrop. Sir Condy is shaving 'at the cracked glass over the chimney-piece' (*Rackrent* 65). By placing himself carefully, Thady is also able to see both parties in the mirror, and so can tell us what is said and describe how the couple react to one another.

Thady's very name is distorted and ambiguous, hinting at his dual role of faithful servant/subversive. In eighteenth-century Ireland, Catholics often found it expedient to adopt English names for self-protection. Surnames were often translated: McGowans, sons of the smith, became Smiths. Forenames were changed to an English form that sounded somewhat similar: Dermot to Jeremiah, Conor to Cornelius. Thady is in fact Teague or Teig, in Irish *Tadhg*, a common name but one with political and even literary overtones. Teague became Anglo-Ireland's general name for any Irishman after about 1640 (Duggan 168); later Teague became the generic name for an Irish man-servant (Duggan 242). Teague is still used by Unionists in Northern Ireland to refer to Irish nationalists, presumed to be treacherous, dirty, lazy, over-endowed with children, controlled by the Pope, and ever eager to kill Protestants.

Ireland was called 'Teagueland' as early as 1690 (Owens 72). Teague's identity as Irish, Catholic, and treacherous was established in the famous 'Lilli Burlero', the anti-Catholic marching-song during the seventeenth-century Williamite wars—until recently played nightly to announce the news on the Northern Ireland BBC. In the song, one Irish Catholic addresses another: 'Ho! brother Teague, dost hear de decree', and looks forward to cutting English throats and subduing 'de heretics'.

Thady's name, then, carries a hint of its sinister and conspiratorial associations. But at the same time, Teague had evolved on the English stage, from the generic name for an Irish man-servant to a sentimental dramatic cliché, the loyal servant who follows his master in adversity (Duggan 252). Thady ambiguously fulfil's both roles, at once rebel and loyalist, schemer and faithful servant.

Castle Rackrent is Maria Edgeworth's first novel, and her best. Brief and episodic, it records the careers of several successive lords of Castle Rackrent: Sir Patrick, Sir Murtagh, Sir Kit, and Sir Condy. They are all fools and wastrels, so bedazzled with their own power and prestige that each in his own way wastes the estate. Sir Patrick is a drunkard, whose chief claim to fame is the invention of raspberry whiskey. Sir Murtagh's vice is litigation, spending vast sums to win worthless judgments. Sir Kit is an absentee, a duellist, a spendthrift. Sir Condy, who can hardly be troubled to sign a business document, eagerly adopts the vices and follies of all his predecessors, and loses the estate at last to his scheming lawyer, Jason Quirk—Thady's son.

Before *Castle Rackrent*, Maria Edgeworth's writing consisted almost entirely of contributions to *The Parent's Assistant* (1796) and *Practical Education* (1798), in collaboration with her father, Richard Lovell Edgeworth (1744–1817), father of twenty-two children—twenty survived infancy—by four wives (Butler 133, 178, 489). Edgeworth was an Anglo-Irish gentleman of means, possessed of a comfortable estate in County Longford, granted to the Edgeworths by James I. After a long residence in England, Edgeworth settled permanently in Ireland in 1782, determined, he tells us in his *Memoirs*, 'to dedicate the remainder of my life to the improvement of my estate, and to the education of my children; and further, with the sincere hope of contributing to the melioration of the inhabitants of the country, from which I drew my subsistence' (*Memoirs* 259). Maria became his principal assistant both in managing the estate and in his educational projects.

Richard Lovell Edgeworth was an enlightened educational theorist, drawing on the theories of Rousseau. Both as landowner and as educator, he tried to be rational. He believed that Irish peasants, if treated fairly and allowed to prosper under the guidance of their landlords, would accept the landlord system for practical reasons. Their grievances would vanish with their poverty, and so would their nostalgic dreams of a vanished paradise, Ireland before the English came. The Irish would accept English rule for its practical blessings and in time become indistinguishable from English yeomen. As for children, they were eager to learn, and would do so gladly if lessons were adapted to their understanding. Edgeworth's fair treatment of his tenants and provision of schools for them earned him the suspicion of many of his Anglo-Irish neighbours. So did his conviction that the Penal Laws against Catholics should be repealed. After he took refuge with his family in Longford during the French invasion of 1798, a Protestant mob tried to lynch him as a French spy. When Catholic rebels left Edgeworthstown House unharmed, he became even more suspect (Butler 136–9).

While Maria Edgeworth was learning estate management at her father's side, she was also observing the tenants who came on business. Father and daughter were both gifted mimics, and amused the rest of the family with 'characters' they encountered among the peasantry (*Memoirs* 440). Maria was particularly good at imitating the accent and gestures of John Langan, the Edgeworths' steward, who became the model for Thady Quirk (Butler 126, 244).

As her father's education assistant, Maria taught her younger siblings in accordance with his theories. She also wrote little didactic tales, intended to teach children the difference between rational and irrational behaviour in a mildly amusing way. Her protagonists have names like Lazy Lawrence and Simple Susan, and usually learn the error of their ways after various mishaps. 'The Purple Jar', an early story from *The Parent's Assistant*, is at once typical of her method and, in its presentation of the foolish beguiled by the worthless, a prototype for *Castle Rackrent*. Young Rosamond, the protagonist, has a limited sum of money to spend as she chooses. She needs shoes, but buys instead a beautiful purple glass jar displayed in a shop window. As a result, she misses a treat because she lacks proper shoes, and finds the purple jar is plain glass filled with coloured water. The Rackrent choice of appearance over substance is here in miniature.

Though *Castle Rackrent* is a didactic novel, it is not obviously one. Maria Edgeworth tells the story of each Rackrent in turn, leaving it to the reader to grasp the moral, to perceive as absurd the actions Thady so enthusiastically admires. Her immediate target was presumably Anglo-Irish landowners, who would get her point: Irish landlords, learn your trade. To treat your estate as the Rackrents treat theirs is to lose it—and to those you consider your inferiors, the dispossessed Irish.

In her later Irish novels, Maria Edgeworth is more directly didactic, introducing exemplars who lecture the protagonist about sound estate management. Richard Lovell Edgeworth has often been blamed, perhaps unfairly, for these obtrusive and rather boring passages, which certainly present his ideas and values. We know that he usually read his daughter's work in progress and, with her agreement, 'corrected' it, though *Castle Rackrent* escaped his supervision (Butler 435).

Two voices, two cultures are competing in *Castle Rackrent*, Caliban's and Prospero's, servant's and master's, the insincere deferential voice of Thady Quirk and the rational utilitarian voice of Richard Lovell Edgeworth, with Maria Edgeworth as a kind of rebellious Miranda mediating between them. Thady's voice is the only one she allows us to hear directly, as she herself heard John Langan's voice dictating the story as she wrote, making her a kind of medium for the voiceless Irish. She heard Richard Lovell Edgeworth's voice all the time, with its message of prudence and common sense. In *Castle Rackrent* that omnipresent voice is paradoxically heard by not being heard. We hear its lessons about rational behaviour only by adding them ourselves, as we recognize the absurdities of the Rackrent way of life. 'Look for me in *The Absentee*' (Butler 457), Maria once advised, oddly equating absence with presence in a way that suggests an Irish Bull, but in fact defines her own simultaneous absence and presence, and her father's, in *Castle Rackrent*.

We who now read *Castle Rackrent* read with the advantage of hindsight, and so we know what Maria Edgeworth only suspected, that Richard Lovell Edgeworth's optimistic vision of an Ireland rationally accepting English rule and a shared prosperity would not be achieved in his terms. Though she gives him the last word in the last few paragraphs of *Castle Rackrent*, by summarizing his favourable expectations about the 1800 Act that would safeguard English rule by uniting the British and Irish parliaments, Maria Edgeworth's tale, written more than a century before English rule ended, makes it clear that the Ascendancy her father hoped to reform was doomed. For the last two hundred years, Irish writers—Carleton, Lover and Lever among her contemporaries, later Somerville and Ross, Elizabeth Bowen, Molly Keane, William Trevor—have been chronicling the Ascendancy's decay, essentially by re-writing *Castle Rackrent*. By leaving the reader to supply the rational advice of Richard Lovell Edgeworth, Maria virtually silences him, and implies that nothing can be done to save Anglo-Ireland. By giving Thady the power to narrate, Maria Edgeworth gives him the power to rule the story, and so to plot the future of the Rackrents, the Quirks, and the future of Ireland.

Thady lives inside a powerful story, that myth about themselves the Anglo-Irish told themselves. He can subvert that story only by exaggeratedly accepting, repeating, embellishing it, and by exaggeration making it absurd. The counter-story is the events of 1798, which revealed that Anglo-Ireland stood on a quaking bog; the self-destruction of the independent Irish Parliament, which voted for the Act of Union in 1800 in return for guarantees of protection against further Irish rebellions; the activities of the Catholic Committee towards repeal of the Penal Laws. It would continue in the activities of O'Connell and Parnell, the 1916 Rising, the War of Independence.

Thady is probably the first, certainly a very early example of the servant-subject as both central character and narrator. He is also a demonstration of self-fashioning. 'Having out of friendship for the family', he begins, 'upon whose estate, praised be Heaven! I and mine have lived rent free time out of mind, voluntarily undertaken to publish the Memoirs of the Rackrent Family, I think it my duty to say a few words, in the first place, concerning myself' (*Rackrent* 7). Under the guise of celebrating the Rackrents, Thady is writing his own autobiography. He presents himself as a paragon of loyalty, the ever-faithful servant. If the Rackrents are a sustained parody of an already familiar literary type, the reckless impecunious Anglo-Irish gentleman who never counts his money or his acres, and cares only for cutting a dashing figure, Thady presents himself as another literary cliché, the faithful Irish servant. In inventing him, Edgeworth examined the process by which the colonized subject simultaneously feigns loyalty, manipulates his rulers, and subverts their control. Inventing the Irish novel, she invented the colonial novel as well.

Thady dubs himself '*honest Thady*' and 'faithful Thady', while continually exploiting his masters' weaknesses for his own benefit (Newcomer 1967: 144–51). He resents Sir Murtagh's lady because she keeps careful watch on the household supplies; Sir Condy's lady is praised as 'very liberal in her house-keeping' (*Rackrent* 48), that is, indifferent about what was purchased for the house and where it went.

Along with petty pilfering and constant eavesdropping, Thady joins forces with his son Jason, by Sir Condy's time an attorney, to obtain the tenancy of a good farm (*Rackrent* 22). Thady reveals a sophisticated knowledge of Sir Condy's financial and legal problems. He watches Jason batten off the estate, first with the farm, then with 'fee simple of a good house for him and his heirs forever for little or nothing' (*Rackrent* 54), until Jason finally owns Castle Rackrent and the entire Rackrent estate. Though Thady comes to reprove Jason for his successful disloyalty to 'the family' and 'wash my hands of his doings' (*Rackrent* 8), both Quirks have treated the Rackrents as geese to be plucked. They differ in tactics and scope. Thady is a servant, and can only use a servant's tricks of flattery, petty theft, and spying. Jason builds on the privileged position his father has attained, and Thady's intimate knowledge of the Rackrents' affairs. His training as a lawyer enables him to use this knowledge to steal the estate legally.

At the beginning of Thady's chronicle, he tells us that Sir Patrick changed his name from O'Shaughlin to Rackrent in order to inherit the estate (*Rackrent* 9). O'Shaughlin is not possible as an Irish surname, but it is certainly not Anglo-Irish. Thady assures us that the O'Shaughlins were 'related to the Kings of Ireland' (*Rackrent* 8–9)—perhaps to the Ó Maoil-sheachlainns, who ruled Meath, including Edgeworthstown, until 1173, and continued to claim the kingship into the fifteenth century (Edgeworth, *Essay* xxii). The change from Irish-sounding O'Shaughlin to Anglo-Irish sounding Rackrent almost certainly marks a change of religion (Flanagan 70). Sir Patrick inherits Castle Rackrent by converting from Catholicism to the Protestant faith at a time when the Penal Laws stipulated that a Catholic estate must be divided among the immediate male heirs, unless one of them turned Protestant. If he did convert, he would inherit the whole estate.

Edgeworth never tells us that the Quirks are Catholics, but their servant/tenant status suggests that they are—though Jason may change his religion as he prospers. But the Penal Laws closed the legal profession to Catholics until 1792, one indication that *Castle Rackrent* is not really about Irish life *before the Year 1782*. Maria Edgeworth's shrewd assessment of Anglo-Ireland's future lets her hint how dangerous a Catholic attorney might be to Anglo-Ireland. One of the first beneficiaries of the 1792 act allowing Catholics to practise law was Daniel O'Connell, 'the Liberator', who would destroy Anglo-Ireland politically in 1829 by devious but legal methods. Like O'Connell, Jason wishes to be a master, not a servant. Edgeworth's inherited belief that fair dealing would reconcile the Irish to their subordinate position faded with the rise of O'Connell, when even some of the Edgeworth tenants voted contrary to the wishes of 'the family', among them one of John Langan's relatives (Butler 453).

In the old corrective sense of *A Mirrour for Magistrates*, Maria Edgeworth holds up a mirror to an irresponsible ruling class. The Edgeworths had watched the outbreak of the French Revolution with enthusiasm. Though she revered her kinsman, the Abbé Edgeworth, the Catholic priest who attended Louis XVI on the scaffold, Maria Edgeworth was loyal to the reforming principles of the Revolution's early years for most of her long life (Butler 111, 391). She does not endorse the grievances of the subject Irish, but she does portray Anglo-Ireland's incompetent misrule. A country governed by Rackrents will be lost, as Castle Rackrent is lost.

By letting Thady praise every foolish extravagance, from Sir Patrick's raspberry whiskey to Sir Condy's indolence, Edgeworth develops a further dimension to her parody of a naive narrator who turns each absurdity into a manifestation of 'the honour of the family'. She was a friend and neighbor of Charlotte Brooke (*c.* 1740–93), whose pioneering *Reliques of Irish Poetry* (1789) collected and translated traditional poems in Irish. Irish poetry is particularly rich in celebratory and elegiac verse. In Gaelic Ireland, every chieftain had his hereditary poet, who was highly privileged. The poet preserved the chieftain's genealogy and celebrated the chieftain and his ancestors in verse, praising their strength, bravery, importance, wealth, and especially their generosity and abundant hospitality towards equals and inferiors. By Maria Edgeworth's time this celebratory tradition had become the keen (*caoin*), praising and mourning the deceased at a funeral. This is the 'fine whillaluh! you might have heard . . . to the farthest end of the county' (*Rackrent* 11) when Sir Patrick died. Edgeworth glosses *whillaluh* with a citation from Giraldus Cambrensis and her own observations:

> The genealogy, rank, possessions, the virtues and vices of the dead were rehearsed, and a number of interrogations were addressed to the deceased: as, Why did he die? If married, whether his wife was faithful to him, his sons dutiful, or good hunters or warriors? If a woman, whether her daughters were fair or chaste? If a young man, whether he had been crossed in love? or if the blue-eyed maids of Erin treated him with scorn? (*Rackrent* 100–1).

Sir Condy hopes to hear something like this mixture of grief and praise when he pretends to be dead so he can see how people talk about him. Thady provides a prose *caoin* in his 'History of Sir Condy Rackrent', but Thady's lament for the Rackrents parodies the traditional lament form. The genealogy he celebrates is a degeneration, and as practised by the Rackrents, the traditional chiefly virtues of open-handed generosity and indifference to cost are in fact vices. To practise them is to lose one's estate, and to die. Sir Condy cannot survive the loss of Castle Rackrent, which involves the obliteration of his identity. Judy M'Quirk, Thady's grandniece, defines the situation succinctly. She has been Sir Condy's mistress, and apparently the mother of his children. Asked would she 'refuse to be my lady Rackrent' if Sir Condy asks her, she scorns the chance: 'Why what signifies it to be my lady Rackrent and no Castle? sure what good is the car and no horse to draw it: . . . to be like some folk, following the fortunes of them that have none left' (*Rackrent* 92).

Castle Rackrent has two parts. Part I, the histories of Sir Patrick, Sir Murtagh, and Sir Kit, 'must have been written between the autumn of 1793 and 1796, probably early in that period' (Butler 353). Edgeworth herself relates it to her fascination with John Langan's mannerisms and dialect; 'I began to write a family history as Thady would tell it . . . [Langan] seemed to stand beside me and dictate and I wrote as fast as my pen could go.' As for the characters and incidents, most of them she found in her own family's history. Sir Kit's marriage to a 'Jewish' and her imprisonment has its origin in an eighteenth century Irish scandal, as Edgeworth's own note tells us (Butler 241–2). It is potentially a Gothic novel, which we must wait for Sheridan Le Fanu's *Uncle Silas* (1864) to read.

Part II, 'The History of Sir Conolly Rackrent', was written two years after the completion of Part I (Butler 353–4). A 'Continuation of the Memoirs of the Rackrent Family' (*Rackrent* 38), it chronicles Sir Condy's decline and fall. Thady, Jason, and Judy are in at the kill: Thady who has pandered to his pride, Jason who has pandered to his laziness, and Judy who has satisfied his lust. Sir Condy dies penniless, abandoned by all save Thady and Thady's 'shister' (*Rackrent* 95–6).

The separation of Parts I and II suggests that Part I is the history of the Rackrent family, not just as told to us. It is the tale Thady told to the future Sir Condy, who, as a boy,

> would slip down to me in the kitchen, and love to sit on my knee whilst I told him stories of the family and the blood from which he was sprung, and how he might look forward, if the *then* present man should die without childer, to being at the head of the Castle Rackrent estate (*Rackrent* 39).

Supposedly written at Thady's dictation (*Rackrent* 3–4), Thady's story, as told to Condy, retains the feel of an oral performance, dialect, malapropisms, and all, just as Maria Edgeworth believed she heard John Langan telling it. Thady and Jason cultivate young Condy when they suspect he might inherit the estate. Thady tells Condy about his predecessors in such a way as to prepare him to be the kind of master Thady wants—foolish, imprudent, careless with money and possessions, indifferent to details of estate management. While Jason does Condy's school work for him, training him to a desirable idleness and incapacity for business, Thady uses his considerable narrative power to create Condy's absurd eagerness to prove himself worthy of his name by emulating all his predecessors in their varied follies. Thady tells a didactic tale, like those Maria Edgeworth wrote for *The Parent's Assistant*, here told not to inculcate prudence but to thwart the development of that virtue. Sir Condy becomes the first audience—the first 'reader'—of the histories of Sir Patrick and the rest. He is a naive reader, who embraces Thady's major theme, that profligate behaviour is expected of gentlemen, and in fact authenticates their claim to be gentry. Thady's plot is the effect he rightly judges his stories will have on Condy, whose emulation of his predecessors shows how well he has learned the lessons Thady teaches.

Maria Edgeworth developed from didactic storyteller to invent a didactic storyteller whose lessons are the reverse of those she wishes to teach. Her invented narrator is her own anti-self. Thady is used to teach Sir Condy how to govern an estate badly; Sir Condy's disastrous reign teaches the reader how to govern correctly.

We must therefore take Thady seriously as the author of *Castle Rackrent*. The novel works by creating a tension between its internal and external authors, whose different aims Edgeworth has both separated and combined—a sophisticated device for a beginning novelist. She has made Thady at once naive and complex by endowing him with the double insights that allow him to glorify the Rackrents and at the same time subvert them. He endorses their opinions about their own importance and their self-absorption, reflecting that false image of themselves they wish to see. To do this he has entered fully into the Rackrents' myth about themselves even as he cynically manipulates that myth. In literature as in life, it is wise to mistrust one who adds to his name the epithet 'honest'.

The mistreated wife, the colonial subject, the servant, all learn to feign deference and admiration for the master, and at the same time study and exploit his weaknesses. As a woman, marginalized in Anglo-Irish society, and further marginalized by her dependent status at Edgeworthstown, Maria Edgeworth knew something about subjection. Her brief periods as mistress there were cut short by the arrivals of her father's successive brides, the fourth and last of them a year younger than herself. At the same time, she was her father's servant, confidant, assistant, estate agent, companion, flatterer, and eventually would become his biographer, living out aspects of Thady's role. Richard Lovell Edgeworth was no Rackrent, but he had his obsessions, and was in no doubt about his own importance in the general scheme of things. Maria never explicitly criticizes her father, but continually praises him. Is there perhaps some connection between her lavish praise and Thady's glorification of the Rackrents? Some connection between Thady's resentment at the arrival and behaviour of each new Lady Rackrent and the recurring arrival of a new Mrs Edgeworth?

Personal dimension or not, I find it significant that a woman writer is the first to give a voice to the subject Irish at a time when women were essentially voiceless, severely restricted in their activities and opportunities. 'As a woman, my life, wholly domestic, cannot afford anything interesting to the public', she declared in 1847, refusing a request for biographical information; '. . . I have no story to tell' (Butler 9). If colonial novels portray those not in control of their own destiny, Maria Edgeworth, as a woman living in eighteenth-century Ireland, was well qualified to write one. She drew on her own experiences as a dependent as well as her observations of the Edgeworth tenants. Thady's exploitation of his masters' weaknesses is a kind of handbook for the subversion of Anglo-Ireland. Edgeworth reveals how thoroughly the underclass understands and utilizes the masters' incompetence. Once their weaknesses are recognized, the myth that the masters have a special gift for ruling is demolished—a myth that Edgeworth tried to sustain in her later Irish novels, where her Anglo-Irish landlords learn how to govern. Daniel O'Connell disliked those novels, on the grounds that efforts to reform the Anglo-Irish, if successful, would maintain them in power (McDonagh 300). But he may have borrowed from Thady his tactic of frequently proclaiming his loyalty and deference to British authority while exploiting every weakness or loophole to end the political power of the Anglo-Irish.

Maria Edgeworth performs one final act of subversion by letting Thady show Sir Condy as attractive and pitiful as well as foolish, and making Jason cynical and sinister. Jason *has* learned how to act rationally and practically. He will make Castle Rackrent profitable, but will treat the tenants harshly. Jason has learned some of the practical lessons about management that Richard Lovell taught.

In portraying Jason as she does, Maria Edgeworth hints at a kind of ambiguity about her father and his ideas which is contrary to her usual professions of allegiance to them. Richard Lovell Edgeworth hoped that Irish national sentiment, the Irish sense of themselves as not English, would disappear under fair and rational treatment. Though he voted against the Act of Union in protest at the bribery which ensured its passage, he spoke in its favour, and believed it would bring about an assimilation of the Irish until they were no longer distinguishable from their fellow subjects (Butler 180–1). 'It is a problem of difficult solution to determine whether an Union will hasten or retard the amelioration of this country', Maria remarks, in the penultimate paragraph of *Castle Rackrent* (*Rackrent* 97), suggesting that she did not fully share her father's enthusiasm for the Union. By announcing that her story takes place '*before the Year 1782*', the year in which the Irish Parliament achieved the independence that the Act of Union would abolish, she seems to imply that independence put an end to the bad old ways and made 'the race of the Rackrents . . . extinct' (*Rackrent* 4).

Writing as 'Editor' of Thady's narrative, Maria endorses her father's hopes about the probable effects of the Union, observing that 'Nations as well as individuals gradually lose attachment to their identity . . . When Ireland loses her identity by an union with Great Britain, she will look back with a smile of good-humoured complacency on the Sir Kits and Sir Condys of her former existence' (*Rackrent* 5). Nevertheless she goes on to invent the national novel, creating Irish characters who show little likelihood of ever assimilating to English norms of behaviour. In his General Preface to his collected novels (1829), Sir Walter Scott traced his Scottish novels to her example:

> I felt that something might be attempted for my own country, of the same kind with that which Miss Edgeworth so fortunately achieved for Ireland— something which might introduce her natives to those of the sister kingdom in a more favourable light than they had been placed hitherto, and tend to procure sympathy for their virtues and indulgence for their foibles (Scott xx).

Scott's example, in turn, led to the popularity of the national novel all over Europe. Through him we can include among Maria Edgeworth's literary descendants Balzac, Pushkin, Manzoni, and Sienkiewicz. Turgenev seems to have studied her work (Butler 389–91).

When Maria Edgeworth and her father collaborated on *Essay on Irish Bulls* (1802), they mocked contemporary Irish historians who were claiming that the Irish language derived from Carthaginian Punic, and that the medieval historians who described the Irish as originating in Spain were to be taken at face value:

> it is a matter of indifference to us whether the Irish derive their origin from the Spaniards, or the Milesians, or the Welsh: we are not so violently anxious as we ought to be to determine, whether or not the language spoken by the phoenician slave, in Terence's play, was Irish . . . we are more interested in the present fate of it's inhabitants, than in the historian of St Patrick . . . the renowned Brien Boru . . . Diarmod; Righ-Damnha; Labra-Loingseach; Tighermas; Ollamh-Foldha . . . by this declaration we have no fear of giving offence to any but rusty antiquaries (*Essay* 313–14).

Despite this dismissal of any interest in Irish tradition, in her later Irish novels Maria's protagonists must understand and accept it, must become Irish rather than English. Richard Lovell Edgeworth's principles of rational estate management and assimilation are presented as sermons to the protagonists who accept them and settle on their Irish estates to put them into practice. But Lord Colambre, in *The Absentee*, must learn something of Irish history and tradition from the nationalist antiquary, Count O'Halloran, who also brings the marriage plot to a satisfactory conclusion. O'Halloran is a composite figure based on the three most conspicuous antiquaries of the day. He takes his name from Sylvester O'Halloran

(1728–1807), whose writings described a glorious Irish civilization before the Normans came; his ancient Irish lineage and his Catholicism evoke Charles O'Conor of Belanagare (1710–91), then the most distinguished of Irish antiquaries; and his other profession, of military architect, suggests General Charles Vallancey (1721–1812), who argued that a Punic speech in Plautus's *Poenulus* was actually Irish. Harry Ormond learns Irish ways from his Gaelic-speaking Irish kinsman, King Corny of the Black Islands, whose relationship with his tenants is tribal rather than rational. Ormond eventually chooses to settle in the Black Islands as Corny's successor, where he will rule in the spirit of Irish traditions.

We began with Caliban, the first colonized subject in English literature. Let us end with his angry words to Prospero, who has seized his island: 'You taught me language, and my profit on't/Is, I know how to curse' (*Tempest* 1.2.363–4). Incorrigibly other, Caliban can learn his masters' language, but he cannot, will not assimilate into their world. Nevertheless, he is left in possession of the island. Thady Quirk has also learned the masters' language. He deploys it with great skill to control the masters' story and even to control their lives, recasting their language into the Hiberno-English dialect that is one sign that their identities are different. Maria Edgeworth obediently listened and wrote as John Langan seemed to dictate *Castle Rackrent* to her, his employer who became his amanuensis, a kind of metaphor for Thady's manipulation of the Rackrents. Edgeworth made Langan/Thady heard, to reveal both the power of the servant/subject and the existence of an Irish identity that would survive.

Delivered as a lecture (February 1994) at the Center for Literary Studies, The Hebrew University of Jerusalem, in 'Rereading Texts/Rethinking Critical Presuppositions', a lecture series honouring Professor H.M. Daleski. Reprinted with permission, in revised form, from *Rereading Texts/Rethinking Critical Presuppositions: Essays in Honor of H.M. Daleski*. Ed. Shlomith Rimmon-Kenan, Leona Toker and Shuli Barzilai. Frankfurt am Main/Berlin/ Bern/New York/Paris/Wien: Peter Lang, 1997.

2

Maria Edgeworth and Lady Morgan

Legality versus Legitimacy

Maria Edgeworth's first Irish novel, *Castle Rackrent* (1800), ends with a funeral. Her three other Irish novels, *Ennui* (1809), *The Absentee* (1812), and *Ormond* (1817), end with weddings, but there is a puzzling ambivalence about her treatment of these weddings. Each one resolves a plot and represents a conventional happy ending, but the novelist herself seems uneasy about the rewards she confers. As the end of each novel approaches, she deliberately foils the plot she has been developing—the marriage which seems inevitable and desirable—and creates an alternative marital outcome. At the same time, she contrives to suggest that somehow the earlier plot and marriage have not been foiled after all and have indeed been validated and brought to a successful conclusion.

There is a strong didactic element in all four Irish novels, though didacticism is often tempered by Maria Edgeworth's eagerness to exploit the more bizarre aspects of her material. This conflict is presumably due to her own awareness of having not one audience but two. Her didactic material is aimed at readers of her own class, at other Anglo-Irish land-lords. She explains to them how to succeed—in *Castle Rackrent*, how to fail—as landlords. But she is also conscious of English readers, and for them she emphasizes the strange and flamboyant—that is, the un-English —nature of Irish life, those very habits and traits which work against the prudent husbandry she is endorsing.

In all four novels the basic issue is how the relationship between Anglo-Irish landlords and Irish tenants can be improved. Maria Edgeworth urged her Irish readers to practise fair dealing and careful husbandry. Landlords, she suggests, will prosper if their tenants prosper; tenants will prosper if their landlords treat them fairly and introduce them to efficient farming methods. Landlords and tenants must recognize mutual interests and will in time develop mutual loyalty. The Irish will lose their foreign 'identity' and become more like their English fellow subjects (*Castle Rackrent* 5).

It is a decent, rational aspiration, but Maria Edgeworth was too shrewd an observer of the Irish scene to believe that things could be settled so sensibly. She knew how irresponsible many landlords were, how lazy or how greedy. And she knew well what barriers of religion, race, tradition, and sometimes even language prevented landlords and tenants from recognizing a mutual loyalty. These barriers were higher and stronger than ever in the aftermath of the 1798 Rising and its brutal repression, which had revealed an implacable hatred between the two classes. Anglo-Irish landlords were well aware that they were a minority surrounded by a disaffected majority and that their legal right was not backed by any freely accepted social contract which would lead Irish peasants to concede that their Anglo-Irish landlord's claim to his place was in harmony with the legitimate and natural order of things. 'Confiscation is their common title', announced the Earl of Clare, describing the Anglo-Irish landowners in his speech advocating the Act of Union in 1800, 'and from their first settlement they have been hemmed in on every side by the old inhabitants of the island, brooding over their discontents in sullen indignation.' Clare's intention was to frighten the Anglo-Irish into voting for the Union by persuading them that they 'never had been, and . . . never could be, blended or reconciled with the native race' (Lecky 5:372). He succeeded in his purpose, but he was not wholly wrong in his evocation of Irish resentment, and the structure and plots of Maria Edgeworth's Irish novels suggest that she was well aware that Irish tenants were not going to forget their wrongs easily, nor accept the legitimacy of the Ascendancy order of things.

Her four Irish novels are simple in structure. *Castle Rackrent* is a chronological account of successive owners of the Rackrent estates, whose follies and extravagances become an object lesson in how *not* to be an Irish landlord. In *Ennui* the owner of an Irish estate is taken on a tour of Ireland, during which he learns something of Irish life and Irish resources, and observes examples of proper and improper estate management. Maria Edgeworth found this tour structure so useful for her didactic purposes that she employed it again in *The Absentee* and in *Ormond*. After *Ormond* she wrote no more Irish novels, though she continued to gather material for one during the 1820s, until O'Connell's successful appeal to Catholic-Irish identity led her to believe that her themes of reconciliation would be unacceptable.

In both *Castle Rackrent* and *Ennui* the Anglo-Irish landlords are depicted as Lord Clare depicted their class, 'hemmed in on every side by the old inhabitants of the island'. The decline of the Rackrents, from Sir Patrick through Sir Murtagh and Sir Kit to Sir Condy, the last of the line, is narrated by Thady Quirk, who controls the story by choosing what he will tell us and how he will tell it. But Thady is well aware that the more foolishly the Rackrents behave, the more he and his family will prosper. He delights at any carelessness with money or land. Thady's praise of extravagance and scorn of prudence hints at his own prosperity as that of the Rackrents declines, and he deliberately shapes the behaviour of the last Rackrent, Sir Condy, by instilling in him the desire to live up to the family tradition of waste.

Sir Condy proves an apt pupil and manages to emulate the different fooleries of all his predecessors until he loses the estate to his attorney Jason Quirk, Thady's son. Jason would rather be owner. In any case, the Rackrents are surrounded by the predatory Quirks, eager to rob them in one way or another. Along with Thady and Jason, there is Judy M'Quirk, who is Sir Condy's mistress and who almost becomes Lady Rackrent. One way or another, the Irish peasants will take back the land from its Anglo-Irish owners—the nightmare of Anglo-Ireland.

In *Ennui* Maria Edgeworth combines her instructive series of good and bad examples of estate management with a bizarre plot that simultaneously allows and refuses to allow the estate to fall into the hands of the Irish peasantry. Lord Glenthorn is bored and unhappy; his marriage has ended in divorce. He resolves to visit his Irish estates and thereafter undergoes a course of instruction in Irish mores and estate management. The novelist emphasizes the strangeness of Irish life and its dangers to landlords: rebellion—presumably the '98—breaks out, and Glenthorn is threatened by the rebels and then scorned by his fellow landlords when he does not seek bloody vengeance. Literally surrounded by the peasantry, Glenthorn describes himself as 'kept a state prisoner in my own castle, by the crowds who came to do me homage, and to claim my favour and protection. In vain every morning was my horse led about saddled and bridled; I never was permitted to mount' (*Ennui* 182). These comic sieges prepare us for the rebels in the countryside and the hostility of the Anglo-Irish.

Glenthorn is also in search of a wife, and eventually he proposes to the vivaciously Irish Lady Geraldine. Marriage with her seems to offer him a chance to assume an Irish identity and to manage his estates justly, but also with due regard for Irish tradition and Irish sensibility. Her name suggests an identification with the great family of Fitzgerald (the Earl of Surrey's love poems to 'the fair Geraldine' addressed one of the Fitzgeralds). From the revolt of 'Silken Thomas' Fitzgerald in 1534 to that of Lord Edward Fitzgerald in 1798, that family often supplied leaders for Irish rebellions against the English. Marriage with Lady Geraldine will give some direction to Glenthorn's life and presumably will make him a better landlord and a true Irishman.

But Lady Geraldine rejects Lord Glenthorn and eventually marries someone else. And then Glenthorn discovers that he is not Lord Glenthorn at all. He is Christy O'Donoghue, an Irish peasant, and the true Earl has been brought up in a peasant cottage as Christy O'Donoghue; the infant Earl's nurse substituted her own child for her noble charge. The false Earl insists on relinquishing title and estates to their rightful owner, and sets off for London, where he works hard, passes the bar, and then returns to Ireland to practise law. His honesty and industry attract favourable notice, and he marries the rather vapid Cecilia Delamere, a character introduced into the novel in its antepenultimate chapter for this purpose. He recognizes as legitimate her mother's objections to the name O'Donoghue and agrees to accept the name and arms of Delamere. Meanwhile, the true Earl is unable to overcome his peasant upbringing and live up to his position. His son and heir becomes a drunkard, sets fire to the Castle, and perishes in the flames. The Earl relinquishes his position to return to his smithy, begging the pseudo-Earl to 'come to reign over us again' (*Ennui* 323). As it happens, Cecilia Delamere is heir-at-law to the Glenthorn estates; the Delameres rebuild the Castle and resolve to settle there.

This resolution ends the novel, but it raises a number of questions. Why is Lady Geraldine shunted away, especially when the hero remarks at the end of the book that she and the man she married 'first awakened my dormant intellects, made me know that I had a heart, and that I was capable of forming a character for myself'? and why does he consider their presence the only 'wish of my heart that remains ungratified'? (*Ennui* 321). If Lady Geraldine is Maria Edgeworth's self-portrait, perhaps she cannot be shown as happily married to the hero. But I suspect a political motive for her banishment.

The plot calls into question certain assumptions about the role of the Anglo-Irish and their mandate to rule. The true Earl's birth is not enough to make him a gentleman. His failure undermines the whole notion of hereditary rank, hereditary right, and of the natural capacity for leadership, which the Anglo-Irish allegedly possessed and the Irish allegedly lacked. The pseudo-Earl's instinctive nobility and honesty is equally subversive. Properly educated, the Irish can rule.

When the novel ends, the Irish peasant has changed his name, has learned how to rule, and has the legal right to do so through his wife. It is not the *national* right that marriage with Lady Geraldine would have conferred—there is nothing personally or characteristically Irish about Cecilia Delamere. But the peasants know the hero and respect him as a gentleman and as one of their own. He is triply legitimized by his education, his legal right, and his Irish identity. Once again an Anglo-Irish estate has fallen into Irish hands; the process is more honourable than in *Castle Rackrent*, but the result is similar—the Anglo-Irish have failed to hold on to what they had. In its tortuous way the plot undercuts all the sensible advice about fair dealing and prudence which the didactic portion of the book offers so freely. Good husbandry is not enough, it seems. The plot suggests that some other vaguely defined legitimacy is needed: the commitment to Irish tradition, which Lady Geraldine seems to represent and from which Maria Edgeworth draws back; or an unhyphenated Irish identity, which the hero half embodies, half evades.

There is some uncertainty as to precisely when Maria Edgeworth finished *Ennui*. She describes herself as 'finishing *Ennui*' in a letter written in April 1805, but a striking description of an Irish hackney chaise and driver in chapter 6 is apparently based on a conversation with Humphry Davy in July 1806. Later Richard Lovell Edgeworth assured a correspondent that the novel had undergone 'patient changes' and had been 'totally rewritten' (Butler 237, 247, 366–7, 291). We can probably assume that she worked on *Ennui* between 1804 and 1807 or 1808, though not continuously. It was during that period that Sydney Owenson—not to become Lady Morgan until her marriage in 1812—published her successful *The Wild Irish Girl* (1806). We do not know precisely when Maria Edgeworth read that novel, nor her initial opinion of it; later, in *Patronage* (1814), she was to caricature Lady Morgan as a governess turned author, and later still to deplore 'a shameful mixture' in Lady Morgan's *Florence Macarthy* (1818) of 'the highest talent and the lowest malevolence and the most despicable disgusting affectation and *impropriety* . . . Oh that I could prevent people from ever naming me along with her—either for praise or blame . . . God forbid as my dear father said I should ever be such a thing as that—' (Butler 448, 258). But it is probable that the character of Lady Geraldine in *Ennui* represents both a response to and a rejection of a theme Lady Morgan develops in *The Wild Irish Girl*, a theme Maria Edgeworth again develops but then again rejects in *The Absentee*.

The Wild Irish Girl is an epistolary novel in which Horatio, second son of the Earl of M——, describes his banishment to his father's Connaught estates. Horatio has wasted time and money, played the libertine, is heavily in debt, and is addicted to 'polite literature and belles lettres' to the detriment of his legal studies (Morgan, *Wild Irish Girl* 1:xiv). In a half-ruined castle by the sea, Horatio discovers the aged Prince of Inismore, last of a line of ancient Irish chieftains, and his lovely daughter, the Princess Glorvina. The estates of Lord M—— were once the estates of the Prince's ancestors, confiscated in Cromwell's time when the ancestor of the M——s, a Cromwellian soldier, killed the then Prince in his own castle.

Horatio conceals his identity and gains admission to the castle, first as an invalid—he hurts his leg trying to spy on Glorvina—and later as the Princess's drawing master. There he hears and duly reports a series of lectures on the Irish language, Irish history, antiquities, grievances, and customs from the Prince, Glorvina, and Father John, the Prince's chaplain. He also falls in love with Glorvina, only to find that he has a rival, his own father. The Earl has long felt guilty about his own prosperity and the Prince's poverty, but the Prince has refused any communication or help from his hereditary enemy. The Earl has also managed to enter the castle by concealing his name and pretending to be an Irish rebel fleeing after the 1798 Rising. He has persuaded the aged Prince and Glorvina to agree to a marriage, so that Glorvina can live in a way appropriate to her rank, and so that the ancient wrong of murder and confiscation can be righted. But the Earl gladly relinquishes Glorvina to Horatio and gives the young couple those estates which were once her ancestors' domain. She and Horatio will rule them together with a double right: to his legal right she adds her own traditional right, and from her he will learn respect for Irish history, Irish ways, and Irish tradition. Their children will be both Anglo-Irish and Irish, heirs to both rights and both traditions. The peasantry will accept them as legitimate masters in a way they have never accepted the M—— family alone, for peasant loyalty has always been with the 'old' Catholic-Irish family.

In her subsequent Irish novels Lady Morgan introduces other descendants of ancient Irish families and emphasizes the strength of their traditional claims on their confiscated lands and on the loyalty of their peasantry. These are far stronger than the merely legal rights of the Anglo-Irish, and the very nature of those legal rights—based as they are on confiscation and usurpation—is a barrier to their acceptance as legitimate and binding by the peasantry. Only the restoration of the old Irish heir or an intermarriage that will merge Irish and Anglo-Irish claims, Catholic and Protestant, legal rights and traditional attitudes, can evoke that loyalty which guarantees that a landlord will be eagerly obeyed and even loved and thus assuage that 'sullen discontent' which Lord Clare described.

This happy coalescence of apparently mutual and irreconcilable enmities makes an attractive literary and political solution, and it became almost a cliché in the novels of Walter Scott, as when Catholic Stuart-supporting Diana Vernon marries Protestant Hanoverian Frank Osbaldistone in *Rob Roy* (1817), or when Saxon and Norman are reconciled in *Ivanhoe* (1819). Scott acknowledges a debt to Maria Edgeworth in his 'postscript, which should have been a preface' to *Waverley* (1814), and in the 'General Preface' to his novels (1829). His chief debt is to *The Absentee* (Butler 394–5), but I suspect an unacknowledged debt to Lady Morgan—unacknowledged because Scott was a Tory, Lady Morgan a notorious Whig, and even, according to her sister, 'an elegant artist, / A radical slut, and a great Bonapartist' (Stevenson 250).

Maria Edgeworth seems to be grooming Lady Geraldine to be a less flamboyant version of Glorvina before she exiles her from *Ennui*. If this is so, Edgeworth is not just toying with Lady Morgan's plot device of inter-marriage. She is close to admitting that legal title and fair dealing are not enough to justify an Anglo-Irish landlord's possession of his estates. He must also make some emotional appeal to the deeper traditional loyalties of his peasants, must become in some way a part of the older tradition. An irrational element must be added to Richard Lovell Edgeworth's rational recipe. But to the Edgeworths, as Marilyn Butler points out, 'Irish tradi-tions meant . . . the survival of irrational and inefficient habits: they thought that extensive education among all classes was the best remedy for tradition' (Butler 364). To endorse Lady Geraldine's Irishness by marrying her to the hero would be to accept and endorse Irish tradition and Irish identity. Clearly Maria Edgeworth's instinct as a novelist, as well as her own awareness of the Ascendancy's failure to put down roots in Ireland and failure to evoke loyalty from the Irish, impels her toward such an endorsement of Irish tradition and Irish identity. But at the same time, her acceptance of Richard Lovell Edgeworth's principles makes her draw back from such an endorsement and, ultimately, deny it. As a novelist, Maria Edgeworth values Irish tradition and Irish strangeness; as an economist, she deplores these things and justifies her hero's success by his hard work, seriousness, and his marriage to the legal heir to the Glenthorn estates. But there is a perfunctory air about this resolution.

The uncertainty about what we may call the Glorvina solution—the intermarriage/assimilation of Irish and Anglo-Irish, of modern efficiency and ancient tradition, of legal right and traditional loyalty—is even more marked in Maria Edgeworth's third Irish novel, *The Absentee*, in which she first develops, then denies, and finally suggests such a solution. The structure of *The Absentee* is once again that of the exemplary tour. Lord Colambre, son and heir of the absentee Lord Clonbrony, visits Ireland and sees both well-managed and badly managed estates, including some of the properties he is to inherit, which he visits incognito. His tour also provides Maria Edgeworth with an opportunity to portray Dublin society, considerably lowered in tone since the Union, and the consequent depar-ture of lords and commons to Westminister. Colambre learns the evils of absenteeism and the necessity for economy and prudent management.

But there is also a plot. Lord Colambre is looking for a wife as well as a definition of his duty. He has two imperative conditions about his mar-riage: he will not marry for money, as his mother wishes him to do—'if you don't marry Miss Broadhurst'—an heiress—'we can't live in Lon'on another winter,' she declares (Edgeworth, *Absentee* 19); and he will on no account marry a woman who is not of legitimate birth. He has, we learn, 'the greatest dread of marrying any woman whose mother had conducted herself ill. His reason, his prejudices, his pride, his delicacy, and even his limited experience, were all against it' (*Absentee* 112). Though even some contemporary readers described this attitude as 'prudery' (Butler 333, n. 1), this attitude is for Colambre a basic principle and one that Maria Edgeworth endorses both here and, more elaborately, in *Patronage* (1814): a child brought up by an unchaste mother will be subtly corrupted, and so rendered unfit to raise her own children properly, an attitude in keeping with the Edgeworth's educational theories about the effect of environment and early training on character.

Colambre has allowed himself to fall in love with his mother's ward, Grace Nugent. Grace is beautiful, intelligent, and 'not a partisan, but a friend' to Ireland (*Absentee* 73). She is the last heir of the old Irish family that once owned the Colambre estates. But there is a question about her legitimacy. In a plot whose complexity hints at Maria Edgeworth's uneasiness with some of its implications, Grace Nugent's parentage is explored and her legitimacy established in such a way as to suggest her relationship to the old Catholic owners of the estates and to deny that relationship. Grace is initially introduced as Colambre's cousin, the daughter of his 'uncle Nugent', whose place in the family tree is never explained; we never learn if he is a paternal or a maternal uncle. We do, however, hear that the Nugents were an ancient Irish family who once owned the Colambre estates; the squalid local village is still called 'Nugent's town'.

During his travels Lord Colambre meets an Irish gentleman, Count O'Halloran, who is a Catholic aristocrat. He received his title after a distinguished career in the Austrian army. (Irish gentlemen traditionally served in the army of one of the Catholic powers, since they were not allowed to be British officers.) Now retired to Ireland, he spends his time advising the government about defence against Napoleon and studying Irish antiquities. O'Halloran represents Colambre's first encounter with Irish tradition. Learned in Irish history, culture, and even fauna, the Count has reassembled the skeletons of an Irish elk and a moose-deer, and his pets are 'an eagle, a goat, a dog, an otter, several gold and silver fish in a glass globe, and a white mouse in a cage'; the dog is 'a tall Irish greyhound—one of the few of that fine race, which is now almost extinct' (*Absentee* 113–14).

When a British officer who accompanies Colambre stumbles over the goat, the eagle attacks him until O'Halloran summons the bird; then 'his first care was to keep the peace between his loving subjects and his foreign visitors. It was difficult to dislodge the old settlers, to make room for the new comers: but he adjusted these things with admirable facility; and with a master's hand and master's eye, compelled each favourite to retreat into the back settlements' (*Absentee* 116). This episode suggests the same reconciliation with the older Catholic and Celtic Ireland that was Lady Morgan's theme. Count O'Halloran is a slightly more plausible version of the Prince of Inismore, endowed, like the Prince, with ancient lineage, antiquarian lore, aristocratic but not English manners, and loyalty to an older tradition. He too is of a 'fine race . . . now almost extinct'. He saves the British officer from the eagle, a hint at his role in assisting Britain against Napoleon; and he mediates between native and foreign, 'old settlers' and 'new comers'. Colambre and the Count become friends, and he offers Colambre another model for success as an Irish landlord. Fair dealing is important, but so is a knowledge of and a respect for Irish tradition.

The Count has noticed Colambre's interest in a black-letter book open on the table to a chapter entitled 'Burial-place of the Nugents', and he presents him with an urn 'enclosing ashes . . . lately found in an old abbey ground' where the Nugents are buried (*Absentee* 117, 120). It is a symbolic gift representing Colambre's initiation into the Irish tradition and foreshadowing that restoration of legitimacy which his marriage with Grace Nugent, like Horatio's to Glorvina, will bring about. And the scene implicitly endorses that irrational Irish obsession with tradition which made Maria Edgeworth and her father uneasy.

But then Colambre discovers that Grace Nugent is not Grace Nugent at all. She was born before her mother's marriage to 'uncle Nugent', who 'adopted the child, gave her his name, and, after some years, the whole story' of her mother's premarital affair 'was forgotten' (*Absentee* 123). Grace seems to be the illegitimate daughter of one Captain Reynolds and a Miss St Omar. The St Omars are described to Colambre by Lady Dashfort, who has her own reasons for preventing his marriage to Grace, as '*that* family, where, you know, all the men were not *sans peur*, and none of the women *sans reproche*' (*Absentee* 110).

But Count O'Halloran saves the day. He has already shown Colambre the way to a kind of national legitimacy by his example and by his gift of the burial urn. Now he is able to establish that Grace *is* legitimate. Her father, Captain Reynolds, was a young Englishman in the Austrian service and O'Halloran's friend. Her mother, also English, was educated in a Viennese convent. The couple were properly and provably married. When O'Halloran and Colambre call upon Grace's English grandfather and show him the certificate of marriage, he immediately agrees to recognize Grace as his granddaughter and heiress. There are no further obstacles to her marriage with Colambre, and even her poverty has been magically removed.

But she is no longer Irish, and her English legitimacy removes her apparent ability to reconcile two traditions and to add the legitimacy of the old Irish owners of the land to Lord Colambre's legal rights to his estates. Maria Edgeworth has worked towards Lady Morgan's resolution, then foiled that solution. She has drawn back from the implications of her own plot; Count O'Halloran, despite appearances, is only the guarantor of formal legality, not of traditional rights. A legal title and prudent habits are, after all, sufficient to justify Colambre's rule of his estates and his choice of Grace as a wife.

But even as she changes the story's direction and implication in this way, Maria Edgeworth simultaneously continues to hint that Grace is, after all, somehow Catholic, Irish, and the heir to ancient traditions. Her father, we are told, has been in the Austrian service with Count O'Halloran—why? We know that Irish Catholics often entered the Austrian army and why they did so. The Irish-Catholic aristocrat who has served in the army of one of the Catholic powers is almost a cliché in Lady Morgan's novels. But why would an Englishman do so? There is an unmistakable hint of the Irish-Catholic aristocrat about Reynolds despite his English identity. And what of Miss St Omar? Sometimes English Protestant girls were educated in Catholic convents abroad, but in context she too has a vaguely Catholic aura. Her name confirms this suspicion. St Omer, in France, was the location of a famous Catholic seminary, where priests were trained to serve in England and Ireland during the Penal Times—Father John, the chaplain in *The Wild Irish Girl*, has studied there (*Wild Irish Girl* 1:250). Finally, why did Maria Edgeworth, in establishing Grace's parentage, decide to call her Grace *Reynolds*? The name had some recent unpleasant notoriety in Irish history: Thomas Reynolds was the informer who caused the arrest of the United Irish leaders, his friends and companions, in March 1798. At their trial John Philpot Curran denounced him as 'a vile informer, the perjurer of a hundred oaths, a wretch whom pride, honour and religion cannot bind' (Pakenham 328, 50–2, 87–8). He was particularly hated for his role in the betrayal of Lord Edward Fitzgerald. Does the name suggest Maria Edgeworth's uneasy awareness that she had in some way betrayed her Irish theme? or is it one more example of her ambivalence? Her juxtaposition of the names Nugent and Reynolds seems to point, not to the traitor Thomas Reynolds, but to the Irish nationalist poet George Nugent Reynolds (1770?–1802), the descendant of an ancient family of Catholic landowners in County Leitrim. Reynolds's once popular poem, 'The Catholic's Lamentation', also known as 'Green were the Fields where my Forefathers dwelt O', addresses that very dispossession of the old Irish families that is a partially submerged theme in *The Absentee* (*DNB*; O'Sullivan 1958, 1:39, 247; 2:66).

By advancing and then denying Grace Nugent's Irish identity, Maria Edgeworth seems at cross purposes with her own intentions, but she implicitly continues to assert that Irish identity by hinting at a Catholic and implicitly Irish identity for Grace's parents. In the last few pages

Grace seems inescapably Irish despite all we have previously heard. The novel ends with a letter from Larry Brady, a postilion at Clonbrony Castle, to his brother Pat in London, describing the triumphant homecoming of Colambre and Grace. The letter, which gave Maria Edgeworth a chance to return to a narrative voice like that of Thady Quirk, was a last-minute solution to the problem of how to end the novel, and was approved, perhaps even suggested, by Richard Lovell Edgeworth (Butler 285, 375). It has the effect of giving an Irish voice the final word and of letting one of the tenants express the satisfaction that he and his fellows feel at the coming reign of Grace and Colambre. The evil bailiff is gone. The tenants have been offered fair leases. An enthusiastic welcoming crowd takes the horses out of the traces and pulls Colambre, his parents, and Grace up the avenue, and then 'the blind harper, O'Neil, with his harp, . . . struck up "Gracey Nugent"' (*Absentee* 264), a song by the famous Carolan, described by Goldsmith in an essay as 'The Last of the Irish Bards'. 'Gracey Nugent', like many of Carolan's songs, celebrates the daughter of one of the old Irish families who were his patrons; Maria Edgeworth would have known it from its inclusion in the first collection of poems translated from Irish, Charlotte Brooke's *Reliques of Irish Poetry* (1789), which printed the original Irish as well as a verse translation, and which quotes from the brief life of Carolan in Joseph Cooper Walker's *Historical Memoirs of the Irish Bards* (1786). The song is also included in Miss Owenson's [Lady Morgan's] *Twelve Original Hibernian Melodies; with English Words, Imitated and Translated from the Works of the Ancient Irish Bards* (1805). Charlotte Brooke cites one of Walker's notes that identifies the subject of the song as 'sister to the late John Nugent, Esq; of Castle-Nugent, Culambre' (Brooke 246; O'Sullivan 1:221; 2:66–9)—presumably the source of Lord Colambre's title. Culambre or Colambre is Coolamber in County Westmeath, near the Longford border. Harper and song are a traditional celebration strongly suggesting an old Irish restoration, as does the general air of enthusiasm and good will among the people. And everyone continues to refer to Grace Reynolds as Grace Nugent despite the change in her identity.

The Absentee represents Maria Edgeworth's most elaborate development of the Lady Morgan plot, with its potential endorsement of the legitimate rights of the old Irish to their lands despite the legal ownership of the Anglo-Irish. It also represents her most tortuous refusal to let that plot and its implications fully work themselves out. She simultaneously hints that the Anglo-Irish order must connect itself with the older tradition if it is to evoke that loyalty which is essential to its survival. After nervously contemplating the displacement of the Anglo-Irish Rackrents by the Irish Quirks in *Castle Rackrent*, and the ambiguous identities of lord and peasant, Anglo-Irish owner and Irish tenant, in *Ennui*, and after creating, then destroying, then obscuring an heiress to the old Irish tradition for the hero of *The Absentee* to marry, she is equally if less tortuously evasive in *Ormond*, her last Irish novel.

As young Harry Ormond, her hero, enters adult life, he is offered three models for possible emulation: Sir Herbert Annaly of Anglo-Irish stock, an enlightened landlord who strongly resembles Richard Lovell Edgeworth; Sir Ulick O'Shane, an Anglicized Irishman, Scottish on his mother's side, who is a government lackey and an unscrupulous speculator with his own and other people's money; and Cornelius O'Shane, known as King Corny of the Black Islands, an old Irish chieftain, Catholic, who lives among his people in the traditional manner and is a less sentimental version of Lady Morgan's Prince of Inismore. Choosing to combine elements of Sir Herbert and King Corny, Ormond will be a prudent agriculturalist but will practise his Edgeworthian virtues on the Black Islands, which he purchases after King Corny's death. Corny had earlier proclaimed him Prince of the islands. Ormond refuses to buy Sir Ulick's more prosperous estate, which is also available. His choice indicates at least a partial allegiance to the traditions King Corny represents.

Maria Edgeworth's treatment of Ormond's marriage once again approaches and then retreats from the Lady Morgan solution of intermarriage and the consequent achievement of legitimacy by uniting a legal owner of land with the heiress of older and more sentimental rights. Ormond falls in love with King Corny's daughter, Dora O'Shane. But Corny has promised her to White Connal, a son of Connal of Glynn. Corny prefers Ormond as his son-in-law and heir, but his word is sacred to him, even after White Connal breaks his neck on an unmanageable horse; Dora is then offered to Black Connal, White Connal's twin brother.

Dora is sardonic about some of the ancient customs maintained at King Corny's castle, and she is a coquette. When Ormond pities her during her first engagement, she responds with a believable mixture of pride, annoyance, and tears. She is perhaps Maria Edgeworth's most interesting Irish woman, and the interest she arouses seems to bar her from the role of heroine. Ormond is most attracted to her when she is safely unavailable and he can pity her as a sacrifice. When she is unexpectedly free because of White Connal's death—in his excitement Corny has temporarily forgotten Black Connal—Harry becomes as ambiguous about Dora as Maria Edgeworth seems to be, and as uncomfortable:

> What were his feelings at this moment? They were in such confusion, such contradiction, he could scarcely tell. Before he heard of White Connal's death . . . he desired nothing so much as to be able to save Dora from being sacrificed to that odious marriage; he thought, that if he were not bound in honour to his benefactor, he should instantly make that offer of his hand and heart to Dora,

which would at once restore her to health and happiness, and fulfil the wishes of her kind, generous father. But now, when all obstacles seemed to vanish, when his rival was no more, when his benefactor declared his joy at being freed from his promise, when he was embraced as O'Shane's son, he did not feel joy: he was surprised to find it; but he could not. Now that he could marry Dora, now that her father expected that he should, he was not clear that he wished it himself.

Quick as obstacles vanished, objections recurred; faults which he had formerly seen so strongly, which of late compassion had veiled from his view, reappeared: the softness of manner, the improvement of temper, caused by love, might be transient as passion. Then her coquetry, her frivolity. She was not that superior kind of woman, which his imagination had painted, or which his judgment could approve, in a wife (*Ormond* 142).

One might well ask, who is being coquettish here? And Maria Edgeworth has already made, in her authorial voice, the same sardonic comments about the arrangements at King Corny's castle that Dora offends Ormond by making.

Once again Maria Edgeworth thwarts the marriage she seems to have been preparing us for, though, as with Lady Geraldine in *Ennui*, she has also hinted at some reservations about the lady's vivacity and equated that with a subtly unsuitable Irish quality. Lady Geraldine, we are told, 'was not ill-natured, yet careless to whom she gave offence, provided she produced amusement; and in this she seldom failed; for, in her conversation, there was much of the raciness of Irish wit, and the oddity of Irish humour' (*Ennui* 87). Lady Geraldine is sent off to India to a presumably happy marriage; Dora rejects Ormond and willingly goes to Paris, briefly infatuated with Black Connal and his Parisian elegance—he is an Irish officer in the French service—but her marriage is unhappy. Ormond will rule the Black Islands, but without the legitimacy that marriage with King Corny's daughter would have conferred.

Instead he marries the colourless Florence Annaly, Sir Herbert's sister. But there is an intriguing, almost subversive detail that complicates this resolution of the marriage issue. Florence is without personality and therefore without markedly Irish characteristics. She has been educated in England. But though her name sounds English, it is the name that County Longford bore—Annaly or Analé—until the old Irish families were driven out early in the seventeenth century, to be replaced by 'Britons and Protestants': 'The chiefly names and all survivals of Irish law and custom were to be abolished . . . the intention was to establish English landlordism and its dependent tenures' (Curtis 1936, 233). As Maria Edgeworth well knew, those 'Britons and Protestants' included her ancestor, Francis Edgeworth, who received the six-hundred-acre Edgeworthstown estate (involving a change from the old Irish place name, Mostrim or Mastrim) in 1619: 'This grant was in accordance with James I's policy of settling Protestants of English descent on lands confiscated from Irish Catholics' (Butler 13). Florence's surname seems almost a desperate though concealed attempt to reintroduce that theme of legitimacy through marriage into the older Irish tradition, which the plot of the book has explicitly rejected.

Maria Edgeworth's flirtations with the theme of intermarriage indicate her awareness of Lady Morgan's themes. They seem to have attracted her strongly, yet she could not bring herself to yield to that attraction, deterred perhaps by her implicit reservations about the position of the Anglo-Irish. Her gingerly handling of the theme suggests how uneasy she must have been about the estrangement between Anglo-Irish and Irish, Protestant and Catholic, legality and ancient traditionary right, landlord and tenant. It suggests too her bleak sense that this estrangement could not be made to vanish by an appeal to mutual interest and mutual fair dealing, longer leases and improved agricultural methods. Perhaps she feared that the Anglo-Irish were incapable of creating among their tenants those emotional ties and loyalty and even love that would make their position secure by connecting them with Irish tradition.

There is one final element in the theme of legitimate rule through marriage with the heiress of ancient rights that Lady Morgan and even Maria Edgeworth may have partially sensed. We can only guess how much each novelist knew about ancient Ireland and its ideas about legitimate chieftainship. Maria Edgeworth, as we have seen, professed little interest in tradition; Lady Morgan sentimentalized it. But both would certainly have been aware of certain echoes of these ancient ideas that can be heard in popular Irish songs of the seventeenth, eighteenth, and early nineteenth centuries. Maria Edgeworth's knowledge of the Irish language was probably very slight. Lady Morgan did know Irish, though we cannot be sure how much or how well: her *Twelve Original Hibernian Melodies* (1805) is described on its title page as 'Imitated and Translated from the Works of the Ancient Irish Bards'. But by 1800 the themes of older nationalist songs in Irish were being reworked in English and were being sung and printed all over Ireland in that language.

A favourite form for these songs, in both languages, concealed a patriotic theme under the guise of a love poem or a poem describing a vision—*aisling*—of a beautiful maiden. The maiden is Ireland, alone, defenceless, robbed of her rightful inheritance, and the poem promises her a strong husband—successively James II, James III, Bonnie Prince Charlie, Napoleon, even L'Aiglon—who will rescue her, restore her lands, marry her, and father strong children upon her (Zimmermann 31–3, 54). She is variously named—Banba, Kathleen ni Houlihan, Rosaleen,

Granuaile or Granu Waile—but fairly consistently depicted: the frontispiece to *Paddy's Resource*, later subtitled *The Harp of Erin*, a booklet of patriotic songs published in Belfast in 1795, is 'Ireland as a woman standing under the Tree of Liberty, holding a harp and a pike topped with a Phrygian cap, some broken chains at her feet: a fairly complete epitome of the contents' (Zimmermann 38).

Kathleen ni Houlihan and the other popular female personifications of Ireland are not merely a convention of eighteenth-century poets. They are also a recollection, faded and altered over the centuries, of the ritual which legitimized an ancient Irish king or chieftain, the source of his right to rule over his lands and people. 'The inauguration of the [ancient Irish] king', writes Myles Dillon, 'was a symbolic marriage with Sovereignty, a fertility rite for which the technical term was *banais rígi*, "royal wedding". Sovereignty was imagined as a goddess whom the king must wed, presumably to ensure the welfare of his kingdom . . . There are many Irish tales in which this idea is expressed, and it persisted into modern times . . . In the seventeenth century Ó Bruadair refers to a king as "the spouse of Cashel". Even in the eighteenth century the poets called Ireland the spouse of her lawful kings' (Dillon and Chadwick 93). Ancient Irish literature has many references to such symbolic matings between a king and 'the sovereignty of Ireland' or the sovereignty of a local area.

Lady Morgan's Glorvina, with her harp, embodies the iconography of Ireland as it was known at the end of the eighteenth century in song and emblem; she is a twin for the figure in a song written to mourn the death of Robert Emmet (1803):

> Despair in her wild eye, a daughter of Erin
>   Appeared on the cliff of a bleak rocky shore,
> Loose in the winds flowed her dark streaming ringlets
>   And heedless she gazed on the dread surge's roar,
> Loud rang her harp in wild tones of despairing,
>   The time past away with the present comparing,
> And in soul-thrilling strains deeper sorrow declaring,
>   She sang Erin's woes and her Emmet's no more
>   (Zimmermann 175–6).

And Glorvina—elusive, mysterious, hardly a real woman—clearly represents a memory of that old tradition by which marriage with the local tribal goddess gave a chieftain legitimacy. In *The Wild Irish Girl* she can legitimize even an Anglo-Irish 'chieftain' and evoke for him a traditional loyalty that Grace Nugent and Dora O'Shane can only remotely hint at. But Maria Edgeworth refuses to let Grace and Dora fulfil the roles they seem destined for, though she is also reluctant to relinquish those roles entirely for them.

Both writers seem to grasp intuitively the broader importance of the theme. For the Anglo-Irish to rule, it is not enough to have legal right or British protection. It is necessary to connect in some way with Irish tradition, to recognize and respect that tradition and the attitudes it embodies, to become a part of it. 'History', exclaims a character in William Trevor's story 'Beyond the Pale' (1981), 'is unfinished in this island'. That uneasy awareness was to become the subject of most of the Anglo-Irish writers as they examined their role and their rule as a privileged but endangered minority.

Reprinted from *Nineteenth-Century Fiction* 40:1 (June 1985), pp. 1–22. Copyright 1985 by The Regents of the University of California; permission granted.

3

Fiery Shorthand

The Banim Brothers at Work

The Banim brothers, John (1798–1842) and Michael (1796–1874), are not well known among students of nineteenth-century fiction, perhaps not even among those particularly interested in the Irish novelists of the period. Maria Edgeworth virtually invented the Irish, or Anglo-Irish, novel with *Castle Rackrent* (1800) and its successors. Lady Morgan, quick to scent a trend, followed with her own flamboyant fictions. But they both wrote about the gentry—the Anglo-Irish gentry, or the old decayed Irish gentry—and usually from an upper-class point of view. The Banim brothers were the first novelists who were Irish rather than Anglo-Irish—Banim is a Tipperary-Kilkenny variant of Bannon, Ó Banáin. They write of the 'strong' (prosperous) farmers of the southeast, of struggling tenants, of the people of the roads, and of the various secret organizations that attacked landlords and tithe collectors in late eighteenth- and early nineteenth-century Ireland: Whiteboys, Rockites, Caravats, Shanavests, groups led by Captain Rock, Captain Moonlight, Captain Starshine, or by John Doe and Richard Roe—names the peasants knew all too well from their unwilling experiences with legal documents and proceedings. The brothers were genuine collaborators, each adding to the other's manuscripts. John improved clarity, Michael added details of custom and idiom.

Like all Irish writers, the Banims hoped for English readers, and they tried to describe Irish grievances, and the savage reprisals those grievances sometimes provoked, without appearing to condone violence. There is always a didactic element: Irishmen must abandon their sectarian rivalries to form a united nation, Protestants must surrender their privileges, Catholics their long-cherished resentment. Men and women of good will have been preaching the same doctrine in Ireland ever since, with some success, but Northern Ireland shows us that it is still needed, and the Banims' fiction is unfortunately still valid as a kind of political guide to the problems of that unhappy province.

When they began their career, with the pseudonymous *Tales by the O'Hara Family* (1825), the 'mere' Irish were only a generation removed from the Penal Laws, which inhibited Catholicism and condemned Catholics to poverty by restricting the land and property they could hold, the professions they could enter. Daniel O'Connell was abroad in the land, and the cause of Catholic Emancipation was up, with all the hopes of equality and material progress that it seemed to offer. The Banims usually set their stories a little before their own time, usually in the late eighteenth century, perhaps to remind their readers that there had not been much improvement in Irish conditions for a long while. They supported Emancipation, but as late as 1833, in *The Ghost-Hunter*, Michael is eager to reassure Protestant or English readers that Emancipation will not bring about a Catholic tyranny or acts of revenge. James II, he remarks, had tried to make Catholicism the established religion, but when James lost the battle of the Boyne, 'away, also, went the political existence of the religion he had tried (in our modest opinion) to scandalize, by unnaturally connecting it with political power . . . That no evil chance may ever confer on it the favours he failed in perpetuating to it, is our honest and hearty prayer' (*Ghost-Hunter* 64).

The Boyne Water (1826), John's most important novel, is about Ireland in the time of James II and the defeat of James and the Catholic Irish by William of Orange at the battle of the Boyne (1690), a defeat that Banim rightly saw as continuing to define the conditions of Irish life in his own times. Banim matches the fanatical Protestant George Walker, who took command of Derry during the Catholic siege of the city (in modern Derry, Catholic and Protestant neighbourhoods are to some extent still determined by the lines of that siege), with the equally fanatical Catholic priest, O'Haggerty. Both preach a gospel of sectarian hate and both die in the battle, each by the other's hand. Banim tries to balance these figures with a quartet of lovers: young Robert Evelyn, Protestant, loves Catholic Eva M'Donnell; Robert's sister, Esther Evelyn, loves Eva's brother Edmund. All four respect individual human qualities rather than sectarian distinctions. The situation seems to promise some kind of symbolic reconciliation by marriage, as when Scott—whose influence is strong in *The Boyne Water*—reconciles Saxon and Norman by marriage at the end of *Ivanhoe*, or Catholic/Stuart and Protestant/Hanoverian at the end of *Rob Roy*. But Ireland does not permit such a resolution. The book ends with Edmund M'Donnell an exile from an Ireland where a Catholic gentleman can no longer live. Esther dies in the siege of Derry, a victim of the Catholic siege and the Protestant refusal to surrender. Robert Evelyn, writing on the last page to the exiled Edmund, can only express the hope that 'Englishmen will yet pay their fathers' debt of faith to Ireland'—presumably by granting Catholic Emancipation.

In 1827 Gerald Griffin, concluding his *Tales of the Munster Festivals*, criticized the Banims for drawing 'pictures . . . more striking than favourable' by depicting Irish peasants in 'moods of troubled gloom and of rude excitement' and by emphasizing 'the violent and fearful passions of the people' (Griffin, *Rivals*, unpaged 'Conclusion'). The remark tells us more about Griffin's fears than about the Banims, but it does point out a persistent feature of their work, a sense that savage violence lurks just below the surface of Irish life, ever ready to break out. William Carleton, John Synge, and Sean O'Casey were later to dwell on the same bleak truth. In *Croohore of the Bill-Hook*, written almost entirely by Michael, the sinister dwarf Crohoore is first introduced sharpening the instrument which gives him his name, seated a little apart in a genre picture of a strong farmer's kitchen but still in the glow of the firelight. Later in *Crohoore*, a tithe proctor's ears are cropped with grim humour: 'bud it isn't none o' your blades that's fit for nothin' but cuttin' butther . . . 'twould take the horns iv a ten-year-old bull, not to spake iv a poor proctor's ears, though them same does be hard enough in regard of all the prayers they won't hear, an' all the lies they tell . . . I'll do the thing nate an' handy . . . I'd whip the ears iv a bishop, not to talk of a crature like you, a darker night nor this . . . an' wouldn't bring any o' the head wid me, neither. . .' (*Tales*, 1st series 1:219–20). Unarmed peasants trample a dragoon to death during a battle; Whiteboys cut the throats of a farmer and his family. A jailer's apartment features 'many ponderous keys, polished from constant use; not rusty, as they used to be in the old romances.' The Banims knew well that Irish jail keys never became rusty from disuse (*Tales*, 1st series 2:84).

Crohoore is a savage tale of violence and superstition in which a farmer and his family are murdered and their daughter, Alley, abducted. Crohoore is suspected of both crimes, but there is also a band of Whiteboys in the neighbourhood, who attack farmhouses at night to protest the tithes they must pay to support the Protestant church—or to pay off old grudges under the guise of political action. Their leader has committed the murders in order to abduct Alley, but Crohoore has in fact saved her by spiriting her away to a half-buried cabin in the hills. The peasants assume she has been abducted by 'the good people' and hidden underground in one of their raths—the old grave mounds so common in Ireland. With considerable skill, Banim combines truth and superstition in his plot. Alley is safe for a time because the peasants are afraid to search for anyone the good people have stolen, but the Whiteboy leader continues to search, claiming possession of a fairy charm which will protect him. Crohoore's demonic aspects have been emphasized, and the tale is able to play on all the legends, about demons and the *sidhe*, the people of the mounds who carry mortals away underground—legends that play their part in the *Táin* and the eighth-

century *Echtrae Chonali Choím* (The Journey of Connla the Fair), in Le
Fanu's *Carmilla*, in Stoker's *Dracula*. Alley *has* been taken underground by
a demon, at least an apparent demon. She *has* been out of the world. An
improbable and melodramatic device becomes more plausible because it is
part of the mental atmosphere that the book sets out to convey.

Both Banims, but especially Michael, had a good ear for Irish dialect
and, like their fellow countrymen Boucicault and Shaw, the varied speech
of Englishmen. 'Tis the Hoirish cry, as 'em calls it, what such loike woild
Hoirish always howls, dom 'em,' says a Yorkshireman, confronted by an
Irish funeral; and a cockney replies, 'Demme, though . . . if them 'ere
vimen, what are arter the coffin, ben't on a lark, like, east-why, they don't
come down a tear, for all they clap hands, and hollar, the velps . . .' (*Tales*,
1st series 1:234). They sprinkle their pages with Irish words and phrases,
reminding the reader that this is a foreign world, emphatically not English,
and that Irish peasants, who often sound comic when speaking in English
to soldiers and magistrates, have another language when they are at home.
Before Terence Delany, a dispossessed peasant, dies in *Crohoore*, he delivers
a moving speech, and Michael comments, 'if the language uttered . . .
appear too refined for one in his situation of life, it is ascertainable as only
in strict unison with the genius and idiom of the language in which he
spoke, and from which we have literally translated; in the Irish, there is
nothing of what is known by the name of vulgarism; its construction even
in the mouths of the peasantry, who to this day use it, has been and can be
but little corrupted; nor could the familiar colloquy of the meanest among
them, be rendered, in English, into common-place or slang' (*Tales*, 1st
series 1:247–8). A man is not, of course, upon oath when defending his
national language. John, who had the task of seeing *Croohore* through the
press in London, comments drily, 'It is tremendous work to compel
English types to shape themselves into Irish words' (Murray 152–3).

The Banims' social status, as sons of a small tradesman and farmer in
Kilkenny, gave them a greater insight into the life of the poor and at the
same time made them more eager than Maria Edgeworth had been to
assert Irish rights. They condemn terrorism, but remind their readers that
Whiteboys and similar groups exist because the Penal Laws left the Irish
leaderless and ignorant, and the unjust tithes have made them poor. Tithes
ought not to be protested with violence, but they ought to be abolished.
When Maria Edgeworth raises the question of tithes in *Ormond* (1817),
King Corny, her Catholic gentleman, has no fondness for tithes, but hopes
for 'no quarrels' and insists that quarrels imply 'Faults on both sides'. The
priest who argues that 'it don't become a good Catholic to say that' about
tithes is seen as boorishly contentious. In a subtle way the Banims are
often contentious (*Ormond* 183). When a British officer praises a girl's

beauty in John Banim's *John Doe* (1825), an Irish listener agrees, 'considerin' sich as them that lives on phatoes one an' twenty times in the week' (*Tales*, 1st series 3:31–2). In the same novel another officer comments to a travelling priest on the superiority of Italian over British scenery, and the priest concurs; the Italian landscape is more beautiful than the English 'owing . . . to the influence of atmosphere . . . and from the scarcity of trees in Ireland, much more so than the Irish one' (*Tales*, 1st series 3:87). The English deforestation of Ireland is one of Ireland's long remembered grievances: the forests were destroyed first because they sheltered the survivors of James II's armies, later because the British navy needed Irish oak. 'What shall we do for timber?/The last of the woods is down . . . The crown of the forest has withered/And the last of its game is gone'—so, in Frank O'Connor's version (O'Connor 100–1), runs one of the most famous Irish laments, composed in the seventeenth century to mourn the passing of the old Irish great houses, the woods, and the old Irish aristocracy. Deforestation bulks large in the Citizen's diatribe in *Ulysses*. Banim underlines his introduction of this controversial item by letting his English officer protest 'he could not understand why—unless it was attributable to the indolence of its people—Ireland should be so "shamefully deficient in trees"' (*Tales*, 1st series, 3:87). Michael trails the same coat in *Crohoore*, sending Crohoore and Alley across a range of hills with 'here and there a stunted oak, the relics of the large woods, that about fifty or sixty years before [that is, about 1715, since the story takes place about 1775] had overspread the district' (*Tales*, 1st series, 55–6).

John Banim was perhaps a little more moderate than his brother, and a little more inclined to seek his heroes and heroines among the gentlefolk—though *The Nowlans*, in *Tales*, Second Series (1826), presents farmers and clerks. Probably his most successful work, it is a bleak tale of a young priest who breaks his vows and marries a Protestant girl, though he believes that by marrying he has lost his soul. In *The Fetches*, John's first contribution to the 1825 *Tales*, a genteel young couple see one another's fetches—a fetch is an apparition of a living person, and its appearance means that that person is about to die. Young Harry Tresham and his Anna spend far too much time discussing the Irish superstitions which Harry has learned about from his peasant nurse. When they see the fetches, they become ill and are separated. But at the end the couple meet by a waterfall, the fetches reappear, and the young people plunge to their deaths. The story is partly a psychological study of those who frighten themselves by brooding too much over superstitions, but it partly endorses those superstitions. Other people see the fetches too. They are real. And they have risen out of the dirt and ignorance of the peasant cabin where Harry learned about them to destroy this educated and amiable young Anglo-Irish couple. Irish superstition is based on ignorance, which in turn is caused by misgovernment. It is as fatal as the diseases which breed in Dickens's slums. In *John Doe*, his other contribution to the 1825 *Tales*, John Banim is more ambivalent. The local tithe proctor is a monster of cruelty, but when the Whiteboy hero kills him, the deed makes him unworthy of the heroine. Instead she chooses a lawfully licensed killer, the English officer Graham, who is hunting the Whiteboys.

John Banim's *The Anglo-Irish of the Nineteenth Century* (1828) is almost a rewrite of Maria Edgeworth's *The Absentee* (1812), and endorses her belief that Ireland needs better, but not fewer, landlords. The plot—letting an absentee Irish landlord visit his estate incognito, see the abuses carried on in his name by unjust stewards, and resolve to live at home and make the system operate more justly and more efficiently—became almost a cliché among nineteenth-century Irish novelists,—there is even Alice Milligan's *A Royal Democrat* (1892), in which the Prince of Wales comes to examine his Irish 'estate' and decides to rule Ireland more benevolently in future. John Banim's hero arrives at the same resolve. He comes to accept, and to accept with pride, the Irish element in his identity—previously he has called himself Anglo-Irish or English-Irish, emphasizing the English element. Despite absurdities of plot depending on mistaken identity, near doubles, and deliberate mystification by the hero's pro-Irish sister, the hero's conversion is believable. And perhaps even the constant disguises, incognitos, half-glimpsed figures, and whispered warnings can be defended as contributing to a picture of an incohesive society swarming with spies, outlaws, and assassins.

The Banims owed a debt to Scott, as Scott admitted a debt to Maria Edgeworth. But in exploring the human potential for savage behaviour, the controlling power of superstition, and especially in their awareness of the crushing effect of history on individuals, they anticipate—although they remain minor novelists—some of the great Russian writers who were also members of an incohesive society. 'Go to the Arran [*sic*] Islands,' Yeats ordered Synge, when they met in 1896, 'express a life that has never found expression'. It had been expressed already by the Banims, and by other nineteenth-century Irish writers. Yeats had forgotten his own words to Father Matthew Russell in 1889: 'Carleton and Banim . . . had a square-built power no later Irishman has approached. They saw the whole of everything they looked at . . . the brutal with the tender, the coarse with the refined . . . The old men tried to make one see life plainly but all written down in a kind of fiery shorthand that it might never be forgotten' (*Letters* 143).

Reprinted with deletions from *Nineteenth-Century Fiction* 35:2 (September 1980), pp. 193–9. Originally a review of reprinted novels by the Banim Brothers. Copyright 1980 by The Regents of the University of California; permission granted.

4

Self-Fashioning as Pseudo-History

Roger O'Connor's *Chronicles of Eri*

In the eighteenth century, a small group of Irish historians tried to refute the view of Irish history shared by most English, Scottish, and Anglo-Irish historians of the period: that the Irish were a savage and undisciplined race, who had never developed a legal system or a system of government; that Ireland owed what civilization she displayed to the English, who imposed order on Irish chaos after 1169. She owed literacy and Christianity to St Patrick, who was probably British. The argument served as a justification for English rule of Ireland.

To the eighteenth-century mind, civilization implied literacy. In his *Dissertations on the Antient History of Ireland* (1753), Charles O'Conor of Belanagare, the most distinguished Irish antiquarian in the second half of the century, argued that the Irish had been literate long before St Patrick. He was seconded by Sylvester O'Halloran in several works, commencing with *Insula Sacra* (1770), and, less soundly, by Colonel Charles Vallancey, whose *Essay on the Antiquity of the Irish Language* (1772) claimed that the Irish and Punic languages were closely related. Vallancey's evidence was some eighteen lines of Punic in Plautus's *Poenulus*, which he insisted could be read as Irish.

Charles O'Conor and his circle were for a time convinced that Vallancey was right, and he also received some support from the great linguist, Sir William Jones. The theory was given plausibility by the tradition, recorded in *Lebor Gábala* and other early texts, that the ancestors of the Irish had come to Ireland from the Near East via Spain. Since the extensive Carthaginian settlements in Spain were well attested, it did not seem unreasonable to expect cognates between Irish and Punic. The Carthaginians had certainly been literate at a respectably early date in history, and were descended from the Phoenicians, who had invented the alphabet. In addition, by arguing a Carthaginian and then Spanish origin for the civilization of pre-Patrician Ireland, the Irish could deny any debt to that Roman

civilization which the English so much revered. Though Rome had destroyed Carthage, her language and culture had escaped to Ireland, there to
flourish until destroyed by the English—a notion Brian Friel touches upon
lightly at the end of his *Translations* (1980). By arguing that Ireland had
not been civilized by Rome via England, any notion of a cultural debt to
England was repudiated, and England's moral right to rule Ireland implicitly questioned. Anglo-Irish writers critical of O'Conor and Vallancey were
quick to reassert the 'Northern' theory, that Ireland had been settled and
civilized from England. In the heady days of Grattan's independent Irish
Parliament, the Punic theory had some vogue. Vallancey himself never
explicitly abandoned it, but ceased to talk about it after he had become
converted to Sir William Jones's theory that Irish was an Indo-European
language descended from Sanskrit.

When Roger O'Connor (1762–1834) revived the Punic theory in his
Chronicles of Eri (1822), he coolly appropriated Charles O'Conor's ideas
about a pre-Patrician Irish civilization and Vallancey's arguments about
the affinities of Irish and Punic, without acknowledging either O'Conor or
Vallancey. He even reprinted Vallancey's Irish reading of the passage from
Plautus as his own. In doing so, he concocted a literary fraud in which he
himself, heavily disguised, figured as Ireland's king, law-giver, and historian.
The history of Ireland, as he narrates it, turns into a disguised and fantastic
autobiography, a compensation for the shady and rather futile activities
that figure in his biography.

Roger O'Connor was a bad son, a bad brother, a bad husband, a bad
tenant, and a bad neighbour. He was a liar, a swindler, a thief, and a pla-
giarist. His extra-literary activities make him seem like a character escaped
from the pages of *Castle Rackrent*, or Sir Jonah Barrington's memoirs.
There was, for example, his hold-up and robbery of the Galway coach in
1812, an action he claimed had been carried out to secure letters which
might embarrass his friend, Sir Francis Burdett. A debt collector who
succeeded in collecting money from O'Connor was immediately set upon
and robbed only a few steps from O'Connor's door. Having rented Dangan
Castle from its owners, he insured it heavily in his own name, after which
the castle immediately burned down. When his brother, the United Irishmen's leader Arthur O'Connor, went into French exile, Roger plundered
Arthur's estate which he had been trusted to manage. Twice married, he
also ran off with a barrister's wife, then abandoned her. At the end of his
life, his companion was a peasant girl from Kerry; he claimed she was the
direct descendant of ancient Irish kings, and referred to her as the Princess
of Kerry (Madden 599).

Charles O'Conor of Belanagare was a close relative of the O'Conor
Don, and provably descended from the O'Conor kings of Connaught.

Roger O'Connor, no relation, was descended from no one in particular: a Bandon merchant named Conner, allegedly of English origin, who had purchased an estate near Dunmanway in County Cork (Webb 382). His father, also named Roger, was a tithe proctor. It may be that Roger O'Connor identified in some way with Charles O'Conor of Belanagare and his genuinely royal lineage. Roger, we are told, was

> naturally morose—a man of self-concentrated thoughts—given to brood over old recollections and traditions, and to ruminate on past glories of ancient families he desired to find evidence of having once been in alliance with his own . . . he assumed, in his manners, air, and look, the frankness, ease, open-heartedness, blandness, and amenity and dignified bearing of a high-born gentleman: such as became one lineally descended from Irish kings. He professed the most ardent patriotism, and proclaimed his readiness 'to do or die' for his country; but he was incapable of an act of high daring for any great object that could be turned to a national account. He professed to love truth more than life—and yet he spent a large portion of that life forging lies, concocting deliberate schemes of imposture, and promulgating literary forgeries with a view of hurting the principles of Christianity (Madden 590–1).

As a young man, Roger O'Connor was 'an ultra-loyalist, a terrorist, a peasant-hunter'. Later, perhaps influenced by his brother Arthur, he joined the United Irishmen, though he was never a leader in that organization, except in his own fantasies. He was, however, compromised by his brother's prominent role, and further compromised when another brother, greedy for his property, accused him of treason. This led to a series of arrests, and a six-month imprisonment in Cork before he was tried and acquitted. A visit to London, where he petitioned to visit his imprisoned brother Arthur, led to further arrests and ultimately to imprisonment with the United Irishmen's leaders at Fort George (Madden 591–5).

The dream of royal ancestry, and the exaggerated sense of his own political importance that arose from the government's treatment of him as a United Irishmen's leader, seem to have persuaded O'Connor that he was Ireland's natural chieftain, indeed her rightful king. In his bombastic *Letters to the People of Great Britain and Ireland* (1799) he claims that the Irish Secretary told him that, while there was no real evidence against him, he was to be imprisoned because the government knew 'of *his power*, and their opinion of an inclination (on his part) to give them opposition'. The remark is probably as imaginary as the power, though the jittery government of the day were also capable of self-delusion about Ireland. 'Time and place were favourable to his pretensions', recalled an acquaintance, writing in 1828:

> the confusion of Irish history, the national prejudices of the people, and their eagerness to grasp at delusions, were so many inducements to a cunning mind to seek the gratification of low ambition; and accordingly, Roger O'Connor

assumed a place in society to which he had no claim. He did this, however, with mean timidity, with a spirit which showed that he was not a daring soul, and with a littleness which would have rendered results harmless, had not a silly, stupid government forced notoriety upon him (Madden 593–5).

Politically irrelevant, except in his own imagination, O'Connor eventually turned to concocting a history of the Irish people with himself as hero: his two volume *Chronicles of Eri; being the History of the Gaal Sciot Iber: or, the Irish People; Translated from the Original Manuscripts in the Phoenician Dialect of the Scythian Language* (London: 1822). The author is simply 'O'Connor', and his frontispiece-portrait, showing him clutching a royal crown and one of the 'original manuscripts', is modestly captioned, 'O'Connor Cier-rige [beloved king] Head of his Race, and O'Connor, chief of the prostrated people of his Nation. *Soumis pas vaincus* [beaten but not conquered].'

'This is the fourth effort which I have made, to present to the world a faithful history of my country', he declares, in a preface that proclaims his own political importance, his imprisonments and persecutions, and connects the *Chronicles* with these vicissitudes. Imprisoned in Dublin for treason in 1798–99, he refused 'an earldom and a pension' rather than desert the Irish cause. Writing in prison, he had brought Irish history 'down to a very late period' when the guards seized all that he had written, together 'with such ancient manuscripts as I had then by me', which 'have never since been recovered'. A second version, completed in Fort George, was burned at his wife's request, lest the authorities use it as a pretext to return him to prison. After returning to Ireland in 1803, 'having availed myself of the earliest opportunity of reclaiming from the bowels of the earth the most ancient manuscripts of the History of Eri, I recommenced my pursuit upon a more enlarged scale.' He had reached AD 1315 when that version perished in the fire at Dangan Castle (1809). Finally, after he was tried and acquitted of the Galway coach robbery in 1817, O'Connor set to work again and produced the text we have, 'a literal translation into the English tongue, (from the Phoenician dialect of the Scythian language,) of the ancient manuscripts which have, fortunately for the world, been preserved through so many ages, chances, and vicissitudes.' He concedes that the manuscripts themselves may not be contemporary with the events they record, but insists they are 'faithful transcripts from the most ancient records; it not being within the range of possibility, either from their style, language, or contents, that they could have been forged' (*Chronicles of Eri* 1:viii–ix).

O'Connor's translated text is preceded by a 360-page 'Demonstration' correcting the errors of ancient authors and of Scripture. The *Chronicles* begin with 'The Writings of Eolus', who ruled Gael-ag (Galicia in Spain) from 1368 to 1335 BC. Eolus briefly narrates the history of the Scythians from 5357 BC the emigration to Spain of a group of them led by Calma in 1490 BC, and continues to his own time. The 'Chronicles of Gael-ag' describe their sojourn in Spain, where they become the Gael or Celt-Iberians, until a second migration, this time to Eri or Ireland, in 1006 BC. The 'Annals of Eri' are the history of Ireland until 7 BC. In his preface, O'Connor promised three more volumes, one bringing Ireland's history to AD 1169, one covering the period from 1169 'to the day of my birth', and a final volume giving

> the history of my own times . . . which five volumes will be a complete continued history of this noble island, under the names of Eri, to the year 1169, and of Ireland from that epoch, from the most remote time to the instant on which I shall drop my pen (*Chronicles* 1:xi).

O'Connor clearly identifies with Eolus, who is at once his people's king and their historian, preserving for them their past and legislating wisely for their future. Eolus emerges as an eighteenth-century rationalist of royal ancestry, a learned antiquarian, and one who writes in Biblical cadences if not with Biblical authority. He is at once a portrait of the ideal ruler and an idealized self-portrait. His double role as hero and narrator persists even in those portions of the *Chronicles* allegedly written long after his death: the 'Writings of Eolus' are read aloud each year at the great assembly of Tara. Wise kings turn to them in moments of crisis; when they are ignored, priestcraft and anarchy flourish.

O'Connor 'would talk whole pages of Voltaire's *Philosophical Dictionary*, as if he was improvising a new theology' (Madden 597). As Eolus he preached a kind of rational deism, and denied the possibility of revelation, or of any communication between God and man, either directly or through a priesthood:

> It is said BAAL formed everything from the earth, the water, and the air, and into man alone breathed the spirit of fire, pure essence of himself, the effect whereof is reason.
> Thus it is said, who knoweth how truly? With whom did BAAL hold talk?— At what time did he draw nigh unto the children of men? Which one of the sons of man did ever approach BAAL? Who is he that ever heard the sound of the voice of BAAL, that he could distinguish the words of his breath? Doth BAAL speak aloud to make man affear'd? Who can tell his words?—none.
> Man imagineth.—Are the thoughts which he divulgeth to his fellow just?
> For myself I ask, and none can tell, how came BAAL himself? Is he not composed of materials the same as all other living beings, his huge dimensions, his might and power, effects of combinations unknown to man?
> Many are the things beyond the reason which man possesseth: he may fancy—what availeth fancy? It is of no avail: reason and wisdom reject such, as misconceptions of vanity.

> Man would be thought to know all things . . . and for lack of wisdom flieth
> to deceitful fancy . . . My son,—Do thy utmost to attain to the certain
> knowledge of things of this world within the scope of thy understanding. List
> not to idle dreams of airy fantasy . . . (*Chronicles* 1:1–4).

Eolus added a set of fifteen commandments, forbidding murder, theft, lying, envy and flattery, urging 'praise to BAAL, the author of light and life', respect for parents and siblings, care for widows, orphans, strangers, and the poor, mercy towards 'every living creature', control over the passions, and finally, 'Preserve the glory of thy race, die, or live free.' He also established a college of OLAM or wise men, to preserve and teach his writings; the OLAM are to be a safeguard against the priests of BAAL, with their false claims to supernatural knowledge.

So far, so good. There is little to object to in O'Connor's moral maxims, except perhaps that in composing them he has taken the roles both of God and of Moses. The orthodox Christian might object to the denial of divine revelation, but the warning against letting priests meddle in politics is understandable. Ireland would soon see Daniel O'Connell's crusade for Catholic Emancipation become increasingly sectarian, and eventually lead to the powerful role of the Catholic clergy in Irish politics.

Preserved and proclaimed by wise OLAM, obeyed by wise kings, the teachings of Eolus become the basis of Irish law. The king is a constitutional monarch, ruling together with an annual assembly or parliament, which ratifies or denies his decrees. Though there are occasional usurpations or civil wars, and weak kings sometimes allow the priesthood too much power, O'Connor describes for us an Irish people who are usually well-governed, literate, rational, and determined to preserve their freedom.

The teachings of Eolus, supplemented by other wise kings and teachers, and the democratic institutions they create, constitute the spirit of O'Connor's narrative. Its body is the history of the people of Eri from their origin 'on the left side of the sun's rising, beyond the sources of the great waters'. Perhaps the most striking aspect of their early history is the identification of the 'Phoenician dialect of the Scythian language' with the Irish language. When they spread themselves 'from the flood of SGEIND even to the banks of TETH-GRIS', that is, from the Indus to the Tigris, we learn that SGEIND, from Irish *sgeim*, foam, is the original Irish name for the Indus; Tigris is from *teth-gris*, sparks of heat, and Euphrates from *affraighe*, swelling. As the ancestral Gaels wend their way northwards, then westwards to Spain and eventually Ireland, they move through a landscape linguistically Irish. Driven from Mesopotamia by invading Assyrians or EIS SOIR, 'multitude from the east', they settle in Armenia, ARDMIONN, Irish for 'the summit of the height', named from Mount Ararat or, in Irish *Air-rearacht-mionn-e*, 'This is the place of ascent'. The Irish Armenians eventually rule from the Black Sea (Mare Euxine, from Irish *moir eis-amhan*, 'sea of the multitude of rivers') to the Caspian. In 1950 BC Glas, a prince of the royal house, establishes a new kingdom in the Caucasus, called IBER, 'the place of ER, land of heroes'. Glas's successor, File ('poet') refuses to pay tribute to his Armenian relatives, establishing Iberian independence. The place name Iber is later transferred to Spanish Iberia, and later to Hibernia (*Chronicles* 1: 5–6; cli–cliv; clxii).

Two brothers claim the Iberian throne in 1492 BC. Calma is the people's choice, but his brother surrounds the hill of Tobrad—'hill of election', from *tagh-barrachd*, the prototype for Tara—'with chosen bands, mad with strong drink'. Calma leaves peacefully, taking with him 'all of the GAAL of SCIOT of IB-ER'. They visit Phoenicia or *Aoi-Mag*, the country of knowledge, where they overawe the treacherous King of Sidon— named, we learn, from Irish *sgadan*, herring. The Phoenicians ferry them to Spain (*Eis-feine*, multitude of Phoenicians), where they resolve to 'die, or live free', a slogan O'Connor often repeats. One might argue that it proves the Hiberno-Scythian origins of New Hampshire (*Chronicles* 1:22–8).

In the middle of all this, O'Connor, not content with revising history, corrects the Bible as well. That migration from Mesopotamia to Mount Ararat, when the Assyrians invaded, is the true version of what Scripture presents as Noah's flood. Eolus describes the invasion in figurative language: 'a multitude . . . poured in upon the land of our fathers . . . even as a torrent of mighty waters'. Fortunately Ard-fear, 'chief of the race', escaped up the Euphrates, floating 'on the bosom of blessed AFFREIDG-EIS, and the waters bare up his little skiff, till he alighted on the plain of ARD-MIONN'. When he later dies, he is coffined in the skiff, and a huge cairn raised over him. He is posthumously hailed as Naoi, 'ship' in Irish, which the writers of Scripture have perverted into Noah while misunder-standing the whole event as a literal flood (*Chronicles* 1:6–8).

It is not surprising that words we take to be Hebrew are in fact Irish. *Talmud* is *Tuil-mead*, 'the improved augmentation'. Goliah of Gath, 'the haft of whose spear was like a weaver's beam', and after him the Goths, are named from *goth* or *gath*, a long spear. Halleluiah is Irish *uail-ol-uagh*, 'a mournful loud cry or howling'. The Hebrew word means 'praising the Lord joyously', O'Connor concedes, 'but were not all their religious ceremonies sad and mournful? did they not thanksgive piteously and whiningly?' (*Chronicles* 1: clx, clxv, clv).

In his 'Demonstration' O'Connor frequently corrects the errors of classical authors, who have misrepresented the Scythians or the Irish. As editor of his own text, he even sometimes corrects himself. When the sons of Iolar die rebelliously attempting to extend their domains, and the text describes their ghosts as wandering because no grave marker commemorates them, O'Connor adds a footnote: 'This was the religious idea, but always combated by the *Olam*, who held, that the immortality of the spirit was the perpetuity of the knowledge and wisdom which man imparted and left (to use their expression) amongst men on earth' (*Chronicles* 2:20) Erac of Munster challenges Erial of Leinster with fighting words:

> 'Doth the blood of the horseman pored out on *Ceseol* yet smell in the nostrils of the eaglets? Attempt not too high a flight, lest thy wings be clipped, and a hook be put in thy nose, brood of Iolar.'

'This passage, in the original, is full of keen satire', O'Connor comments. '*Marcad*, the original name of *Iber*, signifies a horseman; and Iolar means an eagle' (*Chronicles* 2: 20, 22–3). When the *Ard Olam* reads the chronicles before High King Fionn (516–507 BC), the King points out that a recent landslide has been omitted, and so 'I, Urla' inserts it, occasioning O'Connor to note, 'In the original the memorial of this event is written on a slip of skin attached to the roll' (*Chronicles* 2:265).

It would be tedious to follow O'Connor's circumstantial account of the next 4000 years of Irish history, describing the reigns of twenty-two kings of GAEL-AG/Galicia, and eighty kings and one sovereign queen of Ireland. The story resembles that of the Israelites in the Old Testament, who behave themselves for a time, then inevitably backslide, disregard the law and the prophets, seek after strange gods, until God punishes them and they return to their obedience. The High Priests of Baal continually struggle to achieve political power, which inevitably involves diminishing the power of the Ard Olam and his fellow wise men. Sometimes they even prevent the ordained reading of Eolus's writings. After each priestly victory, sooner or later there is an inevitable reaction, and another wishful projection of Roger O'Connor, either as king or as Ard Olam, restores the constitution.

The most conspicuous of these later self-portraits is Eocaid King of Ulster, who becomes Eocaid Olam Fodla (703–663 BC), the first Ard-ri or High King of Ireland. He institutes a national assembly to meet each year at Tara. Eocaid, known in *Lebor Gabála* and other traditional accounts as Ollamh Fodhla, begins his Ulster reign by invading Munster, whose King Noid has slandered the Ulster royal family. He defeats and kills Noid, but is generous in victory. He even attends his enemy's funeral (*Chronicles* 2:72–5), thus inaugurating an Irish political tradition that still survives.

Eocaid reminds his fellow kings of their common ancestry and persuades them to accept the common code of laws he draws up, and to participate in the national assembly over which he will preside. O'Connor reports the seating arrangements for the opening ceremonies in great detail:

And the chief secretary of *Eri* sat between the throne and the table, close thereunto:

And the chief secretary of *Mumain* [Munster] sat between the king of *Mumain* and the table.

And the chief secretary of *Gaelen* [Leinster] sat between the king of *Gaelen* and the table.

And the chief secretary of *Ullad* [Ulster] sat between the seat of the king of *Ullad* and the table.

And the princes of the race of *Iber*, the first-born of the hero, and the princes of *Ith*, sat on the right and left of the king of *Mumain*.

And the princes of the race of *Iolar*, sat on the right and left of the king of *Gaelen*.

And the princes of the race of *Er* sat on the right and left of the seat of the king of *Ullad*.

And the nobles sat behind the princes of the nations, to which they belonged.

And the *Olam*, and the heads of the people, sat behind the nobles of their lands.

And on the table in their midst were the rolls of other times closed, and the writings of *Eolus*, and the chronicles of the *Gaal*.

And rolls open to receive the words of the days as they pass, for the eye of the children of the land that are to come (*Chronicles* 2:97).

As Dr Johnson remarked about Macpherson's Ossian, 'a man might write such stuff for ever, if he would *abandon* his mind to it' (Boswell 1207). When we remember that the 'writings of *Eolus* and the chronicles of the *Gaal*' are in fact the writings of Roger O'Connor, their pride of place in the assembly is endearingly absurd. Many years later, when Queen Maca or Macha (310–309 BC) builds the palace of Armagh, the writings of O'Connor are borne there by three chariots in solemn procession, 'with mirth and joy, and music, dancing, and festivity' (*Chronicles* 2:357).

In his inaugural address as High King, Eocaid successfully proposes a rational code of laws, with rights for all. He rejects the laws which the priests claim are from Baal, which protect the rich against the poor by threatening the poor with supernatural punishments. He establishes an independent judiciary, endows a number of colleges for the *Olam*, and invents the principle of Tanistry, reserving the kingship to descendants of Er, his ancestor, but denying a king's eldest son any guaranteed right to succeed to the throne; instead, each king is to choose as his *Tanaiste* or successor the most capable among Er's descendants. As we know, that wise innovation has endured (*Chronicles* 2:98–109).

'Is it not good that the roll of the laws be spread out, and the book of the chronicles be opened, and the words read aloud?' Eocaid asks, in a later speech:

Therefore, what if for times to come we make the usage,
That the roll of the laws of *Eri* be spread out, and the words read, and the custom of *Tainistact* be repeated on the third day [of the annual assembly]?
And the writing of *Eolus*, and the chronicles of *Gaelag* on the second day?
And the chronicles of *Eri* on the day before the assembly doth separate and the doors of the high chamber shall be closed?
For myself I say, my ear doth like to hold the words, as it doth delight in the lengthened note of the delicious harp (*Chronicles* 2:233).

It is so agreed, and thenceforth O'Connor's writings are read annually—at this point, they amount to almost 350 printed pages—and greeted with acclamation.

If the first Eolus, king, lawgiver, and chronicler of his people, is O'Connor's idealized self-portrait, Eocaid Olam Fodla is his ideal reader, never weary of hearing the chronicles read aloud yet again. As the wise Eolus, as various *ard-olam* who preserve and continue the chronicles, as Eocaid Olam Fodla who makes them part of the legislative procedure, O'Connor is continually present in his own text. That text, in turn, is the life of the Irish nation—the nation's biography, but also its Bible, constitution, code of law, its wisdom, preserver, and moral-political guide, a Palladium invoked to pacify and unite Ireland not by force of arms but by its own moral authority. O'Connor has forged in the smithy of his soul the conscience of his race. In an ultimate wish-fulfilment, he imagines himself ruling the Irish forever by successfully exhorting them to conform to his own free-thinking and republican principles.

Delivered at the joint meeting of the American Conference for Irish Studies and the Canadian Association for Irish Studies, The Queen's University of Belfast, June 1995.

5

Sheridan Le Fanu and the Unmentionable

SHERIDAN LE FANU'S chief interests were Ireland and the supernatural, interests which often coalesced. Though a Dubliner for most of his life, he spent part of his boyhood at Abington, in County Limerick, after his clergyman father's appointment as Dean of Emly. At Abington he was exposed to the richness of Irish oral legend, especially the tales of a gifted local storyteller, Miss Anne Baily of Lough Guir. Supernatural stories described encounters with demons and fairies. There were also legends about the Irish past—the exploits of Finn MacCumhal, or of the more recent Cromwellian and Williamite wars, the latter ending with the siege of Limerick (1690–1), which marked the final defeat of the Stuart and Catholic cause in Ireland. Two of Le Fanu's historical novels, *The Cock and Anchor* (1845), and *The Fortunes of Colonel Torlogh O'Brien* (1847), have the Williamite wars as their setting, and describe their aftermath: the confiscation of Catholic estates, which were then granted to Protestants; the fate of the old families, who either fled abroad, or hovered dispossessed in the vicinity of their old homes.

Le Fanu was also a journalist, and for some years proprietor and editor of the *Dublin University Magazine*, a journal with some claim to speak for Conservative Protestant Ireland. Le Fanu initially had some sympathy with Irish nationalism, and was personally friendly with Isaac Butt, Parnell's predecessor as head of the Irish Home Rule supporters in Parliament. But he wrote no editorials on the chief crises of the late 1860s, the Fenian Rising (1867), and the Gladstone government's disestablishment (1869) of the Church of Ireland. Le Fanu seems to have sunk into a political apathy resembling the lethargy and despair that often afflicts the haunted characters of his supernatural stories. In their helplessness, those lethargic characters may in fact represent his response to Irish events, at a time when his own class seemed less and less capable of preserving the power and privileges which it had once enjoyed or of considering itself the 'Ascendancy' it had once proclaimed itself. Le Fanu's supernatural tales are among the best in this genre. But they are also at once personal confessions and expressions of political and social anxieties.

The supernatural tale, as a deliberate literary form distinct from the popular folk-tale, came into existence about the time the educated classes ceased to believe in ghosts and witches and so began to find them entertaining. The last English trial for witchcraft took place in 1712; the accused was convicted, but not executed. The last execution of a witch in Scotland was in 1722; in Germany a witch was executed as late as 1793. By 1764, Horace Walpole was ready to invent the gothic novel with *The Castle of Otranto*. His example was quickly followed by Clara Reeve, Ann Radcliffe, 'Monk' Lewis, and the writers of the numerous 'horrid' tales Jane Austen ridicules, as she does their readers, in *Northanger Abbey* (1818).

The ghosts in these stories are real, usually appearing to right some wrong connected with the ownership of real estate. But Mrs Radcliffe had developed an important innovation as early as *The Castles of Athlin and Dunbayne* (1789). Her supernatural manifestations eventually turn out to be elaborately contrived frauds, concocted to terrify the heroine into surrendering her virginity, her property, her sanity, or even all three. In *The Monk* (1796), Lewis explored the tale of terror's many opportunities for sexual titillation, especially if the story featured monks and nuns.

Though *Melmoth the Wanderer* (1820), by the Dublin clergyman Charles Robert Maturin, enjoyed considerable popularity, the tale of terror as developed by Walpole and his successors had already ceased to attract many readers. Sir Walter Scott used the supernatural sparingly. By the 1830s it was clear that the writer of supernatural fiction needed a new method. Charles Dickens and Le Fanu seem to have discovered that method independently, at about the same time, though Dickens has priority. But the Irish novelist realized that Dickens's sceptical narration could be used not to undermine a supernatural story but to enhance it, to make it more mysterious and perhaps more terrifying.

In the fifth number of *Pickwick Papers*, published in August 1836, the Pickwickians hear a story about a bagman's encounter with a talking chair; in the tenth number (January 1837), Mr Wardle tells the story of Gabriel Grub, the sexton carried off by the goblins. Neither story attempts to be frightening, and both are presented sceptically: the bagman and Grub have been drinking before their encounters with the supernatural. Le Fanu's 'The Ghost and the Bone-Setter', his first published story, appeared in the *Dublin University Magazine* in January 1838, to be followed by several other supernatural tales: 'The Fortunes of Sir Robert Ardagh' (March); 'The Drunkard's Dream' (August); and 'Strange Event in the Life of Schalken the Painter' (May 1839). In two of these stories, those who see ghosts have been drinking. In 'Sir Robert Ardagh' Le Fanu sets the folk legend against the 'true' story; each admits either a natural or a supernatural explanation. With 'Schalken the Painter' Le Fanu had clearly mastered a new kind of supernatural tale, which accepts and utilizes the reader's scepticism. Schalken's adventure barely allows for a natural explanation. He loses Rose to a sinister, rich, corpse-like old man; Rose flees from her husband, with an incoherent story, but then vanishes; later Schalken sees her, or thinks he sees her, living in a tomb. The sinister old man may simply be an old man, not an animated corpse; the frightened heroine may be hallucinating, or hysterical; doors can slam shut by other than super-natural agency; Rose may have leaped from a window to her death, not been carried off through the air; Schalken has fallen asleep before he sees her in the tomb. Like Schalken, the reader assumes the supernatural element, involving marriage with the dead, but we cannot be sure. The story marks Le Fanu's first completely successful use of the new method, building the story on both doubt and fear, leaving the supernatural presence unexplained and still powerful—or, in other words, creating a mystery and then maintaining that mystery. As with so many speculations about the supernatural, whether religious or merely superstitious, we finally do not know.

M.R. James (1862–1936), himself a distinguished writer of supernatural tales, considered himself Le Fanu's disciple. James has left us brief but valuable comments about the supernatural genre, drawn both from his work and that of his master. 'It is not amiss sometimes to leave a loophole for a natural explanation,' he remarks; 'but, I would say, let the loophole be so narrow as not to be quite practicable' (James vi). Most of the stories collected under the title *In a Glass Darkly* (1872) include the narrow loophole, to tease us with its failure to reassure. There are demons in Le Fanu's world. We cannot always see them, but when we do, they take shape from our guilt, or from our obsessive fears. 'Can't you see them?' cries the haunted protagonist of T.S. Eliot's *The Family Reunion* (1939); '*You* don't see them, but I see them, / And they see me' (Eliot 232).

Le Fanu usually hints at the possibility of hallucination, and of mental or even physical illness in his victims. 'I agree that ghosts appear only to the sick,' argues Dostoevsky's Svidrigaylov, another haunted murderer, 'but that proves only that they cannot appear to anybody else, not that they have no real existence' (Dostoevsky 244). More flippantly, Scrooge tries to dismiss Marley's ghost as 'an undigested bit of beef, a blot of mustard, a crumb of cheese, a fragment of an underdone potato' (Dickens, *Christmas Carol* 18). Between them they more or less define the types of narrow loophole Le Fanu sometimes allows. Mr Jennings's apparition may be due to his addiction to green tea. Captain Barton and

Mr Justice Harbottle have guilty consciences. They are all sick men, and suspect they are sick, for all three consult physicians, as does Laura in 'Carmilla'.

Le Fanu's early supernatural stories were supposedly drawn from among the papers of the Reverend Francis Purcell, an Irish Catholic priest who was also an antiquarian and folklore collector. Father Purcell's ghostly calling, and the association of Catholic priests with supernatural events in Gothic novels, suggest that the stories he has collected are true. *In a Glass Darkly* contains five cases collected by Dr Martin Hesselius, a physician interested in 'metaphysical' medicine. Hesselius is willing to take seriously those who suffer from threatening apparitions—though he loses the only patient he actually treats. He is a doctor for the mind, a forerunner of the modern psychiatrist. As scientist he certifies the stories. But under certain circumstances he is willing to admit that supernatural forces can invade ordinary lives, that the barriers which normally separate us from the world of spirits can dissolve.

Strictly speaking, none of these stories are about ghosts. But they are about hauntings. Even though Beckett, in 'The Room in the Dragon Volant', encounters nothing supernatural, he is nevertheless haunted—tracked, followed—by Count and Countess St Alyre, and obsessed by the Countess's beauty. Jennings is haunted by a small black monkey, Barton and Harbottle by men they have murdered. As for Carmilla, she has apparently watched her intended victim for some time. In Ireland, incidentally, the word 'follow' is often used to suggest that a supernatural being is attached to a certain family over many generations: 'a banshee always follows the O'Sheerans'. As a descendant of the Sheridans, Le Fanu himself could claim a banshee (Lysaght 124).

Le Fanu's ideas about the world of spirits, in so far as they shape *In a Glass Darkly*, are based to some extent on the teachings of Emanuel Swedenborg (1688–1772), the Swedish scientist, theologian, and visionary. After the death of his young wife Susanna in 1858, Le Fanu turned to Swedenborg's writings, which are reassuring about death by describing it as merely a change, to some extent a continuation of ordinary life. We can understand the comfort he found when we read, in *Uncle Silas* (1864), the description of the afterlife Le Fanu put into the mouth of a Swedenborgian teacher:

> a beautiful landscape, radiant with a wondrous light, in which, rejoicing, my mother moved along an airy path, ascending among mountains of fantastic height, and peaks, melting in celestial colouring into the air, and peopled with human beings translated into the same image, beauty, and splendour (*Uncle Silas* 14).

But there are less comforting visions and ideas in the writings of Swedenborg, and they shape 'Green Tea', 'The Familiar', and 'Mr Justice Harbottle'. Swedenborg taught that everyone has an 'inner eye', a non-sensual mode of vision. When opened, the inner eye helps us to read Scripture properly, to discern its hidden or non-literal meanings. The inner eye also lets us see into the world of spirits, which interpenetrates our own world, and even into the heaven of the angels. Swedenborg's religious teachings and his accounts of his visionary experiences depend on this inner sight, as do the visions of William Blake, at one time a reader of Swedenborg.

Le Fanu cites only one of Swedenborg's works in *In a Glass Darkly: Arcana Caelestia* (1749–56), a commentary on the books of Genesis and Exodus. Though the work is mentioned only in 'Green Tea', Swedenborg's ideas about vision also pervade the two following stories, and may play some part in 'Carmilla'. The *Arcana* also provides Hesselius with a literary model. It contains the biblical texts of Genesis and Exodus, Swedenborg's commentary on those texts, and from time to time descriptions of Swedenborg's own visionary experiences. Hesselius, we learn, 'writes in two distinct characters. He describes what he saw and heard as an intelligent layman might', but then 'returns upon the narrative, and in the terms of his art and with all the force and originality of genius, proceeds to the work of analysis, diagnosis and illustration' (*In a Glass Darkly* 5)—a double narrative, suited to stories where two worlds intersect.

Swedenborg's *Arcana* explains how we are to read Scripture, and how we are to read the world, texts we believe we can read with only sensual vision. Genesis is not just an account of man's origin. It is an elaborate allegory (Swedenborg, *Arcana Caelestia* paragraph 167): Eve represents self-love, Adam is the rational principle, the serpent is sensual rather than revealed truth (*Arcana* paragraphs 192, 196). The tree is intellectual as opposed to intuitive knowledge (*Arcana* paragraph 202). Noah's flood was not an actual inundation but 'an inundation of evil and of the false', which 'drowned' antediluvian man (*Arcana* paragraphs 660, 257).

The passage in 'Green Tea' that Jennings marks and Hesselius reads expresses those darker teachings of Swedenborg which Le Fanu uses. We are born with both interior and external or ordinary sight. In most people, the interior sight or 'inner eye' is never opened. They see only the physical world around them. The inner eye, when opened, allows us to see the spirits which surround us, to peer into Heaven and hell, to enjoy intercourse with angels. But, as Swedenborg warns, if evil spirits become aware that they are perceived by—are in communication with—corporeal men, they strive to destroy them. This is apparently what happens to Jennings. Evil spirits take the form of savage beasts. The malevolent monkey has become aware of Jennings, and knows that Jennings can see it. Actuated by innate malice, it leads him to self-destruction—though Hesselius offers several other explanations for Jennings's fate.

'Green Tea' emphasizes the arbitrary and apparently unprovoked nature of Jennings's visitation. His inner eye has been opened accidentally, perhaps by his indulgence in green tea. He is terrified by the spirit-monkey, which haunts him with increasing frequency, interfering even with his religious duties, eventually driving him to suicide. Dr Hesselius loses his patient, partly because of his own irresponsible behaviour. Hesselius assures Jennings that he will be at his disposal, then disappears to a remote country inn to meditate upon the case, while Jennings's demon destroys him. Hesselius rather meanly excuses his failure by quibbling: Jennings was not yet really his patient, Hesselius's treatment—sure to succeed—had not yet begun. At the same time, he gives us too many explanations for Jennings's fate. Jennings drank too much green tea; his father had seen a ghost, and so Jennings had inherited a 'suicidal mania'; Jennings's studies in pagan metaphysics had made him vulnerable. In effect, Hesselius blames the victim.

Jennings does perhaps spend too much time in his study, where his interests resemble those of George Eliot's Mr Casaubon. Too much tea, green or not, can bring about a nervous state. His studies have led him into pagan mythology, to half-realize that the gods and goddesses of Greece and Rome are metaphors for a sensuality he can neither accommodate nor confront: Venus is unbridled desire, Mars unbridled rage, Bacchus licentiousness, Pan sheer animality. Jennings's unintended invasion of the world of spirits causes him to see or imagine a metaphor for his own suppressed erotic self, his animal nature. When Stevenson's Dr Jekyll creates an alternate self so that he can indulge his baser nature while continuing to pose as a paragon of virtue, Mr Hyde is ape-like, with long simian arms. Hyde mocks and reveals Jekyll's repressions. Jennings's haunting monkey is an aspect of himself, from whom there is no escape—in Othello's words, 'As if there were some monster in his thought / Too hideous to be shown' (III iii. 106–7).

The monkey may reflect Victorian anxieties after Darwin's unwelcome suggestion that man was of simian ancestry. Crudely popularized versions of Darwin's theory served to argue that certain races—Australian Bushmen, sub-Saharan Africans, the Irish—were still close to their gorilla ancestors. Le Fanu would have been well aware of the simian Irish who were common in Victorian political cartoons, especially in the pages of *Punch* (Curtis 1971). Supernatural stories often reflect their authors' own anxieties. Written shortly after an abortive Fenian rising, and in the year when Gladstone abandoned the Church of Ireland, and by implication the

Anglo-Irish, to their fate, 'Green Tea' with its monkey may hint at Anglo-Ireland's anxieties about the unhyphenated Irish, their violence and probable malevolence. Members of Le Fanu's family had been attacked during the Tithe Wars (protests by Catholic tenants against being taxed to support the Protestant Church of Ireland) in 1832–6 (W.R. Le Fanu, *Seventy Years* 58–68). There was some monster in Le Fanu's thought, not too hideous to be glimpsed but perhaps too hideous to be confronted directly.

Le Fanu titled his collection from St Paul: 'For now we see through a glass, darkly; but then face to face: now I know in part, but then shall I know even as also I am known' (I Cor. 12). A clergyman's son, we can be sure he did not misquote scripture lightly. The glass of his title is not a window-pane through which we glimpse dim intimations of a spiritual world, or of divine truth. It is a mirror in which we glimpse our own darker nature.

Captain Barton, the haunted victim of 'The Familiar', has a cruel act on his conscience, and is perhaps more clearly responsible for invoking the footsteps which follow him, and the man shrunken 'in all his proportions, and yet [preserving] his exact resemblance to himself in every particular' (*In a Glass Darkly* 54) who terrifies him. His approaching marriage suggests to him the memory of the 'guilty attachment' he had formed with the daughter of one of his own crew members, her father's resentment, and Barton's use of his powers as captain to destroy the man.

Le Fanu dates 'The Familiar'—a slightly revised version of 'The Watcher', a story he had published in 1851—with apparent precision, 'Somewhere about the year 1794', and places it in his own city of Dublin. The story gives him a chance to display his own knowledge of the city and its development. In *The Cock and Anchor* (1845), *The Fortunes of Colonel Torlogh O'Brien* (1847), and *The House by the Church-Yard* (1861–3), he recreated seventeenth-century Dublin and eighteenth-century Chapelizod, a Dublin suburb, reminding the reader from time to time that the seventeenth-century gallows stands where St Stephen's Green is later to be, and that outlaws frequent the wild acres of Phoenix Park. In 'The Familiar' Captain Barton is pursued through the laid out but as yet unbuilt streets of the city in which Le Fanu is writing the story. We know that *The House by the Church-Yard* is one of the texts underlying *Finnegans Wake* (Atherton 110–13), partly because of frequent references to the River Liffey in Le Fanu's novel, and partly because the novel is about different kinds of resurrection. Since *Finnegans Wake* is about the city of Dublin existing simultaneously at every period of its history, past, present, and future, it may also owe something to Le Fanu's phantom city of the future through which Captain Barton is pursued by his past.

Le Fanu's planned but partially unbuilt Dublin is historically accurate. There was a building boom, and considerable speculative building in

Dublin during the 1790s, when Grattan's Parliament made the city a true capital, in the period before the Act of Union (1800). Lady L—is genteelly poor, but nevertheless participates in the contemporary migration of the nobility and gentry from south to north of the Liffey. Barton lives in south Dublin, presumably in the then newly built Merrion Square—perhaps at Number 18, Merrion Square South (now Number 70), where Le Fanu was living when he wrote the story.

For *In a Glass Darkly* Le Fanu retitled 'The Haunted House in Westminster' (1872) as 'Mr Justice Harbottle', to place the emphasis on his protagonist and what he sees, or thinks he sees. The story is a drastically rewritten version—so drastically as to be almost a new story—of Le Fanu's 'An Account of Some Strange Disturbances in Aungier Street', published in the *Dublin University Magazine* in December 1853. The earlier version is set in Dublin's Aungier Street, where Le Fanu was married, south of the Liffey near Dublin Castle, in the oldest part of the city. Le Fanu is again meticulous about dates. The Aungier Street house 'was sold, along with much other forfeited property . . . in 1702; and had belonged to Sir Thomas Hacket, who was Lord Mayor of Dublin in James II's time.' Presumably the house was confiscated in the aftermath of the Williamite victory over James II, that is, at that pivotal moment of Irish history to which Le Fanu also returned in his two historical novels. Many of his stories, supernatural or otherwise, portray the dispossessed Catholic gentry of Ireland after the Williamite triumph: 'The Fortunes of Sir Robert Ardagh', 'The Last Heir of Castle Connor', 'Sir Dominick's Bargain', 'Ultor de Lacy'. Charles Le Fanu de Cresserons, Le Fanu's ancestor, had fought for William at the Battle of the Boyne, and the family cherished a portrait of the king which he was supposed to have personally presented to Cresserons (T.P. Le Fanu, *Memoirs* 28). As Le Fanu contemplated his own class's loss of power in the aftermath of Daniel O'Connell's successful campaign for Catholic Emancipation (1829), and increasing Catholic political economic power, he seemed to imagine the Ascendancy's future by examining the Catholic gentry's dispossessed past, to recognize that the Williamite revolution, which had given the Le Fanu family lands and prestige, was being altered by another revolution which would reverse the earlier one. The rumoured Jacobite plot—a plot to restore the Catholic Stuarts—in 'Mr Justice Harbottle' is an oblique recollection of this historical obsession.

'Disturbances in Aungier Street' shares with 'Mr Justice Harbottle' a cruel and sensual judge—Judge Horrock in the earlier story—who hangs himself in a stairwell, where his ghost re-enacts that hanging. But the story is primarily about two young men who see the apparition, a century or so after Judge Horrock's suicide. In 'Mr Justice Harbottle' this survives only in the lodger's brief account of what he has seen. The story is really about Harbottle himself, and the way he is either supernaturally visited or is worked upon by his own guilt. He is certainly visited by the mysterious Hugh Peters, and later a child sees the avenging Pyneweck, and the kitchen maid sees a monstrous blacksmith. Dr Hesselius comments on the 'contagious character of this sort of intrusion of the spirit-world upon the proper domain of matter' to explain these supplementary apparitions (*In a Glass Darkly* 83). Harbottle sees not only the apparition of his victim. He also has a terrifying vision of his own cruelty, and must recognize his own guilt, when he is judged by Mr Justice Twofold—a crueller and more arbitrary image of himself.

In a Glass Darkly follows these three short stories with two of considerable length, 'The Room in the Dragon Volant' and 'Carmilla'. Both differ drastically in kind from their forerunners. In the briefer stories, Le Fanu always supplies the narrow loophole M.R. James recommends. Jennings, Barton, and Harbottle may all have been hallucinating. All three may have frightened themselves to death. Jennings may have inherited a disposition to suicide. Barton may have died in terror because a pet owl invaded his room and his curtained bed. Harbottle may have examined—prematurely— Hogarth's *Industry and Idleness* (1747) and created, from the print depicting the Idle Apprentice's execution, a vision of his own execution. But at the same time, the stories powerfully suggest that some barrier between the natural and the supernatural worlds has been breached, that what Le Fanu's haunted protagonists see is real though uncanny.

'The Room in the Dragon Volant' is not a supernatural story at all, though the thieves who conspire against Richard Beckett pretend to necromancy to further their plot, and know that lodgers in a certain room at the Dragon Volant often vanish into thin air. 'Carmilla' is unequivocally supernatural, without a loophole. Carmilla really is a vampire, tracked down at last and destroyed in the tomb where she lies in seven inches of blood. But both stories retain the earlier theme of breached barriers between two worlds. Beckett swallows one of the mysterious draughts Hesselius cites in his preliminary note, draughts which induce a catatonic state resembling death. The names of such draughts combine natural and supernatural: *Vinum letiferum*, the wine of Lethean oblivion; *Somnus Angelorum*, the sleep of the Angels. Beckett is taken into the realm of the dead, if only a little way; he is undead, conscious that he is in his coffin but unable to move or speak, and aware that he will be placed in the grave. Carmilla is also undead. She moves easily between the world of the living and the world of the dead, at ease in both, in ballroom or tomb. Her freedom to disregard any boundary between life and death is what makes her terrifying.

Young Beckett, in France a few weeks after Waterloo, is eager for a sexual adventure and aggressive about seeking one. He is an easy mark for a gang of criminal conspirators, and the lovely bait they offer, the Countess de St Alyre—with verbal overtones of allure. Beckett has brought his near-burial alive on himself, by his belief that he is irresistible as a lover, and by his willingness to run off with another man's wife. Unlike Jennings, Barton, and Harbottle, he survives his ordeal, rescued by a zealous French police agent. The official nature of his rescue is noteworthy. Jennings, Barton, and Harbottle represent three institutions that maintained Victorian Britain, the Church, the Navy, and the Law. None of these can offer protection against rampant evil. Perhaps they do order these matters better in France.

Though Beckett is explicitly described as an Englishman, he bears the name of an old and well-known Anglo-Irish family, of Huguenot origin like the Le Fanus. In his silence, impotence, and immobility it is tempting to see a foreshadowing of some of Samuel Beckett's themes and situations. Joyce, incidentally, drew on the story once or twice for *Finnegans Wake*: 'he urned his dead, that dragon volant' (*Finnegans Wake* 25.05); 'Shutmup. And bud did down right well. And if he sung dumb in his glass darkly speech lit face to face on all around (*Finnegans Wake* 355.8–9). Le Fanu's subject, a sleep that is like death induced by quaffing a potion, resembles the ballad of 'Finnegan's Wake' and Joyce's drunken, dreaming publican.

'Carmilla' is an undead survivor from the late seventeenth century, that period that fascinated Le Fanu because of the Williamite victories in Ireland. Her portrait, as Mircalla, Countess Karnstein, is dated 1698. Modern readers have often been surprised at the remarkably overt lesbian theme pervading this tale of a young woman threatened by a vampire—who is also a young woman. In fact, sexual anxiety pervades the whole story, and Le Fanu deliberately heightened this anxiety by introducing a kind of sex he would have considered illicit in order to emphasize the unnatural in his supernatural tale.

Laura, the destined victim in 'Carmilla', is troubled when she is suggestively embraced and kissed by Carmilla, more troubled when she begins to sense that she is the target of some mysterious and uncanny agency. Both reactions are plausible. But perhaps these anxieties at once suggest and mask Le Fanu's deeper anxieties. These anxieties are neither supernatural nor primarily sexual, though sex and a troubled religious faith play their part. They are primarily social and political, aroused as the Catholic Irish begin to assert themselves, especially in terms of the central issue in nineteenth-century Ireland, the ownership of land. Political issues can be rephrased in supernatural terms when religion is intermixed with politics. They can be rephrased in sexual terms when racial tension is added. Both factors were abundantly present in nineteenth-century Ireland, to be encoded in Carmilla's pursuit of Laura.

The story is set in Styria, on the borders of Austria and Hungary—traditional vampire territory. Laura, who tells the story, begins by stressing her English nationality. Though she has never been there, she thinks of England as 'home'. Her father, also English, has retired from the Austrian service. They speak English together, read Shakespeare to keep up the language, and drink tea in the English manner. Their castle is in the midst of a vast forest. There are no neighbours—that is, no neighbouring gentry—and even the local peasantry are few and far between.

The nearest village is roofless and abandoned, clustered around a ruined church and the ruined castle of the Karnsteins, now extinct but once lords of the territory. Laura's dead mother was related to the Karnsteins.

This insistent Englishness, their social isolation, strongly suggest the lives of many Anglo-Irish landowners in the eighteenth and nineteenth centuries. The abandoned village suggests Ireland after the Great Famine of 1845–9. The people have been removed by what Laura's father calls the 'infection' of superstition, their fear of vampires—a recollection of the fever that accompanied the Famine. Many have chosen exile.

In her introduction to a reprint of *Uncle Silas*, Elizabeth Bowen, herself an Anglo-Irish landowner, declared that *Uncle Silas* is an Irish novel, despite its explicit Yorkshire setting: 'The hermetic solitude and the autocracy of the great country house, the demonic power of the family myth, fatalism, feudalism and the "ascendancy" outlook are accepted facts of life for the race of hybrids from which Le Fanu sprang.' Bowen notes Le Fanu's earlier use of the *Uncle Silas* plot in 'Passage in the Secret History of an Irish Countess' (*Dublin University Magazine*, November 1838). She describes his choice of an English setting as 'inscrutable' (Bowen 101), but the research of W.J. McCormack has uncovered the reason. Richard Bentley, who published most of Le Fanu's fiction after 1863, considered Irish stories unpopular, and insisted on stories 'of an English subject and in modern times' (Bentley to Le Fanu, 26 February 1863; McCormack 1980, 140–2). So Mr Jennings, of Kenlis, becomes an English clergyman, Dublin's Aungier Street becomes 'a dark street in Westminster', Laura is settled in Styria, where Le Fanu had never been, but where he knew there was a popular belief in vampires. He drew also on the vampire tradition as it already existed in English literature: John Polidori's *The Vampire* (1819), written during that competition to write a ghost story which produced Mary Shelley's *Frankenstein* (1818); and the interminable *Varney the Vampyre*, serialised in the early 1840s, and written by James Rymer or Thomas Prest. These in turn drew on the Balkan tradition of the undead, the vampire able to leave the grave at will, sustained by sucking the blood of the living, and apparently capable of sexual relations with the living.

Drawing on both the literary vampire tradition and the folklore tradition, 'Carmilla' in turn helped to shape *Dracula* (1897), by Le Fanu's fellow

Dubliner, Bram Stoker (1847–1912). Both were 'Anglo-Irish', though Le Fanu's ancestry was French and Stoker's Dutch, and both were sons of Dublin's Protestant professional class. Stoker's short story, 'The Judge's House' (1914), draws on a situation similar to that in Le Fanu's 'Strange Disturbances in Aungier Street'. In *Dracula* his Dr Van Helsing, scientist, physician, and vampirologist, is a more effective Dr Hesselius. Stoker had signalled his debt to 'Carmilla' in what was intended to be the opening chapter of *Dracula*, deleted because his publisher thought it revealed the vampire theme prematurely. In that chapter, Jonathan Harker, en route to Castle Dracula, wanders in the vicinity of Munich on Walpurgis-Nacht (1 May), when the witches hold their revels. He arrives at a great tomb, inscribed as that of 'Countess Dolingen of Gratz in Styria', who 'sought and found death, 1801.' An iron stake transfixes the tomb and the corpse inside. A violent storm arises, Harker sees 'a beautiful woman, with rounded cheeks and red lips, seemingly asleep on a bier,' and then a lightning bolt strikes the stake, rousing the dead woman 'for a moment of agony, while she was lapped in the flame, and her bitter scream of pain was drowned in the thundercrash.' The tomb is destroyed; Dracula himself must rescue Harker, partly by a timely telegram, but also by assuming the shape of a grey wolf and guarding him (Stoker 9–11; Wilson xi–xii).

Carmilla is at once vampire and Irish banshee, *ban sí*, woman of the *sí*, of the tumulus or mound—a woman who dwells in one of the ancient burial mounds so common in the Irish countryside, a woman of the dead (Lysaght 30). In comparatively recent tradition, the banshee is a highly respectable appanage of certain old families, a wailing spirit who foretells or announces and laments the deaths of family members. In an earlier tradition, she is seen by doomed warriors on their way to battle, washing corpses or bloodied shirts. Other legends describe intermarriage between a mortal man and a woman of the *sí*. Conn the Hundred-Fighter is seduced by such a woman, as is Muircertach mac Erca and the poet-warrior Oisin. These relationships are seldom happy or long-lasting; sometimes the human partner begins to waste away (Cross 491–502; 518–32; 439–56).

Sí (genitive plural *sídhe*) is usually translated as fairy, but Irish fairies are more sinister than Shakespeare's Mustardseeds and Peaseblossoms. They crave human beings, especially children, but also young men and women, luring them away to live a kind of half-life under the earth. In some way they live on—or through—these captives, as vampires live on blood. The *sí* themselves are not easily classified as living or dead. Like vampires, they are undead and hungry. Yeats calls them 'the unappeasable host' (*Variorum Poems* 146).

Carmilla has affinities both with the traditional banshee and the *sí*. Like the banshee, she is attached to Laura's family, and is her ancestress, though she does not limit herself to that family; the banshee is often assumed to be an ancestress of the family she warns. In some versions, she is an old woman, in others young and beautiful. Carmilla's beauty, white garments, and nocturnal habits are those of the banshee, and she is certainly a harbinger of death to the families she visits. In 'The White Cat of Drumgunniol' (1870), presumably drawing on oral tradition, Le Fanu describes a malevolent banshee eager to destroy the Donovans, whose ancestor wronged her.

In another traditional story he retells, 'The Child that went with the Fairies' (1870), set in County Limerick near Abington, the child is lured away by a beautiful lady in a coach, attended by servants with 'faces of cunning and malice' (Le Fanu, *Ghost Stories* 140–1). In the coach with the lady there is a 'black woman, with . . . a sort of turban of silk striped with all the colours of the rainbow . . . a face as thin almost as a death's-head . . . and great goggle eyes, the whites of which, as well as her wide range of teeth, showed in brilliant contrast with her skin.' Carmilla arrives at Laura's door in essentially the same coach, with servants who look 'wicked . . . lean, and dark, and sullen'. She too is accompanied by 'a hideous black woman, with a sort of coloured turban on her head . . . with gleaming eyes and large white eye-balls' (*In a Glass* 257). The woman of the *si* who seduces and destroys Muircertach mac Erca feeds him food that wastes him away, and further wastes his strength by sending him to battle blue warriors (Cross 524)—in Irish, for complex reasons, a Negro is *fear gorm*, a blue man.

In her eagerness for a sexual relationship with Laura, Carmilla resembles the predatory *si* of Irish legend, as well as the Balkan tradition of the vampire. Marriage with the dead is a common theme for Le Fanu, used in 'Schalken the Painter', 'Ultor De Lacy' (1861), and the 'fairy' tale, 'Laura Silver Bell' (1872), hinted at in 'A Chapter in the History of a Tyrone Family' (1839). For 'Carmilla' he adds the lesbian element.

At the same time, Carmilla is outside the banshee/*si* tradition in certain ways. The *si* do not suck blood, nor are they destroyed with stakes and bonfires. Le Fanu combined aspects of Irish tradition with his reading of Dom Augustin Calmet's treatise on vampires, and the other books of vampire lore which Baron Vordenburg lends to Laura's father in the story, and with memories of Polidori and *Varney the Vampyre*. He recognized and used the sexual element that is so strong in both vampire lore and vampire fiction (Lawson 415–16; Barber 9). Freud's disciple, Ernest Jones, discusses the sexual aspects of the vampire at length in his *On the Nightmare*. 'The latent content of the belief yields plain indications of most kinds of sexual perversions,' Jones declares; '. . . the belief assumes various forms according as this or that perversion is more prominent.' Citing mostly German sources, Jones points out that 'Vampires always visit relatives first . . . The belief is, in fact, only an elaboration of that in the Incubus, and the essential elements of both are the same—repressed desires and hatreds.' Jones notes Freud's theory 'that morbid dread always signifies repressed sexual wishes . . . The explanation of these phantasies is surely not hard,' he concludes:

> A nightly visit from a beautiful or frightful being, who first exhausts the sleeper with passionate embraces and then withdraws from him a vital fluid: all this can point only to a natural and common process, namely to nocturnal emissions accompanied with dreams of a more or less erotic nature. In the unconscious mind blood is commonly an equivalent for semen . . . in the Vampire superstition . . . the simple idea of the vital fluid being withdrawn through an exhausting love embrace is complicated by more perverse forms of sexuality, as well as by the admixture of sadism and hate (Jones 98, 102–3, 106, 116, 119–20).

'Death and Love, together mated, / Watch and wait in ambuscade,' sings the seductive Countess in 'The Room in the Dragon Volant'; '. . . Burning sigh, or breath that freezes, / Numbs or maddens man or maid.' Laura is vulnerable because she is lonely, and dreams of a companion, perhaps a lover. To dream is dangerous in Le Fanu's world. Uncomfortable at Carmilla's embraces and ardour, Laura even imagines that she might be a man in disguise: 'What if a boyish lover had found his way into the house, and sought to prosecute his suit in masquerade?' (*In a Glass* 265).

In 'The Circus Animals' Desertion' (1939), Yeats, remembering the themes of his early poems, calls them 'Themes of the embittered heart', especially 'The Wanderings of Oisin' (1889), 'starved for the bosom of his fairy bride . . . Heart mysteries there.' Le Fanu's wife Susanna, who died at the age of 35, seems to have been the model for Maud Ruthyn in *Uncle Silas*, Laura, and his other lethargic protagonists. These women seem passive, without energy, half in love with easeful death. They are incapable of taking action to protect themselves—though Maud Ruthyn does rise to her final crisis. Susanna Le Fanu suffered from mysterious and probably psychosomatic illnesses, especially a nervous disorder which ended with her death during an attack of hysteria. She was morbidly afraid that anyone she loved would die, and had come to doubt both her husband's love for her and any religious promises of salvation.

In the weeks after her death, Le Fanu describes her in letters and a diary as 'so lowly in her thoughts of her spiritual state . . . so abject, so self-accusing, so prostrate in spirit . . . the idea of death was constantly present to her mind' (McCormack 1980, 122–33). In Le Fanu's description of her plight, we can recognize the mixture of fear and failure of nerve afflicting Mr Jennings and Captain Barton, the inability to act that grips Beckett in his coffin. We can particularly find a resemblance to Laura's mixture of fear and fatal attraction. Does Le Fanu represent his sense of his own guilt in Carmilla's mixture of sexual ardour and selfish exploitation? Is he the 'boyish lover' in disguise? are the bloodsucking and the suggestion of lesbianism masks for his own role as husband? To paraphrase Edgar Allan Poe, is this terror not of Styria, but of the soul?

Victor Sage argues that the English horror story originates in Protestant doubt, and represents 'a form of "theological uncertainty", an anxiety which is recognizable at many different levels of consciousness' (Sage xvii). Le Fanu had witnessed his wife's anguished theological uncertainty, and turned, like Mr Jennings, to Swedenborg for possible relief. But 'Carmilla', which draws on Irish as well as Balkan superstitions, is not about theological anxiety. Le Fanu was creating myth, and myth often represents social anxieties.

In the threat that Carmilla poses to Laura, we can see a fear of female sexuality which reappears in *Dracula*. The tale also represents Le Fanu's anxiety about the future of his own class as Catholic Irish nationalists began to assume a dominant role, and reveal a new militancy. In the late 1860s his letters show an increasing fear of Catholic power; in 1868 he described Anglo-Ireland as resting upon 'a quaking bog' (McCormack 1980, 219–20). He was also anxious about money. The family fortune, never very large, did not recover from losses sustained during the Tithe Wars. He was worried about mortgages, which swallowed the income from the little land that was left, and even about his inability to pay the rent on his own Dublin house. These political, social, and financial anxieties—the latter connected with the loss of land and home—have some bearing on Carmilla and the threats she represents, as Le Fanu turns his anxieties into myth.

As *ban sí* and as member of the ancient family who once owned a great local estate, Carmilla is a native of the terrain she haunts. She is one of the ancient lords of the land, whose descendants, reduced to peasant/tenant status, often haunted the Anglo-Irish estates confiscated from their ancestors, which they considered rightfully their own. Carmilla threatens the new English landowners with death, with a kind of demonic possession, sexually with a kind of double miscegenation—basic fears among the Anglo-Irish gentry as they saw their control of Ireland slipping away. Though Le Fanu himself was not of the landed gentry, he had relatives who were. He tended to respect and defend the landowning class as Ireland's natural rulers; W.B. Yeats was to revere them as the natural arbiters and guardians of Ireland's culture. Carmilla will destroy these pleasant, well-meaning people, or enthrall them, or drive them away. In Ireland, as in the vampire legend's basic element, the past survives to torment the present.

In this context, the role of the antiquarian Baron Vordenburg is important. His 'curious lore' and knowledge of the past makes it possible for him to destroy the vampire and the threat she represents. Antiquarians are significant figures in Anglo-Irish fiction, beginning with the Prince and his daughter Glorvina in Lady Morgan's *The Wild Irish Girl* and Count O'Halloran in Maria Edgeworth's *The Absentee*. These three, survivors of the Old Irish Catholic gentry, study and preserve relics of the Irish past. Their role is to teach the Anglo-Irish to understand and respect that past. To do so is to legitimize the Anglo-Irish presence. By collecting folklore, or manuscripts, or studying the ruins of old churches and monasteries, the Anglo-Irish earn their membership in 'Ireland', restoring to the Irish their own lost past—a programme advocated, or embraced, with individual variations, by Sir Samuel Ferguson, Sir William Wilde, Douglas Hyde, Yeats, Synge, and Lady Gregory. In his 'Scraps of Hibernian Ballads', published in the *Dublin University Magazine* (June 1839), Le Fanu himself called his readers to 'the pleasurable and patriotic duty of collecting together the many, many specimens of genuine poetic felling, which have sprung up, like its wild flowers, from the warm though neglected soil' (Le Fanu, *Purcell Papers* 2:256). Baron Vordenburg, whose antiquarian lore saves Laura and destroys the vampire, hints at that commitment to Ireland and the Irish tradition which could help the Anglo-Irish to remain a vital force in Irish life.

But Le Fanu only half believes his happy ending. In a note to his poem 'The Host of the Air' (1893), Yeats tells us that falling 'into a half-dream' is characteristic of those who have been 'touched' by the *sí*. They 'grow indifferent to all things, for their true life has gone out of the world, and is among the hills and forts of the Sidhe' (*Variorum Poems* 804). The lethargy, almost apathy of Laura, the 'touched' victim, seems a kind of death-wish. She is frightened and repelled, but she is also ready to yield—willing to die, the title of Le Fanu's last novel. A chorus in his verse drama *Beatrice* (1865) sings of 'Corruption that is beautiful, / And sadness that is splendid' (Le Fanu, *Poems* 31). Even after Carmilla has been exposed and destroyed, Laura thinks of her 'with ambiguous alternations' and sometimes hears, listens for, her 'light step'. In Laura's failure to resist we can perhaps discern Le Fanu's deepest anxieties about his own class, and his fear that the revenants of Irish history can never be laid to rest.

Originally published as the introduction to the Oxford World's Classics edition of Le Fanu's *In a Glass Darkly* (Oxford: Oxford University Press, 1993).

6

That Rooted Man

Yeats, *John Sherman*, and *Dhoya*

Rather unwillingly, Yeats included his two short novels of 1887–8 in the 1908 *Collected Works*. He never subsequently republished them. Perhaps he discarded them as mere 'prentice work, or as failures, or because his own identification with Sherman was all too obvious, and he preferred the revised version of his early life presented in *Reveries over Childhood and Youth* (1914) and *The Trembling of the Veil* (1922). Nevertheless, they are seminal works. In them Yeats explored in prose various themes and issues which would shape his later poetry and plays: the divided self, the evanescence of love and the loved one.

'There is more of myself in [*John Sherman*] than any thing I have done', Yeats told Katharine Tynan (*Collected Letters* 1: 245–6). T.R. Henn and Richard Ellmann, among others, have recognized in the novel's two main characters a kind of divided self-portrait (Ellmann 1948, 78–9; Henn 26). Yeats portrays conflicting aspects of himself which will spur his quest for Unity of Being, aspects which he will later blur in his autobiographical writing while paradoxically elevating them into a system, the Self and Anti-Self of *A Vision*. John Sherman leaves Ballah (Sligo) for the greater world of London, hoping for financial success and a rich wife, but is always homesick. He is clearly Yeats, even to that encounter with a little water-jet in a shop-window which triggered 'The Lake Isle of Innisfree' (*Autobiography* 103). Sherman is a lounger and a dreamer. But his friend William Howard is that other Yeats who founded the Abbey Theatre and eventually became 'A sixty-year-old smiling public man' whom Auden imagined as an unctuous cleric stepping through 'The parish of rich women' (Auden 197). The Yeats who left Ireland for London was homesick. He was shy and sometimes awkward. But he was also ambitious for conspicuous literary success. For much of his life he was willing to accept living in England as the price of such success. Howard is that eagerly public Yeats, thinly disguised as a High Church curate—a reminder of Yeats's delight in rituals. In his room hangs a Raphael 'Madonna', perhaps the one Yeats will ponder in 'Among School Children' and elsewhere.

Howard's dream of success is really the dream of a man of letters: 'Not too near or too far from a great city, I see myself in a cottage with diamond panes, sitting by the fire. There are books everywhere and etchings on the wall. On the table is a manuscript essay . . .' (*John Sherman* 9). To be sure, the essay is 'on some religious matter', but then, so are many of Yeats's essays and poems. Howard loses a curacy because he had 'preached a sermon to prove that children who die unbaptized are lost. He had been reading up the subject and was full of it'. 'He had a habit of getting his mind possessed with some strange opinion,' Yeats adds, '. . . and of preaching it while the notion lasted in the most startling way . . . It was not so much the thought as his own relation to it that allured him' (*John Sherman* 50, 53). This is the Yeats who at various times celebrated Rosicrucianism, metempsychosis, the intellectual achievements of eighteenth-century Ireland, eugenics, and the Steinach operation for rejuvenation. The difference lies in Yeats's ability to incorporate these temporary obsessions into a central organizing vision or myth, as he recognizes in a striking passage about Howard:

> his efficiency gave to all his thought a certain over-completeness and isolation, and a kind of hardness to his mind. His intellect was like a musician's instrument with no sounding-board. He could think carefully and cleverly, and even with originality, but never in such a way as to make his thoughts an allusion to something deeper than themselves. In this he was the reverse of poetical, for poetry is essentially a touch from behind a curtain (*John Sherman* 54).

Richard Finneran reminds us that William M. Murphy has persuasively identified Rev. John Dowden, brother of Edward Dowden, as the model for Howard (*John Sherman* xxv). But Dowden was no more than the armature for a more complex and honest self-portrait. In the dialogues between Sherman and Howard, Yeats anticipates the divided self of 'Ego Dominus Tuus' (1917) and 'A Dialogue of Self and Soul' (1929).

'Heart-mysteries there' indeed. But the divided self Yeats presents is not merely divided psychologically and socially, bold town mouse and shy country mouse. Howard has a moment of acute self-analysis. He recognizes a deeper division when he compares himself to Sherman in terms that anticipate Isaiah Berlin's categories of hedgehog and fox. 'The fox knows many things', Berlin declared, citing the Greek poet Archilochus; 'but the hedgehog knows one big thing' (Berlin 1). 'You Shermans are a deep people, much deeper than we Howards', Howard tells Sherman. 'We are like moths or butterflies, or rather rapid rivulets, while you and yours are deep pools in the forest where the beasts go to drink' (*John*

Sherman 60). Though Howard, perhaps sensing he has revealed too much, abandons this metaphor for another, he had it right the first time. Yeats had always to resist that centrifugal tendency ('All things can tempt me from this craft of verse'), even as he struggled for Unity of Being. In *John Sherman* the hero finds at last his 'centre of unity' (*John Sherman* 70). He almost succumbs to London and the shallow affected Margaret Leland. She is *not* Maud Gonne, as Finneran rightly reminds us. Maud Gonne descended on Bedford Park on 30 January 1889; Yeats wrote *Dhoya* in the autumn of 1887, and finished *John Sherman* early in December 1888 (*John Sherman* xi, xiv). John Butler Yeats described Laura Armstrong as the model for 'the wicked heroine' in *John Sherman*. We know comparatively little about her. Yeats 'first became infatuated with her when he saw her driving a dog cart at Howth, her red hair blowing in the wind.' In a letter to Katharine Tynan (21 March 1889), Yeats denied that he has 'taken up with Miss Gonne', but goes on to compare the two women:

> . . . she [Maud Gonne] had a borrowed interest, reminding me of Laura Armstrong without Laura's wild dash of half insane genius. Laura is to me always a plesent [*sic*] memory she woke me from the metallic sleep of science and set me writing my first play. Do not mistake me she is only as a myth and a symbol . . . She interests me far more than Miss Gonne does and yet is only as a myth and a symbol . . . 'Time and the Witch Vivien' was written for her to act. 'The Island of Statues' was begun with the same notion though it soon grew beyond the scope of drawing room acting. The part of the enchantress in both poems was written for her. She used to sign her letters Vivien (*Collected Letters* 1: 155).

Writing to Tynan on 31 January, the day following his first meeting with Maud Gonne—whom he prophetically calls 'Miss Gone'—Yeats describes her own unconscious invitation to identify her with Laura Armstrong: 'she says she cried over "Island of Statues" fragment but altogether favoured the Enchantress and hated Nachina' (i.e. Naschina; *Collected Letters* 1: 134).

Sherman evades Margaret by a rather Gilbertian device, successfully donating her to Howard. The pull of Ballah is too strong. He returns there to Mary Carton, a kind of Protestant *genius loci*. They will live in a thatched cottage with a green door, and the bee-hives (*John Sherman* 69) specified in 'The Lake Isle of Innisfree'.

Mary Carton barely exists as a character, but she embodies Yeats's commitment to a national literature based on local associations rather than to a cosmopolitan literature, as 'Lucy' embodied Wordsworth's commitment to being an *English* poet nourished by his native Lake District. Finneran aptly cites Yeats's contemporary dicta: 'Cosmopolitan literature is, at best, but a poor bubble'; 'There is no great literature without nationality' (Yeats, *Letters to the New Island* 12, 30). When Mary Carton rejects him, Sherman makes a Yeatsian pilgrimage to the top of Knocknarea, and keeps vigil all night on Queen Medb's cairn. Returning just before dawn, he encounters Mary again, a pale ghost in her garden, and she accepts him, not very convincingly.

Mary Carton even keeps a Protestant singing-school. When Sherman visits, 'Outside a child of four or five with a swelling on its face was sitting . . . opposite the school door, waiting to make faces at the Protestant children as they came out' (*John Sherman* 16). By stressing Mary's religion—she is the Rector's daughter—Yeats confronts the challenge he was to face so often, questioning his right, as a Protestant of English ancestry, to present himself as an Irish poet. Yeats saw his Sligo connections as legitimizing his claim to be Irish rather than 'Anglo-Irish'. His great-grandfather John Yeats had been Rector at nearby Drumcliffe; his grandmother Middleton came of a family long established in Sligo. Yeats rightly insisted on Protestant membership in the Irish nation, defying those who used the terms Irish and Catholic as synonymous, most notably in his 1925 Senate speech on Divorce. As portrayed here, Mary Carton embodies Ballah and therefore Ireland. Protestant or not, Yeats implies that she is as valid an embodiment of Ireland as Kathleen ni Houlihan. John Sherman's return to her and to Ballah is Yeats's resolve to be an Irish poet, one with 'Davis, Mangan, Ferguson'; Margaret Leland is the possibility of literary success in London, writing on English or cosmopolitan themes, which briefly tempts Yeats from what he already understood instinctively to be his true path.

Ballah/Sligo is so strongly associated with Mary Carton that, at the moment when Sherman realizes he loves her, he comes to that realization by remembering Margaret Leland's disdain for the place, a disdain he recognizes as an assault on his own Irish identity:

> This had been revealed: he loved Mary Carton, she loved him. He remembered Margaret Leland, and murmured she did well to be jealous. Then all her contemptuous words about the town and its inhabitants came into his mind. Once they made no impression on him, but now the sense of personal identity having been disturbed by this sudden revelation, alien as they were to his way of thinking, they began to press in on him (*John Sherman* 46).

Yeats anticipates a passage in his 'Village Ghosts' (*The Celtic Twilight*, 1893; *Mythologies* 15–16) to send Sherman, re-visiting Ballah, past

> rows of tumble-down thatched cottages; the slated roofs of the shops; the women selling gooseberries; the river bridge; the high walls of the garden where it was said the gardener used to see the ghost of a former owner in the shape of a rabbit; the street corner no child would pass at nightfall for fear of the headless soldier; the deserted flour-store; the wharves covered with grass.

To this Yeats adds a bold claim to belong: 'All these he watched with Celtic devotion, that devotion carried to the ends of the world by the Celtic exiles, and since old time surrounding their journeyings with rumour of plaintive songs' (*John Sherman* 42). With that audacious 'Celtic devotion', emotional rather than genealogical, Yeats declares his own membership in the unhyphenated Irish and equates his 'exile' in London with the exile of those dispossessed by the Famine or poverty. It is a powerfully stated claim, which Yeats will spend the rest of his career advancing and defending.

'I have an ambition to be taken as an Irish novelist not as an English or cosmepolitan [*sic*] one choosing Ireland as a background', Yeats told Katharine Tynan (2 December 1891), suggesting to her that in reviewing *John Sherman* she

> say that Sherman is an Irish type . . . I studied my characters in Ireland & described a typical Irish feeling in Sherman's devotion to Ballah. A West of Ireland feeling I might almost say for like that of Allingham for Ballyshannon it is local rather than national. Sherman belonged like Allingham to the small gentry who in the West at any rate love their native places without perhaps loving Ireland. They do not travel & are shut off from England by the whole breadth of Ireland with the result that they are forced to make their native town their world. I remember when we were children how intense our devotion was to all things in Sligo . . . I claim for this & other reasons that Sherman is as much an Irish novel as anything by Banim or Griffen [*sic*; Gerald Griffin] (*John Sherman* xvii–xviii; *Collected Letters* 1:274–5).

Yeats returns to this self-defining localism in *Estrangement: Extracts from a Diary Kept in 1909*, to distinguish 'two different kinds of love of Ireland', William Allingham's 'entire emotion for the place one grew up in' and Thomas Davis's more abstract and 'artificial' love for the intellectual idea of Ireland (*Autobiography* 319). He blames Davis for thwarting or misdirecting that instinctual love of one's place which leads to psychological integrity. *John Sherman* celebrates that sense of belonging which nourished Yeats in Sligo, and later at Coole Park and the tower at Ballylee.

Yet Sherman moves through Ballah as solitary as he moves through London, in it but hardly of it. 'In your big towns a man finds his minority and knows nothing outside its border', he tells Howard; 'He knows only the people like himself. But here one chats with the whole world in a day's walk, for every man one meets is a class' (*John Sherman* 9). Sherman notes local quaintnesses as he moves through the town, and remembers local legends. He is gratified when he is occasionally acknowledged with a bow or a nod. But he speaks to no one. Apart from his mother and Mary Carton, he has no conversation with anyone in Ballah except a waiter at the Imperial Hotel. 'All my life I have been haunted with the idea that the poet should know all classes of men as one of themselves', Yeats tells us in

Estrangement. 'Fifteen or twenty years ago I remember longing, with this purpose, *to disguise myself as a peasant* and wander through the West, and then to ship as a sailor. But when one shrinks from all business with a stranger, and is unnatural with all who are not intimate friends, because one underrates or overrates unknown people, one cannot adventure forth' (*Autobiography* 318; italics mine).

Insofar as Ballah has an aristocracy, Sherman is of it, a lounger who need not work. Like Allingham, he is of the 'small gentry', slightly above the class Yeats came from. In a phrase Yeats was to use many years later, he has been 'born into the Anglo-Irish solitude' (*Explorations* 325), cut off alike from the Catholic peasantry and townspeople, and from the land-owning gentry of the Big Houses. Visiting the Gore-Booths at nearby Lissadell, in November 1894, Yeats told his sister of the 'impressive house inside with a great sitting room as high as a church & all things in good taste' (*Collected Letters* 1: 414). When he recalled that visit in his *Memoirs*, he explained how unusual it was for someone of his background to be received there:

> In my childhood I had seen . . . the grey stone walls of Lissadell among its trees. We were merchant people of the town. No matter how rich we grew, no matter how many thousands a year our mills or our ships brought in, we could never be 'county', nor indeed had we any desire to be so. We would meet on grand juries those people in the great houses . . . and we would speak no malicious gossip and knew ourselves respected in turn, but the long-settled habit of Irish life set up a wall . . . But . . . I had written books and it was my business to write books and it was natural to wish to talk to those whose books you like, and besides I was no longer of my grandfather's house (*Memoirs* 77).

In Sherman's solitude, Yeats admits an important aspect of the Anglo-Irish dilemma as it affected the little-scrutinized business and professional class in the small towns of the West. Unlike the landed gentry, titled or untitled, they had scant contact with the peasantry, since they rarely had tenants. They usually comprised a tightly knit little local group who con-trolled most of the business in each town, and had some capital to invest. Caught between the gentry, who condescended to them, and the rural or urban poor, who resented their power and had only business dealings with them, they turned in upon themselves, as the lives of such Yeats relatives as George Pollexfen and Henry Middleton exemplify, especially as a Catholic middle class began to assert itself late in the nineteenth century.

When they went to England, even members of the gentry suffered an identity loss, as novelists from Maria Edgeworth to Elizabeth Bowen have shown us. Their local distinction was meaningless, and they became simply 'Irish'. Middle-class Anglo-Irish away from their own little worlds were even more decidedly anonymous, as Yeats learned when a Hammersmith schoolboy (*Autobiography* 20). That identity Sherman felt to be threatened is partly the symbolic relationship Yeats felt for what he sometimes called 'my native place' (*Collected Letters* 1:102). But on a merely social level it is the shock of urban anonymity after living in a small town as one of those who were, or believed themselves to be, entitled to recognition and even deference. 'You are going to London', a Pollexfen aunt told the nine-year old Yeats in 1874. 'Here [in Sligo] you are somebody. There you will be nobody at all' (*Autobiography* 16). In *John Sherman* this becomes, 'Why are ye goin' among them savages in London, Mister John? Why don't ye stay among your own people?' and is spoken by an old peasant woman. How appropriate it was that *John Sherman* and *Dhoya* should have first been published anonymously by Fisher Unwin, to Yeats's frustration, as part of what the poet called his 'Pseudonym Library' (*John Sherman* xv). Yeats characteristically signed the book 'Ganconagh' (*Geancánach*), literally a snub-nosed individual, but here a 'love-talker', a fairy given to amorous dalliance with shepherdesses and milkmaids. In *Irish Fairy Tales* (1892), Yeats lists 'The Ganocer or Gancanagh' as one of 'The Solitary Fairies' (Yeats, *Fairy and Folktales* 384–5).

Finneran reminds us that Joyce owned a copy of *John Sherman*, and probably discussed the book with Yeats at their famous meeting in 1902. He quotes a remark by Brendan O Hehir, that the Joyce who was writing *Dubliners* had little to learn about prose fiction from Yeats (*John Sherman* xxvi, xxxii). True enough, but nothing was ever wasted on Joyce. Can we perhaps see in 'A Little Cloud' a partial parody of Yeats's contrasting stay-at-home and cosmopolite? The 'vague shadows of houses, seeming like phantoms gathering to drink' (*John Sherman* 6) which Howard observes from Ballah bridge, conscious of his own literary and imaginative gifts, may be echoed, and deflated, when Little Chandler on Grattan Bridge pities 'the poor stunted houses. They seemed to him a band of tramps, huddled together along the river-banks, their old coats covered with dust and soot, stupefied by the panorama of sunset.' Chandler dreams of being recognized as a poet 'of the Celtic school by reason of the melancholy tone of his poems' and wishes his name was 'more Irish-looking'. Joyce is having his fun with Yeats's crises of identity. In 'A Painful Case', Mr Duffy decides that 'Love between man and man is impossible because there must not be sexual intercourse and friendship between man and woman is impossible because there must be sexual intercourse' (*Dubliners* 73–4, 112), a balder version of Margaret Leland's refusal to 'believe in friendship between a man and a woman' (*John Sherman* 39). As Stephen Dedalus makes his way through Dublin to the University in *Portrait*, he screens out the sordid reality by associating each stage of his journey with selected passages from Hauptmann, Newman, Cavalcanti, Ibsen (Joyce,

Portrait 176). For Yeats's Howard, 'who had read much, seen operas and plays, known religious experiences, and written verse to a waterfall in Switzerland, and not for those who dwelt upon its borders their whole lives', Ballah's river raised 'a tumult of images and wonders'. As he contemplates the river, 'his mind had strayed from the last evening flies, making circles on, the water beneath, to the devil's song against "the little spirits" in *Mefistofele*' (*John Sherman* 7).

Neither *John Sherman* nor *Dhoya* suggests that a great novelist was lost when Yeats committed himself to poetry and verse drama. But there is no doubt that he had some gift for social fiction. *John Sherman* is competently structured, if a little predictable, and Yeats has taken pains with his minor characters: that child lurking to stone the Protestant children, another child who prattles away to Sherman when he calls on Mary, the Shermans' old servant who 'did not stop peeling the onion in her hand' when told that the family will move to London, but 'In the middle of the night . . . suddenly started up in bed with a pale face and a prayer to the Virgin whose image hung over her head' (*John Sherman* 21). He fixes Howard with his choice of books: 'Cardinal Newman and Bourget, St Chrysostom and Flaubert'; Margaret reads the *Imitation of Christ* 'between a stuffed parroquet and a blue De Morgan jar' (*John Sherman* 55, 62); Victorian bric-a-brac and Bedford Park chic. Yeats even undercuts Sherman's declaration of love to Mary with a believable little detail:

> 'I loved you all along,' he cried. 'If you would marry me we would be very happy. I loved you all along,' he repeated—this helplessly, several times over. The bird shook a shower of seed on his shoulder. He picked one of them from the collar of his coat and turned it over in his fingers mechanically. 'I loved you all along' (*John Sherman* 74).

John Sherman fulfils John Butler Yeats's demand for 'a story with real people', expressed after his earlier suggestion that Yeats 'write a story' had elicited *Dhoya*, 'a fantastic tale of the heroic age' (*John Sherman* x). But in *Dhoya* we can discern anticipations of *John Sherman*, as well as what Richard Ellmann calls 'another of [Yeats's] half-symbolical autobiographies' (Ellmann 1948, 78). The setting is the vicinity of Sligo, though so long ago that the mountains were not yet named, 'Long ago, before the earliest stone of the Pyramids was laid' (*Dhoya* 81). Like Sherman, Dhoya is solitary, abandoned by his comrades who fear his fits of fury. He lives a more primitive version of the life Sherman and Yeats imagined themselves living on Innisfree. Yeats draws on Polyphemus and Caliban—Browning's as well as Shakespeare's—to create him. Though he reminds us that Dhoya lived long before Diarmuid and Gráinne, something of their sylvan idyll shapes his story.

Yeats also draws on the many Irish legends about mortal men who fall in love with fairy women, women of the *sí*. Finneran points out that *Dhoya* shares this theme with 'The Wanderings of Oisin' (1889; *John Sherman* xi). Yeats identifies himself with Oisin in 'The Circus Animals' Desertion' (1939): '. . . I that set him on to ride, / I, starved for the bosom of his faery bride'—another of the 'Heart-mysteries' the later poem acknowledges. John Sherman's solitude ends when Mary Carton—shade more than woman, more image than a shade—accepts him. Dhoya's solitude is relieved when a young woman, beautiful but uncanny, joins him. 'I have left . . . My people', she announces. '. . . They are . . . always happy, always young, always without change. I have left them for thee, Dhoya, for they cannot love. Only the changing, and moody, and angry, and weary can love' (*Dhoya* 86). She is drawn to Dhoya's moodiness, sadness, harshness. But because she is always young, changeless, their love must be evanescent. 'Eternity', Blake reminds us, 'is in love with the productions of time.'

Yeats begins *Dhoya* with that reference to a time before the pyramids, and other references to long ago events: 'before the Bo tree of Buddha unrolled its first leaf . . . before the ravens of Thor had eaten their first worm together.' Among them he includes, 'before a Japanese had painted on a temple wall the horse that every evening descended and trampled the rice-fields' (*Dhoya* 81). Those horses reappear, in almost the same words, in *The Trembling of the Veil* (1922), recalled from 'a pamphlet on Japanese art . . . I had found when a boy,' with an added detail: 'Somebody had come into the temple in the early morning, had been startled by a shower of water drops, had looked up and seen painted horses still wet from the dew-covered fields, but now "trembling into stillness"' (*Autobiography* 126).

The anecdote seems to endorse a kind of realistic art usually not congenial with Yeats's theories. But it more powerfully suggests that relationship between art and magic that shaped his development as a poet. Is Dhoya's woman a creation of his own imagination, a projection of his own felt needs? Does he create a fairy woman and so doom himself to lose her? Is that loss his recognition that he is not capable of sustained intimacy, that his instinct is for solitude? Does he also imagine the man of the *sí* who fights with him for the woman, then wins her back by defeating Dhoya at chess? John Sherman is playing chess against himself when he finally manages to 'lose' Margaret Leland to Howard.

Dhoya shares with Yeats a powerful fictive imagination. In describing his solitude, his imaging of a 'faery bride', and his loss of that bride, Yeats is telling another story about himself. Here again the woman is not Maud Gonne, who had not yet entered Yeats's life, though she is a kind of prefiguring of the relationship he would have with Maud Gonne, a relationship that Yeats can be seen to have craved, and to have controlled imaginatively. Dhoya's woman represents Yeats's ability to externalize his romantic dreams.

Yeats's early dream women, and many of the real women who were important to him in his youth, had some aura of the supernatural. Maud Gonne joined the Order of the Golden Dawn; Olivia Shakespear was 'psychic' (Ellmann 1948, 147); Helen Blavatsky and Annie Besant were active Theosophists; Florence Farr, Annie Horniman, and George Hyde-Lees were all members of the Golden Dawn. Spiritualism, Theosophy, and other esoteric efforts to communicate with and manipulate supernatural powers were among the ways certain Victorian women rebelled against their circumstances and sought power. They were often associated with agitation for political change: Annie Besant worked for Indian independence, Maud Gonne for a free Ireland. Yeats was attracted to women who were at once assertive and mystical, the combination he recognized in himself and examined in the contrasts between John Sherman and William Howard, Mary Carton and Margaret Leland. At the same time, the young Yeats was intimidated by the assertiveness, while the 'mystical' side of Maud Gonne and Olivia Shakespear seemed to justify an avoidance of physical love. When Olivia Shakespear first 'gave me the long passionate kiss of love I was startled and a little shocked', Yeats remembered. A virgin until he was thirty, he 'was impotent from nervous excitement' when they first went to bed; 'A week later she came to me again, and my nervous excitement was so painful that it seem best but to sit over our tea and talk.' Yeats describes his embarrassment when they went together to purchase a bed, and credits her sympathy and patience with overcoming his anxieties and allowing 'many days of happiness' (*Memoirs* 85–9). Maud Gonne's rejections of his proposals nerved him to repeat them, and to accept her claim that they had 'a spiritual marriage' (*Collected Letters* 1: 490).

When Yeats first describes her (*Autobiography* 82), Maud Gonne is, in a single paragraph, a Sybil, 'a classical impersonation of the Spring', and evokes Virgil's description of Venus dressed like a huntress in *Aeneid* 1:314–409, disappearing at the moment when her walk reveals her supernatural identity—a detail Yeats would remember when writing *Cathleen Ni Houlihan* (1902). Venus wears red boots, which Yeats elsewhere called 'The colour of magic in every country . . . The caps of fairies and magicians are well-nigh always red' (*Dhoya* 102, n. 8). Oisin sees 'a phantom hound' with one red ear. Dhoya's fairy woman wears a white dress, 'save for a border of feathers dyed the fatal red of the spirits' (*Dhoya* 85). Virgil's description of Venus stresses her athletic appearance, dressed to pursue the deer; at an early encounter, Margaret Leland plays tennis aggressively, and wears a red feather in her cap (*John Sherman* 28). Laura Armstrong, her prototype, had red hair and drove a dog cart. Yeats thought Maud Gonne resembled her, if only in manner, and he identified both women with Vivien, who beguiled Merlin but in Yeats's play dies herself, and with the Enchantress of his *Island of Statues*, who turns the men who seek her into stone statues. The real and imagined women share supernatural tokens and strenuous physical activity.

Significantly, Dhoya's fairy woman appears just after the moon has rejected his sacrifice, and his prayer that he be protected from evil spirits. She is dangerous and unhallowed. She watches him 'with eyes no ardour could rob of the mild and mysterious melancholy that watches us from the eyes of animals—sign of unhuman reveries' (*Dhoya* 86).

'All creation is from conflict, whether with our own mind or with that of others' (*Autobiography* 380). Dhoya's fairy woman infatuates him, and her loss destroys him. Is Yeats already imagining that evanescent and emotionally turbulent love, 'The troubling of my life' (*Memoirs* 40) that Maud Gonne was to embody, a lover who could only satisfy aesthetically? His early love poems, before and after he met her, describe human love as fleeting and unfulfilling. Love is 'A meteor of the burning heart, / One with the tide that gleams, the wings that gleam and dart' ('The Indian to His Love', 1886). Love wanes in 'The Falling of the Leaves' and 'Ephemera' (both 1889). A young bride is enticed away in 'The Host of the Air' (1893) and *The Land of Heart's Desire* (1894). Wandering Aengus (1897) has only a brief glimpse of the maiden before she 'faded through the brightening air'. The Queen will not listen to the jester-poet ('The Cap and Bells', 1894). Other poems of the period have titles like 'The Lover mourns for the Loss of Love' (1898) and 'He Remembers Forgotten Beauty' (1896). In the first version of *The Shadowy Waters* (1900), a song has made Forgael dissatisfied with all ordinary love: 'When I hold / A woman in my arms, she sinks away / As though the waters had flowed up between' (Yeats, *Variorum Plays* 749). He seeks a purer love 'That shall burn time when times have ebbed away.' God 'has made me the friend of your soul,—/ Ah he keeps for another your heart,' Yeats wrote in October 1891, in one of the poems presented to Maud Gonne in the vellum book (Ellmann 1948, 155).

All these poems of evanescence and unfulfilment are narratives of desire, but a desire that finds a voice by emphasizing its own failure to achieve satisfaction. 'Yeats makes a cult of frustration', Ellmann remarks, 'and courts defeat like a lover' (Ellmann 1948, 82). Maud Gonne successfully embodied that hopeless desire, as Yeats recognized. Her arrival at Bedford Park clarified Yeats's imagination by focusing that readiness to fail which he had already portrayed in *John Sherman*, that fatal determination to lose he had portrayed in *Dhoya*.

When Yeats put Olivia Shakespear 'into a condition between meditation and trance' and solicited advice from 'A certain symbolic personality who called herself, if I remember rightly, Megarithma,' he partly rejected the message he was given. 'I believed that this enigmatic sentence came from my own daimon, my own buried self speaking through my friend's mind.' He goes on to claim the mind's power to control or alter external events:

> My friends believed that the dark portion of the mind—the subconscious—had an incalculable power, and even over events. To influence events or one's own mind, one had to draw the attention of that dark portion, to turn it, as it were, into a new direction (*Autobiography* 247).

'Who thought Cuchulain till it seemed / He stood where they had stood?' Yeats asks in his last play (Yeats, *Variorum Plays* 1093). Did he 'think' Maud Gonne before she appeared, imagining one who would evoke that hopeless yearning he turned into poetry, as Dhoya's loss sends him on a wild and fatal ride? *Dhoya* remains an enigmatic text, hinting at secrets of Yeats's imagination as the fairy woman initially hints at her presence by a touch, a whisper, a partial fleeting glimpse. To re-read it in Richard Finneran's superb edition is to feel, to use Yeats's terms, a trembling of the veil that conceals his secrets, almost a touch from beyond the curtain.

Reprinted with deletions from *Yeats: An Annual of Critical and Textual Studies* 11 (1993), pp. 247–60. Originally a review of Richard Finneran's edition of Yeats's *John Sherman* and *Dhoya* (New York: Macmillan, 1991).

7

Long Division in the Long Schoolroom

Yeats's 'Among School Children'

From the national point of view W.B. Yeats occupies an almost unique position in Irish life; for he is virtually the first man since Swift who has been able to bring the Anglo-Irish tradition into line with positive nationalism.
The Irish Times, 14 June 1935, noting Yeats's 70th birthday

It has been my principal purpose . . . to lay beside the essential unity of Ireland a no less essential diversity . . . This was the true anarchy that beset the country . . . an anarchy in the mind and in the heart, an anarchy which forbade not just unity of territories, but also 'unity of being' . . .
F.S.L. Lyons, *Culture and Anarchy in Ireland 1890–1939*

And all real unity commences
In consciousness of differences.
W.H. Auden, 'New Year Letter'

The Yeats who visited St Otteran's School in Waterford, in February 1926, and wrote 'Among School Children' over the next few months, had always been acutely aware of the basic division in Irish life, which separated Anglo-Irish Protestants from their unhyphenated Catholic fellow countrymen. Yeats himself, as Irish nationalist, as Protestant poet in a Catholic nation, had struggled to overcome that division, confronting the hostility of the Anglo-Irish, who saw him as a traitor to his class, and at the same time confronting the hostility of Catholic nationalists, who doubted his loyalty to their cause and continually challenged his right to consider himself Irish—a term they reserved for those who were Gaelic, Catholic, and preferably of peasant stock.

In 1917, Yeats bought his 'castle', the Norman tower he renamed Thoor Ballylee (Hanley 13; 22). He spent parts of most summers there between 1919 and 1928. He had not previously owned property in Ireland. In 1922 he purchased a house in Dublin. Both purchases represented a commit-ment to living and working in Ireland, and a determination to play a part in the new Ireland shaped by the events of 1916.

The tower was more than a summer home. It became a poem, 'The Tower', finished in October 1925; the 1928 collection that takes its title from that poem; and in 'Blood and the Moon' (1928) Yeats would 'declare this tower is my symbol'. The tower 'satisfied his desire for a rooted place in a known countryside, not far from Coole and his revered friend Lady Gregory', T.R. Henn suggests; 'To live in a Tower completed, perhaps, his alignment with a tradition of cultivated aristocracy which he had envied' (Henn 5). Built by a descendant of Norman invaders, the tower was also associated with the Irish poet Raftery, prototype for Yeats's mask of 'Red Hanrahan', with Mary Hynes, the Galway beauty Raftery celebrated, and with the wise-woman Biddy Early, neatly encapsulating Yeats's awareness of his own 'outsider' ancestry, his eagerness to be a nationalist poet, and his interest in supernatural traditions. But a tower is at once a stronghold and an assertion. The Yeats who felt increasingly besieged by the moral and political priorities of the Free State could take refuge there, keep watch from its battlements. The tower is at once part of the landscape and imposed upon it, separate from it. And a tower is an assertion: I am here, and I intend to stay here.

In 1926 Yeats was particularly and painfully aware of these Irish divisions. His own Irish identity had been recognized by the new Irish Free State when President Cosgrave appointed him to the Senate in December 1922, as one of three Senators who were responsible for advising the government on education, literature, and the arts (Pearce 11). But at the same time that very Senate eagerly passed laws imposing censorship and abolishing divorce, accommodating the new state to rural narrow-mindedness and Catholic doctrine, in ways that denied the Anglo-Irish rights they had until now enjoyed. 'I think it is tragic that within three years of this country gaining its independence we should be discussing a measure which a minority of this nation considers to be grossly oppressive,' Yeats declared, debating the Divorce Bill in the Senate in June 1925;

> I am proud to consider myself a typical man of that minority. We against whom you have done this thing are no petty people. We are one of the great stocks of Europe. We are the people of Burke; we are the people of Grattan; we are the people of Swift, the people of Emmet, the people of Parnell. We have created the most of the modern literature of this country. We have created the best of its political intelligence (Pearce 99).

The new government's tendency to legislate in ways that would please the Catholic Church and a rural electorate, excluding the Anglo-Irish and their traditions, was paralleled outside the walls of the legislature by those who denied Yeats and his Abbey collaborators the right to call themselves Irish writers. 'The Irish nation is the Gaelic nation'; the *Catholic Bulletin* insisted in 1924; 'its language and literature is the Gaelic language . . . All other elements have no place in Irish national life, literature and tradition' (Brown 1981, 63). In *The Hidden Ireland* (1924) and *Synge and Anglo-Irish Literature* (1931), Daniel Corkery, attempting to depict the Gaelic literary tradition and rescue it from neglect, passed over into denying the Anglo-Irish any place in a national literary tradition: 'what chance of expressing the people of Ireland have those writers who, sprung from the Ascendancy, have never shared the Irish national memory, and are therefore just as un-Irish as it is possible for them to be?' (Corkery, *Synge* 15). 'The usual sort of thing' Yeats remarks of an *Irish Press* article in 1932; 'only the Gael or the Catholic is Irish' (*Letters* 791). Kate Alcock, the Anglo-Irish heroine of Lennox Robinson's *The Big House*, performed at the Abbey in September 1926, repudiates such efforts to exclude her and her class from the new Ireland: 'Ireland is not more theirs than ours' (Robinson 196), she insists. Joyce had already noted assertive Gaeldom's eagerness to exclude, to define the Irish community narrowly, by depicting in *Ulysses* (1922) the Citizen's refusal to consider Bloom Irish. The Citizen's Ireland is a policy from which Bloom is excluded, and the novel's brief moments of communion between Bloom and Stephen are limited and temporary, a provisional unity between two rejected outsiders.

Yeats saw the Bill forbidding divorce as 'a wedge . . . put . . . into the heart of this nation' (Pearce 92), marginalizing the Anglo-Irish and denying their centrality to any Irish tradition. He specifically connected the Bill with another divisive act, the division of Ireland into two separate political entities, the twenty-six county Irish Free State and the six-county Northern Ireland, one Catholic and one Protestant dominated. The Protestant North, he told the Senate, would never reunite 'If you show that this country . . . is going to be governed by Catholic ideas, and by Catholic ideas alone' (Pearce 92). For Yeats the political division of Ireland along sectarian lines as settled in 1925 was a betrayal of Ireland's traditional identity as a single kingdom. In practice, the division denied the Free State a substantial Protestant minority that might have impeded the imposition of Catholic doctrine as national laws.

'If there is a distinctive Irish experience, it is one of division', Denis Donoghue comments, and goes on to list the various Irish forms of division: Catholic/Protestant, Gaelic/Anglo, Irish language/English language, 'the visible and the hidden Ireland . . . the Big House and the hovel' (Donoghue 1986, 16). Given this endemic divisiveness, and the intensely asserted and felt divisions of the 1920s, it is hardly surprising that divisions and separations should be much on Yeats's mind in the year of 'Among School Children', and should have marked, indeed shaped that poem. These divisions were particularly insistent in February 1926, when Yeats visited St Otteran's. A few days before his departure, ultra-nationalists demonstrated to protest the performance of Sean O'Casey's *The Plough and the Stars* at the Abbey. Some of the demonstrators were angered because the men of 1916 were not portrayed as conventional heroes, others that one of the characters was a prostitute. 'You have disgraced yourselves again', Yeats told the Abbey audience (McCann 15), remembering the *Playboy* riots. 'Yeats, as mad as the maddest there, pranced on the stage', O'Casey later recalled, 'shouting out his scorn, his contempt; his anger making him like unto an aged Cuchullain in his hero-rage' (O'Casey 1949, 175–6). The demonstrations were followed by reasoned, though hardly more reasonable attacks on the play as 'Anglo-Irish' (O'Casey 1949, 181) and the Abbey Theatre as 'Cromwellian' (Yeats, *Uncollected Prose* 2:466– 70), and by demands for theatrical censorship (McCann 152). There was also a well-orchestrated movement to censor books and magazines, particularly 'foreign' work but also highly suspicious of Anglo-Irish writers. Kevin O'Higgins, the Free State Minister for Justice, set up a Committee of Enquiry on Evil Literature in 1926 (Brown 1981, 68), and in the same year Yeats protested the public burning of an English magazine containing the 'Cherry Tree Carol', declared indecent and anti-Catholic by a zealous Christian Brother (*Uncollected Prose* 2:461). The extremist *Catholic Bulletin* described Yeats's Nobel Prize as awarded, not to an Irishman, but to a member of 'the English colony in Ireland' as a reward for 'paganism in thought and word' (Brown 1981, 72). Yeats unsuccessfully opposed film censorship in 1923, and, retired from the Senate, published an eloquent attack on the Censorship of Publications Act (Pearce 175–80).

   Even the committee established in the spring of 1926, with Yeats as chairman, to select designs for the new Free State coinage, needed to protect itself against, in Yeats's phrase, 'all Gaels and ultra-Nationalists' (Hone 1943, 388). The committee rejected shamrocks, round towers, wolfhounds, and explicitly Catholic symbols in favour of native birds, fish, and animals, images that would not be politically or religiously divisive, only to be charged, as Yeats reported, with being 'under the influence of the Freemasons who wanted to drive out of Ireland all traces of the Christian religion' (Hone 1943, 389). Yeats is still sometimes excluded from the magic circle of Irishness. Writing in 1996, Thomas Kinsella quoted Corkery with approval and described Yeats as isolated from Irish life: 'his living tradition is solely in English . . . He refuses to come to terms with the real shaping vitality of Ireland where he sees it exists.' For Kinsella it exists among the Catholic 'Gaels': 'Daniel O'Connell's children . . . De Valera . . . Paudeen at his greasy till . . . Yeats had a greatness capable, perhaps, of integrating a modern Anglo-Irish culture, and which chose to make this impossible by separating out a special Anglo-Irish culture from the main unwashed body' (Kinsella 62–4). In his 1984 Field Day pamphlet *Heroic Styles: the tradition of an idea*, Seamus Deane described the 'Irish Protestant writers', especially Yeats, as seizing for themselves an Irish cultural tradition as their ancestors had seized Irish lands. Yeats's 'programme . . . was not, finally, a programme of separation from the English tradition. His continued adherence to it led him to define the central Irish attitude as one of self-hatred . . . The pathology of literary unionism has never been better defined' (Deane 7–10).

Kinsella and Deane do not, of course, deny Yeats's greatness. They are examining his separation, as a Protestant of English ancestry, from certain attitudes and experiences that define the Irish majority. 'The typical Anglo-Irish boy . . . learns that he is not quite Irish almost before he can talk'; wrote Vivian Mercier, who had been such a boy; 'later he learns that he is far from being English either' (Mercier 1977, 26). For Yeats, as for all Anglo-Irish writers, the central fact, perhaps even the impetus to writing, was this separation from the unhyphenated Irish, the nation he wished to speak for and to as its national poet. Throughout his career he struggled to transcend this separation without repudiating his own Anglo-Irish identity. He did this by choosing themes and situations from a legendary Ireland, pre-Christian and long antedating any English invasion, where Catholic/ Protestant and Anglo-Irish/Gaelic categories were irrelevant, celebrating Fergus, Cuchulain, Deirdre, at once Irish, heroic, and aristocratic. He also celebrated a pre-Christian or a-Christian element which he found among the tales and visionary experiences of the peasantry, which allowed him to present his own interests as essentially Irish. In 'To Ireland in the Coming Times' (1893), Yeats declared himself a national poet, 'one/With Davis, Mangan, Ferguson', despite the contrast between their explicitly nationalist themes and his own preference for the occult, the visionary Rose:

> When time began to rant and rage
> The measure of her flying feet
> Made Ireland's heart begin to beat.

In the 1920s, disappointed with the small-mindedness, intellectual timidity, and clerical domination of the Free State, Yeats became less diffident about his own Anglo-Irish tradition as the new state ignored or marginalized it. He added Swift, Goldsmith, Berkeley, and Burke to Cuchulain and Deirdre as exemplary Irish heroes. In 1904 he had insisted that 'Swift, Burke, and Goldsmith . . . hardly seem to me to have come out of Ireland at all' (*Uncollected Prose* 2:328; Torchiana 1966, 169). Goldsmith and Burke had once 'come to seem a part of the English system' and Swift insufficiently romantic (*Explorations* 344). Now he demanded that the Free State recognize the Anglo-Irish thinkers

of the eighteenth century as representative of the central Irish tradition, and sought in their work a merging of his own thought and the
national tradition:

> now I read Swift for months together, Burke and Berkeley less often but always
> with excitement, and Goldsmith lures and waits. I collect materials for my
> thought and work, for some identification of my beliefs with the nation itself,
> I seek an image of the modern mind's discovery of itself, of its own permanent
> form, in that one Irish century that escaped from darkness and confusion.
> I would that our fifteenth, sixteenth, or even our seventeenth century had been
> the clear mirror,

he concludes, aware that he is trailing his coat by proclaiming the glories of
what Irish nationalists would consider the period of their defeat and degra-
dation under the Penal Laws, 'but fate decided against us' (*Explorations*
344–5). The passage is from Yeats's preface to his 1934 play about Swift,
The Words upon the Window-Pane. In returning to Swift and the other
eighteenth-century thinkers, Yeats was returning to the ideas of his early
mentor, John O'Leary, and his generous definition of the Irish community.
'You must give your days and nights to our Swifts, Goldsmiths, Berkeleys
Burkes . . . you will be told by narrow-minded or ignorant people that
there is little that is Irish about all or most of them', O'Leary told an
audience in 1886. 'But if you begin by freeing yourself from narrow-
mindedness, you have made a great (perhaps the greatest) step towards
freeing yourself also from ignorance' (Torchiana 1966, 108). O'Leary's
lecture was entitled *What Irishmen Should Know. How Irishmen Should Feel.*

'We have as good blood as there is in Europe', Yeats insisted in *On the
Boiler* (1939), that strange meditation on eugenics and racial purity.
'Berkeley, Swift, Burke, Grattan, Parnell, Augusta Gregory, Synge, Kevin
O'Higgins, are the true Irish people . . . If the Catholic names are few
history will soon fill the gap' (*Explorations* 442). O'Higgins aside, these
names represent those who had given Ireland cultural leadership, political
leadership, or intellectual leadership. 'We Irish' must define ourselves
politically in terms of Burke and Grattan as well as Daniel O'Connell, must
imitate Swift and Berkeley in audacity of thought—a challenge to those
who would censor books and films according to the prejudices of rural
Catholicism. The Big House and the peasant cabin belong equally to the
Irish tradition; their mutual exclusion is temporary and mistaken. 'Ireland,
divided in religion and politics, is as much one race as any modern country'
(*Explorations* 347), Yeats reminds us. In doing so he is not only asserting
the Irishness of his own people. He is asserting their centrality to any Irish
tradition—and asserting his own centrality to that tradition and his right to
speak for it.

Yet inevitably, even as he insisted on the cultural, intellectual, and even political centrality of the Anglo-Irish, Yeats implicitly recognized their separation from the other Ireland. Goldsmith and Berkeley, Swift and Burke may have 'walked the roads/Mimicking what they heard, as children mimic,' and learned 'that wisdom comes of beggary' ('The Seven Sages', 1932), but they are still apart from the beggars they observe, even as Yeats asserts their community, imagined as preserved in the folk memory. The Yeats who asserts the Irishness of the Anglo-Irish also asserts his own pride of race. He makes the Old Man in *Purgatory* (1938), son of a marriage between Anglo-Irish lady and groom in a training-stable, murder his own son, 'A bastard that a pedlar got/Upon a tinker's daughter in a ditch' (*Variorum Plays* 1044), lest a mongrel race perpetuate itself. He admires Parnell's ability to lead the Irish and yet maintain a proud isolation from them (*Autobiography* 156). In his essay 'Ireland, 1921–1931', Yeats connects his renewed interest in Protestant Ireland, and increasing sense of identity with it, to the setting up of the Free State. So long as English rule lasted he

> had seen nothing in Protestant Ireland as a whole but its faults, had carried through my projects in face of its opposition or its indifference, had fed my imagination upon the legends of the Catholic villages or upon Irish mediaeval poetry; but now my affection turned to my own people, to my own ancestors, to the books they had read. It seemed we had a part to play at last . . . we alone had not to assume in public discussion of all great issues that we could find in St Mark or St Matthew a shorthand report of the words of Christ . . . our eighteenth century had regained its importance . . . From Berkeley I went to Swift, whose hold on Irish imagination is comparable to that of O'Connell [Yeats is presumably remembering folk anecdotes about both men; cf. Ó Súilleabháin 521–2]. The Protestant representatives in Dáil and Senate [during the Civil War] were worthy of this past; two or three went in danger of their lives; some had their houses burnt; country gentlemen came from the blackened ruins of their houses to continue without melodrama or complaint some perhaps highly technical debate in the Senate. Month by month their prestige rose (*Uncollected Prose* 2:489).

In a practical vein, Yeats took care to ensure Protestant control at the Abbey through Lennox Robinson and Ernest Blythe, regularly collecting them before meetings of the Abbey board to instruct they what to say and how to vote (interview with Ernest Blythe, June 1972).

Yeats insisted that the Anglo-Irish were an integral part of the Irish tradition and the Irish community. They could not and must not be excluded nor denied full membership in the nation. But at the same time, Yeats recognized their separation from the unhyphenated Irish, and even described the Anglo-Irish as a superior race, alone entitled to define Irishness. They were Ireland's natural leaders, culturally, perhaps even politically. They would shape the political traditions of the new state: 'Now that Ireland is substituting traditions of government for the rhetoric of agitation our eighteenth century had regained its importance' (*Uncollected Prose* 2:489; Hone 1939, 494). Members of the new national legislature would come to see themselves as the heirs of Burke and Grattan, who had sat in the last independent Irish legislature. While eager to employ the inclusive phrase, 'We Irish', Yeats nevertheless continually employed an exclusive we/they or I/they duality in the 1920s and 1930s. This tension between an imagined national unity and a perceived, even cherished duality, shapes the only poem originating out of his duties as a Senator and the inevitable political issues they raised. Though not overtly a political poem, 'Among School Children' is about Irish separation and Yeats's struggle to reconcile it with his vision of Irish unity.

Conscientiously informing himself about Irish educational conditions in preparation for Senate debates on a new School Attendance Act, Yeats visited a number of schools, among them St Otteran's School in Waterford, a primary school for Catholic girls, run by the Sisters of Mercy. In 1920 the nuns had reorganized the school to adopt the educational theories and methods of Maria Montessori, with their emphasis on cleanliness and orderliness: Montessori wanted to train children to become responsible citizens. In a letter to Lady Gregory Yeats described St Otteran's as 'a very remarkable convent school. Waterford is becoming the centre of Irish school reform and will remain so if it can be protected from the old-fashioned ideas of the inspectors. It is having the fight we have all had'— Yeats meant the struggle to be innovative and intellectually audacious— 'Our work is being embodied in the programme . . . The children had no idea who I was' (Hone 1943, 378).

Yeats visited St Otteran's in February 1926, a few days after the demonstrations over *The Plough and the Stars*. Around 14 March, while reading reports on schools, he noted a 'Topic for poem—School children and the thought that life will waste them perhaps that no possible life can fulfil our [Parkinson "their own"] dreams or even their teacher's hope. Bring in the old thought that life prepares for what never happens' (Jeffares 1968, 299; Parkinson 93). The poem slowly emerged from its rough cancelled versions, and was essentially completed by 14 June—though stanza six was not quite in its final form as late as 24 September, when Yeats sent it to Olivia Shakespear, telling her, 'Here is a fragment of my last curse upon old age. It means that even the greatest men are owls, scarecrows, by the time their fame has come' (*Letters* 719). *The Dial* and *London Mercury* published the poem simultaneously in August 1927.

Yeats's preoccupation with Irish divisions dictates the basic structure of the poem, as the poet, ageing, masculine, Protestant, separates himself from the Catholic girls in their Catholic classroom, escaping from the

Catholic here and now into a deceptively Anglo-Irish there and then—deceptive because the escape into a reverie of Maud Gonne as 'Ledaean body', child, and the old woman she is now invokes an image of Irish unity that anticipates the chestnut tree and the dancer of the final stanza. Anglo-Irish, yet passionate Irish nationalist, Maud Gonne herself evades excluding sectarian and genealogical categories, most specifically through her participation in Yeats's art by playing the title role in his most nationalistic play, *Cathleen ni Houlihan* (1902), and so herself personifying the Irish nation. As 'Poor Old Woman' who is also 'a young girl' with 'the walk of a queen' (*Variorum Plays* 227, 231) Maud Gonne as Cathleen was at once old and young, foreshadowing her presence as simultaneously young and old in stanzas two, three, and four of 'Among School Children'. If she personifies popular Irish myth as Cathleen, she also personifies the larger European myth of Helen of Troy, that daughter of the swan who set Troy ablaze—a myth that Yeats nationalized in 'No Second Troy' (1908):

> Why should I blame her that she filled my days
> With misery, or that she would of late
> Have taught to ignorant men most violent ways,
> Or hurled the little streets upon the great,
> Had they but courage equal to desire?
> . . . .
> Why, what could she have done, being what she is?
> Was there another Troy for her to burn?

Maud Gonne had played a prominent part in the attack on *The Plough and the Stars*.

Invoking Leda invokes the act of begetting, of lives beginning, that Yeats examines in stanza five, and also invokes the beginning/begetting of a new social order. For Yeats, the rape of Leda engendered not only 'The broken wall, the burning roof and tower/And Agamemnon dead' ('Leda and the Swan' 1924). It also brought about a whole new political order. Troy's fall caused the founding of Rome, and so began one of the three ages, each originating in an act of miscegenation: that begun by the sexual union of Leda and the god Zeus, that begun by the sexual union of God the Father and the Virgin Mary, and that to come, which will conceive the 'rough beast' of 'The Second Coming' (1919).

In Yeats's mind, Leda was associated with Mary, as she is in the 'Dove or Swan' section of *A Vision* (1925). In Leda and in Mary, divine and human meet and beget, with profound political consequences, a new political order that manifests itself in art. 'Leda and the Swan', written in September 1923, almost immediately precedes 'Among School Children' in *The Tower* (1928), the two poems separated only by 'On a Picture of a Black Centaur by Edmund Dulac' (1920), a poem celebrating a hybrid being who is the successful unity of two different ancestries. Are that poem's 'horrible green parrots' those 'Irish Irelanders' who loudly and repetitiously denied Yeats's Irishness?

Yeats thought of 'Leda and the Swan' as a poem about a 'violent annunciation', and AE, realizing that it treated the Virgin Birth in explicitly sexual terms, refused to print it in his *Irish Statesman* (*Variorum Poems* 828). The poem appeared in the short-lived Dublin magazine *To-morrow* (August 1924), founded to protest the narrow Catholicism of the Free State. 'We are Catholics, but of the school of Pope Julius the Second and of the Medician Popes', Yeats declared in the magazine's manifesto, and praised those Popes' tolerance and artistic taste, their employment of great artists to reconcile 'Galilee and Parnassus' upon the ceiling of the Sistine Chapel. 'Leda and the Swan' did indeed provoke a clerical uproar (*Uncollected Prose* 2:438, 463), intensified because the same issue of *To-morrow* contained Lennox Robinson's story about an Irish country girl, raped by a tramp, who believes she is to be the mother of God, the vessel for Christ's second coming.

Having already defined the Anglo-Irish as the *true* Irish, Yeats declared himself a truer Catholic than the Catholic clergy in 'The Need for Audacity of Thought' (*The Dial*, February 1926), an essay AE also refused to print. Yeats described the *To-morrow* controversy and the Christian Brother's attack on the 'Cherry Tree Carol', and explained them as clerical squeamishness at the physiological implications of God become man, born of mortal woman: 'God, in the indignity of human birth, all that seemed impossible, blasphemous even, to many early heretical sects . . . I have thought it out again and again and I can see no reason for the anger of the Christian Brothers, except that they do not believe in the Incarnation. They think they believe in it, but they do not, and its sudden presentation fills them with horror' (*Uncollected Prose* 2: 462–3). Again Yeats is more Catholic than the Church.

'Leda and the Swan' and later 'The Mother of God' (1932) imagine the physical impact when divinity mates with humanity. In both cases the result is a being or beings who are at once human and divine or, like Castor and Pollux, at least semi-divine. Mary's son and Leda's progeny unite in themselves ancestries more drastically different than Anglo-Irish and unhyphenated Irish. Both poems wonder what union with divinity was like for the women involved, and speculate about their possible infusion with divine qualities or attributes. Did Leda, 'Being so caught up,/So mastered by the brute blood of the air,/. . . put on his knowledge with his power?' In 'The Mother of God' Mary understands 'that I bore/The Heavens in my womb'.

Leda, then, is linked in Yeats's mind with a unity of human and divine, and so with the Virgin Mary. Maud Gonne's 'Ledaean body' and identification with Helen prepares us for the 'youthful mother' of stanza five, seated with her child 'upon her lap', and for the images worshipped by 'nuns and mother' of stanza seven.

Yeats was notorious in the Dublin of his day for seeming to be lost in a poetic reverie, indifferent to his surroundings, only to reveal suddenly that nothing had escaped him. Yeats composed out loud, 'blooming and buzzing like a bumble bee' in Maud Gonne's phrase (Hone 1943, 330), and found the long tram ride from the city centre to his home in Rathfarnham a congenial setting for humming and buzzing out a poem in its early stages. One day his daughter Anne boarded the tram with some of her school mates, and was embarrassed to find her father seated behind the driver, buzzing away at a poem. She hurried past, pretending not to know him; he seemed oblivious. But when both descended at their stop, and she followed him to their gate, he turned to her with well-feigned surprise, asking, 'Did you wish to see someone?' The absorption in the poem was real, but he was at the same time well aware that she had treated him as a stranger, and so treated her in the same way (conversation with Eilís Dillon, July 1988).

In 'Among School Children' Yeats depicts himself as escaping in reverie from the schoolroom to 'dream of a Ledaean body' and speculate about childhood and old age. He seems only briefly aware of the room and the children in it. Nevertheless, a month later he was able to tell the Senate, 'I have seen a school lately in a South of Ireland town managed by the Sisters of Mercy, and it is a model to all schools . . . the part of the house that is used frequently is washed once a week and brushed daily. The children are perfectly clean.' Yeats praised the 'Italian system' of education, presumably that of Maria Montessori: 'There is one large primary school managed by nuns . . . which has adopted practically the entire Italian system and which is carrying it out with great effect, and has found that it is applicable, and that its teachers do not need special training to carry it out' (24 March 1926; Pearce 108, 111). Nor did Yeats miss the details of 'the long schoolroom'. Like all Montessori schools it displayed a copy of Raphael's 'Seated Madonna' ('Madonna della Seggiola', also known as 'Madonna della Sedia'; Torchiana 1965, 124): the Virgin seated, the infant Christ on her lap, the child St John the Baptist beside them—a 'youthful mother, a shape upon her lap'. Maria Montessori had declared this picture 'the emblem' of her schools:

> In this beautiful conception, Raphael has not only shown us the Madonna as a Divine Mother holding in her arms the babe who is greater than she, but by the side of this symbol of all motherhood, he has placed the figure of St John, who represents humanity . . . In addition to this beautiful symbolism, the picture has a value as being one of the greatest works of art of Italy's greatest artist (Montessori 82).

Montessori saw the painting as representing maternity, the connection of human and divine in unity, and a work of art by a national genius. Yeats has spotted and understood the picture. It partly underlies his poem, which also combines the human and the divine in a single composition, and meditates on that Incarnation the Christian Brother seemed to fear and deny. The union of human and divine, logically impossible, can be achieved only through miracle or through art—though art that expresses the nationality of the artist, and in doing so helps to create that nationality. In 'The Municipal Gallery Revisited' (1937) the portraits of Casement, Griffith, Lady Gregory, Synge, Kevin O'Higgins, and Hugh Lane become the icons defining the Irish tradition, the school where future generations will learn what it is to be Irish. Maria Montessori hung the Madonna in her classrooms for similar reasons, to develop a sense of national identity, as well as evoke a religious mystery. 'Among School Children' evokes the same religious mystery of divine-human unity and does so to evoke other unities. The natural unity of the chestnut tree, echoing Edmund Burke's metaphor of the tree as the state, invites a vision of achieved national unity. The poem ends with a vision that is doubly aesthetic: the dancer inseparable from the dance, and the completed poem.

Yeats develops the poem by emphasizing his own separation from this time and this place, from the Catholic schoolroom and the Catholic schoolgirls. In doing so he asserts and demonstrates the power of the imagination over temporal and local reality, substituting an imagined Maud Gonne for the children before his eyes. That separation creates the poem, and provides a metaphor for Yeats's ambiguous attitude towards Anglo-Irish and unhyphenated Irish, mutually exclusive categories and yet a single nation, as the poem moves to its aesthetically achieved unity.

The opening lines establish the dichotomies which govern the poem: 'I walk through the long schoolroom questioning;/A kind old nun in a white hood replies.' The children are present but hardly noticed. They are narrated rather than seen. They stare 'In momentary wonder' but are not much interested in the 'sixty-year-old smiling public man'. The children are passive, static; Yeats keeps moving, as he so often does in poetry ('I will arise and go now'; 'And therefore I have sailed the seas'; 'I climb to the tower-top'). His mind is also peripatetic, escaping into his 'dream of a Ledaean body'.

In the schoolroom Yeats is an outsider, an invader, the very thing his opponents considered him to be in Ireland. Here he is Anglo-Irishman among Catholics, adult among children, man among women: the nun, the girls, the pictured Madonna, Leda, Maud Gonne, the chestnut-tree (a less masculine image than its origin, Burke's oak), the dancer. To achieve unity, he must move from outsider to shared identity, and to achieve this he must move from spectator/spectacle to visionary. His separation is a kind of freedom. Unbound by the discipline of the schoolroom, he is free to dream of the Ledaean body and then to arrive at the vision of the chestnut-tree and the dancer. 'The children learn to cipher'—to count, distinguish categories—'and to sing', to celebrate in art. Yeats's dream of Maud Gonne contains categories that can be logically and verbally distinguished, her childhood, young womanhood, and old age, but they merge in her unity as the same woman, as Maud Gonne was at once Cathleen ni Houlihan old and young, and as the chestnut-tree can be verbally and logically separated into leaf, blossom, and bole, yet transcend these categories in its indivisible unity.

Yet, to attain his vision of unity, Yeats must be outside, separate, an exile, a nomad. He wanders in his reverie through time and space, as Bloom wanders through Dublin. In *The Tower*, 'Among School Children' is followed by 'Colonus' Praise', Yeats's translation of a chorus from *Oedipus at Colonus*. The poem reiterates the images of dancer and dance ('Immortal ladies tread the ground/Dizzy with harmonious sound') and sacred olive tree, the tree 'that gives/Athenian intellect its mastery', and recalls related themes from *Oedipus at Colonus*: Oedipus, a foreigner, is an outsider at Colonus, an invader of a spot sacred to the local gods. He is initially unwelcome, urged to depart, but once accepted he is a sacred possession by which Athens shall maintain herself and flourish, politically and intellectually. The outsider must be recognized as such but not excluded; he must instead be cherished for his otherness, the special gifts and qualities he brings.

The ability to escape into dream, and the vision that it brings, is Yeats's gift to Ireland. 'One night I had a dream almost as distinct as a vision', he told Lady Gregory, in his dedication to her of *Cathleen ni Houlihan*,' of a cottage where there was well-being and firelight . . . and into the midst of that cottage there came an old woman in a long cloak. She was Ireland herself' (*Variorum Plays* 232). That vision became both art and politics, a play which Yeats imagined as the impetus for the Easter Rising and Ireland's independence: 'Did that play of mine send out/Certain men the English shot?' ('The Man and the Echo'). Yeats recalls the play through his dream of Maud Gonne, to recall his own claims to membership in Ireland—then moves to reassert the claims of the Anglo-Irish by invoking Berkeley and Burke. 'We have in Berkeley and in Burke a philosophy on which it is possible to base the whole life of a nation', he declared in 'The Child and the State' (*Irish Statesman*, December 1925), a lecture written and delivered a few months before his visit to St Otteran's, describing his ideas about Irish education: 'Berkeley proved that the world was a vision, and Burke that the State was a tree, no mechanism to be pulled in pieces and put up again, but an oak tree that had grown through centuries' (Pearce 172).

If Burke's tree is to be part of the poem's culminating vision of unity, Berkeley shows Yeats how to achieve that vision. Berkeley could make the material world vanish by changing his thought, as Yeats erases the schoolroom to dream of the 'Ledaean body':

> And God-appointed Berkeley that proved all things a dream,
> That this pragmatical, preposterous pig of a world, its farrow that so solid seem,
> Must vanish on the instant if the mind but change its theme
>   ('Blood and the Moon', 1928)

Esse est percipi, as Beckett liked to remind us: to be is to be perceived.

The unity that is Maud Gonne, three in one, woman, child, and hag, is presented in three stanzas (2–3–4), and initially creates another image of unity. Recalling her 'Ledaean body, bent/Above a sinking fire', Yeats also recalls 'a tale that she/Told of a harsh reproof, or trivial event/That changed some childish day to tragedy'. More importantly, he recalls a moment of unity with her as both responded to that tale: 'Told, and it seemed that our two natures blent/Into a sphere from youthful sympathy'—a perfect sympathy, like the organic unity of an egg, 'yoke and white of the one shell'. Yeats remembers Leda's eggs, from which came Helen and the warrior demigod Pollux: 'from one of her eggs came Love and from the other War' (*Vision* 181) he tells us in *A Vision* (1925). The uniting sympathy is based on a tale of reproof. Recalled oppression blends them into one; Cathleen ni Houlihan too has her tale of loss and oppression in Yeats's play.

Though the thought of 'that fit of grief or rage' brings Yeats back to the schoolroom and its inhabitants, it is only to wonder if Maud Gonne ever 'stood so at that age', and to recognize at once a likeness and a contrast: '. . . even daughters of the swan can share/Something of every paddler's heritage'. These children are ugly ducklings, paddlers, perhaps alliteratively paddies, peasants, the raw material from which Yeats assembles an image of Maud Gonne 'as a living child'.

Stanza 4 describes Maud Gonne now, 'Hollow of cheek'—Yeats's less than gallant version of Thomas Moore's 'Believe me if all those endearing young charms'. Nor does he spare himself: 'And I though never of Ledaean kind/Had pretty plumage once.' Again there is a subtext in Yeats's plays. If Maud Gonne is at once Helen and Cathleen ni Houlihan, Yeats's antiself and mythic projection is Cuchulain, like Helen and Christ begotten by divinity upon a human woman, and like them with ornithological ancestry. In Lady Gregory's *Cuchulain of Muirthemne* (1902), the god Lugh changes Cuchulain's mother into a bird; in Yeats's *On Baile's*

Strand (1906 version), Cuchulain remembers 'that clean hawk out of the air/That, as men say, begot this body of mine/Upon a mortal woman' (*Variorum Plays* 485); later the Fool, Cuchulain's other self within the play, puts feathers in his hair (519). 'Heart-mysteries there', Yeats remarks in 'The Circus Animals' Desertion' (1938), admitting the self-revelation in the play. Cuchulain figured in the first version of 'The Hero, the Girl, and the Fool' (1922), originally 'Cuchulain, the Girl and the Fool', printed in *The Tower* as the next poem but one to 'Among School Children'. He appears as masculine strength, in opposition to feminine beauty. Cuchulain is also the masculine counterpart of Cathleen ni Houlihan as an icon of the Easter Rising. 'Pearse and some of his followers had a cult' of Cuchulain, Yeats told Edith Heald in 1938; 'The Government has put a statue of Cuchulain in the rebuilt post office to commemorate this' (*Letters* 911). Padraic Pearse had hung a painting by Edwin Morrow at the entrance to his school, St Enda's, portraying Cuchulain and inscribed with the hero's words on first taking up arms: 'I care not though I were to live but one day and one night if only my fame and my deeds live after me' (Lyons 1982, 87).

The meditation on ageing invites Cuchulain into the poem. 'Helen never ages, Cuchulain never ages', Yeats told Frank Fay, who was to be Cuchulain in *On Baile's Strand* (1904), noting also in the character 'The touch of something . . . self assertive yet self immolating' (*Letters* 425–5). In 'Dove or Swan', Book III of *A Vision* (1925), Yeats moves in a single page from 'the annunciation . . . as made to Leda' to her eggs, from which came Love and War, to ask, 'Did the older civilisation like the Jewish think a long life a proof of Heavenly favour that the Greek races should affirm so clearly that those whom the Gods love die young, hurling upon some age of crowded comedy their tragic sense?' (*Vision* 1925, 181). A rejected passage links Cuchulain with Achilles, two heroes who chose a brief heroic life and the eternal fame that the poets can confer, rather than long life (*Vision* notes 46). The same page begins a discussion of statues and their relationship to individual and national beauty, drawing on Plato and Aristotle. Cuchulain, like Achilles, performed heroically to be transformed aesthetically, to give 'the long-remembering harpers . . . matter for their song' (*Green Helmet, Variorum Plays* 453).

Helen and Cathleen ni Houlihan instigate heroic action, Achilles and Cuchulain perform such actions. All are heroic figures recreated in art by Homer or Yeats; Maud Gonne is 'A Woman Homer Sung' in Yeats's 1910 poem, published with *The Green Helmet*. Yeats's *Cathleen ni Houlihan* instigates the Easter Rising, and she had promised that those who die for Ireland will be remembered in song (*Variorum Plays* 228–9, 231), a promise Yeats redeems in 'Easter 1916', a poem that is not a political but an aesthetic statement: 'A terrible beauty is born'. Maud Gonne as 'Quattrocento' painting or statue, the implicit reference to Raphael's 'Madonna della Seggiola' lead to the 'images' of stanza seven, that mock the promise and beauty of beginnings, and replace transient human identity and beauty with the permanent identity and beauty of art. Art satisfies in a way that life cannot; imagination can create an aesthetic vision which is also political, a dream of a unified seamless society: the tree and the dancer of the final stanza.

The poem has developed by creating separations, then turning them into unities: I/the children, apart, yet linked by the poem; the absent Maud Gonne, imagined into a moment of unity; the blended yolk and white; Maud Gonne then/Maud Gonne now; 'Her present image . . . hollow of cheek'/'a comfortable kind of old scarecrow'. In stanzas five, six, and seven the childhood/age separation, which is also merging, develops that theme of life as wasting youth and beauty, Yeats's original 'Topic' for the poem, and his notion that 'no possible life can fulfill our dreams'. The separations which are also mergings continue as well: Plato/Aristotle/Pythagoras, a trinity in the middle of the poem to match the three ages of Maud Gonne at the beginning and the leaf/blossom/bole at the end; 'nuns and mothers'; 'marble or . . . bronze repose'; passion/piety/affection, another trinity.

Yeats's theme of disappointment after promising beginnings hints at his disappointment at the restrictive atmosphere of the Free State, born out of the 'terrible beauty' of 1916 to become 'A little potato-digging republic' (*Uncollected Prose* 2: 446). His task is to offer an aesthetic vision of the state as perfect unity, of shared Irishness. '. . . Help the two Irelands, Gaelic Ireland and Anglo-Ireland, so to unite that neither shall shed its pride', he wrote in 1930. 'Study the great problems of the world, as they have been lived in our scenery, the re-birth of European spirituality in the mind of Berkeley, the restoration of European order in the mind of Burke' (*Explorations* 337). That vision itself becomes a force, an energy brought into the world.

In the last stanza, perhaps not part of the poem's original plan (Parkinson 94), school and schoolchildren forgotten, Yeats imagines unity, body with soul, labour with joy. Body and soul need not be at odds—a hit, perhaps, at the Christian Brothers and their allies, who deny the Virgin's body its role in the Incarnation. Beauty and wisdom are gifts, not to be achieved by struggling for them; Yeats may have been recalling his 'The Sphere of Women', published in *The Irish Times* a few months earlier (17 November 1925): he argued that women could not and should not provide masterpieces, but be content to be beautiful. 'Why, then, should she toil for many years to produce a masterpiece? Looking into her glass, she saw a greater masterpiece than had ever been created in art or in sculpture. Why should she toil?' (Torchiana 1966, 211). The stanza, and the poem, culminate in a final double vision of unity:

> O chestnut-tree, great-rooted blossomer,
> Are you the leaf, the blossom or the bole?
> O body swayed to music, O brightening glance,
> How can we know the dancer from the dance?

The tree cannot be divided, separated into parts. It is completely itself in every part, a natural unity. The dancer cannot be separated from the dance. The tree is a natural unity, the dancer and dance an aesthetic unity. Yeats liberates himself and the poem from separating categories and distinctions, to combine images of political or national unity with aesthetic unity—a striking summary of the role of Maud Gonne/Cathleen ni Houlihan in the poem, at once political and aesthetic. Earlier, Yeats himself, as recording consciousness, stood at the centre of the poem ('I walk . . . I dream'), in his favourite stance, artist/aristocrat alone before a crowd of ignorant plebians. 'Many are beginning to recognise the right of the individual mind to see the world in its own way', he had declared in 1907; 'to cherish the thoughts which separate men from one another, and that are the creators of distinguished life' (*Explorations* 229–30). Even that 'Ledaean body' is an Ascendancy rebuke to the unlettered and a taunt for the Christian Brothers. But at the end of the poem Yeats relinquishes separation and centrality, abolishing self for a larger utterance, imagining the chestnut-tree and the dancer transcending all the poem's *dramatis personae*, all the categories of Irish life.

Thomas Parkinson has commented on the apparent ease of these lines, their assurance and fluency, despite Yeats's many revisions, and the obvious effort the rough drafts show (Parkinson 96, 104). Writing about effortless grace, he managed also to exemplify it, to create an idiom as 'natural' as the chestnut-tree he celebrates, and the organic unity it embodies.

The chestnut-tree—a hawthorn in some early drafts (Parkinson 107)—is a natural unity, but for Yeats it is also a metaphor for political and social unity, that is, for erasing the sectarian and genealogical categories which made the Free State exclusive rather than inclusive. It is, with a botanical shift from oak to chestnut, Burke's state as 'a tree, no mechanism to be pulled in pieces and put up again, but an oak tree that had grown through centuries' (Pearce 172, 19).

In 'Blood and the Moon', written in August 1927 in response to the July assassination of Kevin O'Higgins, Free State Vice-President, Minister for Justice and External Affairs, Yeats invokes his Anglo-Irish heroes, Goldsmith, Swift, Berkeley, fellow inhabitants of 'this tower' that 'is my symbol', fellow-climbers of 'This winding, gyring, spiring treadmill of a stair . . . my ancestral stair':

> And haughtier-headed Burke that proved the state a tree,
> That this unconquerable labyrinth of the birds, century after century,
> Cast but dead leaves to mathematical equality.

Burke's tree image for the state had been in Yeats's mind for many years, since as early as 1893 (Torchiana 1966, 192), though initially he seems to have found the tree as a metaphor for organic unity in Blake (Kermode 96–103). In his Senate years it became closely connected with his insistence that the Anglo-Irish were an integral part of any Irish tradition, and that the new Free State must recognize this in its laws and institutions. A state that curbed their rights, even their privileges, denied the reality of Anglo-Ireland's role in Irish history. 'A State is organic', Yeats wrote in 1930; '. . . We owe allegiance to the government of our day in so far as it embodies that historical being' (*Explorations* 318). 'This country will not always be an uncomfortable place for a country gentleman to live in, and it is most important that we should keep in this country a certain leisured class', he had told the Senate in 1923, debating the question of compensation for Anglo-Irish 'Big Houses' burned during the War of Independence (1919–21) and the Civil War (1922–23). '. . . On this matter I am a crusted Tory. I am of the opinion of the ancient Jewish book which says "there is no wisdom without leisure"' (Torchiana 1966, 196–7; Pearce 38–6). As we have seen, Yeats found in Berkeley and in Burke 'a philosophy on which it is possible to base the whole life of a nation' (Pearce 172), equating them with Gaelic folk literature as essential in developing the Irish intellect and the Irish imagination. 'Feed the immature imagination upon that old folk life, and the mature intellect upon Berkeley and the great modern idealist philosophy created by his influence, upon Burke who restored to political thought its sense of history, and Ireland is reborn, potent, armed and wise,' Yeats declared in 'The Child and the State' (November 1925), reminding his listeners that Burke had 'proved the state a tree, no mechanism to be pulled in pieces and put up again, but an oak tree that had grown through centuries'. Religion, civic duty, and history should be taught 'as all but inseparable . . . the whole curriculum of a school should be as it were one lesson and not a mass of unrelated topics.' Religion, so touchy and divisive a subject in Ireland, should be taught as it is in Italy, 'that it may not be abstract, and that it may be a part of history and of life itself, a part, as it were, of the foliage of Burke's tree' (Pearce 172–3).

Burke's image of the state as a tree is to some extent Yeats's own extrapolation, though very much in the spirit of Burke. In his *Reflections on the Revolution in France* (1790), Burke dismisses British admirers of the Revolution as 'several petty cabals, who attempt to hide their total want of consequence in bustle and noise, and puffing, and mutual quotation of each other', and declares them in no way representative of British public opinion: 'Because half a dozen grasshoppers under a fern make the field ring with their importunate chink, while thousands of great cattle, reposed beneath the shadow of the British oak, chew the cud and are silent, pray do not imagine, that those who make the noise are the only inhabitants of the field' (Burke 1790, 181). It is Yeats who elaborates Burke's glancing metaphor of the sheltering oak into a vision of the state as tree, rejecting in the process the all too British oak, and offers that vision, in 'The Child and the State', 'Among School Children', and 'Blood and the Moon' as a central metaphor for an Irish unity that reconciles or transcends diversities. The pastoral scene, where the oak shelters the future roast beef of old England— already noted as Irish by Leopold Bloom (*Ulysses* 81)—vanishes into the chestnut's surge from root to blossom, a particularly potent metaphor for Ireland when we remember that England's destruction of Ireland's forests was a constant grievance among Irish nationalists (*Ulysses* 268–9), and that the Free State immediately embarked upon an ambitious programme of reforestation. For Yeats the chestnut tree represents liberation from social and political categories that define the Irish nation. Though it owes little to Burke, it does recall his disdain for the petty tyranny of the eighteenth-century 'Ascendancy'—a word he ridiculed (McCormack 1985, 61–96)— and Burke's own conviction that Ireland could only be ruled justly when Catholic and Protestant are equal (Deane; McCormack 62–5). Burke had insisted on the rights of Catholics; Yeats now implicitly insists on the rights of Protestants, as he had done explicitly in his Divorce Bill speech.

Those among the Anglo-Irish who considered themselves Irish often defined themselves negatively, in terms that Mr Podsnap would have accepted: Not English. Yeats saw Bishop Berkeley as the beginning of independent Irish thought because he had written 'We Irish do not think so' after a list of propositions drawn from the writings of Hobbes and Locke (*Uncollected Prose* 2: 458, 484; *Essays* 396). 'Every one I knew well in Sligo despised Nationalists and Catholics', Yeats recalled in *Reveries over Childhood and Youth* (1914), 'but all disliked England with a prejudice which had come down perhaps from the days of the Irish Parliament . . . everybody had told me that English people ate skates and even dog-fish, and I myself had only just arrived in England when I saw an old man put marmalade in his porridge' (*Autobiography* 21–2). His literary career had been an attempt to create a positive Irish identity for Anglo-Irish as well as unhyphenated Irish: 'if we had a national literature that made Ireland beautiful in the memory . . . I thought we might bring the halves'— Catholic Ireland and Protestant Ireland, each incomplete—'together' (*Autobiography* 68). In his 1925 speech on the Divorce Bill, he offered a positive but still defensive claim: 'We . . . are no petty people. We are one of the great stocks of Europe' (Pearce 99). To do so, he had to admit Anglo-Ireland's separate status. With the chestnut-tree he imagined instead an organic unity, its divisions merely verbal categories. Leaf, blossom, and bole are one tree. Yeats never used the word *shamrock* in a poem or play. The closest he comes is the trefoil of 'The Seven Sages'. By 1931 he had come to terms with the colour green and the harp as national symbols; they had been legitimized by the Free State's ability to preserve order. But the shamrock continued to disgust him, 'as though the ascent of the other symbols had left the shamrock the more alone with its associations of drink and jocularity' (*Uncollected Prose* 2: 486–7). As Yeats well knew, the shamrock was St Patrick's botanical representation of the Trinity, three in one, one that is three, perfect unity. Leaf, blossom, and bole offer a new representation of unity, national rather than theological.

Like the shamrock, the tree as state dissolves the logical/verbal categories of either/or, to Yeats 'the mechanical philosophy of England' (Pearce 172), which he blamed for the Industrial Revolution and dialectical materialism:

> Locke sank into a swoon;
> The Garden died;
> God took the spinning-jenny
> Out of his side.
> ('Fragments', 1931).

Locke's crime was separating 'the primary and secondary qualities; and from that day to this the conception of a physical world without colour, sound, taste, tangibility, though indicted by Berkeley as Burke was to indict Warren Hastings . . . and proved mere abstract extension, a mere category of the mind, has remained the assumption of science . . . It worked, and the mechanical inventions of the next age, its symbols that seemed its confirmation, worked even better.' Only in 'communities where . . . solitaries flourish' can men think unity rather than separation:

> Born in such a community, Berkeley with his belief in perception, that abstract ideas are mere words, Swift with his love of perfect nature, of the Houyhnhnms, his disbelief in Newton's system and every sort of machine, Goldsmith and his delight in the particulars of common life that shocked his contemporaries, Burke with his conviction that all States not grown slowly like a forest tree are tyrannies, found in England the opposite that stung their own thought into expression and made it lucid ('Bishop Berkeley', *Essays* 401–2).

Yeats's chestnut-tree discards those 'English' categories of either/or and chooses instead to emphasize both/and, what Joyce called 'two thinks at a time' (*Finnegans Wake* 583). 'The Irish mind remained free, in significant measure, of the linear, centralising logic of the Graeco-Roman culture . . .

based on the Platonic-Aristotelian logic of non-contradiction which operated on the assumption that order and organisation result from the dualistic separation of opposite or contradictory terms', Richard Kearney has suggested;

> Hence the mainstream of western thought rested upon a series of fundamental oppositions—between being and non-being, reason and imagination, the soul and the body, the transcendentally divine and the immanently temporal and so on . . . In contradistinction to the orthodox dualist logic of *either/or*, the Irish mind may be seen to favour a more dialectical logic of *both/and*: an intellectual ability to hold the traditional oppositions of classical reason together in creative confluence . . . We have here not meaninglessness but another kind of meaning, not confusion but another kind of coherence . . . Joyce subverted the established modes of linear or sequential thinking in order to recreate a mode of expression which would foster rather than annul heterogeneous meanings (Kearney 9–10).

Plato separating what is from what we see, Aristotle asserting the reality of nature, its separation from spirit, yield to the creative unity of Pythagoras's music, Yeats's poem. Yeats's vision of the chestnut-tree re-conceptualizes 'the ancient ideology of order, involving a subtle equilibrium between spiritual/cultural cohesion and socio-political diversification' (Kearney 16). In doing so, Yeats moves out of logic into mythopoesis. Ironically, he reverses Arnold's categories of dreaming Celt and logical Saxon: the Irish children 'learn to cipher', their Anglo-Irish visitor dreams of 'a Ledaean body' and of the chestnut-tree. At the same time he declares his own mind 'Celtic' in Arnoldian terms, to merge those categories of Celt and Saxon that Arnold had distinguished. 'Among School Children' recognizes and develops, indeed deliberately cultivates separate categories of isolation, space, time, to dissolve those categories triumphantly in the images of the chestnut-tree and the dancer. In doing so, the poem as it concludes dissolves its own scaffolding, the opposed categories of ageing Senator and schoolchildren, Anglo-Irish and Catholic, attentive pupils and dreamer, to create a new poetic that includes a new politic. 'People are trying to found a new society', Yeats told Edmund Dulac in January 1924. 'Politicians want to be artistic, and artistic people to meet politicians . . . I want to begin arranging performances . . . It seems to be the very moment for a form of drama to be played in a drawing-room' (*Letters* 702). Yeats wanted these politicians to see his Nō plays, written for drawing-room performance and culminating in a dance: *At the Hawk's Well* (1917), *The Only Jealousy of Emer* (1919), *Calvary* (1920). The dancer takes her place to engender the New Ireland.

'All thought moves by a series of conflicts', Yeats told American audiences in 1932 ('Modern Ireland', 263). 'Among School Children' recognizes, asserts, even celebrates the divisions of Irish life—I/they—to celebrate unity, building on logical/categorical irreconcilables to reach an aesthetic unity which offers an image of social and cultural unity. Yeats develops his final images of organic unity by recognizing division in order to transcend them, as the final coming together of the Old Man's father and mother in an incandescent blaze of passion at the end of *Purgatory* (1938) transcends those divisions—Catholic/Protestant, stableboy/ lady— which torment the solitary class-conscious Old Man and cause him to cancel the future.

The poem ends with a vision of aesthetic unity, dancer and dance, and the poem itself achieves that unity, as 'Easter 1916' simultaneously achieves and asserts an aesthetic triumph—'A terrible beauty is born'— which does not depend on the Easter Rising's practical political conse- quences or even relevance: '. . . England may keep faith/For all that is done and said'. The poem unites leaf, blossom, and bole into tree, dancer and dance, into a single aesthetic unity which is the aesthetic identity of the poem itself, and retroactively unifies its apparently separate entities: Yeats and the children, viewer and viewed. The poem incorporates, reconciles, and validates its own socially, physically, and psychologically separate entities. The children people the poem's achieved world as much as the poet and the dancer do, or Maud Gonne, or the traditional poetic image of Leda and the Swan, separated by ten lines which in fact link them.

The speaking voice in the poem initially seems self-indulgent, solipsistic, telling itself its favourite story, another story about Maud Gonne. It resem- bles the lonely Anglo-Irish voice of Molloy, Malone, The Unnamable, talking to create its own existence. But the voice breaks free of solipsism, soliloquy, solitude, and enters a vision of shared identity, of community, that is the poem—a vision of shared identity that we then realize the voice has been talking about all along, by invoking Maud Gonne in her com- munal identity as Cathleen ni Houlihan, or by unifying her triple aspect as child, young woman, old woman—bole, blossom, leaf. The speaking voice finds Maud Gonne in the schoolroom by locating details of her childhood appearance in 'one child or t'other there', a process that simultaneously shares out her individual traits among them.

A solitary individual merges into a vision of 'Mother Ireland', then into the exuberant natural plenitude of the tree, and at last into the exuberant aesthetic order of the dance, a metaphor for the poem, the single dancer now merged into a unity, a completeness, the perfection of 'There' (1935), the Thirteenth Cone of *A Vision* (1937), a 'sphere . . . sufficient to itself . . . even conscious of itself . . . like some great dancer, the perfect flower of modern culture, dancing some primitive dance and conscious of his or her own life and of the dance' (*Vision* 1937, 240; Jeffares 1968, 429):

> There all the barrel-hoops are knit,
> There all the serpent-tails are bit,
> There all the gyres converge in one,
> There all the planets drop in the Sun.

The politically and socially impossible can be accomplished aesthetically. The poem can resolve all divisions, all opposition. As usual with Yeats, poetics and politics are one.

Delivered as a lecture to the Yeats Summer School, Sligo, in August 1993; part was earlier delivered at the 1992 meeting of the International Association for the Study of Anglo-Irish Literature, Trinity College, Dublin.

8

Intelligible on the Blasket Islands

Yeats's *King Oedipus*, 1926

IN the 1980s, Irish poets, especially those associated with Field Day, have found in Greek tragedy a form and metaphors adequate to convey the dilemmas of contemporary Ireland. Field Day has staged Tom Paulin's *The Riot Act* (1984) and Seamus Heaney's *The Cure at Troy* (1990), versions of Sophocles's *Antigone* and *Philoctetes*. Tom Paulin's *Seize the Fire* (1989), which reworks Aeschylus's *Prometheus Bound*, was broadcast on BBC2. Aidan Carl Mathews's *Antigone* (1984) and Brendan Kennelly's *Antigone* (1986) appeared in Dublin, as did Kennelly's *Medea* (1988). This return to Greek models may seem like one more rebellion against the hegemony of W.B. Yeats and his expectation that Irish writers would follow his example by using native mythic materials. Cuchulain and Deirdre were to supersede, or at any rate rival Ajax and Orestes, Hecuba and Electra, in a word-centred theatre sparing of gesture and austere in decor.

But Yeats, like all great writers, was great enough to be inconsistent. His Irish dramas are sometimes Greek in form, with choruses, flawed heroes, and divine or supernatural interventions—elements he was aware of before he found them again in the Japanese Nō play. His preference for physical inaction on stage recalls the necessarily limited movements of the Greek actor, masked, robed, and wearing the inhibiting buskin. Theories about the origins of tragedy in primitive ritual, as expressed by Sir James Frazer, Jane Harrison, and William Ridgeway, helped to shape Yeats's own dramaturgy, and allowed him to recognize that the sacred caves and woods of Greece, like Ireland's holy mountains and wells, were places where man might commune with earthbound but potent spirits.

The most conspicuous result of his interest in Greek drama was his translation of both Sophocles's *Oedipus Tyrannos* (1926) and *Oedipus at Colonus* (1927). Yeats chose each partly as an act of homage, partly for complex personal reasons, and partly because each play could challenge prevailing attitudes in the newly established Free State. His long preoccupation with *Oedipus Tyrannos*, or *King Oedipus*, has been splendidly charted by two well-known scholars of Yeats's texts, David R. Clark and James B. McGuire, in their *W. B. Yeats: The Writing of Sophocles' King Oedipus* (1989).

In 1916 Yeats began an autobiography with recollections of Oedipal conflict, or rather of Laius-like aggression, incidents that had occurred in his early twenties. 'I began to read Ruskin's *Unto this Last*', he tells us,

> and this, when added to my interest in psychical research and mysticism, enraged my father . . . One night a quarrel . . . came to such a height that in putting me out of the room he broke the glass in a picture with the back of my head. Another night when we had been in argument over Ruskin or mysticism . . . he followed me upstairs . . . He squared up at me, and wanted to box, and when I said I could not fight my own father replied, 'I don't see why you should not' (Yeats, *Memoirs* 19).

These recollections suggest that Yeats had personal reasons for his interest in *Oedipus*, especially when we note the recurrence of father-son conflicts in his work—conflicts in which the son dies. Cuchulain kills his son in *On Baile's Strand* (1904); the Old Man in *Purgatory* (1938), already a parricide, kills *his* son; Jonathan Swift, in *The Words Upon the Window-Pane* (1930), has avoided fatherhood, lest he 'add another to the healthy rascaldom and knavery of the world'. These plays recognize the power and aggressive supremacy of fathers. Oedipus, we remember, killed his father Laius only after provocation—the old man first tried to kill him.

The 1922 death of John Butler Yeats, and Yeats's own success, acknowledged now by the Nobel Prize and a Senate seat, may have freed him to return to an earlier project and, in 1926, complete his version of Sophocles's play—'Heart mysteries there', in this renewed preoccupation with 'a man who murdered his da'. Synge, incidentally, was reading *Oedipus* and thinking about a possible Abbey production while he worked on *The Playboy of the Western World* (Clark/McGuire 12).

Yeats declares that he was drawn to Sophocles's *Oedipus Tyrannos* as a way of asserting the Abbey's—and Ireland's—independence from English laws which controlled theatrical performances by requiring that each play be licensed by the Lord Chamberlain, acting through his deputy, the Examiner of Plays. In England the Examiner had refused to licence *Oedipus* at the end of the 1890s because of its incest theme. Yeats successfully defied this process—the Lord Chamberlain had no jurisdiction in Ireland—by producing Shaw's unlicensed *The Shewing-up of Blanco Posnet* at the Abbey in 1909. Like Shaw's play, *Oedipus* would be conspicuously controversial and defiant, and Yeats had hoped for an Abbey *Oedipus* as early as 1904. In 1909, he thought of producing the play with or soon after *The Shewing-up*, as a sequential challenge to the authorities. By 1912 he had resolved to translate *Oedipus* himself, despite his lack of Greek, by turning R.C. Jebb's version 'into simple speakable English'. He planned for an Abbey production of his version, but, after completing a draft of all the dialogue, with the choruses still to do, Yeats abandoned the project in the spring of 1912. He did not complete his version until 1926.

Clark and McGuire have carefully collated the extant manuscripts and typescripts of Yeats's *King Oedipus*. They show us the poet at work, making verbal and dramatic choices to develop a direct and rhythmic stage speech which would be immediately intelligible, and yet believable as the speech of mythic men and women. We can also see a steady subversion of Sophocles's play, as Yeats displaces it with is own, imposing a statuesque immobility on the actors and turning the choruses into mighty lyric outbursts rather than commentary on the developing crisis. Richard Murphy, who supplied translations of passages Yeats had omitted for Michael Cacoyannis's 1973 *King Oedipus* at the Abbey, described Yeats's encounter with the older poet as 'a battle, a ritual battle almost, which Yeats made sure he won' (Murphy 12). Perhaps there was another Oedipal conflict in Yeats's struggle with Sophocles.

'I have made [*Oedipus*] bare, hard and natural like a saga', Yeats told Olivia Shakespear in 1926. He had indeed, especially in the dialogue. Here is part of Oedipus's effort to persuade the prophet Tiresias to interpret the oracle, as translated by Jebb (1887), Gilbert Murray (1911), and by Yeats:

Jebb:

OEDIPUS. For the love of the gods, turn not away, if thou hast knowledge: all we suppliants implore thee on our knees.

TIRESIAS. Aye, for ye are all without knowledge; but never will I reveal my griefs—that I say not thine.

OEDIPUS. How sayest thou? Thou knowest the secret, and wilt not tell it, but art minded to betray us and to destroy the State?

TIRESIAS. I will pain neither myself nor thee. Why vainly ask these things? Thou wilt not learn learn them from me.

OEDIPUS. What, basest of the base,—for thou wouldst anger a very stone,—wilt thou never speak out? Can nothing touch thee? Wilt thou never make an end?

TIRESIAS. Thou blamest my temper, but seest not that to which thou thyself art wedded: no, thou findest fault with me (Jebb 14–15).

Murray:

OEDIPUS.

Thou shalt not, knowing, turn and leave us! See.
We all implore thee, all, on bended knee.

TIRESIAS.
Ye have no knowledge. What is mine I hold
For ever dumb, lest what is thine be told.

OEDIPUS.
What wilt thou? Know and speak not? In my need
Be false to me, and let thy city bleed?

TIRESIAS.
I will not wound myself nor thee. Why seek
To trap and question me? I will not speak.

OEDIPUS.
Thou devil!

Movement of LEADER to check him.

   Nay; the wrath of any stone
Would rise at him. It lies with thee to have done
And speak. Is there no melting in thine eyes!

TIRESIAS.
Naught lies with me! With thee, with thee there lies,
I warrant, what thou ne'er has seen nor guessed (Murray 19–20).

Yeats:

OEDIPUS. For God's love do not turn away—if you have knowledge. We suppliants implore you on our knees.
TIRESIAS. You are fools—I will bring misfortune neither upon you nor upon myself.
OEDIPUS. What is this? You know all and will say nothing?
You are minded to betray me and Thebes?
TIRESIAS. Why do you ask these things? You will not learn them from me.
OEDIPUS. What! Basest of the base! You would enrage the very stones. Will you never speak out? Cannot anything touch you?
TIRESIAS. The future will come of itself though I keep silent
(Yeats, *Variorum Plays* 817–18).

Yeats's debt to Jebb is evident, as is the simple revision which pruned away Jebb's pseudo-archaisms and wisely rejected Murray's shackling couplets, at odds with the primitive passions of the play. More puzzling, but, as we shall see, consistent, is Yeats's deliberate excision of Tiresias's final hint about incest—'that to which thou thyself art wedded' and 'with thee there lies . . . what thou ne'er hast . . . guessed'—replacing it with an all-purpose gnomic utterance.

Yeats took significant liberties with Sophocles's text, particularly by omitting certain passages. These omissions call into question Yeats's plan to challenge authority by producing a play officially banned as indecent.

Clark and McGuire convincingly argue that Yeats did not abandon his plans for a 1912 *Oedipus* for the reason he gives us: 'the English censorship withdrew its ban, and when the pleasure of mocking it and affirming the freedom of our Irish uncensored stage was taken from me, I lost interest in the play'. It was, rather, the success of Max Reinhardt's spectacular London production of *Oedipus Rex*, in Murray's translation, at Covent Garden in January 1912, with Sir John Martin-Harvey and Lillah McCarthy as Oedipus and Jocasta—'the most imaginative production of a play I have ever seen', Yeats told Lady Gregory just after seeing it. After Reinhardt's success, an Abbey production might well have seemed shabby, and anticlimactic (Clark/McGuire 32–3).

It seems to me equally likely that Yeats, in 1912, was nervous about the Irish reception of the play. The Abbey audience had been outraged when Nora, in Synge's *In the Shadow of the Glen* (1903), left her cross old husband for another man, and outraged again at the theme of parricide in *The Playboy of the Western World* (1907), even at Christy's reference to 'a drift of chosen females, standing in their shifts itself, maybe'. How might a Dublin audience respond to incest?

In 1931, Yeats remembered that he had first been drawn to *Oedipus* during his American lecture tour of 1903–4, when he learned that the University of Notre Dame 'at Illinois' had presented the play:

> The play was forbidden by the English censorship on the ground of its immorality; Oedipus commits incest; but if a Catholic university could perform it in America my own theatre could perform it in Ireland. Ireland had no censorship, and a successful performance might make her proud of her freedom, say even, perhaps, 'I have an old historical religion moulded to the body of man like an old suit of clothes, and am therefore free'
>
> (Clark/McGuire 4–5).

Oedipus offered Yeats a chance to please Irish nationalists by defying England and to silence conservative Catholics, always suspicious of the Abbey, by emphasizing that a Catholic university had sponsored the play.

Yeats, as Frank O'Connor memorably recalled, was 'very devious', and we should always be wary about his own explanations of his motives. 'Four or five years ago', Yeats told listeners to a 1931 broadcast, 'my wife found [the uncompleted 1912 version] and persuaded me to finish it and put it on to the Abbey Stage' (Clark/McGuire 5). Perhaps. But by 1926 there was a new censorship—this time Irish rather than English. In Ireland, Yeats felt an increasing hostility towards literature, art, and any idea not already held by conservative rural Catholics, led, according to Yeats, by 'Ecclesiastics, who shy at the modern world as horses in my youth shied at motor-cars'. In the Senate Yeats had voted against the censorship of films (1923), and was opposed to the planned censorship of publications, which became law in 1929. His speech against the law forbidding divorce deplored efforts to legislate so that 'this country [is] governed by Catholic ideas, and by Catholic ideas alone' (Yeats, *Senate Speeches* 175; 92).

In February 1926, the Abbey audience rioted against Sean O'Casey's *The Plough and the Stars*, on both patriotic and moral grounds: the men of 1916 were not portrayed as conventional heroes, and the prostitute Rosie Redmond in the pub with Citizen Army men and their flag gave great offence. In the same year, Kevin O'Higgins, the Free State Minister for Justice, set up a Committee of Enquiry on Evil Literature. In December 1925, a Dublin Christian Brother had publicly burned an English magazine containing 'The Cherry Tree Carol', claiming that the ancient carol was indecent and anti-Catholic—charges Yeats mocked in 'The Need for Audacity of Thought' (*Dial*, February 1926).

In this climate, it seems likely that Yeats saw a chance to bait the 'unco guid' by presenting a play that would shock them. Yet *Oedipus* was read in Catholic colleges and seminaries, and had been performed at a Catholic university. Its antiquity and classic status would make protest laughable. Nevertheless, Yeats deliberately toned down the play by removing explicit references to incest. Goaded by Oedipus's insults during the escalating quarrel we have already watched commence, Tiresias leaves the stage after revealing what he had earlier promised to conceal:

> He shall be exposed as his own children's father and brother,
> Son and husband at once to the woman who bore him,
> Who took his father's life, his father's wife.
> Ponder these things when you have gone inside,
> And if you find that what I say is wrong,
> Call me unskilful at the prophet's art (*Oedipus Tyrannos*, lines 457–62; trans. Robert Tracy).

In Yeats's version, these remarks should come between lines 356 and 357, but they do not. Yeats gives us the preceding lines describing Oedipus as Laius's murderer, 'a native Theban', rather than 'an alien', and those predicting Oedipus's blindness. But then Yeats elides to lines 460–2: 'so you go in and think on that, and if you find I am in fault say that I have no skill in prophecy'. Despite his alleged eagerness to challenge the English censors, and later the Irish censors, Yeats carefully omitted the lines which make Oedipus's plight explicit—though the Covent Garden audiences had received them calmly enough in Murray's version.

Later on, Yeats is equally prudent. 'How will the Catholics take it?' he wondered, writing to Olivia Shakespear a few hours before the first performance (Clark/McGuire 35). He had anticipated them, by cutting both Oedipus's anxious question, 'Should I not shrink in fear from my mother's bed?' and Jocasta's flippant reply:

> Why should a man, who is subject to chance, be afraid,
> When nobody knows for sure how things will turn out?
> It is best to live life as it comes, in what way you can.
> Do not be afraid of marrying your mother,
> For many a man has dreamed about sex with his mother.
> The man who ignores such things bears life easiest (*Oedipus Tyrannos* 11. 976–83; trans. Robert Tracy).

It is only fair to note that Murray treats these lines very timidly: '. . . fear not thy mother. Prophets deem / A deed wrought that is wrought but in a dream' (Murray 56). Yeats's omissions made the play less of a challenge to conservatives in his audience. Of course, most of his auditors knew the story of Oedipus, and, as the play develops, the incestuous relationship becomes clear. But Yeats avoids stating it explicitly, verbalizing it, as long as he can— perhaps remembering how the *Playboy* audience erupted at the word 'shifts'. To compensate, as the ending of the play draws near, Yeats becomes finally more explicit that his predecessors—indeed, more explicit than Sophocles:

> But, looking for a marriage-bed, he found the bed of his birth,
> Tilled the field his father had tilled, cast seed into the same abounding earth;
> Entered through the door that had sent him wailing forth.
>
> Begetter and begot as one! How could that be hid?
> What darkness cover up that marriage bed?
> (*Variorum Plays* 844).

If Yeats sometimes altered or omitted out of caution, he also subtly realigned the play by making the plague, and its effect on the people of Thebes, less prominent. In Sophocles's text, Oedipus's opening speech and the Priest's speech in reply make it clear that a crowd of suppliants have come to Oedipus's palace. Though Yeats's text implied an accompanying crowd, the audience saw only the Priest, not the distressed citizens of a city in agony. Sophocles's crowd embodied the collective distress that the Priest describes—at length in Jebb's accurate if unspeakable translation:

> For the city, as thou thyself seest, is now too sorely vexed, and can no more lift her head from beneath the angry waves of death; a blight is on her in the fruitful blossoms of the land, in the herds among the pastures, in the barren pangs of women; and withal the flaming god, the malign plague, hath swooped on us, and ravages the town; by whom the house of Cadmus is made waste, but dark Hades rich in groans and tears (Jebb 4).

and tersely in Yeats's version:

> . . . for the city stumbles towards death, hardly able to raise up its head. A blight has fallen upon the fruitful blossoms of the land, a blight upon flock and field and upon the bed of marriage—plague ravages the city
> (*Variorum Plays* 810).

Having seen Reinhardt's *Oedipus*, Yeats may have remembered its spectacular opening effect: after the audience was seated, a huge crowd of panicky suppliants poured down the aisles shrieking and gesticulating, to flow out across a broad open area to the steps of the palace. Just as they were about to engulf the steps, the doors sprang open, and Oedipus stepped out to stop them and command silence with one imperious gesture (*The Times*; Carter 1914, 211; 217–19). This was theatre dominated by effect and movement, not by poetry. Yeats's dialogue between Oedipus and the Priest emphasizes language, even by expanding Jebb's 'hard songstress' to 'that harsh singer, the riddling sphinx'.

A little later, Yeats omitted Sophocles's twenty-line description of the city in plague time from the first choric ode, perhaps because he thought it repeated the Priest's description; instead, Yeats minimized public distress by incorporating only a few details into a choric prayer. He saw in the device of the Chorus a way to make the audience listen to verse without any danger of distracting stage movement. The Greek Chorus seemed to answer beautifully to his notion that actors should be heard but not seen—or at any rate, not draw attention to themselves and away from the play's language. Yeats's Chorus 'must stand stock still' (Yeats 1928, v). In keeping with Yeats's theories of drama, the real action of his *King Oedipus* is verbal; Yeats's language is the real hero.

Yeats used a six-man Chorus, a Leader and five others. Clark and McGuire unfortunately do not print Lennox Robinson's brief specifications for the Chorus, found in the first edition of the play, which explain that 'The Leader's voice should be of a tenor quality, the Second Voice a baritone, the Third Voice a bass, the other voices—there can be as many as the producer likes—should be bass' (Yeats 1928, 55). Though Robinson directed the first performance, Yeats was at his side during most rehearsals, and informally shared direction, as he often did at the Abbey. Any indications of how the play was performed under Yeats's eye are an essential part of the record, though technically not part of Yeats's text. Nor do they print the first edition's music for the Chorus, which does indicate the rhythm to which Yeats wanted the choruses to be chanted, and the disposition of the lines among Yeats's 'liturgical singers'—a term Yeats continually wrestled with in successive versions of his preface. Yeats saw Oedipus as a kind of sacrificial victim. His play was a sacrifice to be performed like a Mass. 'In rehearsal I had but one overwhelming emotion,' he told Olivia Shakespear, 'a sense as of the actual presence in a terrible sacrament of the god' (Clark/McGuire 35).

Here is part of the first chorus (Yeats 1928, 56–7) as spoken by the several voices:

2ND VOICE.

A - pol - lo chase the God of Death that leads no shout-ing men,

Bears no ratt -ling shield and yet con - sumes this form with pain,

Fa -mine takes what the plague spares, and all the crops are

lost; No new life fills the emp -ty place, ghost flits af -ter

ghost to that god-trod-den west-ern shore, as flit be - night-ed birds.

Sor - row speaks to sor - row and finds no com-fort in words.

3RD VOICE.

Hur - ry him from the land of Thebes with a fair wind be - hind,

Out on to that form - less deep, where not a man can find

Hold for an an -chor fluke, for all is world - en - fold - ing sea,

Mas - ter of the thun - der - cloud, set the light - ning free,

And add the thun - der - stone to that and fling them on his head.

For Death is all the fash - ion now, till ev - en Death be dead.

Yeats sometimes evaded Sophocles's text completely, to replace it with a lyric outburst of his own. 'What monstrous thing our fathers saw do the seasons bring? / Or what that no man ever saw, what new monstrous thing?' asks the Chorus Leader, speaking 'Not slow, nervously' in the first chorus (Yeats 1928, 55), after Creon has summarized the oracle's message: Thebes is plague-ridden because it harbours the murderer of King Laius. The lines, preceded by a reference to 'the riddling Sphinx', echo 'The Second Coming' (1920).

Richard Murphy has described Yeats as turning 'the Chorus away from being public commentators on events and mak[ing] them more of the kind of Choir that takes part in a ritual' (Murphy). Perhaps the most faithful staging of Yeats's *Oedipus*—apart from the original Abbey production—was Tyrone Guthrie's, first performed at Stratford, Ontario in 1954, with James Mason as Oedipus. Guthrie aimed 'to present the Tragedy as Ritual . . . the actors commemorate and comment upon the sacrifice of Oedipus—one man whose destruction was expedient that his people may live—in a manner analogous to Christian priests' commemoration and comment upon Christ's sacrifice' (Guthrie). The actors were depersonalized and their movement impeded by masks, platform shoes, and stiff sacerdotal robes. Guthrie, Irish himself, grasped Yeats's purpose. Does Yeats's Chorus as ritual commentator echo that role he assigned to the Irish peasantry in his preface to Lady Gregory's *Gods and Fighting Men* (1904)? When 'an English-speaking aristocracy' replaced the old Gaelic aristocrats in Ireland, 'it felt about it in the popular mind an exacting and ancient tribunal', Yeats tells us, 'and began a play that had for spectators men and women that loved the high wasteful virtues' (Yeats, *Explorations* 27).

When he returned to *Oedipus*, Yeats was still fresh from his great divorce speech of 1925 protesting the imposition of Catholic law on all Irish citizens: 'We against whom you have done this thing are no petty people' (*Senate Speeches* 99). In the new Free State, Irishness was being ever more narrowly defined as Catholic and Gaelic. Yeats and other Protestant writers were seen as non-Irish, and his 1924 Nobel Prize was described in the *Catholic Bulletin* as awarded 'to a member of the English colony in

Ireland' (Brown 1981, 72). Yeats found in Oedipus a protagonist who is at once native and alien to the city he leads: 'He seems . . . an alien; yet he shall be found a native Theban'. Oedipus's power, like Yeats's, is based on his mastery of words: he solved the Sphinx's riddle. Now he is revealed as the polluting presence responsible for the plague. His nationality is ambiguous, as Yeats's was to some of his fellow citizens, as Bloom's was to the Citizen.

Clark and McGuire quote from letters that show Yeats, buoyed by the success of *King Oedipus*, embarking immediately on a version of *Oedipus at Colonus*, to be 'less literal[!] and more idiomatic and modern' (Clark/McGuire 36). In *Oedipus at Colonus*, the Thebans have exiled Oedipus, and so Thebes has plunged into anarchy. His sons fight a fratricidal war over his abandoned power. Belatedly, the Thebans realize they need Oedipus, not to rule them, but as a sanctifying and protective presence. But Oedipus refuses to return. Because Theseus of Athens has given him sanctuary, he bestows the gift of his presence on Athens. At Athenian Colonus he enters the Wood of the Furies, and there the Athenian earth itself opens to accept him: 'some messenger carried him away or the foundations of the earth were riven to receive him, riven not by pain but by love' (*Variorum Plays* 897).

For Yeats, the Oedipus myth may have resonated satisfyingly in an atmosphere where certain Irish nationalists questioned his right to belong to Ireland or to Irish literature. Commenting on the Oedipus plays in 1933, he slyly spoke of 'altering every sentence' in *King Oedipus* 'that might not be intelligible on the Blasket Islands'—sacred ground to zealous nationalists, because the islanders were Catholic and Gaelic-speaking. He went on to stress the affinities between ancient Ireland and ancient Greece, affinities which Roman culture and perhaps the Roman church obscures:

> When I say intelligible on the Blasket Islands I mean that, being an ignorant man, I may not have gone to Greece through a Latin mist. Greek literature, like old Irish literature, was founded upon belief, not like Latin literature upon documents. No man has ever prayed to or dreaded one of Vergil's nymphs, but when Oedipus at Colonus went into the Wood of the Furies he felt the same creeping in his flesh that an Irish countryman feels in certain haunted woods in Galway and in Sligo. At the Abbey Theatre we play both *Oedipus the King* [*sic*] and *Oedipus at Colonus*, and they seem at home there (Yeats, 'Plain Man's Oedipus', *Letters* 527).

Originally published as a review of *W.B. Yeats: The Writing of Sophocles'* King Oedipus, by David R. Clark and James B. McGuire (Philadelphia, 1989). Reprinted with permission from *Eire-Ireland* 28:2 (Summer 1993), pp. 116–28.

9

Merging into Art

The Death of Cuchulain and the Death of Yeats

Pride, like that of the morn,
When the headlong light is loose,
Or that of the fabulous horn,
....
Or that of the hour
When the swan must fix his eye
Upon a fading gleam,
Float out upon a long
Last reach of glittering stream
And there sing his last song.
And I declare my faith:
....
Death and life were not
Till man made up the whole,
....
And further add to that
That, being dead, we rise,
Dream and so create
Translunar Paradise.
                              'The Tower.'

I think that all happiness depends on the energy to assume the mask of some other self; that all joyous or creative life is a re-birth as something not oneself. . .
                              Yeats, 'The Death of Synge', XXV (1928)

. . . even love and death and old age are an imaginative art.
                              Yeats, *Ideas of Good and Evil* (1903)

'When I was young', Yeats tells us,

I had not given a penny for a song
Did not the poet sing it with such airs
That one believed he had a sword upstairs
('All Things can Tempt Me', 1909).

That brief lyric reminds us of two consistent elements in Yeats: his frequently expressed impatience with the poet's limited role as witness and recorder of heroism, and his habit of thinking and imagining in opposites. The two combine in his own moments of political action, and in his restrained eagerness to be himself a man of action, a hero. Sean O'Casey, remembering him, chose the right metaphor: 'among the fighting for higher thought, finer literature, and fairer art', O'Casey writes, 'none bore a tougher shield, a brighter sword, or a loftier crest than W.B. Yeats, the poet . . . Yeats, dreaming his life away, did and did as heartily as any king . . . spent far more of his life in doing things than in dreaming about them' (*Blasts* 183–4).

Yeats's habit of thinking in opposites, and of organizing poems, plays, and the system of *A Vision* in an antithetical way, is a feature of his work from the beginning. We move from the Happy and Sad Shepherds of 1885 through Fergus and the Druid, the Blind Man and the Fool, Cuchulain and Conchubar, King and no King, those who 'burn damp faggots' and those others who 'may consume/The entire combustible world in one small room/ As though dried straw' ('In Memory of Major Robert Gregory'), Michael Robartes as Yeats's alter ego, Hic and Ille, 'That . . . country' of 'sensual music' and Byzantium, Self and Anti-Self or Man and Mask in *A Vision*. Yeats's poetry and his thought are alike sustained on a structure of antitheses.

Yeats accepts the Irish poet's traditional task of celebrating the heroic, and sees that celebration as the creation of heroic images to inspire later potential heroes. '. . .The poets hung/Images of the life that was in Eden/About the child-bed of the world', Seanchan's pupil declares in *The King's Threshold* (1904), 'that it,/Looking upon those images, might bear/ Triumphant children'. He goes on to compare 'The world that lacked' such images to 'a woman/That, looking on the cloven lips of a hare,/ Brings forth a hare-lipped child' (*Variorum Plays* 264–5)—an early hint at that linkage of art and eugenics pervading *On the Boiler* (1939) and 'Under Ben Bulben'. In 'The Municipal Gallery Re-visited' (1937), Yeats hints that art can provide 'approved patterns' of heroism and nobility to contemplate and perhaps emulate. In 'The Statues' (1939), statues planned by Pythagorean numbers bring 'boys and girls pale from the imagined love/Of solitary beds' to press 'at midnight in some public place/Live lips upon a plummet-measured face'. Such 'broad-backed marble statues . . . gave to the sexual instinct of Europe its goal, its fixed type' (*On the Boiler* 37). Art offers heroic or physical ideals, to provoke an eagerness to behave heroically or arouse sexual desire. The artist's task is to preserve or imagine heroism and sensual beauty for later generations to imitate if they dare and can.

But, as the imagined poet with his imagined sword suggests, there is a sense of the road not taken, that life of heroic action which is the antithesis to the poet's life of witnessing, remembering, recording. Yeats regularly speaks of his own preference for action, his eagerness to be the hero. In 'Sailing to Byzantium' the aged man must turn from the active sexual life to seek the contemplative world of art, but his abdication is a wistful one, at least initially, and even in art he seeks a different fiery passion. Yeats's King Goll eagerly remembers his days of power and heroism; poetry has not fully compensated him for that loss. Yeats placed 'Politics' last among his poems, and ends it, '. . . O that I were young again/And held her in my arms'.

At intervals throughout his career, Yeats celebrated the hero Cuchulain, whose prowess on the battlefield is matched with sexual prowess in the *Táin Bó Cúalnge*, though Lady Gregory makes them less prominent in her *Cuchulain of Muirthemne* (1902). Yeats reminds us of Cuchulain's lovers in *The Only Jealousy of Emer* (1919), when Emer, Eithne Inguba, and the Woman of the Sidhe compete for him at his sick bed. Their competition is more striking when we remember that the Woman of the Sidhe is a version of Maud Gonne, Eithne Inguba a version of her daughter Iseult, the two women Yeats proposed to unsuccessfully not long before (Skene 84). *On the Boiler* twice draws our attention to 'Great bladdered Emer' and reminds us that 'Her violent man/Cuchulain' chose her as his wife because 'the strength and volume' of the bladder 'were . . . considered signs of vigour' (*On the Boiler* 24, 31).

Why did Yeats chose Cuchulain as the hero he would celebrate and offer as heroic example? He rejected the better known and more popular Finn Mac Cumhal. There were various reasons for the choice: Finn is a buffoon in later versions of his legend, he had been exploited by earlier poets, he was less aristocratic. But Yeats was particularly attracted by three things. Unlike Finn, Cuchulain was sexually as well as militarily successful. He was, like Achilles, pure hero, apparently indifferent to his own physical survival, eager for the glory that the 'long-remembering harpers' (*Variorum Plays* 453) can confer, a hero looking for a poet (as Yeats was a poet looking for a hero). And Cuchulain as hero had a third important advantage: his remoteness in time, before the Reformation, before the Norman invasion, before the beginnings of Christianity in Ireland. For a Protestant poet who was creating himself as the poet of the Irish nation, a hero without party or sectarian associations was essential. In celebrating Cuchulain, Yeats could develop an Irish hero too early for Irish controversy, and therefore, at least in theory, acceptable to all Ireland, Orange or Green, Protestant or Catholic, Anglo or unhyphenated, an ikon to embody the cultural nationalism he imagined, free of Gaelic or Catholic shibboleths.

Yeats also came to identify with Cuchulain, a kind of projection and a kind of alter ego, as he tells us in 'The Circus Animals' Desertion': 'And when the Fool and Blind Man stole the bread/Cuchulain fought the ungovernable sea;/Heart mysteries there'. Yeats placed 'The Circus Animals' Desertion' between 'Man and the Echo' and 'Politics' as the last three poems in *Last Poems and Two Plays* (Dublin: Cuala Press, 1939). 'The Man and the Echo' suggests that Yeats's poems have instigated action: 'Did that play of mine send out/Certain men the English shot?' 'The Circus Animals' Desertion' identifies Cuchulain as a projection of Yeats's own 'Heart mysteries'. 'Politics' records a momentary sexual impulse.

Poetry, then, celebrates heroism in bed or on the battlefield, reveals 'Heart mysteries', and can provoke further heroism in potentially unending reiteration. The poet, if only at second hand, is a man of action. But Yeats seeks a heroic metamorphosis that is more direct and more satisfying. In 'Sailing to Byzantium' he imagined a posthumous and eternal existence for himself, re-embodied as a golden bird, an imperishable artifact that would never wear out or break down, but would be 'set upon a golden bough to sing/To lords and ladies of Byzantium/Of what is past, or passing, or to come'—to record the past, comment on the present, and warn about the future. The conventional metaphor of poet as singing bird becomes a metaphor for the poet's permanent survival in his poems, after his mortal life has ended.

But this is still a spectator's and commentator's role, perpetuated in the artifice of bird and poems. It does not take into account Yeats's belief in a series of reincarnations, which he expresses in *A Vision*. Nor does it offer that escape or merging into one's anti-self that the man of each phase yearns for in *A Vision*. In his very last poems, facing death with the self-possession of his centenarian in 'In Tara's Halls' (1939), Yeats moves toward a more daring way of perpetuating and re-inventing himself, by becoming hero instead of poet, becoming Cuchulain, his own anti-self.

'Haunted by certain moments' of 'tragic ecstasy' from his own plays or those of his friends which he had 'seen . . . greatly played', he opined that 'These things will, it may be, haunt me on my deathbed' (*On the Boiler* 14). 'I know for certain that my time will not be long', he wrote to Lady Elizabeth Pelham on 4 January 1939, less than a month before his death:

> I have put away everything that can be put away that I may speak what I have to speak and I find 'expression' is a part of 'study'. In two or three weeks . . . I will begin to write my most fundamental thoughts and the arrangement of thought which I am convinced will complete my studies. I am happy, and I think full of an energy, of an energy I had despaired of. It seems to me that I have found what I wanted. When I try to put all into a phrase I say, 'Man can embody truth but he cannot know it'. I must embody it in the completion of my life (*Letters* 922).

He must re-embody himself so as to experience tragic ecstasy rather than describe it. Paradoxically, this re-embodiment or re-incarnation can be achieved only through poetry.

Yeats planned the order of the poems and plays in the 1939 Cuala *Last Poems and Two Plays* during the last week of his life. The last poem he actually wrote is 'The Black Tower', dated 21 January 1939. Two days before he died, he made corrections in 'Under Ben Bulben' and in the recently completed *The Death of Cuchulain*. 'The Black Tower', then, is Yeats's last poem, and *The Death of Cuchulain* his last play, though he did not place them to emphasize their lastness in *Last Poems and Two Plays*. 'The Black Tower' is the third item in the table of contents, after 'Under Ben Bulben' and 'Three Songs to the one Burden'; it is followed by 'Cuchulain Comforted', dated 13 January. There are nineteen poems, followed by two plays, *The Death of Cuchulain* and *Purgatory*. The order of the poems is drastically altered in the 1940 Macmillan *Last Poems and Plays*, and the order of the two plays is reversed.

I call attention to the placement of the two plays because Yeats's effort to 'embody truth . . . in the completion of my life' cannot be understood unless we recognize that the poems and the plays are integrally related. Yeats regularly included plays in his collections of poems, always because they are related thematically to the accompanying poems. *The Countess Cathleen* appears in *Poems* (1895), *On Baile's Strand* in *In the Seven Woods* (1903), three plays—*The Shadowy Waters, On Baile's Strand, The King's Threshold*—in *Poems 1899–1905* (1906), *The Hour-Glass* in *Responsibilities* (1914), *The King of the Great Clock Tower* and *A Full Moon in March* in the collections (both 1935) which they name. By publishing poems and plays together, Yeats urges us to consider them together, as mutually complementary. He stresses this by subtitling *In the Seven Woods* 'Being Poems Chiefly of the Irish Heroic Age', and, in a note, connecting poems and play alike with the Seven Woods of Coole: 'I made some of these poems walking about among the Seven Woods . . . and I thought out there a good part of the play which follows. The first shape of it came to me in a dream, but it changed much in the making, foreshadowing, it may be, a change that may bring a less dream-burdened will into my verses'. The *Green Helmet* volume (1910) is subtitled 'and other poems'. In *The King of the Great Clock Tower*, the poem 'God guard me from those thoughts men think', later retitled 'A Prayer for Old Age', is part of the preface to the play. The commentary to the play includes another poem, 'He had famished in a wilderness'. Both are thematically related to the play. 'A Prayer for Old Age' is particularly important, not only for *The King of the Great Clock Tower* but for that whole theme of passionate old age and wild old wickedness Yeats dwells on at the end:

God guard me from those thoughts men think
In the mind alone;
He that sings a lasting song
Thinks in a marrow-bone;

From all that makes a wise old man
That can be praised of all . . .

Asked for a message to India in 1937, Yeats answered, 'Let 100,000 men of one side meet the other. That is my message to India, insistence on the antimony'. Then he unsheathed Sato's sword and shouted, 'Conflict, more conflict' (Hone 463).

Passion, then, is an antidote to old age. Poetry is a way of evading death. How are they to be combined? They are combined in Yeats's final theme, which lets him perform a kind of substitution trick by disappearing into his own work, specifically into Cuchulain, the mask or alter ego he has so carefully constructed for himself with words. There is a hint of this at least as early as *The Only Jealousy of Emer*, where a changeling, a man of words, usurps the body of the dying Cuchulain, and where Cuchulain himself almost disappears into the supernatural world of 'the Country under Wave' (*Variorum Plays* 549) with the Woman of the Sidhe.

Let us return for a moment to Yeats's last two completed poems, 'Cuchulain Comforted' and 'The Black Tower', and to his last two plays, *Purgatory* and *The Death of Cuchulain*. As we have seen, Yeats did not plan to print them in the order of their composition, but placed 'The Black Tower' before 'Cuchulain Comforted' and *The Death of Cuchulain* before *Purgatory*—though that may not represent his final intentions about the order of the two plays. All were to appear in a volume which he himself may have named *Last Poems* (Sultan 20; but see Finneran, *Editing Yeats's Poems*, 66–7). As his letter to Lady Elizabeth Pelham shows, he knew he was writing his final culminating work.

In Yeats's case, the title *Last Poems and Two Plays* is thematically accurate. Under the guise of stating biographical and bibliographical fact, it signals the end of making poems, a shift from art to heroic action. In reading the title we should emphasize the second word. But the title is also a misnomer because it implies finality. Yeats devised these poems, written as he lay dying, to be, if only metaphorically, a way of prolonging life. They allowed the poet to contrive his own posthumous survival in art, becoming one with his poems and plays, and changing places with his created anti-self, Cuchulain. Auden is wrong about many things in his 'In Memory of W.B. Yeats', but instinctively right when he says, 'The death of the poet was kept from his poems'. Yeats's last poems and plays are, again metaphorically, a device to evade death and control the reincarnation in which he professed to believe.

How did Yeats go about this complex and ambitious project? We can compare him, I think, to the ancient Egyptians who planned for and designed their own posthumous survival through works of art—tomb paintings, ship models, statues of servants, the great epic poem of posthumous survival. *The Book of the Dead*, of which each dead Egyptian becomes the hero. These texts, statues, paintings promised survival through art, life prolonged by objects created by an artist's imagination. For the ancient Egyptians, this survival was a holding operation. At some remote period, after successfully encountering various posthumous trials and ordeals, the soul would apparently merge into the godhead, as, in the eschatology of *A Vision*, the soul will at last escape the round of reincarnation at the dark of the moon. Perhaps for Yeats too, the survival in art he projected was not to be eternal. Even art, he reminds us in 'Lapis Lazuli', does not survive forever, though it does offer an escape from the merely transient. But in 'A Dialogue of Self and Soul', written in the spring of 1928, he had rejected the Soul's suggestion that he seek

> . . . ancestral night that can,
> If but imagination scorn the earth
> And intellect its wandering
> To this and that and t'other thing,
> Deliver from the crime of death and birth.

Self remains enamoured of Sato's sword and the embroidery which wraps it, 'things that are/Emblematical of love and war', sex and heroic death, and claims '*as by a soldier's right*/A charter to commit the crime' of reincarnation 'once more' (italics mine; Sultan 25–6). Self is not ready for the ultimate release from the round of reincarnation, is determined to be re-embodied. *Last Poems and Two Plays* declare and portray that process of re-embodiment.

There are analogies between 'The Black Tower' and *Purgatory*: an 'old black tower' and a ruined house; the 'oath-bound men' of the tower's garrison and the son of that house's return to carry out his self-imposed sacred duty, the release of his mother's soul; 'old bones' that 'shake . . . upon the mountain' and the sexually active ghosts. 'I have embodied my thoughts about this life and the next in my play', Yeats told the Abbey audience after the first performance of *Purgatory* (10 August 1938); that single sentence constituted his entire speech, and his last words from the Abbey stage (Holloway 12). A letter to Dorothy Wellesley a few days later (15 August) gives a slightly different version: 'I have put nothing into the play because it seemed picturesque; I have put there my own conviction about this world and the next' (*Letters* 913).

Along with *Purgatory*, the Abbey also performed *On Baile's Strand* on that occasion, perhaps bringing Cuchulain back into Yeats's mind—where he was never absent for long. 'A fine performance', he told Dorothy Wellesley. '"Cuchulain" seemed to me a heroic figure because he was creative joy separated from fear'. In the same letter he followed this immediately with a first version of the lines which were to end 'Under Ben Bulben' and become his epitaph:

> Draw rein; draw breath.
> Cast a cold eye
> On life, on death.
> Horseman pass by (*Letters* 913).

There is thus a connection between *Purgatory*, Cuchulain, and Yeats's epitaph, and so with that whole theme of survival in language which pervades *Last Poems and Two Plays*.

Yeat's draft table of contents for *Last Poems and Two Plays* ends with *Purgatory*. Mrs Yeats seems to have yielded too readily to Thomas Mark, the Macmillan editor, when she agreed to a different order of poems and plays for the Macmillan *Last Poems and Plays* (1940), notably by moving 'Under Ben Bulben' from the beginning to the end of the collection: 'Certainly put "Under Ben Bulben" at the end . . . Its present position was WBY's, but I t[h]ink now it should undoubtedly be at the end as you suggest'. Here she is clearly accepting an editor's suggestion, a little hesitantly: 'I think'. She is much more decisive in a letter about the two plays, written to Harold Macmillan on the same day (14 June 1939): '"Purgatory" should precede "The Death of Cuchulain" *of course*' (Finneran 1983, 65; italics mine).

Purgatory has made many of Yeats's admirers uncomfortable because it seems to advocate a doctrine of racial purity which is sinister in itself, and particularly so when we remember what was already going on in contemporary Germany, and what was soon to occur in German-occupied Europe. Yeats included the play in *On the Boiler* because it has 'something to do with my main theme' (*On the Boiler* 7), an attack on democracy and the moral and physical degeneration of Europe, the first to be fought by recognizing the leadership of the aristocracy, the second by a programme of eugenics. The arguments echo some of Yeats's claims about the Anglo-Irish gentry and their aptitude for leadership, and they also reflect an Anglo-Irish obsession: fear of miscegenation, of intermarriage with the Irish, and the consequent degeneracy of blood, loss of racial identity, and loss of power and prestige. But *Purgatory* also recognizes the other aspect of that obsession, the Anglo-Irish fascination with that forbidden miscegenation. The daughter of the Big House has eagerly given herself to a drunken groom; their son, for all his pride of race and his sense of shame, has taken 'a tinker's daughter in a ditch' (*Variorum Plays* 1044). Yeats recognizes the earthy attractions of raw sexuality, wantonness, and squalor as early as *Where There Is Nothing* (1902), where Paul Ruttledge leaves his

Big House to join the tinkers. Yeats returns to it in *A Full Moon in March* (1935), when the Queen seeks the 'desecration and the lover's night' (*Variorum Plays* 989) that only the Swineherd can provide.

Purgatory echoes some of Yeats's claims about the special cultural and political skills he saw in Coole Park and the Anglo-Irish Big House generally. It may also hint at his scorn for the democracy of the Free State and its apparent disdain for art and culture, a scorn expressed in more eugenic terms in 'Under Ben Bulben':

> Scorn the sort now growing up
> All out of shape from toe to top,
> Their unremembering hearts and heads
> Base-born products of base beds.

But, while these themes and issues are undoubtedly present in *Purgatory*, the play develops in an unexpected direction, to endorse implicitly the very acts it explicitly scorns. The Old Man rails against the mésalliance which has engendered him. He even tries, with words, to prevent retroactively his own conception. But, ghosts or hallucination, the wanton couple do not hear him. The Old Man imagines their eager desire. Though he kills his son to put an end to that sensual re-enactment, he fails to do so. The Boy is dead, right enough. The miscegenation of lady and groom will have no further 'consequence' in 'pollution' passed on to a third generation. But as the play ends, the lovers are apparently about to copulate again. The fallen lady has not been released from her repeated re-enactments of that eager moment. The Old Man has already wondered how a moment of satisfied sexual desire can be a punishment:

> But there's a problem: she must live
> Through everything in exact detail,
> Driven to it by remorse, and yet
> Can she renew the sexual act
> And find no pleasure in it, and if not,
> If pleasure and remorse must both be there,
> Which is the greater?
>   (*Variorum Plays* 1046)

In *The Words Upon the Window-Pane* (1934), Yeats offers his own unorthodox notions of Purgatory: 'Sometimes a spirit re-lives not the pain of death but some passionate or tragic moment of life . . . If I were a Catholic I would say that such spirits were in Purgatory' (*Variorum Plays* 944).

Though they are socially, and probably religiously and racially, mismatched, the couple's sexual intensity transcends death. They indefinitely repeat their moment of satisfied desire. The Old Man is only a man of words, a talker, a poet. He can watch, describe, imagine, speculate, but he cannot disturb their ecstasy nor can he share it.

For lady, and perhaps groom, their purgatorial punishment seems to be a repeated sexual fulfillment, like that described in *The King of the Great Clock Tower* (1934), when the First Attendant praises the 'heroic wantonness' of the passionate dead:

> All those living wretches crave
> Prerogatives of the dead that have
> Sprung heroic from the grave.
> *A moment more and it tolls midnight.*
>
> Crossed fingers there in pleasure can
> Exceed the nuptial bed of man;
> *What of the hands on the Great Clock face?*
> A nuptial bed exceed all that
> Boys at puberty have thought,
> Or sibyls in a frenzy sought.
>   (*Variorum Plays* 1002–3)

The song has already evoked 'the fierce horsemen' who 'ride . . . from mountain to mountain' in 'Three Songs to the One Burden' (I) and 'Under Ben Bulben' (I) as they had long ago ridden in 'The Hosting of the Sidhe' (1893), and even earlier in a vision of Mary Battelle (Mary Battle), George Pollexfen's housekeeper: 'There is no such race living now, none so finely proportioned . . . I see none as they be' (*Mythologies* 58; *Autobiography* 178). Crazy Jane sees them again ('Crazy Jane on the Mountain') in *On the Boiler* (31), thus implicitly connecting them with *Purgatory* and its themes. In all these cases, the visionary horsemen and women suggest an insatiable and ecstatic sensuality and violence which is heroic. To see it, even in vision, leaves the beholder discontented with all ordinary men and women, tantalized with a glimpse of unattainable potency.

In *Purgatory*, the couple's sexual ecstasy is made permanent by the play's text, recurrent whenever the play is performed. Within the play, their ecstasy may go on nightly, or even permanently, whether or not the Old Man is there. It will certainly repeat itself each time there is an audience to hear him describe them, as the spotlight evokes recurrent performance in Beckett's *Play*. And if the Old Man is a kind of medium, making it possible for them to manifest themselves, as the Medium in *The Words Upon the Window-Pane* enables Swift's ghost to become manifest, he may in fact be a kind of poet, creating the verse play we see. 'Mediumship is dramatisation' (*Variorum Plays* 968), Yeats tells us in his notes to *The Words Upon the Window-Pane*. Describing his evocations of vision as they affected George Pollexfen and Mary Battelle, he stresses their dramatic nature: 'At times coherent stories were built up, as if a company of actors were to improvise, and play . . . Who made the story? Was it the mind of one of the visionaries?' (*Autobiography* 174). 'Whatever flames upon the night/Man's own resinous heart has fed' ('Two Songs from a Play').

Does the play's violence arise out of the contemplation or the experience of violence? The Boy's murder, as the Old Man makes clear, is a direct consequence of the Old Man's own violent begetting: 'This night she is no better than her man/And does not mind that he is half drunk,/She is mad about him' (*Variorum Plays* 1046). Does the thought of his parents' sexual ecstasy provoke the Old Man to stab his son, or does his murderous intention to kill evoke the vision of sexual frenzy, blood lust answering sexual lust and/or vice versa, in a dramatic metaphorical demonstration of the Elizabethan ambiguity of the verb *to die*? The play is about the union of social opposites ('This night she is no better than her man'), and the opening line reminds us of this by uniting 'Half-door, hall door', peasant cabin and Big House. Does the play end with each action evoking and even becoming its opposite, until 'opposites die each other's life, live each other's death' (*On the Boiler* 15)?

For Yeats, sexual ecstasy and the heroic ecstasy of battle were alike: the Irish Airman is driven by 'A lonely impulse of delight'. Artist and poet alike provide heroic images to help 'fill the cradles right' ('Under Ben Bulben'). For Cuchulain, heroic sex and heroic swordplay were parallel modes of delight. The eager embrace of the lady and groom in *Purgatory* matches 'doom eager' Cuchulain's readiness to embrace death in *The Death of Cuchulain*. His death is preceded by a parade of the women he has courted, among them the Morrigu, the crow-headed goddess who represents death in battle. *The Death of Cuchulain* seems to me the work that should end Yeats's last collection, but, because they are so closely related, either *Purgatory* or *The Death of Cuchulain* can adequately conclude his work. Both plays contain Yeats's final '"thoughts about this life and the next"' (Holloway 12). Together they constitute a diptych about the intensity of the heroic act, sexual or marital, its persistence, and its perpetuation in art.

The play-within-a-play arrangement of *Purgatory* is repeated in *The Death of Cuchulain*. An angry Old Man 'looking like something out of mythology' (*Variorum Plays* 1051) introduces the play by railing against modern social and artistic degeneracy as vociferously as his fellow declaimer in *Purgatory* and Yeats in *On the Boiler* rail against degenerate blood. At the end, Cuchulain and the other mythic figures are replaced by ragged street musicians. They close the play with a song that connects the 'thought' of Cuchulain as imagined in art with the heroes of 1916: the Cuchulain of Yeats's plays, of the painting at Pearse's school, and, by 1938, of Oliver Sheppard's statue, placed in the General Post Office to commemorate the Rising. An imagined Cuchulain evoked the 1916 leaders' reckless bravery and willingness to die. But the song also recalls the erotic powers of Cuchulain and others from the age of heroic legend. The eager but frustrated harlot of the song adores and loathes the living men her 'flesh has gripped', but 'can get/No grip' on the fleshless shades of Cuchulain and his peers, much as she desires them:

> The harlot sang to the beggar-man.
> I meet them face to face,
> Conall, Cuchulain, Usna's boys,
> All that most ancient race;
> Maeve had three in an hour, they say.
> I adore those clever eyes,
> Those muscular bodies, but can get
> No grip upon their thighs.
>
> (*Variorum Plays* 1062)

The harlot has shared Mary Battelle's vision of the aerial riders and knows them for the long dead; to see them is at once to 'adore and loathe' the less vigorous modern men she has known: to adore because they too have given sexual satisfaction, to loathe because they fall short of the heroic ideal.

In its two final stanzas, introduced by another burst of music, the song combines that vision of sexual and martial heroism with its own modes of alternate reality, either seen by the visionary or formed by the artist. The mythological heroes, the riders above Knocknarea, still exist, are still present, though they are not there in the ordinary material sense. They also exist in the play, poem, or statue which re-creates them, as the vision does, in a different mode of reality. And they continue to evoke heroism as well as sexual desire, in ways that echo 'The Statues':

> Are those things that men adore and loathe
> Their sole reality?
> What stood in the Post Office
> With Pearse and Connolly?
> What comes out of the mountain
> Where men first shed their blood?
> Who thought Cuchulain till it seemed
> He stood where they had stood?
>
> No body like his body
> Has modern woman borne,
> But an old man looking on life
> Imagines it in scorn.
> A statue's there to mark the place,
> By Oliver Sheppard done.
> So ends the tale that the harlot
> Sang to the beggar-man.
>
> (*Variorum Plays* 1063)

The 'old man looking on life' of the final stanza is at once Yeats himself and his projections, the Old Man of *Purgatory* and the Old Man of *The Death of Cuchulain* prologue.

In *The Death of Cuchulain*, Cuchulain hastens to meet his death, as the lovers hasten to one another in *Purgatory*. Their embrace continues after death, and is also perpetuated in verse. *The Death of Cuchulain* does not end with Cuchulain's death, and he too continues, as vision and as art. As the Blind Man of *On Baile's Strand* prepares to cut off his head, Cuchulain has a vision:

> There floats out there
> The shape that I shall take when I am dead,
> My soul's first shape, a soft feathery shape,
> And is not that a strange shape for the soul
> Of a great fighting-man?
> (*Variorum Plays* 1060–1)

A moment later, as the Blind Man feels to strike, Cuchulain adds, 'I say it is about to sing' and 'the stage darkens'. The curtain falls, then rises to show the Morrigu among six parallelograms, the heads of Cuchulain's killers. She holds a seventh parallelogram that represents Cuchulain's head. Emer 'runs in and begins to dance' among the heads, miming rage against Cuchulain's killers and 'adoration or triumph' before Cuchulain's head. Her actions recall the Queen's dance before the Stroller's severed head in *The King of the Great Clock Tower*. But this head does not sing of Cuchulain and the riders from Knocknarea, as the Stroller's head had done in the 1934 version of *The King of the Great Clock Tower* and in the alternative song Yeats later provided (*Variorum Plays* 1002, 1005), nor does it offer sexual satisfaction and insemination, as the Stroller's head seemed to do, and as the Swineherd's severed head does in *A Full Moon in March*.

Instead, Emer pauses in her dance to listen: 'she seems to hesitate between the head and what she hears. Then she stands motionless. There is silence, and in the silence a few faint bird notes. The stage darkens slowly' (*Variorum Plays* 1062). Then the 'stage brightens' to show the street musicians whose song ends the play.

Yeats called 'Cuchulain Comforted' a 'lyric that has risen out of' *The Death of Cuchulain*, and 'a kind of sequel' to the play, "strange too, something new" (*Letters* 921, 922). The poem is in fact the play's alternate unseen ending, an ending which is at the same time a beginning. We follow Cuchulain into the world of the dead, shrouded 'bird-like things' who are intimidated by his rattling arms and warlike appearance. A Shroud urges him to surrender his heroism and individuality: 'all we do / All must together do'. He should make and wear a shroud, like all the rest. Cuchulain threads his needle.

When he begins to sew, the Shroud offers further instruction:

'Now we shall sing and sing the best we can
But first you must be told our character:
Convicted cowards all by kindred slain

'Or driven from home and left to die in fear.'
They sang, but had nor human notes nor words,
Though all was done in common as before,

They had changed their throats and had the throats of birds.

Cuchulain the hero has become a coward, and at the same time a singer, a poet. He has changed from man of action to man of words, 'to be but artist', one of those 'who express something which has no direct relation to action'. As coward he shares that timidity which Yeats at once deplores in himself and justifies as necessary for his art (*Memoirs* 251, 252–5, 256–8), that uneasiness and wistful envy when confronted by men-at-arms he describes in 'Meditations in Time of Civil War'. Hero has changed places with poet. The bird notes Emer hears occur, as it were, off stage in 'Cuchulain Comforted', synchronized with the end of her dance in *The Death of Cuchulain*. Cuchulain has changed to that bird shape he foresaw as his future shape, an analog to the golden bird/poet of 'Sailing to Byzantium'. Cuchulain has become his anti-self. He has become Yeats.

Yeats perhaps hints at this identity in his prose version of 'Cuchulain Comforted', preserved by Dorothy Wellesley. The prose accurately foreshadows the not-yet-written poem, until its last three sentences: '"We are the people who run away from the battles. Some of us have been put to death as cowards, but others have hidden, and some even died without people knowing they were cowards." Then they began to sing, and they did not sing like men and women, but like linnets that had been stood on a perch and taught by a good singing master' (*Letters . . . to Dorothy Wellesley* 193).

Yeats provides a kind of oblique commentary on *The Death of Cuchulain* and, by implication, 'Cuchulain Comforted', in two letters to Ethel Mannin, written in October 1938 as he worked on the play. He had just read her novel, *Darkness My Bride*, and then 're-read an essay on "the idea of death" in the poetry of Rilke', finding in both texts parallels with 'what I call my "private philosophy" (The *Vision* is my "public philosophy"). My "private philosophy" is the material dealing with individual mind which came to me with that on which the mainly historical *Vision* is based. I have not published it because I only half understand it . . . According to Rilke,' Yeats goes on, a man's death is born with him and if his life is successful and he escapes mere 'mass death' his nature is completed by his final union with it . . . In my own philosophy the sensuous image is changed from time to time at predestined moments called *Initiationary Moments* . . . One sensuous image leads to another because they are never analysed. At *The Critical Moment* they are dissolved by analysis and we enter by free will pure unified experience. When all the sensuous images are dissolved we meet true death . . . This idea of death suggests Blake's design (among those he did for Blair's *Grave* I think) of the soul and body embracing. All men with subjective natures move towards a possible ecstasy, all with objective natures toward a possible wisdom (*Letters* 916–17).

Yeats, subjective, moves toward the possible ecstasy of sex and violence, both presented in *Purgatory* and *The Death of Cuchulain*. Both ecstasies had earlier been imagined when Yeats described the islands Oisin visits in 'The Wanderings of Oisin' (1889). A few days later (20 October 1938), writing again to Ethel Mannin, Yeats tells her that 'My "private philosophy"' is in *The Death of Cuchulain,*

but there must be no sign of it; all must be like an old faery tale. It guides me to certain conclusions and gives me precision but I do not write it. To me all things are made of the conflicts of two states of consciousness, beings or persons which die each other's life, live each other's death. That is true of life and death themselves. Two cones (or whirls), the apex of each in the other's base (*Letters* 917–18).

'God and man die each other's life, live each other's death' (*Variorum Plays* 931) in *The Resurrection* (1931), another play about simultaneously accepting and transcending death, to survive both dead and alive. 'The Heart of a Phantom is beating!' exclaims the Syrian, and that beating abolishes all previous philosophies and logics. Three times in *On the Boiler* Yeats declares that opposites 'die each other's life, live each other's death' (*On the Boiler* 15, 22, 25), and adds that 'death is but a passing from one room into another' (32). So close to Yeats's own expected death, these phrases have a particular resonance and a particular significance. They summarize that 'private philosophy' we are to look for in *The Death of Cuchulain* and the poem which is its sequel, and hint at Yeats's own determination to survive by becoming the Cuchulain he had created out of words, metaphorically changing places with that verbal image. 'Under the frenzy of the fourteenth moon'—that is, exactly halfway through the twenty-eight phase cycle—'The soul', Michael Robartes announces, 'begins . . . To die into the labyrinth of itself!' ('The Phases of the Moon', 1919). 'Nineteen Hundred and Nineteen' (1921) explains that art offers, indeed imposes that reincarnation which Yeats's Self decided to 'claim as by a soldier's right' ('A Dialogue of Self and Soul', 1929):

> A man in his own secret meditation
> Is lost amid the labyrinth that he has made
> In art or politics;
> Some Platonist affirms that in the station
> Where we should cast off body and trade
> The ancient habit sticks,
> And that if our works could
> But vanish with our breath
> That were a lucky death,
> For triumph can but mar our solitude.
>   ('Nineteen Hundred and Nineteen')

In the next stanza he imagines 'a rage/to end all things, to end/What my laborious life *imagined*, even/*The half-imagined, the half-written page*' (italics mine). The imagined poem, preserved on the written page, is a way of evading extinction. In 'Nineteen Hundred and Nineteen' Yeats dreams of rejecting that evasion, but in his last poems and plays he seeks it. The art he has created will keep him alive in a different mode of being.

Knowing that death was near at hand, Yeats deliberately made his own physical deterioration and imminent end a theme. In doing so he created an alternate ending for himself, just as 'Cuchulain Comforted' offers an alternative ending to *The Death of Cuchulain*. In both cases, artist evades extinction by creating a way of continuing in a different mode of being. Cuchulain becomes poet. Yeats becomes Cuchulain, contriving for himself a more heroic posthumous mode of survival than the golden bird of 'Sailing to Byzantium'.

Moving through physical death to the next stage of his existence, Cuchulain changes from hero to coward, from fighter to singer, from subject of poetry to maker of poetry. The change is almost instantaneous. Cuchulain has become a poet. He has become the dying Yeats. He has undergone a metamorphosis, to become a changeling like those in some of the Irish folk tales Yeats collected, or like his own dying false self in *The Only Jealousy of Emer*. Cuchulain begins to die Yeats's life, to live Yeats's death. He joins the cowards and begins to sing.

At the same moment, Yeats dies as poet to reincarnate as hero, to become the heroic figure he had created and towards which he had aspired, to live within the labyrinth of his own art when his poems and plays are read and performed. As Cuchulain dies Yeats's life, Yeats lives Cuchulain's death. In 'The Black Tower' the speaker is not a poet but a man-at-arms, a man of action, a soldier, who refuses to listen to 'The tower's old cook' whom Richard Ellmann considers 'the poetic imagination' (Ellmann 1954, 209), when the cook claims to have heard 'the great king's horn' which will signal the king's return and the garrison's relief. Can we perhaps even discern a circular or cyclic structure to the Cuala

Last Poems and Two Plays, so that Cuchulain as poet sings the collection's first poem, 'Under Ben Bulben', a poem which refers to Yeats in the third person and dissolves the distinctions between life and death? We can imagine, for Cuchulain-poet and Yeats-hero, a further series of reincarnations in which Cuchulain aspires to heroic action and Yeats to poetry, as again and again poet and hero live each other's death, die each other's life, until both finally achieve non-being at the dark of the moon.

Delivered as a lecture in the Yeats Summer School Sligo, August 1988.

10

Living in the Margin

Synge in Aran

He belonged to a very old Irish family and, though a simple courteous man,
remembered it and was haughty and lonely.

W.B. Yeats, *The Irish Dramatic Movement*

To John Synge's conservative relatives his combined interests in literature
and the Irish were a regrettable aberration. Although legend traced
the family name and fortunes to a talented ancestor whose singing was
supposed to have impressed Henry VIII, later Synges had little to do with
any of the arts. They had come from England to Ireland early in the seventeenth century and thereafter ran mostly to clergymen, who found in the
Established Church a profitable and agreeable way of life. Five Synges
became bishops of Irish dioceses (Swift recommended one of them for the
bishopric of Ferns when asked by the Lord Lieutenant for 'a person to
make a Bishop whom I knew was not an honest man').

The family prospered amid the cheerful corruption of eighteenth-century
Ireland, acquiring extensive estates in County Wicklow and elsewhere.
They were thus typical of the 'Ascendancy', the powerful English
Protestant minority in Ireland which called itself Anglo-Irish (Brendan
Behan defines an Anglo-Irishman as 'a Protestant with a horse') and
governed the Catholic Irish majority until early in the nineteenth century.
This class based its power on safe men who could be counted upon to
uphold British over Irish interests and to maintain the Protestant Church
of Ireland. Catholic Irishmen could not hold military rank or public office.
The Ascendancy attitude toward Ireland and the Irish was that of an army
of occupation until well into the twentieth century. Like the colonial
administrators portrayed by E.M. Forster in *A Passage to India*, they
considered their mission to be one of keeping their excitable subjects out of
trouble, and fraternizing with them only on official occasions. But by the
end of Victoria's reign this attitude was no longer very tenable, and the
Ascendancy was in decline. Its monopoly of political power had vanished

with Catholic Emancipation (1829), and most of its economic power disappeared after the Great Famine of 1846–48, which destroyed the basis of landlordism. Only the petrified attitudes of a ruling class remained.

Although most of their money and estates had vanished by the 1870s, when J.M. Synge was born, the Synges still remained staunch supporters of the Anglo-Irish supremacy. One of Synge's brothers took up the traditional family profession of clergyman. Another became a landlord's agent (Greene 7), whose duties included superintending those wholesale evictions of the peasantry that were a conspicuous feature of the nineteenth-century Irish scene, a fact that John Synge's nationalist enemies later recalled with venomous delight. Such an eviction is described—bitterly—in *The Aran Islands*, Synge's mother, herself the daughter of a clergyman, was a woman of formidably evangelical and Unionist views—Low Church Protestantism and the unhindered rule of Ireland by England made up her simple creed. Of his father we know little. A barrister, he died in 1872 when Synge was less than a year old.

In the Ireland of 1900 it was unusual for a young man with such a background to turn away from his inherited English and Anglo-Irish culture, the culture that had produced Berkeley, Goldsmith, Sheridan, Swift, and Burke, and interest himself instead in the despised Celt. Although Matthew Arnold had proclaimed the importance of Old Irish literature in 1867 (and thus unwittingly helped to start the Irish Literary Movement) the Anglo-Irish were not convinced. To them the Irish were a quarrelsome and degenerate race, revolutionary in politics, reactionary in religion, lacking the saving virtues of industry, thrift, and steadiness. It was impossible that such a people should seriously interest a member of the ruling classes, inconceivable that they should produce a literature. Indeed, soon after the turn of the century the Provost of Trinity College, Dublin, the stronghold of the Ascendancy, declared that Old Irish literature was degenerate and 'filthy' and Irish folklore 'at bottom abominable' (Gregory 1913, 56). In Synge's day as a Trinity undergraduate the Irish language was taught by an elderly clergyman, not for literary or even archeological purposes but as a skill which Protestant missionaries would need if they were to wean the Irish speakers of the West from the errors of Rome.

The Anglo-Irish had always produced occasional dissidents who became 'more Irish than the Irish', rebelling against their own class to throw in their lot with the natives. In the sixteenth century 'Silken Thomas' Fitzgerald led the Irish against the English; in the eighteenth century Swift's pen and Grattan's speeches defended Irish rights and Wolfe Tone and Lord Edward Fitzgerald led armed rebellions. Parnell attempted to gain Irish Home Rule through parliamentary action in the nineteenth century, and a few years later Maud Gonne dreamed of being Ireland's Joan of Arc. These leaders were all of Anglo-Irish rather than of unhyphenated Irish blood. They sided against their own class, hoping to free Ireland from restrictive British rule. But after Parnell fell in 1890, neither political nor military methods seemed likely to achieve this freedom. (When it did finally come, in 1922, it came partly because England had been weakened in World War I.) The Anglo-Irish found themselves isolated, their efforts to gain self-government for Ireland within the Empire defeated by the British Parliament and increasingly rejected by the Irish themselves, whose growing sense of nationalism began to lead to dreams of total independence from England.

To some critics and historians the fall of Parnell marks the beginning of the Irish Literary Movement, and to Yeats, especially, the two events are related as cause and effect (Yeats, *Autobiography* 133; Jeffares 1949, 82; Ellmann 1948, 104). Chronologically they are related—the sudden disappearance of Ireland's hope of freedom seems to have coincided with the release of a great deal of creative literary energy. According to Yeats, who was the chief theorist as well as the chief practitioner of the Literary Movement, any sensitive Anglo-Irishman who sympathized with Irish problems found a political career irksome and useless after 1890. Instead, he turned to literature to express his patriotism and his identification with the Irish people. Around 1900 we find Lady Gregory, Yeats, George Moore, Douglas Hyde, AE (G.W. Russell), Edward Martyn, and Synge, all Anglo-Irish save Martyn, combining to make that astonishing constellation of genius that was the Irish Literary Movement. Their purpose, Yeats said, was not political. Their task was to provide the free Ireland of the future with pride in a glorious past, to hang 'images' of heroism around the cradle of the Ireland that was a-borning—the poet's tasks, as Yeats defined it in *The King's Threshold* (1904).

This, at any rate, is Yeats' explanation of the mood and causes of the Movement, and some indication of the way in which this group of writers regarded themselves. But Synge himself suggests a better set of causes in some of his essays. In 'A Landlord's Garden in County Wicklow' he points out the decline of the old landlord class, his own class, and in 'Good Pictures in Dublin' he predicts what its role will be in the Ireland of the future. It will provide not political leaders, for these the emancipated people can now find among themselves, but cultural leaders, who can come only from those families which have a tradition of leisure and culture. After Catholic Emancipation politics soon became a crowded profession but, since it takes far longer to build an educated class than it does to build a group of politicians, the Anglo-Irish remained unchallenged as Ireland's cultural leaders. The great nineteenth-century interest in the past, which had been aroused by the Romantics and especially by Sir Walter

Scott, turned their attention to Irish history. A by-product of this interest in the past, the study of Celtic languages initiated by French and German philologists, led them to Old Irish folklore and literature. Anglo-Irishmen did not take up literature as a substitute for politics. Instead they simply found it a field in which they were unchallenged far longer than in politics, and so they dominated Irish cultural life well into the twentieth century.

Synge himself had no particular interest in Irish politics, although he admired Parnell, and no interest at all in the kind of government a future Ireland would have. He was a member of no group. Unlike Yeats, who was dubbed 'the Great Founder' because of his delight in organizing brotherhoods, societies, and clubs, Synge belonged to no literary clique. Originally he had been a student of languages (at Trinity he won prizes in Irish and Hebrew). Later he decided on a musical career, and then settled in Paris to be a critic and interpreter of French literature. It was here that Yeats found him in December, 1896, in the Hôtel Corneille, a genteel hotel of literary antecedents (Dostoevsky, Thackeray, and Du Maurier's Little Billee had all lodged there), living in a neat bed-sitting room which Yeats ever after insisted on describing as a bohemian garret.

Yeats had visited the Aran Islands briefly that summer. Enthusiastic about the rough and barren life of the remote islanders, he planned a novel, never completed, *The Speckled Bird*, which was to bring 'its central personages from the Aran Islands to Paris'. In the process of abandoning this novel when he met Synge, Yeats reversed his own plot by telling him:

> 'Give up Paris, you will never create anything by reading Racine, and Arthur Symons will always be a better critic of French literature. Go to the Arran [*sic*] Islands. Live there as if you were one of the people themselves; express a life that has never found expression' (Yeats, *Essays* 299).

'I had just come from Arran', adds Yeats, 'and my imagination was full of those gray islands, where men must reap with knives because of the stones'.

Synge went, for six weeks in May and June of 1898. What he found and felt in Aran is the subject of *The Aran Islands*. He visited Aran five times in all, returning each summer until 1902. His book was written during the winters from notebooks kept while on the Islands.

The Aran Islands were the making of Synge as a writer. Everything important he wrote in his brief career is directly traceable to his stay there. He learned how to observe and know the shape and texture of peasant life, its gloom and imminent hysteria as well as its vitality, and with this knowledge he was able to write not only *The Aran Islands* but also his other descriptive studies of the peasant's life and environment. The sketches comprising *In West Kerry*, *In Wicklow*, and *In the Congested Districts* round out the portrait of a race which he began in *The Aran Islands*. Then too, he set down in this book the plots and themes of all but one of his plays, for Synge was his own Holinshed, his own Plutarch. The source hunter can readily discover the seeds of *In the Shadow of the Glen*, *The Well of the Saints*, and *The Playboy of the Western World* in Part I of *The Aran Islands*, and of *Riders to the Sea* in Part III (*The Tinker's Wedding* owes its source to a later essay, 'The Vagrants of Wicklow'). Finally, Synge learned in Aran, as Lady Gregory had learned from the Irish-speaking Kiltartan peasants, the idiom that became the vivid and racy dialect of Abbey Theatre comedy, a language based not on stage Irish, with its *begorras* and its *bedads*, but on the daily speech of those who habitually thought in Irish and whose idiom resulted from mentally translating Irish constructions into English.

For the Aran Islands taught Synge to listen as well as to see, and from the unconscious poetry of their everyday language and the formulaic quality of the Aran speech he formed his own distinctive style. Like Yeats's four heroes, Burke, Goldsmith, Swift, and Berkeley, Synge was one of those who

> walked the roads
> Mimicking what they heard, as children mimic
> (Yeats, *Variorum Poems* 487).

The prose of *The Aran Islands* and of the other descriptive books is just that, an attempt to mimic, to define. Synge tries not only to describe the Aran scene, its exteriors and interiors, as he saw it, but to describe it in the rhythms that he had heard around him as he looked. The book is a series of impressions of Aran conveyed in the faintest possible echo of the Aran idiom, thus uniting matter and manner.

Synge writes a dramatist's prose. He avoids tedious description; instead he illuminates a character or a scene with a sudden flash, and a single object or trait sums up a whole way of life. He depends heavily on the device which Joyce was to christen 'epiphany' and Yeats long after defined as

> Character isolated by a deed
> To engross the present and dominate memory
> (Yeats, *Variorum Poems* 630).

An example of this use of objective and revealing detail is the moment toward the end of Part I of *The Aran Islands*, when Synge leaves Aran and, as he says goodbye to Pat Dirane, notices the old man's hand 'with the mitten worn to a hole on the palm, from the rubbing of his crutch'. Another occurs at the end of 'An Autumn Night in the Hills', where a coffin, strapped to a cart in the rain while its bearers stop for a drink on the road, emphasizes the lonely bleak life of the Wicklow glens. Such objects are not symbols; Synge makes his effect by pure description. Once rendered, objects do not stand for anything but themselves, but the description evokes a whole range of emotion. In his plays Synge uses such objects as

Michael's socks in *Riders to the Sea*, the loy in *The Playboy of the Western World*, and the can in *The Tinker's Wedding* in the same way. They sum up and concentrate much of the action and emotion. Only one or two books in English—James Agee's *Let Us Now Praise Famous Men* is a rare example—rely thus strongly on the revelatory power of objects.

Synge seldom comments. He simply shows us his people and his scene. Except in the series about the Congested Districts he does not care about arousing our sympathy for the hard lot of the Irish peasant. He is neither revolted nor angry, and he requires his reader only to watch and listen. Like Chekhov, whose plays he never read but would have understood (the essay 'A Landlord's Garden in County Wicklow' contains, in brief, the themes of both *Three Sisters* and *The Cherry Orchard*), Synge is content to render a scene, a character, a situation as carefully as possible, and attempts nothing more. John Masefield recalls that 'His mind was too busy with the life to be busy with the affairs or the criticism of life . . . His interest was in life, not ideas' (Howe 28; Masefield 9). George Moore criticized him for this interest in things rather than ideas (Moore 1933, 553), failing to see the importance and exaltation that things took on when Synge turned his attention to them, and the way in which he could use a casual object, fully realized, to illuminate a place, a personality, a life.

The mood of all the Irish sketches is generally sombre, the greyness of a land so barren that all seasons seem one. There is little laughter; instead there is bitter loneliness, struggle and fierceness and always the closeness of death. 'Poetry in unlimited sadness' was Lady Gregory's suggested description of Synge's work (Gregory 1913, 122). Loneliness is especially a prevalent mood. In the Aran Islands, in the remote Wicklow glens, on Dinish Island it is the essential fact of life. And all observers agree on Synge's own air of loneliness. 'A drifting silent man', Yeats calls him (*Essays* 330). To W.A. Henderson of the Abbey Theatre he was 'a dark lonely figure against the skyline' and Masefield notes that 'his place was outside the circle, gravely watching'. 'The lonely returns to the lonely', wrote Yeats—adapting a line from Lionel Johnson (and Proclus)—on the wreath he sent to Synge's funeral.

This loneliness forms the pervasive mood of *The Aran Islands*, of the other travel books, and of the plays. Even among the isolated peasantry at the farthest end of Europe, Synge was an exile, remote from many of their concerns. He excluded himself especially from their religious life and so missed a major preoccupation of the Irish. Frequently in these essays we find him sitting alone while the people are at Mass, awaiting their return but meanwhile self-exiled from the emotional and intellectual core of their communal life. Much of this isolation was deliberate; he told Masefield that when he lived in a peasant house he tried to make the inhabitants 'forget that he was there' (Masefield 28). But in *The Aran Islands* a man genuinely trapped in loneliness speaks for a moment when he describes his remoteness from the Islanders:

> They have the same emotions as I have and the animals have, yet I cannot talk to them when there is much to say more than to the dog that whines beside me in a mountain fog (Synge 78).

And at times, as in 'An Autumn Night in the Hills' and 'The Ferryman of Dinish' the sketches become obsessive studies in loneliness.

Synge's isolation from his own background and from those around him combine in his work with a third quality which made him many enemies during his brief lifetime—a refusal to idealize the Irish peasantry in the way that patriotic nationalist opinion demanded. Because of this, his plays became a focal point for popular protest. The reception of *The Playboy of the Western World* is especially notorious. It was met (January, 1907) with a full week of riots in Dublin, with shillelaghs and tin trumpets in Liverpool, with 'stink pots, rotten fruit and rosaries' in New York, and with the arrest of the entire cast in Philadelphia (Gregory 1913, 204, 224). In all cases the objections were to the 'indecency' (particularly to the inflammatory word *shifts* in Christy's remark about 'a drift of chosen females, standing in their shifts itself, maybe, from this place to the Eastern World'), to the unflattering portrayal of the Irish peasant, and to the suggestion that an Irish girl would spend the night alone in a house with a man to whom she was not married. Only *Riders to the Sea*, the starkest and least ironic of Synge's plays, escaped condemnation in his lifetime.

But Synge had lived among the peasants, and it was impossible for him to idealize them. He knew the crudity and cruelty of their lives, the Elizabethan coarseness of their language, their gloom. In all his work they become, like the author himself, lonely figures in a stark landscape, symbols of man enduring.

Synge's literary antecedents are not difficult to discern. The essays and reviews he wrote for various magazines and newspapers contain numerous indications of his reading and interests. The plays seem to owe little to any previous writer, although at times, in their sardonic picture of hypocrisy and pretence, they recall the Ibsen of *An Enemy of the People* and *Pillars of Society* (It is not entirely an accident that the heroine of *In the Shadow of the Glen*, who is forced out of a loveless marriage, is named Nora). At times, too, there is a trace of Ibsen's later poetic style, and even of Maeterlinck. For the prose the models are less easy to discover. Pierre Loti (1850–1923), who set the fashion, in the 1880s, of exoticizing the harsh life of peasants and exalting the tragic intensity of their lives, had some influence on Synge's Irish sketches. So perhaps did Lafcadio Hearn, a distant relative of whom Synge was very proud, admiring his 'fiery prose style' (Bourgeois 13). Hearn's impressionistic sketches of Japanese and West Indian life probably aided in developing Synge's technique of concentrating on the mood of a person or landscape and rendering that mood, only throwing in a sudden concrete detail now and then to anchor the sketch to the realities of the scene, a material object relieving the mind from a series of reveries and impressions.

But there is another important source of Synge's unique method of realizing a scene in such a way that we have its essentials filtered through his own consciousness. I have described Hearn above as an impressionistic writer. The term is even more applicable to Synge. In Paris the theories of the Impressionist painters—especially Monet, Manet, and Renoir—were constantly being discussed in the circles in which Synge moved. He went to the galleries again and again to look at their paintings, and these paintings were important in determining his way of looking at reality. An Impressionist painter looks at a scene or object and then constructs an image moulded around whatever interests him most in the scene or object. He does not strive for photographic realism. So it is with Synge. An object is emphasized and examined to summarize the total reality of a place or person. He practises what painters call 'blurred definition'. Details are obscured and absorbed in the whole, blurred either by actual or emotional distance, by vapour or smoke in the atmosphere, or by a darkening of the spirit, and we get only those shapes and tones of importance to the interested eye. The rest are sacrificed. There is, perhaps, some lack of precision, even of truth perhaps. The artist who tries for elusive effects cannot at the same time render the external forms of objects exactly. Instead he gives an impression of them. One can see this painter's technique, marvellously adapted to another medium, in use all through Synge's noncritical prose in his descriptions of people, or of interiors and exteriors. Consider his description of a kitchen on Inishmaan where all is subdued and repressed, brown and grey, with 'the continual murmur of Gaelic', and only the glowing red dresses of the women are emphasized (*Aran Islands* 18–20). Or the Aran funeral, where everything is reduced to blurred form save the savage keening and dark shrouded shapes of the old women.

The scenes Synge describes are usually quiet ones, and not very much happens. The reader ends knowing something of how the Islanders lived and felt but far more of how things looked and felt and sounded to John Synge. The tone is the monotone of a single centre of consciousness, heightened here and there by a vivid phrase or a bit of colour or excitement, all held together in the prevailing quiet luminous grey which conveys to us at once the actual atmosphere—the weather, light, smells, sights— and the mood—life lived at a low key with sudden rare flashes of violence or excitement. Even the technique of a series of apparently disconnected jottings, held together only by their common subject, derives perhaps from the Impressionist painters, with their insistence that the artist complete his painting quickly while its subject remains before him unchanged. And Synge's trick of showing the same scene at different times of day can probably be traced to Monet, who once made a dozen paintings of the same haystack because at each hour, as the light changed, the appearance of the haystack changed too. Synge himself talks at times of the visual painterly aspects of his reaction to the Irish scene. 'No one who has not lived for weeks among these grey clouds and seas can realize the joy with which the eye rests on the red dresses of the women', he comments (*Aran Islands* 30).

Some indication of his reliance on the Impressionists can be found by comparing a description of Aran written about 1865 by the Irish novelist Charles Lever with any passage of Synge's description of the Islands. If Synge sees with the eye of an Impressionist, Lever sees with the romantic eye of a follower of Salvator Rosa, and describes 'that great mountain rising abruptly from the sea . . . those wild fantastic rocks, with their drooping seaweed; those solemn caves, wherein the rumbling sea rushes to issue forth again in some distant cleft' (Lever, *Luttrell of Arran* 15).

So much for Synge's method. His subject was all around him, in the unregarded lives of the peasantry, and once Yeats suggested it to him, he never looked back.

Synge's prose is often looked upon as minor work, of interest only as an adjunct to the plays. But it is a mistake to dismiss it so lightly. The prose works stand by themselves as a unique and separate achievement, perhaps the only work of the Irish revival which tries to see the peasant plain and to portray him without bias. They are a full-length portrait of the most primitive way of life in Europe, lived in the bleakest of landscapes, an Impressionistic portrait perhaps, after the manner of Manet or Whistler. They are also intensely personal. Reading them, we get with extraordinary force an impression of the author himself, the retiring man who 'dying took the living world for text', who made it his solitary and lonely task to portray the life of the solitary and the lonely. Padraic Colum remembered Synge's telling him that 'all his work was subjective . . . it all came out of moods of his own life'. Yeats was summing up this peculiarly personal quality of Synge's art when he wrote of him as 'a man trying to look out of a window and blurring all that he sees by breathing upon the window' (Yeats, *Autobiography* 230).

Reprinted with permission from *The Aran Islands and Other Writings* by John M. Synge, ed. Robert Tracy. New York: Random House/Vintage, 1962.

11

Words of Mouth

Joyce and the Oral Tradition

There was an old woman one time who lived at the far end of the parish. She was a widow woman, and she lived alone in a little cabin, with only a little garden and a few chickens. She paid the rent with what she could earn helping farmers at saving the hay or their wives with a bit of sewing.

One day, and it was rent day, she had to walk to the bailiff's house at the other end of the parish with her bit of rent, and then she had to stand in the bailiff's yard with the other tenants for a long time before her turn came to pay. When she started home she was very tired, and so, when she came to the chapel, she thought she would stop in and rest herself and say a prayer. So she went inside and sat down, and didn't she fall fast asleep.

The sexton came to lock up the chapel for the night, and he didn't see her there in her corner. When she woke up it was dark, and she found she was locked in. She was frightened at first, but then she said a prayer, and she moved up near the altar where the sanctuary lamp was burning before the Blessed Sacrament. And that was a comfort to her.

After a while she fell asleep again, but she woke up suddenly at the stroke of twelve. There were two candles burning on the altar. Then the door to the sacristy opened. A strange priest came out, a priest she had never seen before. He was vested for the altar and he held a chalice in his hands.

The strange priest came to the altar rail and looked out into the dark empty chapel. The old woman hunched down in her seat and made herself as small as she could. The priest spoke. 'Is there anyone here who will serve my Mass for me?' he asked. The old woman said nothing. 'Is there anyone here who will serve my Mass for me?' he asked again, and then a third time: 'Is there anyone here who will serve my Mass for me?'. Then he turned and went back into the sacristy, and the candles on the altar went out.

References to Joyce's works are as follows: *D, Dubliners*; *P, Portrait*; *U, Ulysses*; *FW, Finnegans Wake*. For *Finnegans Wake* citations I have given line as well as page.

The old woman didn't sleep any more that night. She was too busy praying. In the morning the sexton opened the chapel and he was very surprised to see her there. As for her, she went straight to the priest's house and asked to see the parish priest.

The housekeeper brought her into the dining-room where the priest was having his breakfast. She told him her story and he listened carefully. Then he had the housekeeper bring her tea and a boiled egg. 'You must stop here with me today', he said, 'and tonight I will watch in the chapel with you so we get to the bottom of this.'

The old woman stayed at the priest's house all day, with the best of everything. The housekeeper gave her meat for dinner and again for supper, and lashings of tea. After supper she dozed for a while in a big soft chair until the priest woke her up. 'You must come to the chapel now with me', he said, 'and we will watch together'.

It was dark when they went to the chapel. The priest unlocked the door and when they were inside he locked the door behind them. He asked the old woman to show him where she had been sitting last night, and they sat down together in the same place.

They sat there for a long time. There was no sound but the sound of the wind outside in the trees. But suddenly, on the stroke of midnight, two candles flared up on the altar, and the strange priest came out of the sacristy with a chalice in his hands, vested for the altar. He came to the altar rail as before and said, 'Is there anyone here who will serve my Mass for me?' 'I will serve your Mass', said the parish priest, standing up. And so he went up to the altar, and he served the strange priest's Mass, making the responses, pouring the water and the wine, ringing the bell, while the old woman looked on and prayed.

When the Mass was over, the strange priest spoke to the parish priest. 'I have been coming out on this altar every night for more than a hundred years', he said, 'asking if there was anyone who would serve my Mass. You are the first to respond and help me. I was the parish priest here long ago. One of my parishioners gave me a pound note to say a Mass for the souls of his dead, but I died before I could say that Mass. Now I have been able to say it at last, and I can rest until the day of Judgement.' With that the strange priest disappeared. He was never seen again.

The story I have just told is well known to European folklore collectors, especially in Spain and France, and to Irish folklore collectors. In Stith Thompson's *Motif-Index of Folk Literature* it appears as motif E 415.3, 'Ghost of priest cannot rest because he failed to say certain masses for the dead' (volume 2), and as motif Q 521.6, 'Penance: holding midnight mass until someone will make responses'. Seán Ó Súilleabháin's *Handbook of Irish Folklore*, organized as a series of questions to be used by local folklore collectors, asks for 'local versions of a story about a deceased priest who required a Mass-server at night in the church' and, under the rubric 'Dead Seek Help', lists 'deceased priest seeks clerk to serve his Mass (promised to be said before he died)' (Ó Súilleabháin 1942, 153, 247). More than 200 oral versions of the legend are in the Folklore Archives at University College Dublin, collected during the 1920s and 1930s (Lysaght 1991b, 194). Patricia Lysaght, who has carefully studied the legend, divides these into what she calls the A-redaction, most common in Munster and south-east Leinster, and the B-redaction, found in most counties but rare in north-east Ulster. Apart from distribution, these redactions differ in length and personnel. In the A-redaction a boy or man falls asleep in the chapel, and is able to respond immediately to the dead priest's request, thus ending both the priest's torment and the story. I have told the B-redaction, in which the old woman's inability to answer the dead priest lengthens the story, introduces a third character, and provides some degree of suspense (Lysaght 1991b,196–200; 203–5).

Lysaght also points out the story's dependence on details of Catholic ritual and Canon Law (Lysaght 1991b, 197). The Council of Trent (1545–63) decreed that all Catholic priests must celebrate Mass in conformity with the ritual as celebrated at Rome, and regulated every detail of the ritual. These decrees remained in force until altered or partially superseded by the Second Vatican Council (1962–65). There must be a cross on the altar, and at least two candles must be lit. The priest must wear the appropriate vestments. He may not say Mass alone. There must be a congregation, or at least an altar-boy or server, male, who utters the prescribed responses to the priest's prayers. These prayers and responses must be recited in Latin. The server also moves the missal when required by the rubric, and pours for the priest the water and wine which are to be consecrated, along with bread, to become, according to Catholic doctrine, the Body and Blood of Christ. In his responses, the server acts as a representative of the congregation, or as a substitute congregation.

'A priest may not celebrate the eucharistic Sacrifice without the participation of at least one of the faithful, unless there is a good and reasonable cause for doing so' (Canon 906); such reasons seem to be limited to the need to consecrate a host for someone who is dying. Earlier versions of Canon Law demand a server: 'a priest is not to celebrate Mass without a server who serves him and responds to him' (1917 Code). The only exceptions are when a priest must consecrate a host as a viaticum for one seriously ill, or to enable the faithful to fulfil their obligation to hear Mass. Furthermore, until recently the server had to be of the male sex. Listing the conditions that would prevent a priest from saying Mass, the *Missale Romanum* (1898) specifies, 'si non adsit Clericus, vel alius deserviens in

Missa, vel adsit qui deservire non habet, ut mulier'; if there is no clerk or other person capable of serving Mass present, or if there is present [only] one not entitled to serve Mass, such as a woman (*Missale* 1i). In April 1836 the Congregation of Sacred Rites decreed that 'A person of the female sex may not serve at the altar itself (e.g. transfer the missal, present the cruets, etc.)' though conceding that 'Women (especially nuns) may, however, answer the celebrant from their places if no male server be at hand' (*Catholic Encyclopedia* 10:20).

This explains the ghostly priest's situation in the folk tale. He can only be released from his ordeal of appearing nightly if he finds a server: a male capable of supplying the appropriate Latin responses to the priest's prayers, and otherwise familiar with the ceremonies that the server at Mass must perform. When someone is finally present at midnight in the chapel to hear his appeal, in the B-redaction it is a woman, barred from serving Mass by Canon Law and presumably by her own ignorance of the Latin responses the server must make. All she can do is fetch another priest, who becomes the hero of the story by enabling the ghost to rest. The old woman is silenced in the story as she is silenced by Canon Law.

Most people enjoy a ghost story, but why should this one be so popular? Apart from its dramatic plot, there also seems to be a didactic element, connected both with the doctrine of Purgatory and the duties of the priesthood. The story is about a dead priest, his failure to perform his duties properly when alive, and his posthumous need of assistance from the living. These aspects reappear, somewhat re-ordered, in Joyce's 'The Sisters', and suggest that the folktale is in part Joyce's source and model.

The Catholic doctrine of Purgatory is one of the major differences between Catholic teaching and the teachings of most Protestant churches. The Protestant Reformation began with Martin Luther's objections to the sale of indulgences to the living, which would diminish their time in Purgatory after death, a practice he considered simony, the buying and selling of sacred things. Catholics believe that, while life on earth earns salvation or damnation, for those not clearly in either category there is a second probationary stage for souls not evil enough to merit Hell. It is a place of great suffering, an ordeal, where the sins committed in life are *purged* away. Prayers and Masses said by the living for those in Purgatory can assist and speed this process of purgation, and so Catholics often request a priest to say a Mass or Masses 'for the repose of the soul' of the deceased, and offer him a stipend for doing so. The Church's 'strict regulation . . . binding under pain of mortal sin' is 'that priests shall not accept more intentions than they can satisfy within a reasonable period' (*Catholic Encyclopedia* 10:21), a regulation the dead priest in the folk tale has clearly violated, and for which he must atone by being earthbound until he can finally say the Mass he has promised. Critics of Catholicism have some-times equated the acceptance of a stipend for saying a Mass with simony—the 'word . . . in the Catechism' which 'had always sounded strangely' in the ears of Joyce's narrator, and which he associates with *paralysis*—Father Flynn's ordeal—and 'the word *gnomon* in the Euclid' (*Dubliners* 9).

Like Father Flynn's conversations, the story emphasizes 'The duties of the priest' (*D* 13). By stressing the priest's obligation to say the Mass requested and promised for one in Purgatory, the story subtly affirms the reality of Purgatory and the priest's ability to assist the dead to leave Purgatory for Paradise. The priest who is unable to rest while the Mass is unsaid is himself in a kind of Purgatory, where he must expiate his failure by his repeated appearance in the darkened chapel. He is in a kind of stasis, a supernatural version of Father Flynn's literal stasis or paralysis. Father Flynn cannot move; the ghostly priest cannot cease repeating the same action for a hundred years, another kind of paralysis.

Joyce was always interested in restless ghosts: Michael Furey in 'The Dead', Bloom's father and son, Stephen's mother in *Ulysses*. He may have heard someone tell the story of the priest's ghost in either the A or B-redaction. More probably, he read it, as 'The Priest's Ghost', in Samuel Lover's *Legends and Stories of Ireland: First Series* (1832). Joyce refers to at least one story from that collection, 'King O'Toole and St Kevin', which features the King's pet goose, in *Finnegans Wake*: 'old Kong Gander O'Toole of the Mountains or his googoo goosth' (557.6–7). Glasheen cites other references to St Kevin and O'Toole. Lover himself appears paired with Charles Lever ('Samyouwill Leaver and Damyouwell Lover' (*FW* 93.34). Joyce also draws on a story from *Legends and Stories of Ireland: Second Series*, 'The White Horse of the Peppers' (*FW* 214.16). Joyce may also have heard someone tell, or rather perform Lover's version of the story. Lover himself (*d.* 1868) had recited his stories 'originally . . . merely for the diversion of a few friends around my own fire-side' (Lover, *First Series* vii), later as a popular entertainment. In his preface to *Legends . . . First Series* he emphasizes their oral nature: 'some of them are essentially *oral* in their character, and, I fear, suffer materially when reduced to writing . . . if I meet but half as good natured *readers* as I have hitherto found *auditors*, I shall have cause to be thankful' (viii). In the days of par-lour entertainments, his versions were often memorized and recited to a domestic audience; his preface contains hints on how best to achieve the appropriate Irish accent (Lover, *First Series* ix).

Lover's 'The Priest's Ghost' differs from both traditional versions I have described in that it does not end with a Mass. Though he remarks that 'the tale was told . . . to prove how sacred a duty the mass for the "soul of the faithful departed", is considered before the eternal judgment-seat' (*Legends*

137), he failed to understand how essential it is that the ghostly priest actually *say* the Mass for which he has accepted a stipend, nor does he seem to have realized that only a male server could give the responses. Lover's protagonist, one Mary O'Malley, falls asleep in the chapel, wakes to see and hear the ghostly priest, and swoons, to be found next morning. After 'as good as a week before she could lave her bed', she tells 'her clargy' what she has seen.

> his Riverince, undher God, was enlightened to see the maynin' of it all; and the maynin' was this, that he undherstood from hearin' of the priest appearin' in black vestments, that it was for to say mass for the dead that he kem there; and so he supposed that the priest durin' his lifetime had forgot to say a mass for the dead that he was bound to say, and that his poor sowl couldn't have rest antil that mass was said; and that he must walk antil the duty was done (Lover, *First Series* 136).

Mary and 'his Riverince' watch in the chapel by night until the ghostly priest appears to ask, 'Is there any one here to answer this mass?' At the third request—'"Is there *no* one here to answer this mass?" poor Mary mutthered out "yis", as well as she could.' At that the ghost smiles

> a lovely smile . . . and looked kindly upon her, saying these remarkable words—'It's twenty years', says he, 'I have been askin' that question, and no one answered till this blessed night, and a blessin' be on her that answered, and now my business on earth is finished,' and with that, he vanished, before you could shut your eyes.

Lover's narrator points the moral:

> So never say, Sir, it's no good praying for the dead; for you see that even the sowl of a priest couldn't have pace, for forgettin' so holy a thing as a mass for the sowl of the faithful departed (Lover, *First Series* 137).

The story is also told in Canon Sheehan's popular novel, *My New Curate* (1898).

'The Sisters' contains major elements of the folk tale, though drastically re-arranged, as the *Odyssey* would be drastically rearranged in *Ulysses*. Indeed, Joyce's simultaneous adoption and concealment of his source material makes 'The Sisters' a kind of rehearsal for his later treatment of the *Odyssey*. Folk tale and short story are about a priest who has failed in his duty. Joyce's Father Flynn has dropped and broken a chalice, and for doing so is literally paralysed with guilt. 'It was that chalice he broke . . . That was the beginning of it', his sister Eliza tells the narrator. 'Of course, they say it was all right, that it contained nothing, I mean. But still . . .' (*D* 17). Though the chalice did not contain Christ's consecrated blood, Father Flynn is haunted by the possibility that he might have failed in those 'duties of the priest towards the Eucharist' which he had described to the narrator as 'so grave . . . that I wondered how anybody had ever found in himself the courage to undertake them' (*D* 13). His 'sin', morbidly exaggerated by guilt and his sense of his own unworthiness, has affected both his mind and his body. His conversations with the narrator dwell obsessively on the proper performance of the Church's ceremonies and on possible failure to perform them properly. His repetitious discussion of these issues resembles the ghostly priest's repetitious appearance and question:

> he had taught me to pronounce Latin properly . . . he had explained to me the meaning of the different ceremonies of the Mass and of the different vestments worn by the priest. Sometimes he had amused himself by putting difficult questions to me, asking me what one should do in certain circumstances or whether such and such sins were mortal or venial or only imperfections. His questions showed me how complex and mysterious were certain institutions of the Church which I had always regarded as the simplest acts . . . I was not surprised when he told me that the fathers of the Church had written books as thick as the *Post Office Directory* and as closely printed as the law notices in the newspaper, elucidating all these intricate questions . . . Sometimes he used to put me through the responses of the Mass which he had made me learn by heart; and, as I pattered, he used to smile pensively and nod his head . . . (*D* 13).

When Eliza tells Father Flynn's story, she describes him haunting a locked and darkened chapel at midnight, like the ghostly priest. He is found in his confessional box—site of another heavy duty he fears he cannot adequately perform: 'And what do you think but there he was, sitting up by himself in the dark in his confession-box, wide-awake and laughing-like softly to himself' (*D* 18). Joyce even juxtaposes this with a tired old woman falling asleep: 'Nannie had leaned her head against the sofa-pillow and seemed about to fall asleep' (*D* 16).

Father Flynn has taught the narrator 'to pronounce Latin properly' and made him 'learn by heart . . . the responses of the Mass', thus preparing him to say or serve a posthumous Mass. Joyce's own sensibilities were receptive to Catholic ceremonies and he was critical when they were carelessly or imperfectly performed. Attending Tenebrae at Dublin's Pro-Cathedral, Stephen Dedalus 'did not like the office which was gabbled over quickly' (*Stephen Hero* 123). In Trieste Joyce attended the Easter liturgy for 'esthetic, not pious' motives (Ellmann 1959, 320). The narrator of 'The Sisters'—and the boyhood self he at once recollects and embodies—is alert to ceremony and ceremonious usage. He knows that the 'evenly' lighted window will give way to the flickering reflection of candles when Father Flynn dies (*D* 9), the 'ceremonious candles in the light of which the Christian must take his last sleep' of the first, or *Irish Homestead* version (13 August 1904) of 'The Sisters' (*D* 243). He declines the proffered cream crackers lest the noise of chewing them seem indecorous in a house of mourning (*D* 15).

The dead priest in the folk tale needs a man or boy to serve his Mass and so release his spirit. When the dead Father Flynn appears to the narrator in a dream, Flynn is another needy spirit, seeking to confess and receive whatever response—or absolution—the boy can provide:

> In the dark of my room I imagined that I saw again the heavy grey face of the paralytic. I drew the blankets over my head and tried to think of Christmas. But the grey face still followed me. It murmured; and I understood that it desired to confess something. I felt my soul receding into some pleasant and vicious region; and there again I found it waiting for me. It began to confess to me in a murmuring voice and I wondered why it smiled continually and why the lips were so moist with spittle. But then I remembered that it had died of paralysis and I felt that I too was smiling feebly as if to absolve the simoniac of his sin (D 11).

He cannot remember 'what had happened afterwards in the dream'—though it seems to have been a waking dream, in a darkened room—but 'remembered that I had noticed long velvet curtains and a swinging lamp of antique fashion'. He imagines he has been 'very far away, in some land where the customs were strange—in Persia, I thought. . .' (D 13–14). But the curtains and lamp also suggest the sanctuary of a Catholic church. If so, both ghostly priests appear in a darkened nocturnal chapel. Father Flynn's confession is incomplete, perhaps because the boy falls asleep, perhaps because, like the old woman in the chapel, he makes no response.

Father Flynn is not a simoniac, but simony becomes paralysis and vice versa by a kind of metaphrasis. Paralysis—a failure to move forward, on to other duties, after dropping the chalice—is the sin Father Flynn tries and fails to confess. We know that he 'had a great wish' (D 10) for the boy, that is, that the boy would grow up to become a priest himself, and so in some way expiate Father Flynn's failure. His ghost pursues the boy to have him perform a priestly ceremony, that of absolution which would free him from sin, or, more accurately, from guilt—a state similar to the ghostly priest's guilt at his failure to say the promised Mass.

Father Flynn wants to confess to the boy his failure in his duty towards the Eucharist. As in the doctrine that the prayers of the living can assist the dead in Purgatory, and in the ghostly priest's need for someone to serve his Mass, the dead need the help of the living. This is very much a part of Irish folklore, as when the *sí* or 'fairies' need at least one human being when they play a hurling match (Lysaght, 1991a, 33–4; MacCana 126).

Father Flynn's need for the assistance of the living boy resonates against his original dropping of the chalice, perhaps caused by his altar boy or server—'They say it was the boy's fault' (D 17). He has possibly spilled Christ's blood, which represents and nourishes eternal life. Spilled or not, his own life, spiritual and physical, has gone with it. The dead priest in the folk tale, himself perhaps in need of a Mass, must appropriately say an omitted mass for the dead, which will free him as well as the soul for whom it was originally requested. Both priests seek grace and pardon, elements ironically linked and punned in the Father Purdon of 'Grace' and his sermon addressed 'to business men . . . in a businesslike way' with its faint undertone of simony (*D* 174).

In the folk tale, the old woman must tell her story to her priest before the dead priest can be helped. Though unable to speak in church, her speech is necessary for his salvation. Lover elaborated the story into a narrated performance. Narrators and narrative ability are ultimately a means of grace in 'the Sisters'. The narrator emerges as gifted both with observation and considerable narrative skill. He notes 'how clumsily' Nannie's 'skirt was hooked at the back and how the heels of her cloth boots were trodden down all to one side' (*D* 14). He records Eliza's mis-pronunciation of the *Freeman's Journal* as *General* and 'pneumatic' as, rheumatic; (*D* 16–17). He is critical of old Cotter's unfinished phrases and vague hints, which thwart the story. Cotter is a failed storyteller. With her brother dead, Eliza becomes a storyteller 'seated in his arm-chair in state' (*D* 14). Though unskilled at narrative, she manages to convey Father Flynn's story, which the narrator skilfully reshapes out of her broken sentences so that we can understand. 'The Sisters' culminates in storytelling (a traditional activity at wakes)—a story about telling a story. With Eliza's telling of his story, Father Flynn can rest:

> She stopped suddenly as if to listen. I too listened; but there was no sound in the house: and I knew that the old priest was lying still in his coffin as we had seen him, solemn and truculent in death, an idle chalice on his breast (*D* 18).

A woman is unable to help the ghostly priest say his Mass. She can only tell her priest what she has seen, though her tale leads to the ghost's release. Joyce's two sisters seem equally limited. They can recall and report, but, it seems, not really help until the narrator takes over. Just as Father Flynn has needed and valued the boy's companionship in life, so he needs his quasi-priestly services after death. 'I think he said more to me than to anyone else', the narrator recalls, in the *Irish Homestead* text of the story;

> He had an egoistic contempt for all women-folk and suffered all their services to him in polite silence. Of course neither of his sisters was very intelligent. Nannie, for instance, had been reading out the newspaper to him every day for years and could read tolerably well and yet she always spoke of it as the *Freeman's General*. Perhaps he found me more intelligent and honoured me with words for that reason (*D* 247).

The folk tale assumes that the old woman cannot herself help the dead priest except by bringing another priest. Joyce's earlier version of 'The

Sisters' is more explicit about the exclusion of the Flynn sisters from their brother's mental world of priestly concerns and duties:

> He used to sit in that stuffy room for the greater part of the day from early morning while Nannie (who was almost stone deaf) read out the newspaper to him. His other sister, Eliza, used to mind the shop. These two old women used to look after him, feed him and clothe him . . . When he was tired of hearing the news he used to rattle his snuff-box on the arm of his chair to avoid shouting at her and then he used to make believe to read his prayer-book. Make believe because whenever Eliza brought him a cup of soup from the kitchen she had always to waken him (*D* 246–7).

Flynn silences Nannie by pretending to turn to one of his priestly duties, the daily recitation of a prescribed office or series of prayers as printed in his breviary. Joyce notes the exclusion of other women from any partic-ipation in Church ritual with Aunt Kate's angry outburst in 'The Dead': 'I think it's not at all honourable for the pope to turn out the women out of the choirs that have slaved there all their lives and put little whipper-snap-pers of boys over their heads.' Her sister, Aunt Julia, is one of the women excluded from taking an active part in Church services by the decree *Motu Proprio* of Pope Pius X, which announced that

> singers in churches have a real liturgical office, and . . . therefore women, as being incapable of such office, cannot be admitted to form part of the choir or of the musical chapel. Whenever, then, it is desired to employ the acute voices of sopranos and contraltos, these parts must be taken by boys, according to the most ancient usage of the church (*D* 194, 502).

Despite this exclusion of women, it is Eliza who speaks and so confesses what the narrator has failed or refused to hear during his waking dream. Since confession must be spoken and heard to obtain absolution, she has articulated for her brother his sin of omission, failing to safeguard the chalice and its possible precious contents—a chalice must be ritually cleansed after it has held Christ's blood. She has also articulated his other, graver sin, that of being 'too scrupulous, always . . . The duties of the priesthood was too much for him' (*D* 17); in the *Irish Homestead* version, 'It was his scrupulousness, you see, that affected his mind. The duties of the priesthood were too much for him—'(*D* 251). Like the ghostly priest, he has been unable to carry out the obligations he has assumed.

The ghostly priest is finally able to say his Mass, but he must also confess his earlier failure to do so. His confession to the old woman and the living priest who have helped him is at once religiously and narratively required: religiously because the Catholic Church requires oral confession, narratively because the story cannot end properly without explaining the ghostly priest's presence. In Lover's version, 'his Riverince . . . was enlightened to see the maynin' of it all', and the explanation is left to the narrator, who reveals it in the middle of his account. Joyce avoids specific explanations to lead us to an epiphany through Eliza's hesitant story of the dropped chalice and the discovery of Father Flynn at night in the locked and empty chapel. It is the boy observer, presumably now grown up, who records Eliza's phrases and fragments of sentences that make that epiphany possible. He has heard the confession he shrank from when the dead Father Flynn appeared to him. Though the narrator does not absolve, the reader does. With his confession finally uttered, and heard, Father Flynn can rest at last—a resolution the *Irish Homestead* version emphasizes in its final words:—'God rest his soul!—'(*D* 252). As in the folk tale, an ignorant woman and a more sophisticated male must cooperate to bring rest to the perturbed spirit.

Though barred from any ecclesiastical function by Canon Law, Eliza and Nannie do in fact parody the two lowest of the four minor orders, to which every Catholic priest is ordained early in his ecclesiastical career. Though these orders are no longer of any practical importance, they remain closed to women. In the final version of the story, Eliza fills the office of Porter or Ostiary, the lowest of the minor orders. Originally, the Porter's duties were to keep the keys to the church, and ensure that it was clean and properly prepared for worship. Eliza is the sister who seems to be in charge of the house in Little Britain Street, and Father Flynn's chief care-giver. Nannie, who reads the *Freeman's Journal* to him, has the next ecclesiastical office, that of Lector or Reader. The narrator combines the remaining minor offices of Exorcist and Acolyte.

A traditional Irish storyteller could be either a *scéalaí* (*sgéalaí, sgéaltóir*), who told stories of magic and the supernatural, and legends about such heroes as Finn Mac Cumhal, or a *seanchaí*, who made 'a specialty of local tales, family-sagas, or genealogies, social-historical tradition . . . and . . . tales of a short realistic type about fairies, ghosts, and other supernatural beings' (Delargy 192). Joyce acts as a kind of *scéalaí* when he retells ancient Irish heroic legends in 'The Dead', *Ulysses*, and *Finnegans Wake*. Initially composed orally, but written down during the Middle Ages, such tales were once part of a storyteller's repertoire. Tales of Finn Mac Cumhal and the Fianna were preserved and told orally until the 1930s. John Kelleher long ago suggested interesting parallels between 'The Dead' and the eighth- or ninth-century 'Destruction of Da Derga's Hostel' (*Tógail Bruidne Da Derga*). More recently, Maria Tymoczko has persuasively argued the relevance of the 'Book of the Takings of Ireland' (*Lebor Gabála Erenn*), 'The Voyage of Bran' (*Imram Brain*), and 'The Cattle Raid of Cooley' (*Táin Bó Cúalnge*) for *Ulysses*, and established Joyce's knowledge of these works, which were described in Arbois de Jubainville's *Le Cycle Mythologique*

Irlandais, translated by Richard Irvine Best, who discusses Shakespeare with Stephen in 'Scylla and Charybdis', and serialized in a paper Joyce read, *The United Irishman* (1901–2). *Lebor Gabála* may explain Bloom's Jewish identity and Molly's Spanish origin. The *imram* or 'rowing around' genre resembles the *Odyssey* in describing a sea voyage punctuated by many landings on mysterious islands, some pleasant, some very dangerous. As for the *Táin*, Queen Medb or Maeve makes her own sexual choices and, like Molly, menstruates and urinates copiously, traditional signs of sexuality. Her husband, Ailill, plays the voyeur when she lies with Fergus Mac Roth, as Bloom imagines for himself a voyeuristic role while Molly is with Blazes Boylan. Ailill steals Fergus's—presumably phallic—sword during the love-making, an event echoed when Bloom mislays the—presumably phallic—key to 7, Eccles Street, a key associated with sovereignty and 'home rule'.

Cuchulain, hero of the *Táin*, has two fathers. One is Lugh, god of arts and crafts, a reasonable avatar for the fabulous artificer Daedalus. The main action of the *Táin* is Cuchulain's series of single combats against the men of Ireland at the ford marking the boundary of Ulster; Stephen and Bloom each fight a series of verbal single combats against well-armed enemies in Dublin, Baile Átha Cliath, the settlement at the Ford of the Hurdles. As we know, *Finnegans Wake* draws on stories of Finn Mac Cumhal and his warrior band, the Fianna or Fenians.

Most of the stories in *Dubliners* are *seanchaí* stories, scandalous episodes from the histories of local families. We learn how Eveline Hill almost ran off with a sailor; how Mrs Mooney and her daughter Polly tacitly conspired to force Bob Doran into matrimony; how badly Mrs Kearney behaved at the *Éire Abu* Society concert. In 'An Encounter' and 'Araby' the narrators tell stories about themselves. Farrington, in 'Counterparts', amazes himself by finding a witty riposte—'I don't think, sir . . . that that's a fair question to put to me'—when his boss asks, 'Do you think me an utter fool?' (*D* 91). He knows that the remark will in future make his life 'a hell' in the office, but it has given him a story to tell, one way of making

> a good night of it . . . As he walked on he preconsidered the terms in which he would narrate the incident to the boys:
> —So, I just looked at him—coolly, you know, and looked at her. Then I looked back at him again—taking my time, you know. *I don't think that that's a fair question to put to me*, says I (*D* 93).

Farrington tells his story several times, to several groups of listeners, and even listens as his story is retold by Higgins, his co-worker:

> Of course [Higgins] had to join in with the others. The men asked him to give his version of it, and he did so with great vivacity . . . Everyone roared laughing when

he showed the way in which Mr Alleyne shook his fist in Farrington's face. Then he imitated Farrington, saying, *And here was my nabs, as cool as you please*, while Farrington looked at the company out of his heavy dirty eyes, smiling and at times drawing forth stray drops of liquor from his moustache with the aid of his lower lip (*D* 93–4).

Tom Kernan's visitors in 'Grace' exchange inaccurate anecdotes and information about Church history and the first Vatican Council. 'Ivy Day in the Committee Room' ends with a poem mourning the death of Parnell, the Chief, a version of the traditional lament or *caoine* once composed by a chieftain's bard, and later improvised by women who were professional mourners.

'The Sisters' is about a family secret and, as we have seen, reworks a traditional story, one that stresses the duties and responsibilities of the priest, the punishment for failing in those duties, and the possibility of posthumous release from that punishment. The story examines its own processes with the inclusion of old Cotter as a failed *seanchaí*, Eliza as a partially successful one. The narrator is finally able to tell the story, and even assert its truth by his own presence as eye-witness—a common device in folk tales. The boys aunt, 'A gossip, a harmless one' in the *Irish Homestead* text (*D* 249), elicits the story by encouraging Eliza to tell it. Encouragement from listeners was common when folk tales were told in a traditional setting.

With careful symmetry, Joyce ends *Dubliners* by balancing 'The Sisters' with 'The Dead', another story about two old sisters, a man who fails in his duty, a woman who tells a story, a restless ghost. Like the priest in need of a server, the dead lover who returns for his bride has his place in Irish folklore (Ó Súilleabháin 1942, 248), as in most folk traditions.

The motif of 'The Dead Lover's Return' or 'The Dead Bridegroom Carries off his Bride' (Aarne-Thompson 365; Stith Thompson E 215) usually involves a promise broken by death; like the priest who failed to say the promised Masses for the dead, the betrothed lover has failed to come for his bride as he had promised (Uí Ógáin 126). The best known literary version is Gottfried Bürger's eerie ballad, 'Lenore' (1773). Seán Ó Súilleabháin and Reidar Christiansen record thirteen Irish versions of the motif, which can be summarized as follows:

A couple are promised to each other; the boy dies without the girl's knowledge. At their planned rendezvous his spirit comes, usually on horseback, to meet her; unsuspecting, she accompanies him. Due to the strange circumstances and conversation she realises that he is a spirit, and becomes afraid. He tries to take her with him into the grave, but she narrowly escapes, sometimes with the help of a blacksmith; the spirit disappears and in some versions, pieces of the girl's clothing are found in shreds on his grave the following morning; frequently the girl dies shortly afterwards (Ó Súilleabháin/Christiansen 86; Uí Ógáin 129).

Joyce uses anecdotes and details about his own family throughout 'The Dead'. His father usually carved the goose at the 'Misses Flynn's' annual Christmas party for their pupils, and made the after dinner speech. The Misses Flynn, Morkans in the story, were Joyce's maternal great-aunts; his great-grandfather Flynn owned the starch mill in Back Lane that figures in Gabriel's mimed anecdote about the treadmill horse and the statue of King Billy (Ellmann 1959, 17, 254–5). Gretta's story, about Michael Furey who stood in the rain outside her window on her last night in Galway, and died soon after, reworks Nora Barnacle's recollections about two of her Galway beaux, Michael (Sonny) Bodkin and Michael Feeney, both of whom died young of tuberculosis (Maddox 15–18; Ellmann 1959, 164, 252).

Joyce intermixes 'The Dead Lover's Return' motif with Nora's anecdote. The Irish Folklore Collection contains four different versions of the motif from Ross barony, County Galway, where 'Michael Furey' is buried at Oughterard 'where his people came from' (*D* 221). These Galway versions (Irish Folklore Commission 920:562–4; IFC 574:430–2; Uí Ógáin 131) are particularly striking in the context of 'The Dead'. In all Irish versions, the girl does not know of the boy's death. She has already decided not to marry him, because she has heard he is 'no good'. He dies of a broken heart 'because the girl has locked the doors against him' (Uí Ógáin 132). The horse and horseback ride are absent as Joyce reworks the story, though Gabriel's and Gretta's cab ride to their hotel takes its place, this time with Gabriel as the dead lover with little to say. Miss O'Callaghan refers to the belief that 'you never cross O'Connell Bridge without seeing a white horse'; Gabriel does see 'a white man', the snow-covered statue of Daniel O'Connell, a sexually energetic man from the west, now habited like a ghost.

If Joyce thought of the Elizabethan equivalence of bed and grave, Gretta escapes the grave. The snowflakes on Michael Furey's grave recall the shreds of the girl's clothing found on the boy's grave in some versions. As Joyce reworks the traditional motif, he makes the dying boy's nocturnal visit to Gretta, when he shivered in the rain-soaked garden, a moment of intense love, so intense that, when Gretta describes it, though Michael Furey is not visible, he is nevertheless present in the Dublin hotel room, lit only by 'A ghostly light from the street lamp' (*D* 216). Bartell D'Arcy has summoned him into Gretta's memory by singing 'The Lass of Aughrim', the song Furey used to sing. The song foreshadows both his last visit to Gretta and the sexual disappointment Gabriel is to undergo: in 'The Lass of Aughrim', the lovers' roles are reversed; it is the woman who asks to be let in, the man who refuses:

> The dew wets my yellow locks,
> The rain wets my skin,
> The babe's cold in my arms,
> Oh Gregory, let me in! (*D* 504).

Furey is no conventional ghost, but he is *there*, so much so that he comes between Gabriel and Gretta. He cannot literally carry her off, but, though he cannot himself possess her, he can thwart Gabriel's amorous intentions.

But Furey also may bring salvation, freeing Gabriel from his death-in-life. Gretta's story makes Gabriel begin to wake from his emotional paralysis. Though his first response to the story is 'A vague terror . . . as if . . . some impalpable and vindictive being was coming against him, gathering forces against him in its vague world' (*D* 220), he overcomes his fear and hears the story out. It helps him to self-knowledge and self-confession. At the end, like the dead man's bride he embarks on that silent nocturnal journey across Ireland to the snowy graveyard in Oughterard.

A Portrait of the Artist as a Young Man begins with Mr Dedalus telling a story, the one about the moocow and Betty Byrne and the 'nicens little boy' who turns out to be baby tuckoo alias Stephen Dedalus—at once the protagonist of his father's story, and of his own. *Portrait* is deliberately self-centred. It excludes all that rich *seanchaí* lore about families and their secrets which is on display in *Dubliners*. We get only an interpolated story here and there, as when Davin tells Stephen of the lonely woman in the Ballyhoura cottage who seemed ready to give herself to him—a dreamy retelling of Synge's *In the Shadow of the Glen*, ironically told by a nationalist student who would probably have demonstrated against Synge's play.

Ulysses is in many ways a return to the *seanchaí* tradition of *Dubliners*. When we talk about *Ulysses*, we mostly talk about Bloom, Molly, and Stephen. We pay less attention to the novel's fourth major character, Simon Dedalus, Joyce's elaborate but in a sense polymorphic portrait of his father, John Joyce. Simon Dedalus/John Joyce is a frequent presence in *Ulysses*, either as himself or as one of his many avatars who share with him the *seanchaí* role: Martin Cunningham, Joe Hynes, the unnamed narrator of 'Cyclops', and other Dublin storytellers. Simon Dedalus and his cronies carry with them all the abundant lore and gossip of Dublin, as the traditional *seanchaí* preserves and narrates the lore and scandal of his bit of countryside. It was Daedalus the father, after all, who built the Labyrinth, and supplied son Icarus with the material for his wings. As one who knows and tells Dublin's stories, Simon Dedalus or each of his various avatars functions as an urban *seanchaí* retailing the folklore of the city. 'What is the city but the people?' Sicinius asks (*Coriolanus* 3.1.199). Simon builds

Dublin as Daedalus built the Labyrinth, and so looks forward to HCE as Masterbuilder of Dublin and of the Tower of Babel—a city of words, a tower of words. Is he Simon because of Christ's pun, which Joyce considered a justification of his punning method in *Finnegans Wake*? (Levin 185). 'Tu es Petrus, et super hanc petram aedificabo ecclesiam meam', Christ declares, when he changes Simon Bar-jona's name to Peter and makes him first among the Apostles: 'thou art Peter, and upon this rock [petram] I will build my church' (Matthew 16:17–18). *Ulysses* is built on the anecdotes of Simon and his cronies.

Doubly disguised as Leopold Bloom and Stephen Dedalus, Joyce himself plays the outsider in Ulysses. Bloom and Stephen are both excluded from the 'real' Dublin, often tantalizingly out of their reach, Bloom excluded because he is a Jew, Stephen because he is an artist. It is Simon Dedalus/ John Joyce, his cronies and avatars, who by knowing all Dublin's stories can tell the story of Dublin. Many stories in *Dubliners* are John Joyce's anecdotes about his own family, or his wife's family (Ellmann 1959, 17, 18–19). As a young man in Cork, before moving to Dublin, John Joyce 'prided himself on knowing the history of every house and householder . . . mastering all the local details'. Once settled in Dublin, he again established himself as an 'encyclopedia of local trivia' (Ellmann 1959, 12–13). When Stephen describes his father to Cranly ('A medical student, an oarsman, a tenor, an amateur actor, a shouting politician . . . something in a distillery, a taxgatherer, a bankrupt, and at present a praiser of his own past', he includes 'a storyteller' among 'his father's attributes' (*Portrait* 241). When John Joyce died, Joyce told a friend that 'The humour of *Ulysses* is his; its people are his friends. The book is his spittin' image' (Ellmann 1959, 21). But *Ulysses* belongs to John Joyce not just because of its humour. He and his friends gave Joyce all that richly detailed Dublin lore and gossip surrounding and sometimes defining the book's major characters, allowing us to see them as citizens as well as individuals.

Simon Dedalus and his cronies are a kind of chorus, busy at the ongoing conversation, richly allusive and circumstantial, which narrates the public and private activities of Dublin's citizens, and so *is* the Dublin of words that is the book. Their narratives often thwart the reader. They seem to impede the development of the story, but in fact they *are* the story. They surround Bloom and Stephen with their city. At the same time, the reader's sense of frustration at fragments of narrative, hints of scandal, arcane allusions to forgotten and often trivial events, means that the reader vicariously experiences that sense of being excluded which we all feel at our father's or grandfather's stories, that we have missed some event or adventure and can never really comprehend it, let alone experience it. The young Stephen is confused and marginalized during the Christmas dinner argument in *Portrait*. In *Ulysses* Bloom and Stephen share a sense of exclusion because they are maringalized by many of the people they encounter. As in so many Anglo-Irish novels and memoirs, there is a strong sense of division, apartness. Bloom and Stephen finally communicate with one another in 'Ithaca'— organized as a neat unequivocal series of questions which corresponds to Odysseus putting his house in order in *Odyssey*, Book XXII.

Bloom's knowledge of Dublin trivia is less extensive than that of Simon and the other gossips. Riding in Paddy Dignam's funeral cortege, he wonders, 'Who was he?' passing Sir Philip Crampton's 'memorial fountain bust' (*U* 76). He knows that a man selling bootlaces is an ex-solicitor, 'struck off the rolls' (*U* 77), but he does not know why, nor does he know if Mr Power really keeps a woman (*U* 77). When he tries to narrate a piece of gossip, 'the awfully good one that's going the rounds about Reuben J and the son', Simon Dedalus interrupts him with interjections, then Martin Cunningham 'thwarted [Bloom's] speech rudely' (*U* 78) and tells the story himself. Mulligan, Lyster, Best, and John Eglinton continually interrupt Stephen's exposition of his Shakespeare theory in 'Scylla and Charybdis', and he is pointedly not included among the *literati* invited to George Moore's that evening.

Stephen is often the subject of a kind of running commentary by Buck Mulligan. Ned Lambert is able to give John Henry Menton a brief but full biography of Bloom (*U* 87–8); later Nosey Flynn gives Davey Byrne a less accurate version (*U* 145–6). Bloom and Stephen and Molly are part of the Dublin narrative, but they neither control it nor express it. Simon Dedalus and his fellow *seanchaithe* tell stories, but the only story about them is the novel itself.

The collective narrative of these *seanchaithe* reflects Vico's theory, that the Homeric poems were not composed by a single author but are the collective product of Homeric society. The narrative is sometimes about public events: the escape of James Stephens, John F. Taylor's speech about the Irish language (*U* 116–17), Sir Frederick Falkiner's soft-heartedness when hearing 'a tale of woe' (*U* 264), the alleged jobbery that thwarted the development of Galway harbour (*U* 27), the possibility that Parnell is not really dead (*U* 93, 530). There are semi-public events—Reuben J. Dodd's stingy reward to his son's rescuer, the 'U.P.' postcard sent to the unsettled Mr Breen (*U* 130–1). But nothing remains private for long in Joyce's Dublin. There is no reason to believe that Blazes Boylan will not boast about his afternoon with Molly, and so make her even more a subject for gossip than she is already.

His affair with Polly Mooney 'would be sure to be talked of and his employer would be sure to hear of it', Bob Doran muses in 'The Boarding

House', just before the marital trap closes on him; 'Dublin is such a small city: everyone knows everyone else's business' (*D* 65–6). The narrator of 'Cyclops', another avatar of John Joyce/Simon Dedalus, proves the truth of Doran's observation—or has read *Dubliners*. 'Fitter for him to go home to the little sleepwalking bitch he married, Mooney, the bumbailiff's daughter', he comments, contemplating Doran drunk in Barney Kieran's pub:

> mother kept a kip in Hardwicke street, that used to be stravaging about the landings Bantam Lyons [who also lodged at Mrs Mooney's; *D* 65] told me that was stopping there at two in the morning without a stitch on her, exposing her person, open to all comers, fair field and no favour . . . Then see him of a Sunday with his little concubine of a wife, and she wagging her tail up the aisle of the chapel with her patent boots on her, no less, and her violets, nice as pie, doing the little lady. Jack Mooney's sister. And the old prostitute of a mother procuring rooms to street couples. Gob, Jack made him toe the line. Told him if he didn't patch up the pot, Jesus, he'd kick the shite out of him (*U* 249; 258).

Even in *Dubliners*, Bob Doran realized that Mrs Mooney's boarding house 'was beginning to get a certain fame' (*D* 66) as a house of ill fame. Now he too has acquired 'a certain fame'. Tricked and trapped into marriage with Polly, he has also become part of the story Dublin tells.

Simon Dedalus's Dublin *arcana* tends to be more allusive than stories the narrator of 'Cyclops' tells, but equally critical. Recalling Buck Mulligan, he sums him up personally, socially, and genealogically:

> That Mulligan is a contaminated bloody doubledyed ruffian by all accounts. His name stinks all over Dublin. But with the help of God and His blessed mother I'll make it my business to write a letter one of those days to his mother or his aunt or whatever she is that will open her eye as wide as a gate. I'll tickle his catastrophe, believe you me . . . A counterjumper's son. Selling tapes in my cousin, Peter Paul M'Swiney's (*U* 73).

Peter Paul McSwiney was John Joyce's first cousin once removed (Ellmann 1959, 12). Simon's threat to write a narrative of Mulligan's misdeeds is carried out by Joyce's unflattering portrayal of Gogarty as Mulligan in *Ulysses*.

Simon Dedalus knows that Paddy Dignam lost a job through drinking (*U* 85). He can hint darkly 'how our friend Fogarty [is] getting on', and comment when Mr Power points out the house where Childs was murdered: 'So it is, Mr Dedalus said. A gruesome case. Seymour Bushe got him off. Murdered his brother. Or so they said' (*U* 82). Dedalus relies on what 'they said'; Mr Power and Martin Cunningham note that the evidence was scanty and 'Only circumstantial'. As part of the continuum of Dublin lore, J.J. O'Molloy praises Bushe's defending speech, 'on the law of evidence' and quotes a passage from it describing Michelangelo's *Moses* (*U* 114–15). It is Dedalus who has told Bloom about Martin Cunningham's 'awful

drunkard of a wife' and described her 'Drunk about the place and capering
with Martin's umbrella' (*U* 80), Dedalus who remarks that 'Mrs Marion
Bloom has left off clothes of all descriptions,' and supplies her maiden
name, parentage ('Daughter of the regiment'), and birthplace, and certifies
her as Irish (*U* 221). Extended as it is through his avatars, his role looks
forward to *Finnegans Wake*, when the two washerwomen wash H.C.E.'s
dirty linen in public, calling his secrets to one another across the Liffey.

In *Finnegans Wake*, Joyce draws on legends of Finn Mac Cumhal, the
ballad 'Finnegan's Wake', the adventures of Parnell, legends of Isis and
Osiris, the resurrection of Tutankhamen with the 1922 discovery of his
tomb, and much else. But he also structures the book around some of
John Joyce's Dublin anecdotes. The elder Joyce often told the story of
Buckley, who, in the Crimean War, aimed at a splendidly uniformed
Russian general, then held his fire when he saw the man had his trousers
down and was defecating, but did fire when the general wiped himself
with a grassy turf (Ellmann 1959, 410–11). Another story from John
Joyce's repertoire that appears in *Finnegans Wake* described the argument
when a suit the Dublin tailor Kerse made for a hunchbacked Norwegian
sea captain did not fit:

> the captain berated the tailor for being unable to sew, whereupon the irate tailor
> denounced him for being impossible to fit. The subject was not promising, but
> it became, by the time John Joyce had retold it, wonderful farce, and it is one of
> the parables of native and outlander . . . which found their way into *Finnegans
> Wake*. If that book ever reached his father in the afterworld, James Joyce once
> said, John Joyce's comment would be, 'Well, he can't tell that story as I used to
> and that's one sure five!' (Ellmann 1959, 22–3).

These Dublin stories weave in and out of the Daedalian verbal
labyrinth that is *Finnegans Wake*. They reinforce the role of anecdote or
urban folklore—that is, gossip—in Joyce's work. *Dubliners*, *Ulysses*, and
Finnegans Wake derive from family secrets, family scandals which
become public, well known to the gossips of Dublin and often repeated.
Bloom's embarrassing secrets are the subject of a public trial in 'Circe';
Finnegans Wake circles endlessly around the possible exposure of H.C.E.'s
scandalous secret or secrets.

In Synge's *Playboy of the Western World*, Christy Mahon is a man with a
dangerous secret that he turns into the 'gallous' public story of how he killed
his father. 'He tells it lovely' (*Collected Works* 4: 103), and the story makes
him the playboy, successful at games and at words. Partly perhaps as reply
to Synge, partly as parody, Joyce supersedes his father by taking over his
father's stories and making them his own. 'Not a word out of you', says
Christy to his once dominant father as they exit at the end of *Playboy*. Old
Mahon has imagined a future of storytelling partnership: 'we'll have great

times from this out telling stories of the villainy of Mayo and the fools is here.' But Christy has another future in mind, with his father 'stewing my oatmeal and washing my spuds . . . Ten thousand blessings upon all that's here', he tells the denizens of Michael James Flaherty's Mayo pub as he exits,

> for you've turned me a likely gaffer in the end of all, the way I'll go romancing through a romping lifetime from this hour to the dawning of the judgment day (*Collected Works* 4: 173).

'The lowquacity of him!' Shaun exclaims, denouncing Shem the Penman: '. . . The last word in stolentelling! And what's more rightdown lowbrown schisthematic robblemint! . . . He store the tale of me shur' (*FW* 424.35–425.2). Stephen Dedalus/Icarus/James Joyce flies past his father, up and away, himself becoming storyteller, Master of Dublin's Secrets, fabulous artificer and artificer of fables.

Delivered as a lecture to the James Joyce Summer School, University College Dublin, July 1995. The portion dealing with 'The Sisters' was earlier delivered at the XIV International James Joyce Symposium, Seville, June 1994.

12

Mr Joker and Dr Hyde

Joyce's Politic Polyglot Polygraphs

Humptydump Dublin squeaks through his norse,
Humptydump Dublin hath a horrible vorse
And with all his kinks english
Plus his irismanx brogues
Humptydump Dublin's grandada of all rogues.
        Joyce, for the dust jacket of *Haveth Childers Everywhere* (1930)

Crackajolking away like a hearse on fire.
        Finnegans Wake (94.04)

When Falstaff reappears in Verdi's opera, he has, like Joyce, learned Italian, and a little Irish. Escaped from Shakespeare's English, he uses his new languages to protest the drubbing—verbal as well as physical— he has received from Mistress Ford and her co-conspirators, and to protest the universal domination of the English language—in Irish, *Béarla*—with a bilingual pun. '*Tutto nel mundo è burla*', he cries (Act 3, scene 2): 'the whole world's a joke', but also 'the whole world's English-speaking'.

To the young Oscar Wilde, the young Douglas Hyde, the young Bernard Shaw, the young John Synge, the young Stephen Dedalus, and certainly the young Padraic Pearse and the young James Joyce, this dominant English loomed as a powerful and challenging opponent. Wilde borrowed from Tennyson on Virgil to proclaim his own self-ennoblement as a 'lord of language' (Wilde 1964, 66), and it is English that he learned to rule. Hyde urged the Irish to abandon English and speak Irish. Shaw uses *Pygmalion* to remind the English that they cannot properly speak their own language; a Dubliner from Synge Street will show them how. Synge creates a new stage language of English words and Irish grammar, adapting the

References to Joyce's works are as follows: *CW, Critical Writings*; *D, Dubliners*; *FW, Finnegans Wake*; *P, Portrait*; *SH, Stephen Hero*; *U, Ulysses*. References to *Finnegans Wake* are to page and line of text.

translation methods of Hyde and Lady Gregory. Pearse follows Hyde, calling upon the Irish to repudiate the English language as well as English rule. Their various theories and methods culminate in Joyce, who masters English only to destroy it. Both mastery and destruction are ultimately political acts. They originate in his recognition that England ruled Ireland linguistically as well as politically, and that linguistic independence was as necessary as political independence. His declaration and achievement of that linguistic independence represents a radical 'exaggeration' (*FW* 3.07) of the efforts of Wilde, Shaw, and the rest, and at the same time parallels and even imitates the methods of contemporary political activists working to achieve Ireland's political independence.

As for Stephen Dedalus, he reminds the English-born Dean of Studies that he lives in 'Lower Drumcondra . . . where they speak the best English', but he is uneasy speaking with 'a countryman of Ben Jonson':

> —The language in which we are speaking is his before it is mine. How different are the words *home, Christ, ale, master,* on his lips and on mine! I cannot speak or write these words without unrest of spirit. His language, so familiar and so foreign, will always be for me an acquired speech. I have not made or accepted its words. My voice holds them at bay. My soul frets in the shadow of his language (*P* 188–9).

Stephen returns to this encounter at the very end of *Portrait*, when he discovers that tundish is 'English and good old English too. Damn the dean of studies and his funnel! What did he come here for to teach us his own language or to learn it from us?' The passage is followed by an encounter with an Irish-speaker (*P* 251), and the two passages together pose the terms of Stephen's dilemma: is he to cast his lot with English, the language of the oppressor, or is he to commit himself to Irish, as Davin urges (*P* 202–3)? Joyce eludes the dilemma. He will write English subversively, first undermining the grammatical and literary forms it has developed, then dissolving the words themselves.

Stephen Dedalus began his rebellion against English rule and language early, subversive even as an infant. When he sings, 'O, the wild rose blossoms/On the little green place,' he turns it into an Irish song and dissolves its language: 'O, the *green* wothe botheth' (*P* 7). He makes the rose green for hope, for Ireland, and, like Dante's brush, for Parnell. A green rose is a little rose or bud, that Dark Rosaleen who is Ireland—with perhaps a recollection of Wilde's defiant green carnation (for *wild* is greened), and even a foreshadowing of Bloom alias Virag alias Flower. At the same time, the English words themselves lose their shape and dissolve, as rose liquefies into wothe and blossoms sinks through bloweth into botheth. Neither text nor language remained fixed.

From the very beginning, then, Joyce and Stephen approach and appropriate the English language subversively, determined to break and bend it
to their own purposes. In his lecture 'Irlanda, Isola dei Santi e dei Savi'
(1907), delivered in Trieste in the language of Falstaff, Joyce describes
Ireland as a colony of Great Britain (*CW* 163), and recalls that the Irish
mocked Prince Albert in 1849 'by imitating the way he was said to lisp
English' (164). He narrates the long list of England's crimes against
Ireland, comparing them to the Belgian crimes against the natives of the
Congo that Roger Casement had recently revealed (166), defends the Irish
right to rebellion and separation, and ends with a vision of an Ireland that
is politically, intellectually, and even linguistically free of Great Britain,
ready to lead Europe spiritually:

> Is this country destined to resume its ancient position as the Hellas of the north
> some day? Is the Celtic mind . . . destined to enrich the civil conscience with new
> discoveries and new insights in the future? . . . It would be interesting . . . to see
> what might be the effects on our civilization of a revival of this race. The eco-
> nomic effects of the appearance of a rival island near England, a *bilingual* [italics
> mine], republican, self-centred, and enterprising island with its own commercial
> fleet, and its own consuls in every port in the world. And the moral effects of the
> appearance in old Europe of the Irish artist and thinker . . . (*CW* 172–3).

He goes on to recall Mangan, who translated Irish poems—that is, revived
them in the English language. Joyce speaks of Ireland 'reviving' or awaken-
ing, and finally imagines this resurrection as verbal, dramatic, aesthetic:
'the play that we have waited for so long' (174). He recognizes the right to
political rebellion, but it must be accompanied by linguistic and aesthetic
rebellion, with European rather than merely national effects.

Joyce's rhetoric of revivals and resurrections is that of the Fenians, the
Gaelic Revival and the Irish Literary Revival, and anticipates the similar—
perhaps inevitable—rhetoric of the Easter Rising, as well as the interlaced
resurrection themes of *Finnegans Wake*. Ireland as a nation will rise again,
this time as a bilingual republic. It will be a talking, teaching republic, bringing words to Europe in a play of talk, like the plays of Oscar Wilde—talk that
embodies subversive unsettling ideas. A political and verbal corpse, a country
dead and dumb, imagined at one moment on its death bed, at another as
long buried in the grave, will arise and speak, to instruct the world in radical
new ways of thought. We remember that Leopold Bloom, in Glasnevin
cemetery, imagines some device that would enable visitors to hear the voices
of the dead (*U* 93). Joyce was always fascinated by Sheridan Le Fanu's *The
House by the Church-Yard* (1863), in which an all-but-dead man is revived
long enough to speak, an episode repeated and parodied in *Finnegans Wake*.

All readers of Joyce are aware of his consistent interest in Irish politics,
and his frequent references to Irish political figures, from Isaac Butt and

Parnell to William Cosgrave and Eamon de Valera. Bloom spends time 'with some of them Sinner Fein', and assures Molly that Arthur Griffith is 'the coming man' (*U* 616); Dublin Castle believes that Bloom 'drew up . . . the Hungarian' plan (*U* 276), that is, developed the plan by which Irish members elected to Parliament would refuse to attend at Westminster, but meet instead in Dublin as the Parliament of Ireland—a proposal Griffith argued in *The Resurrection of Hungary* (1904), and Sinn Féin successfully adopted in the 1918 election. Joyce mocks Griffith's notorious antisemitism by attributing the plan to Bloom. When Joyce began *Finnegans Wake*, in March 1923, he commented obliquely on the new Irish Free State, with Parnell's betrayer, the despised Tim Healy, as Governor-General. In the first pages written (*FW* 380–2; Ellmann 1959, 801), Joyce remembered the last independent Irish King, Roderick or Ruari O'Connor (Ruaidrí Ua Conchobair, High King 1166–83), and at the same time commemorated Rory O'Connor, who began the Irish Civil War by seizing the Four Courts (14 April 1922), and was shot without trial by the Free State on 8 December 1922—two days after the Free State came officially into existence (*FW* 380–2). Later, 'Molochy wars bring the devil era' (*FW* 473): General Richard Mulcahy's forces defeat de Valera's supporters in the Civil War, but de Valera will eventually triumph and create Dev's—or the Devil's—Éire, a prophecy realized when 'Liam failed' (*FW* 25): William Cosgrave's Cumann na nGaedheal party lost the 1932 election to de Valera's party, Fianna Fáil.

But for Joyce literature and language were more important political issues than those commonly raised in revolutionary manifestoes or election addresses. In this he agreed with Yeats, who responded to Parnell's fall, and the consequent failure of parliamentary efforts to achieve Home Rule, by striving to create an Irish cultural identity as a prelude to political independence. Yeats had found a way for literature to be profoundly political without being conventionally propagandist. Yeats's literary nationalism was paralleled by Douglas Hyde's linguistic nationalism: Hyde called for an Irish-speaking Ireland in 1892, the year after Parnell's death, and a year later helped to found the Gaelic League.

The Gaelic League, with its programme of replacing English with Irish, is generally recognized as the nursery of the Easter Rising and of Irish political independence. Despite Hyde's insistence that the League remain non-political, the language issues it raised became intensely political, and are of crucial importance to Joyce's development as a writer. Stephen Dedalus is sardonic about the League's efforts to revive the Irish language, and he fears and flees the old Irish-speaker in the mountain cabin. But Joyce was much more interested in the League and the language issue. We know that he studied Irish more seriously than Stephen did, and for a longer period (O Hehir 1967, vii–x). Though he declined to write in Irish, and remained sceptical about the revival of the Irish language, he recognized the revolutionary implications in the project, for it called into question all assumptions about how one speaks or writes. Joyce, after all, was a teacher of language, living in Trieste, where a choice of language—Italian, German, Hungarian, Croatian—was a political act, where Hektor or Ettore Schmitz would become Italo Svevo. Though Joyce did not embrace Irish, he challenged the hegemony of English in a variety of ways. In *Stephen Hero*, when Madden connects Irish speaking with Irish independence, Stephen insists that he must work out both issues in art:

—And don't you think that every Irishman worthy of the name should be able to speak his native tongue?
—I really don't know.
—And don't you think that we as a race have a right to be free?
—O, don't ask me such questions, Madden. You can use these phrases of the platform but I can't.
—But surely you have some political opinions, man!
—I am going to think them out. I am an artist, don't you see? Do you believe that I am?
—O, yes, I know you are.
—Very well then, how the devil can you expect me to settle everything at once? Give me time (*P* 60).

Only in the slow processes of art can these issues be faced, reshaped, and become themselves the matter of art. Joyce attended Padraic Pearse's Irish class in Dublin, but 'couldn't stand Pearse's continual mockery of the language of the hated Sassenach, . . . particularly Pearse's ridiculing of the English word "thunder"' (Budgen, *Further Recollections* 10). Joyce responds in *Finnegans Wake* by evading English and Irish to create thunder out of all language, to speak, as artist and man of words, in the thunder-language in which God speak, all tongues at once.

Some of Joyce's ideas in his 1907 'Santi e . . . Savi' lecture echo ideas put forth by Douglas Hyde in the 1890s. Though Joyce did not adopt Irish, much of his work through *Ulysses* can, in one sense, be read as an extended meditation on, quarrel with, and revision of Hyde's efforts to promote an Irish culture based on the Irish language and Irish tradition, expressed in lectures, speeches, translations, and especially in Hyde's lecture 'The Necessity for De-Anglicising Ireland', delivered in Dublin in November 1892. *Finnegans Wake* continues the debate with Hyde, but in addition engages Hyde's most conspicuous disciple, Padraic Pearse, and especially Pearse's 1915 oration at the grave of O'Donovan Rossa. For Joyce the Book of Life was always initially the Book of Liffey.

Hyde's 1892 lecture, which led to the founding of the Gaelic League, insisted that the preservation of Irish was the best way to maintain an Irish identity, and heaped scorn upon the negative aspects of Irish nationalism, which abused England and English rule but made no effort to learn Irish or maintain Irish customs. Without Irish, then rapidly vanishing, 'the race will from henceforth be changed' and Ireland will be truly conquered when England has, in terms Hyde adapted from Jubainville, '"imposed upon us her language, that is to say, the form of our thoughts during every instant of our existence"' (Hyde 1986, 159–60). Hyde hints at political independence—he tended to be more explicit when lecturing in America (151)—but his peroration, like Joyce's, emphasizes culture: 'upon Irish lines alone can the Irish race once more become what it was of yore—one of the most original, artistic, literary, and charming peoples of Europe' (Hyde 1986, 170).

If Joyce responds to this by partly echoing it in his 'Santi e Savi' lecture, he responds more critically, and more evasively, in *Stephen Hero* and *Portrait*, as we have seen—though *Portrait* ends, like Hyde's lecture, with a turning towards Europe. In *Dubliners*, Irish, to Hyde 'like a corpse on the dissecting table' (161), is a dead language, and a language of the dead, repeated by Eveline's dying mother 'with foolish insistence:—Derevaun Seraun! Derevaun Seraun' (*Dubliners* 40)—a phrase for which no two Irish speakers can agree on a meaning. Or, alternatively, Irish is portrayed as an appendage of pseudo-culture—Kathleen Kearney, in 'A Mother', learns a little Irish and is said to be 'a believer in the language movement' (*D* 138).

'I have no hesitation at all in saying that every Irish-feeling Irishman, who hates the reproach of West-Britonism, should set himself to encourage the efforts which are being made to keep alive our great national tongue' Hyde declared (Hyde 1986, 160). Though 'West Briton' was a favourite reproach with Irish nationalists, it is the Gaelic Leaguer Miss Ivors who launches it at Gabriel Conroy (*D* 188, 190). Gabriel is 'sick' of his own country, and declares 'Irish is not my language' (*D* 189), but he learns the power of traditional Irish song when he sees Gretta listening as Bartell D'Arcy sings 'The Lass of Aughrim' in 'the old Irish tonality' (*D* 210), *sean-nós*. Though he has refused to join Miss Ivors on a visit to the Irish-speaking West, the song and Gretta's response to it summons Michael Furey from his lonely graveyard in Oughterard, and sends Gabriel himself on an intense imaginative journey across Ireland to a profoundly Irish place.

Michael Bodkin, the prototype for Michael Furey, was buried at Rahoon graveyard in Galway City (Ellmann 1982, 324), not at Oughterard. Joyce placed Furey in Oughterard because the village was associated with nationalist and linguistic issues, especially in Pearse's writings. There had been bitter struggles nearby during the Land War. It had remained Irish-speaking until the early years of the twentieth century, and Gaelic Revivalists deplored its gradual surrender to English; at the same time, in the village community hotels were being built for English-speaking visitors.

Pearse had a cottage at Rosmuc, in Connemara, not far away. In 1903 he championed Colm or Colum Wallace (Colm de Bhailís), a Gaelic poet living in the Oughterard Workhouse. He arranged a lodging and allowance for him, and published his poems, *Amhrai Amhrain Chuilm de Bhailis* (Dublin 1904), supplying a commentary and persuading Douglas Hyde to write a preface (Pearse, *Letters* 74; Edwards 90).

Gabriel Conroy's name may represent a complex theological/linguistic/ personal joke. The Archangel Gabriel announces her destiny to the Virgin Mary, that she is to bear God's son; his trumpet will signal the end of the world, and will raise all the dead. Conroy is a Munster and West of Ireland name, letting Joyce hint that Gabriel's 'people' (*D* 189), like Gretta's, come from Connaught—whence Joyce's own people ultimately derived, and where a Galway district near Oughterard is known as 'Joyce's Country'. Lily the maid pronounces Conroy with 'three syllables' (*D* 177), making him Connery, a frequent Western form of the name, close to Conaire, its Irish form.

In sacred art, paintings of the Annunciation often depict Gabriel with the Virgin, but it is also common to show her with the Dove, the iconograph for the Holy Ghost—the relationship Buck Mulligan celebrates in his 'ballad of joking Jesus' (*U* 16). Gabriel and Dove, then, are iconographically interchangeable. We can expect Joyce to have known that Pearse used the pseudonym 'Colm O Conaire' for stories and prose poems published in *An Claidheamh Soluis*, the Gaelic League's paper, in 1905–6 (Porter 30): Colm (dove) O Conaire, Dove Conroy. Pearse/O Conaire's writings emphasized the West as the real Ireland in ways Miss Ivors echoes (*D* 187–90). These pieces, written in Irish to celebrate an Irish-speaking area, were part of Pearse's campaign to restore the Irish language. As when he mocked Griffith's anti-semitism by making Bloom the originator of the Hungarian plan, Joyce mocks both Gabriel and Pearse by making Gabriel hostile to the West and to the Irish language, and naming him after the enthusiast who praised both.

From the beginning, Joyce characteristically adapted to his own purposes aspects of the movement for the Irish language as promulgated by Hyde and Pearse. He used the language movement, and the self-consciousness about language it developed, as a way of defining and underlining important themes in his own work. This remains true in *Ulysses*, perhaps most obviously in the 'Cyclops' episode, where the Citizen's words and actions present Irish nationalism and the related movements to restore the Irish language and Irish games as chauvinistic and excluding, not a liberation but a closing of ranks. The Citizen denies Bloom's right to call himself an Irishman, meanwhile carrying under his arm recent issues of Griffith's *United Irishman*, which contained Bloom's Hungarian plan

(*The Resurrection of Hungary*), endorsements of the language movement, and praise of those who had boycotted Jewish shopkeepers (Tracy 1965). Joyce uses Irish speaking sardonically: Mulligan, who has brought Haines, the English invader, into the tower, calls him 'The Sassenach' (*Ulysses* 8); Haines addresses the milk-woman in Irish, which she does not understand (*U* 12); the Citizen shouts the Sinn Féin slogan, '*Sinn Fein!* . . . *Sinn fein amhain!*' (*U* 251).

But Irish is used in subtler ways. As Bloom passes the National School, on his way to buy his pork kidney, he hears the scholars 'At their joggerfry', chanting the names of Irish islands, and thinks of his own Irish mountain: 'Mine. Slieve Bloom' (*U* 48). It is and it isn't. Bloom and the mountain share a name in English, and both are translations: Bloom translates Hungarian *Virag*, flower, as Bloom reminds us when he signs his letters to Martha Clifford, 'Henry Flower'. In *Irish Names of Places* (1869–1913), P.W. Joyce derived Slieve Bloom from *bládh* or *bláth*, flower, genitive *bláthanna*: Slieve Bloom, Bloom Mountain, Flower Mountain (three paragraphs later Bloom encounters a namesake, Moses Montefiore). But the mountain is in fact Slieve *bladhma*, the mountain of the flame, the mountain of the blaze (*bladhm*, gen. *bladhma*, flame, blaze): Blazes's Mountain. Joyce combines P.W. Joyce's mistake with Hyde's complaint, in 'The Necessity for De-Anglicising Ireland', that many Irish place-names 'have become almost wholly unrecognisable, through the ignorant West-Britonising of them' (Hyde 1986, 166), to foreshadow Bloom's rivalry with Blazes Boylan, and perhaps to hint that for Molly they are in some ways interchangeable.

In 'Aeolus', Professor MacHugh recalls a speech in defence of Irish originally delivered by John F. Taylor at a meeting of the Trinity College Historical Society, a hostile setting for such a speech, for Trinity strongly opposed any efforts to introduce Irish into the schools (Coffey 66–71, 74). The meeting was chaired by Justice Gerald Fitzgibbon, who was particularly committed to anglicising Ireland (Gifford 1974, 116). Fitzgibbon's speech had poured 'the proud man's contumely upon the new movement. It was then a new movement. We were weak, therefore worthless'. Taylor's extempore reply imagined that Fitzgibbon's arguments for the power and universality of English and the British Empire were spoken by a high priest of ancient Egypt, '*addressed to the youthful Moses*' (*U* 116–17; italics in original).

Both speeches had actually been delivered in October 1901, but Joyce made the situation more dramatic by making Trinity their setting—the actual setting was the King's Inns (Garvin 67). Taylor's speech was reported in several discrepant versions. Joyce's principal source seems to have been Yeats's *Reveries over Childhood and Youth* (*Autobiography* 64), but he altered cadences and language for dramatic effect. In fact, Joyce wrote the speech himself (Garvin 68).

Stephen's response is to think of Daniel O'Connell's speeches at 'monster meetings', which had failed to achieve the Repeal of the Union and are 'Gone with the wind' (*U* 118). Joyce took the speech more seriously. It is bombastic, but a few pages earlier we have been reminded of Michelangelo's Moses, *'horned and terrible'* (*U* 115), at once an image of a leader who had led his people out of bondage and a reminder of the artist's creative power. The speech echoes frequent analogs of Parnell with Moses, notably Lady Gregory's *The Deliverer* (1911), but emphasizes *'the language of the outlaw'*, that linguistic revolt which was Hyde's policy but never Parnell's. '—That is oratory, the professor said uncontradicted' (*U* 118), and Stephen's reverie does not argue. In 1924, Joyce chose this speech as 'the only reading from *Ulysses*' he would record, describing it to Sylvia Beach as 'the only passage that could be lifted out of *Ulysses* . . . and the only one that was "declamatory" and therefore suitable for recital . . . I have an idea that it was not for declamatory purposes alone that he chose this passage from Aeolus', Miss Beach goes on. 'I believe that it expressed something he wanted said and preserved in his own voice. As it rings out— "he lifted his voice above it boldly"—it is more, one feels, than mere oratory' (Beach 171). When Joyce recorded the speech, he was already writing *'in the language of the outlaw'*, rejecting English for the new language of *Finnegans Wake*.

Padraic Pearse's 'Oration at the Grave of O'Donovan Rossa', delivered in Glasnevin cemetery on 1 August 1915, is a political, indeed insurrectionary speech, a kind of verbal overture to the Easter Rising. It boldly proclaims a commitment to Irish independence, and evokes the memory of the 1867 Fenian Rebellion 'by the grave of this unrepentant Fenian' (Pearse 1922, 134).

Pearse deliberately merges issues of political and linguistic independence; three days earlier, Douglas Hyde had resigned as president of the Gaelic League (29 July), after Sinn Féin members, with Pearse's knowledge if not connivance (Edwards 231), had persuaded the League to add to its list of objectives a 'free' Ireland (Coffey 122–3). Pearse emphasized the new alliance of politics and the language movement. He began his speech with four brief paragraphs in Irish, and addressed his hearers as *'Gheala'*, the Irish, a word particularly associated with Irish-speaking and with the Fenians (Dinneen 507). When he shifted to English, it was to praise Rossa as 'that brave and splendid Gael . . . splendid in the Gaelic strength and clarity and truth of him. And all that splendour and pride and strength was compatible with a humility and a simplicity of devotion to Ireland, to all that was olden and beautiful and Gaelic in Ireland, the holiness and simplicity of patriotism of a Michael O'Clery or of an Eugene O'Growney'. The comparisons are instructive: O'Clery (1575–1643) was one of the Four Masters, who collected Irish history and traditions and recorded them in Irish; O'Growney (1863–99) was a founder of the Gaelic League and the author of its Irish lesson book. Rossa's dream, which Pearse endorses, is an 'Ireland as we of today would surely have her: not free merely, but Gaelic as well; not Gaelic merely, but free as well' (Pearse 1922, 135). Throughout the speech, Pearse's rhetoric mingles insurrection and resurrection in ways that are shared with *Finnegans Wake*:

> Life springs from death; and from the graves of patriot men and women spring living nations. The Defenders of this Realm . . . think that they have pacified Ireland . . . They think that they have foreseen everything, think that they have provided against everything; but the fools, the fools, the fools!—they have left us our Fenian dead, and while Ireland holds these graves, Ireland unfree shall never be at peace (136–7).

The prevalence of resurrection themes in *Finnegans Wake* is a critical commonplace. These themes are drawn from many sources, and certainly not from Pearse alone. But Joyce gives Pearse an important role in *Finnegans Wake*, merging him, as Persse O'Reilly/*perce-oreille* with Earwicker, in this manifestation ear-waker, one who penetrates and awakens the sleeping ear, but also Eire-waker or 'Eire-weeker' (*FW* 593.02) and 'Irewaker' (*FW* 59.27), the awakener of dead or sleeping Ireland. As Eireweeker he was out in Easter Week. As Irewaker, he is juxtaposed with Eiskaffier, a pun on the famous French chef Escoffier: 'Eiskaffier said . . . *Mon foie*, you wish to ave some homelette . . . Your hegg he must break himself' (*FW* 59.29–32). The passage combines Humpty Dumpty, the necessary violent action that must be performed to achieve certain results—here the violence of the Easter Rising to achieve Irish independence—and also the resurrection symbolism of eggs at Easter. Though Eiskaffier also puns on iced coffee (German *Eiskaffee*; Bonheim 27), it contains *ei*, egg, and implicitly the plural form, *eier*, an anagram for Eire. The mixture of German and French, and the reference to *foie*, usually associated with Strasbourg/Strassburg, a place of political and linguistic contention between France and Germany, connects the passage with language issues generally, and with that aspect of 'pearse orations' (*FW* 620.24). The connection is strengthened when we remember that the Dublin *Morning Post* disparagingly called Irish 'kitchen Kaffir' in 1905, an association emphasized in the food aspects of the passage. The *Post* was provoked by the Gaelic League's campaign to force postal authorities to accept mail addressed in Irish only, and by Pearse's appearance in court to argue the case of a Donegal man prosecuted for having his name on his cart in Irish. Roger Casement seized on the phrase 'kitchen Kaffir' and waved it like a banner above his own commitment to Irish in a letter to

Douglas Hyde. Hyde showed the letter to Pearse, who published it in *Uladh* (Inglis 120; Nowlan 21–2). The Easter Rising is a 'flasch' at 'pasch' (*FW* 594.16–17) and, punning on sun, 'Sonne fein, somme feehn avaunt! . . . Piers' aube' (*FW* 593.08–9). The Rising was to begin with the explosion of five bags of gelignite at the Magazine Fort in Phoenix Park; the Fort, its store of explosives, and Ireland would rise together. The stored explosives were inaccessible, and the gelignite did no serious damage (Caulfield 65–70), but this episode, and the 'flasch' it would have produced, presumably contribute to HCE's encountering 'a cad with a pipe . . . luciferant' near the Magazine Fort. The Cad addresses him in Irish, then asks the time; Earwicker thinks of 'fenian rising', and 'felt . . . unwishful . . . of being hurled into eternity right then', but gives the time as twelve (*FW* 35.11–33), the hour at which the Magazine was to have been exploded by the *Fianna Éireann*.

As Earwicker/ear-waker, Pearse is also 'the *Bug of the Deaf*' (*FW* 134.36), and therefore connected with Joyce's frequent use of the Egyptian *Book of the Dead*, a book about resurrection and how to achieve it. His mission is to waken Ireland deaf and Ireland dead, partly by raising the Fenians and partly by giving dumb Ireland back her own speech: 'Irise, Osirises! Be thy mouth given unto thee!' (*FW* 493.28). Here Pearse merges with Shem, whose roles include that of *sem* priest, in the *Book of the Dead* the central participant in the ritual of opening the mouth of the dead so that the mummy can speak the necessary formulae of salvation (Budge 1895, cxxxviii–cxli; Troy 75–6): 'he's the mannork of Arrahland oversense he horrhorrd his name in thuthunder . . . Tried mark, Easterlings . . . ledn us alones of your lungorge, parsonifier propounde of our . . . idol worts! . . . we're a drippindhrue gayleague all at ones. In the buginning is the woid' (*FW* 378.06–29).

Pearse's evocation of the Fenian dead, in language that mingles insurrection and resurrection, plays yet another important role in *Finnegans Wake*. One of the best known Fenians was James Stephens (1824–1901), whose escape from Dublin's Richmond Prison and passage out of Ireland, allegedly disguised as a bride, created a Dublin watchword for an ingenious person: 'the man that got away James Stephens' (*U* 56, 259, 395). As a travelling Fenian organizer in 1858, Stephens appears in police records as 'Shook' or 'Shooks', an anglicisation of his Irish *nom de guerre*, *An Seabhac*, the Hawk (O'Donovan Rossa 9; Ryan 1967, 100). In fact, Stephens anticipated those connections between Finn or Fenians rising, the Phoenix, and the *Book of the Dead* which shape so much of *Finnegans Wake*. Immediately after founding the Irish Revolutionary (or Republican) Brotherhood, soon to be known as Fenians, he had recruited most of the members of the Phoenix National and Literary Society, which O'Donovan

Rossa had founded in Skibbereen, ostensibly to preserve the Irish language, but in fact as a mask for organizing a Fenian rising which would revive the Irish nation (Sullivan 128).

Indeed, Stephens himself had risen from the dead. Wounded after serving as William Smith O'Brien's *aide-de-camp* during the Ballingarry rising (July 1848), he had escaped to France while his obituary appeared in the *Kilkenny Moderator* and his family went into mourning (Sullivan 125–6). Like the scribes of the *Book of Kells*—which merges with the *Book of the Dead* as 'our book of kills' (*FW* 482.33)—and the Egyptian scribes, whose hieroglyphs were believed to be a sacred secret script, Stephens used the letters of the alphabet to complicate, conceal, and mystify rather than communicate. His Fenian 'Circles' under four V's (provincial chiefs) were organized in nines: an A ('centre') commanded nine B's (captains), each with 9 C's (sergeants), each leading 9 D's (privates), in order to preserve secrecy (Denieffe 25).

Stephens's 'Hawk' sobriquet associates him with the Egyptian god Horus, the hawk son of Osiris and Isis; he assists her in resurrecting Osiris and is an important agent of resurrection in the *Book of the Dead* (Budge cxiv–cxvi). It also connects him with Dedalus, the fabulous artificer and 'hawklike man flying sunward above the sea' (*P* 169), and so with Stephen Dedalus. Stephens-the-Fenian is among the godfathers of Stephen Dedalus, as James, as Stephens, and as Hawk. Joyce's curious plan that James Stephens, the author of *The Crock of Gold* (1912), take responsibility for completing *Finnegans Wake* (Ellmann 1959, 604–6, 632), a book with no ending, hints at this. Joyce himself is continuing Stephens-the-Fenian's insurrectionary and resurrectionary work, not the other way round.

James Stephens, Douglas Hyde, Arthur Griffith and Padraic Pearse were all committed to the independence of Ireland, a goal they described in terms of resurrection. With varying degrees of intensity, they were also committed to the resurrection of the Irish language as necessary to that independence. The first goal was partly achieved with the setting up of the Irish Free State in 1922. The Free State's domestic and legislative independence more than fulfilled O'Connell's dream of Repeal of the Union, and Parnell's efforts for Home Rule. But it was not the independent Irish Republic for which the Fenians and the men of 1916 had fought. Despite the claim that its name in Irish, *Saorstát Éireann*, was 'the Irish equivalent of "Irish Republic"' (Kohn 37), the Free State was a self-governing British dominion. In Ireland, Republican opposition to the Free State caused the Civil War (1922–3) between de Valera's Republican followers and the Free State army, the Sinn Féin policy of abstention from participation in the Dáil until 1927, and was only partly mollified by de Valera's 1937 republic in all-but-name.

Joyce said comparatively little about Irish politics in his letters and conversations. But *Finnegans Wake* expresses his disappointment with the Free State, where the despised Tim Healy reigned as Governor-General, and later with de Valera's clerical-peasant regime. 'Now be aisy, good Mr. Finnimore . . . and don't be walking abroad,' the risen Finnegan is told. 'Sure you'd only lose yourself in Healiopolis now' (*FW* 24.16–18). Tim Healy's Ireland is no place for Rising Fenians. As for de Valera, Joyce includes him in puns on *Devil*. He is often Shaun, and so Shem's enemy and rival, especially as forger of documents. As Shaun, he is sometimes Set or Seth, the evil god responsible for the death of Osiris in the *Book of the Dead*, where he struggles against Horus, the Hawk. If 'Molochy wars bring the devil era' (*FW* 473.08), Dev's and the Devil's Ireland, 'our own sphoenix spark' (473.18) causes the 'sombrer opacities of the gloom' to be 'sphanished' (*FW* 473.20), a pun on de Valera's name, Cuban ancestry, and broad-brimmed hat. Though devilish, he introduces an *'inquisition . . . Da Valorem's Dominical Brayers'* (*FW* 342.10–11), at once Dominican inquisitors on the alert for heresy, St Dominick's 'canes Dominici', the hounds of the Lord, and the 'Broy Harriers', the anti-Blueshirt squad Colonel Broy created for de Valera in 1933, which quickly became known as the 'Broy Harriers', a pun on the Bray Harriers, a County Wicklow pack of hounds.

Joyce reminds us of de Valera's ability to be pedantically legalistic and yet evade the spirit of a law, by punning on Oliver Cromwell's 'Remove that bauble!', the Mace, when he suspended the House of Commons, and de Valera's removal of the Bible to a couch at 'the other end of the room' (Longford 256) when he signed the oath of allegiance to the King— after first carefully covering the text of the oath—in order to take his seat in the Dáil in August, 1927 (*FW* 71.16; 456.13; 579.10). There are also many references to Document No. 1, the 1921 Treaty that ended direct British rule and prepared for the Free State, and Document No. 2, de Valera's alternative text (*FW* 107.25; 109.12–13; 358.30; 369.24–25; 386.20; 390.29; 482.20; 528.33; 619.19). Joyce also recalls de Valera's acquiescence in the partition of Ireland and the creation of Northern Ireland, a betrayal of the Men of 1916. In many ways, de Valera contended with Tim Healy as the target of Joyce's political scorn (Garvin 136–51; Manganiello 169–89).

Clearly, then, Joyce continued to follow political developments in Ireland, and particularly to note de Valera's methods for subtly sabotaging the constitution of the Free State in order to create the very republic that the Free State had been designed to thwart. Born in the same year, and nourished on the same nationalist history, Joyce and de Valera were well aware that, at least since the Act of Union (1800), Irish political resistance to British rule had been creatively subversive, using British laws and institutions in a pedantically logical way in order to evade them. Daniel O'Connell had used British electoral laws and principles of representative government to obtain a result those laws had never intended, the right of Catholics to sit in Parliament. His simple method was to stand for Parliament, which the laws did not forbid, and then present himself at the bar of the House of Commons as a duly elected Member, thus emphasizing the discrepancy between the electors' right to chose their own representative and the House's initial refusal to seat him. He creatively used the British system and its tradition against itself. Parnell, taking his cue from Joseph Biggar, brilliantly used parliamentary forms and the tradition of unlimited debate to obstruct the work of the House of Commons and so gain attention for Irish problems. Arthur Griffith followed his own—or Bloom's—'Hungarian plan' in 1918, by running Sinn Féin candidates for the British Parliament, who promised that, once elected, they would instead gather in Dublin as the Parliament of Ireland. After inventing complicated ways of taking and not taking the obligatory oath to the King in order to take his seat in the Free State Parliament, de Valera later cynically used that oath during the 1936 Abdication Crisis to remove all references to the British Crown from the Free State Constitution, and abolish the office of Governor-General, creating a President instead. He had already subverted the office of Governor-General by appointing Domhnall Ó Buachalla, 'Don Gouverneur Buckley' (*FW* 375.23), to the post. Ó Buachalla was a Maynooth shopkeeper, whose sole function was to sign documents requiring his signature. He lived in a small suburban house rather than the Vice-Regal Lodge, travelled by bicycle, and made no public or social appearances, in order to diminish the importance of his office (Longford 290–3, 285).

   If Joyce presents de Valera as Devil in *Finnegans Wake*, he also presents him as Shaun, twin brother and alter ego. In his own progress towards literary independence he draws on the same Irish tradition of creative subversion, working within English—and Anglo-Irish—literary forms to subvert those forms, and the English language itself, as Irish activists subverted English political forms. He begins that process of literary subversion with *Dubliners* and *Portrait*, which he wrote more or less in tandem, and which constitute a kind of diptych, one focussing on the artist's environment and the other on his inner life. In *Dubliners* he turns his back on the tradition of explicit fiction to create a reticent form that culminates in an epiphany that is beyond words—or for which, at any rate, Joyce does not supply the words. His attempt to portray Dublin 'in a style of scrupulous meanness' as a 'centre of paralysis' (Joyce *Letters* 2:134) deliberately eschews vivacity of style or content. Though Dublin is 'supposed to be the second city of the British Empire' (*Letters* 2:122), it is a subjected city where action and initiative are impossible. Joyce invented a way of making this lack of action his subject. As for his subject matter, his difficulties with potential publishers indicate how revolutionary *Dubliners* was for anyone conditioned by contemporary English writing—to Joyce 'the laughing-stock of Europe' (*Letters* 2:134). It was equally revolutionary in the context of contemporary Anglo-Irish writing, which ignored urban life and favoured either the mythic past, the Big House, or the peasantry. At the same time, Joyce studied Dublin folkways as eagerly as an Anglo-Irish writer examining rural Ireland.

With *Portrait*, the title deliberately blurs the traditional distinction between literature and painting. The portrait itself is fluid rather than stable. Though *Portrait* is usually classified as a novel, it parodies rather than fulfils our expectations about that form. The form itself shifts from time to time, now a sermon, now a diary, now a philosophic dialogue examining its own aesthetic. And, like *Dubliners* and Joyce's subsequent books, it avoids traditional fixity of closure, pointing instead to insurrection and resurrection.

Yet *Portrait* is closer to the traditional English novel than *Ulysses*, where Joyce collapses—or explodes—the novel form which he pretends to accept. There is no plot in the ordinary sense, characters are daringly proliferated, and conventional narrative form repeatedly dissolves—into stream of consciousness, dramatic dialogue complete with stage directions, parody, catechism. *Ulysses* is made up of episodes, and originated in a short story intended for *Dubliners*; its episodic structure relates it to the Irish novel, which developed in the shade of the nineteenth-century English novel. The English novel developed to present the values of a stable, gradated society, dominated by a middle class. It was therefore unsuited to portraying Irish society, which was patently unstable, sharply divided politically, religiously, and economically, and essentially without a middle class. The English form did not adapt to Irish reality, and Irish novels were formal failures, proliferating episodes only tangentially related to the main plot, and indeed finding plot—a social and situational connective—an embarrassment. Joyce managed to adopt these seeming weaknesses and develop them into a method for portraying his fragmented society.

Joyce also fitted his novel to an older literary form, the epic: not only the *Odyssey*, but also the ancient Irish epic, the *Táin Bó Cúalnge* or 'Cattle Raid of Cooley', thus parodying Yeats's dramas of the heroic age and especially the poet's cult of Cuchulain, the hero of the *Táin*. Joyce alerts us to this material when Mulligan mocks Lady Gregory's version of the *Táin*, *Cuchulain of Muirthemne* (1902), and Yeats's fulsome praise of the book (*U* 177–8). Cuchulain, like Stephen Dedalus, has an avian ancestry, 'that clean hawk out of the air/That . . . begot this body of mine/Upon a mortal woman' (Yeats, *On Baile's Strand*, *Variorum Plays* 485). Stephen's fear of dogs parodies Cuchulain's *geas* or tabu against eating dog (Hyde, *Literary History* 348), his totemic animal. Queen Maeve is married to Ailill, but, like Molly, freely bestows her own sexual favors and dominates her husband. The men of Ulster suffer a mysterious ailment resembling the pangs of childbirth when their country is invaded and their cattle stolen (Gregory, *Cuchulain* 148; Hyde, *Literary History* 294), an episode that partly underlies 'Oxen of the Sun', while Stephen, as 'bullockbefriending bard' (*U* 29), and Bloom's plan for transporting cattle to the docks, hint at the bovine preoccupations of the *Táin*. Bloom's phallic lost key echoes the disappearance of Fergus's sword while he dallies with Maeve (Gregory, *Cuchulain* 157) and Ailill shares Bloom's voyeuristic instincts.

Like O'Connell, Parnell, Griffith, and de Valera, Joyce adopted and subverted English forms, severing his work from the English literary tradition as they had worked to sever Ireland from English governance. 'An Irishman will seldom behave as convention demands'. Joyce told Arthur Power; 'restraint is irksome to him. And so I have tried to write naturally, on an emotional basis as against an intellectual basis.' He goes on to endorse improvisation and lack of literary fixity: 'In writing one must create an endlessly changing surface, dictated by the mood and current impulse in contrast to the fixed mood of the classical style' (Power 95). Joyce adapts the Irish technique of political fluidity to literature, and, even more subversively, to language.

In *Dubliners*, Joyce's 'style of scrupulous meanness' mocks at the language he is using, as when he repeats *nice* in 'Clay', or shows us the banalities of Mr Hynes's poem in 'Ivy Day' and Father Purdon's sermon in 'Grace'. As we have seen, *Portrait* raises the issues of English linguistic rule and of speaking Irish, while 'O, the green wothe botheth' dissolves the sounds and shapes of English words. 'His destiny', Stephen punningly realizes, is 'to be elusive of' linguistic as well as 'social or religious orders' (*P* 162). With his 'usylessly unreadable' (*FW* 179:26–7) *Ulysses*, Joyce extends his war on the English language as well as on English literary form—beginning, ironically, in a martello tower built to defend Ireland from revolutionary ideas, and from any alliance between those ideas and Irish notions of rebellion. In 'Oxen of the Sun' he charts and parodies the rise and fall of written and spoken English, from its halting gestation out of Latin and Anglo-Saxon to deliquescence in the barbaric yawp of 'Alexander J. Christ Dowie' (*U* 349). Molly's soliloquy destroys the categories of sentence and paragraph as developed in English grammar, like a flood washing away all landmarks.

Joyce had no interest in replacing English with Irish, as Hyde and Pearse advocated. But their challenge to English is echoed explicitly in *Portrait*, explicitly and implicitly in *Ulysses*—and it is worth remembering that the Joyce family replaced English with Italian as their domestic language (Ellmann 1959, 401, 499). These challenges to the hegemony of English culminate in *Finnegans Wake*, where Joyce creates his own language in a daring act of linguistic independence: 'Are we speachin d'anglas landadge or are you sprakin sea Djoytsch?' (*FW* 485.12–13). 'I'm at the end of English', he told August Suter late in 1922, and he said it in French: '*Je suis au bout de l'anglais*' (Ellmann 1959, 559).

In *Finnegans Wake* Joyce carries his subversion of the novel form much further, and his assault on the English language becomes total war, or better perhaps total revolution—Stanislaus Joyce called it 'literary bolshevism' (Manganiello 183). English words are jumbled, hustled, buried, reversed, shrunk, exploded. They merge or half-merge into Norse, Irish, French, Italian, Samoan, Swahili. Joyce simultaneously reverses the evolution of the English language back into the inchoate gruntings of the Saxon forests and shapes English into a new 'equoangular trillitter' (*FW* 286.21–2) multilingua, the language that is perhaps yet to be. Multilingual puns create bilocution—'Two-Tongue Common' (*FW* 385.4–5)—or trilocution, a parody of St Patrick's shamrock—though St Patrick seems not to understand Irish (*FW* 54.14). A new quicksilver language constantly shifts and slides and changes shape, as words written in ink spread and blur and alter and flow into each other when the paper is submerged in water.

Here again Joyce is responding to and paralleling Irish linguistic politics. 'Impulsory irelitz' (*FW* 421.27) would exclude rather than include, as the chauvinistic Citizen excludes Bloom from the Irish polity, and lead to an inability to communicate, talking only with one's own mirror image:

> A password, thanks.
> Yes, pearse.
> Well, all be dumbed!
> O really?

There is a footnote to 'O really': 'O Evol, kool in the salg', 'O Love, look in the glas[s]' (*FW* 262.7–10, F2).

With the resurrection of Ireland as the Free State, it was possible to implement Hyde's and Pearse's dream of resurrecting the national language, one of the few issues about which Free Staters and Republicans agreed (Coffey 149). Article Four of the Free State Constitution (25 October 1922) declared: 'The National language of the Irish Free State (Saorstát Éireann) is the Irish language, but the English language shall be equally recognized as an official language' (Kohn 390). De Valera's 1937 Constitution for Éire called Irish 'the national language' and 'recognised' English as a second official language (Lyons 1973, 539). Douglas Hyde became the first President of Éire under this new Constitution. Irish had been introduced as a compulsory subject in Irish schools on 1 February 1922, the day before *Ulysses* was published. By describing the language of the country as other than the one the majority of its citizens habitually spoke, both constitutions raised issues about the use of language which *Finnegans Wake* explores.

Joyce was interested less in the establishment of Irish than in the ouster of English. Irish critics of *Finnegans Wake* were quick to recognize his linguistic rebellion. 'Joyce is . . . in several respects a champion spirit in the new national situation', wrote 'John Eglinton' (W.K. Magee) in 1929. 'In him, for the first time, the mind of Catholic Ireland triumphs over the Anglicism of the English language, and expatiates freely in the element of a universal language: an important achievement, for what has driven Catholic Ireland back upon the Irish language is the ascendancy in the English language of English literature, which . . . is 'saturated with Protestantism' . . . in Joyce literature has reached for the first time in Ireland a complete emancipation from Anglo-Saxon ideals' (Deming 2:459). In the same year, Sean O'Faolain, reviewing *Anna Livia Plurabelle*, responded more skeptically, but he too recognized that Joyce was trying to escape 'from the trammels of our imperfect speech to the greater freedom of a language that is at once virginal and ancient' (O'Faolain 1929, 179). *The Irish Times* described the completed *Finnegans Wake* as perhaps

> a new and wonderful work on English . . . [Joyce] may have considered it necessary to do this service for the language, so as to release it from the clogging effects of conventional accumulation and its tyranny over mind . . . Or he may have thought of taking up the duty . . . of adjusting language generally to the new speeds of earth and air . . . in this book a new language may have been born (*The Irish Times* 3 June 1939; Deming 2:692).

Not surprisingly, Joyce's severest English critic, Wyndham Lewis, condemned his linguistic experiments, a condemnation Joyce rejected in *Finnegans Wake* in political-linguistic terms by parodying Parnell's 'No man has a right to fix the boundary to the march of a nation' and Lewis's Nazi sympathies and Oxbridge accent: 'no mouth has the right to set a mearbound to the march of a landsmaul [*Landsmaal* was a Norwegian language movement resembling the Gaelic League] . . . the beast of boredom, common sense, lurking . . . down inside his loose Eating S.S. collar is gogoing of whisth to you sternly how . . . you must, how, in undivided reawlity draw the line somewhawre' (Manganiello 178; *FW* 292.26–32).

Whether we think of Joyce as sapping, undermining, flooding out English—and here the flow of Molly Bloom's soliloquy and the river theme that Anna Livia represents are important—or as exploding English, as the nineteenth-century Fenian 'professors of dynamite' or Dynamitards tried to blow up buildings to protest British rule—in *Stephen Hero*, Stephen calls his 'exposition of a . . . theory of aesthetic . . . "the first of my explosives"' (*SH* 85–6)—we must recognize the profoundly political implications of his attack on English, and its affinities with the political-linguistic independence which was the Gaelic League's goal as well as the specifically political independence through insurrection that linked the Fenians, the Irish Revolutionary Brotherhood, and Sinn Féin. His subversions of the English language represent a more revolutionary activity than de Valera's deliberate misreadings and rereadings and revisings of treaties and constitutions. De Valera subverted the political vocabulary; Joyce more drastically de-Anglicized Ireland by subverting the English language itself. The two men had more in common—certainly 'Two-tongue Common' (*FW* 385.4–5)—than eye trouble and their Swiss oculist. Each could be called 'the dibble's own doges for doublin existents!' (*FW* 578.13–14).

Joyce was determined to 'wipe alley english spooker, multaphoniaksically spuking, off the face of the erse' (*FW* 178.06–07). But, though the Irish struggle for political and linguistic independence had formed his polyglot politic, he would neither be 'ersed' (*FW* 285.11; 484.09) nor 'rehearsed' (*FW* 55.16), buried in the 'midden Erse clare language' (*FW* 488.25). He was instead 'covetous of his neighbour's word' (*FW* 172.30). 'Capped out of beurlads scoel' but indifferent to 'auracles who parles parses orileys' (*FW* 467.24–29), he expanded, exploded into a language at once individual and universal, hardly more accessible to the English speaker than to any other European. The voices of the dead—dead languages—mutter in the tongues of the living, as Pearse's oxymoronic 'dead generations' participate in the Easter Rising, to dethrone English and replace it with 'Djoytsch' (*FW* 485.13), a language of joyous resurrection. For Joyce, who called himself a socialist (Manganiello 66ff.), world revolution was word revolution, '*The abnihilisation of the etym*' (*FW* 353.22). To dissolve words is to dissolve language, and so to dissolve rhetoric, the straitening formulae of politics, law, and creeds, logical categories which inhibit and imprison—a dazzling and terrifying break into freedom.

In *Finnegans Wake*, Master builder Finnegan falls dead but he also rises from the dead, erection, insurrection, resurrection. Like Balbus, builder and stammerer, he will re-erect the Tower of Babel out of the linguistic divergence that caused it to fall. That tower becomes the new Bloomusalem, where all will be at home, where, as when the gift of tongues descended upon the Apostles (*Acts* 2:1–13), each will hear his own language, at a moment which dissolves all traditional religious, political, philosophic and linguistic categories. The moment and the language are universal. But for Joyce they originate in the ersal.

Reprinted with permission from *LIT* 1:3 (1900), pages 151–69. Copyright 1990 Gordon and Breach Publishers, Lausanne, Switzerland.

13

In the Heart of the
Theban Necropolis

Mummyscripts and Mummiescrypts
in *Finnegans Wake*

all the mummyscrips in Sick Bokes' Juncroom and the Chapters for the
Cunning of the Chapters of the Conning Fox by Tail
Finnegans Wake 156. 05

I am Yesterday; I know Tomorrow . . . I am the keeper of the
volume of the book of things which are
and of things which shall be   *Book of the Dead* 282

'Going to wake up Egypt a little'
Dickens, *Mystery of Edwin Drood*

According to *Lebor Gabála Erenn*, the *Book of Invasions* or *Book of the Taking of Ireland*, the version of their own history that the medieval Irish used to tell themselves, the Irish are descended from Noah through one Fenius, who was among those who tried to build the Tower of Babel. His son, Nel, became a linguist, learned all 72 languages engendered at Babel, and drew upon them all to create the language of the Gaels (*LG* 1:39; 143; 147). The Egyptian Pharaoh invited Nel to open a language academy—a forerunner of the Berlitz School where Joyce was employed in Trieste. So pleased was Pharaoh that he rewarded Nel with an estate beside the Red Sea, and the hand of his daughter, Scota or Scotia.

Scotia is the mother of us all, the Scotti, Irish and Scots, who moreover are all Nel's sons, Nelsons. Scota is specifically the mother of Gaedel Glas, whose name Goidelic and Gaelic preserve:

> Feni are named from Feinius—
> a meaning without secretiveness:
> Gaedil from comely Gaedel Glas,
> Scots from Scota (*Lebor Gahála* 2:87)

References to Joyce's work are as follows: *CW*, *Critical Writings*; *D*, *Dubliners*; *FW*, *Finnegans Wake*; *P*, *Portrait*; *U*, *Ulysses*. References to *Finnegans Wake* are to page and line of text.

In some accounts, it is Fenius or Gaedel who creates the Gaelic language. Settled on the Red Sea shore, Nel and Scota welcomed Moses and the Israelites on the last night of their flight out of Egypt, risking the wrath of the pursing Pharaoh. On that very night, Gaedel Glas was bitten by a poisonous snake. Moses cured him, and promised that when the Gaels came into that 'northern island of the world' (*LG* 2:61) that was destined to be their promised land, they would find it free of snakes and other poisonous creatures.

The Irish, then, are anciently descended from Egyptian royalty, a claim repeated by Geoffrey Keating in the seventeenth century (Keating 2:14–20) and Charles Vallancey in the eighteenth. In his 1907 Trieste lecture, 'Irlanda, Isola dei Santi e dei Savi', Joyce uncritically promulgates Vallancey's belief that the 'religion and civilization' of the ancient Irish 'were Egyptian' (*CW* 156). In the same lecture, he compares the present state of Ireland with that of Egypt, and connects both countries with the idea of resurrection: 'Ancient Ireland is dead just as ancient Egypt is dead. Its death chant has been sung, and on its gravestone has been placed the seal . . . If [Ireland] is truly capable of reviving, let her awake, or let her cover up her head and lie down decently in her grave forever' (*CW* 173–4). That passage contains a germ of *Finnegans Wake*.

An interest in Egypt was not uncommon among intellectuals of Joyce's generation. This was partly due to the rapid developments in Egyptian archaeology. Early nineteenth-century expeditions to Egypt had usually been hunting souvenirs or treasure, a tendency commemorated by the obelisks brought back to adorn London, Paris, and New York. Scientific archaeology really began in the 1850s with the work of Auguste Mariette, who died, a comparatively young man, a year before Joyce was born. Egyptology as a science established itself in the 1880s, developed by such figures as Gaston Maspero, Flinders Petrie, and E.A. Wallis Budge, and attracted popular attention with a series of spectacular discoveries or resurrections: Maspero's discovery of a great cache of royal mummies in 1881 and his clearing of the great temple at Karnak; Petrie's finds, including the lost Greek city of Naucratis in the Delta (1885) and the Temple of Medum (1891). Petrie makes several appearances in *Finnegans Wake*, usually in a context of graveyards and buried kings (*FW* 77.01; 350.27; 481.35; 610.03); Budge may also be present (*FW* 511.30).

These archaeologists became famous in an age of popular journalism. Their discoveries, together with those of Sir Arthur Evans in Crete—which played their part in the naming of Stephen Dedalus (Fortuna 123–5, 134)—were described at length, with lavish illustrations, in the newspapers of the day, culminating in the orgy of press coverage provoked by the discovery of Tutankhamen's nearly intact tomb in 1922.

At the same time, there was a parallel fascination with the supposed occult lore of ancient Egypt. In the Dublin of Joyce's youth, AE's Hermetic Society drew upon Egyptian esoterica, and Yeats was an eager reader of Helena Blavatsky's *Isis Unveiled* (1877). The Tarot pack, so popular with nineties cabbalists, supposedly emblematized the 42 nomes or districts of ancient Egypt and their local deities, and gave access to Egyptian secrets. The search for secret doctrines and secret truths continues vigorously into our own time in the works of such writers as Edgar Cayce, or Peter Lemesurier's *The Great Pyramid Decoded* (1977). That Joyce was not immune from this interest is shown by his early possession of Henry Olcott's *A Buddhist Catechism*, published by the Theosophical Society, and of W. Marsham Adams's 'decoding' of the great Pyramid, *The House of the Hidden Places* (Slocum 177).

Thanks to the recurrent discoveries of tombs and mummies, and the association of Egypt with the occult, there was also a popular strain of horror fiction featuring ancient but effective curses, and mummies coming back to life: H. Rider Haggard's *Cleopatra* (1889), Bram Stoker's *The Jewel of Seven Stars* (1903), Ambrose Pratt's *The Living Mummy* (1911), supplemented by such silent horror films as *La Momie du roi* (1909) and *The Mummy* (1912). These fictions in turn contributed to legends of the Pharaoh's curse on archaeologists, especially in the legend of Tutankhamen's curse, 'Tuttut's cess' in *Finnegans Wake* (29.28), which has been credited with wiping out whole faculties of archaeologists.

As Joyce's comparison of Edwardian Egypt and Edwardian Ireland suggests, Egypt was also of interest to contemporary Dubliners as a political metaphor. Lady Gregory's *The Deliverer* (1911) portrays Parnell as a Moses trying to lead his people out of captivity; they are an all-too-Irish crowd, afraid to follow him to the Promised Land, and instead stone him to death. In *Ulysses*, Stephen listens as Professor MacHugh repeats a speech defending the Irish language, which dramatized the debate as one adressed '*to the youthful Moses*' by an Egyptian high priest. Stephen's response   is his story about two 'Dublin vestals' who climb Nelson's Pillar in O'Connell Street to see the view: '*A Pisgah Sight of Palestine or The Parable of the Plums*' (*U* 117,122); Moses, it will be recalled, failed to enter the Promised Land, and was merely allowed to glimpse it from Mount Pisgah.

Irish nationalists in Joyce's Dublin frequently argued that contemporary Egypt should be free from British rule. Lady Gregory began her literary career with a sympathetic account of the life and activities of Ahmed Arabi Bey, published in *The Times* (London, 23 October 1882) and later as a pamphlet. Arabi's efforts to establish a responsible Egyptian government, and free Egypt from Franco-British financial control, caused the British to bombard Alexandria (11 July 1882), thus laying, as

E.M. Forster put it, 'the basis of our intercourse with modern Egypt' (Forster 24). Arabi was exiled to Ceylon. Lady Gregory was recruited to the Egyptian cause by Wilfrid Scawen Blunt, who simultaneously advocated Egyptian independence and Irish Home Rule. Blunt hired Joyce's friend Fred Ryan to edit *Egypt* (1907–13), a journal opposing British rule in Egypt; as editor, with John Eglinton, of *Danu* (1904–5), Ryan had published Joyce's 'My love is in a light attire', and loaned two shillings to Stephen Dedalus (*U* 25, 176). G.B. Shaw devoted much of his preface to *John Bull's Other Island* (1904) to denouncing an atrocity carried out in Egypt by British officers.

Joyce, who loved to read the topography of Dublin or the seemingly random accumulation of objects as texts, would almost certainly have seen and remembered the juxtaposition, in the Long Room of Trinity College Dublin Library, of a harp, allegedly once the property of Brian Boru, the prototype of the national emblem as depicted on Ireland's coinage; the *Book of Kells*; and a full-sized plaster replica of the Rosetta Stone, which had provided Jacques-Joseph Champollion with the key to understanding Egyptian hieroglyphics. Placed in the Long Room around 1892 by Thomas Kingsmill Abbott, Trinity's librarian, the Stone, in its triplicity of language—hieroglyphs, demotic script, and Greek—was to become, like the *Book of Kells*, a prototype for the polylingual *Finnegans Wake*:

> was I not rosetted on two stellas of little Egypt? had not I rockcut readers, hieros, gregos and democriticos?: triacastellated, bimedallised: and by my sevendialed changing charties Hibernska Ulitzkas made not I to pass through twelve Thread-needles and Newgade and Vicus Veneris to cooinsight? (*FW* 551.30–4).

Rosetta is a diminutive, little rose, or, as she would be called in Ireland, Rosaleen—dark Rosaleen, because the Rosetta Stone is a slab of black basalt. Joyce does not invent but rather discovers—or he invents in the sense that the Church celebrates the Invention—finding—of the Cross. By setting the Rosetta Stone next to Brian Boru's harp and the *Book of Kells*, librarian Abbott suggested an affinity between ancient Egypt and Ireland which Joyce was able to read

Standing on the steps of the National Library in *Portrait*, Stephen Dedalus thinks of 'the hawklike man whose name he bore soaring out of his captivity on osierwoven wings', only to add simultaneously an Egyptian and an Irish element, Egyptian Thoth, 'the god of writers, writing with a reed upon a tablet and bearing on his narrow ibis head the cusped moon . . . he knew that he would not have remembered the god's name but that it was like an Irish oath' (*Portrait* 225)—*thauss* [pronounced *thoth*] *ag Dhee*, God knows (P.W. Joyce 1910, 69; Gifford 1982, 268); or *Tá a fhios* [pron. *thoth*] *ag fia*, heaven knows. Back in the Library in *Ulysses*, Stephen thinks again of

'Thoth, god of libraries, a birdgod, moonycrowned' (*U* 159); in *Finnegans Wake*, Thoth is sometimes Shem the Penman, sometimes Shaun the Post. Joyce's early interest in ancient Egypt is evident from his 1902 purchase of W. Marsham Adams's *The House of the Hidden Places: A Clue to the Creed of Early Egypt from Egyptian Sources* (1895). Adams's book shaped Joyce's perception of the Egyptian doctrine of bodily resurrection. Combined with his later discovery of the *Book of the Dead* in Budge's several editions and translations, and later with the impact of Howard Carter's discovery of Tutankhamen's tomb, Adams's book is one of the primary 'books at the Wake', though not mentioned by James Atherton.

Let us begin with the *Book of the Dead*, which eventually became Joyce's major source for Egyptian doctrines and allusions. Joyce told Miss Weaver (28 May 1929) that he hoped to follow *An Exagmination* with a set of four long essays, one, by Harry Crosby, to connect 'the treatment of night' in *Finnegans Wake* with the *Book of the Dead* and *The Dark Night of the Soul* by St John of the Cross (*Letters* 1:281). Writing, presumably, with Joyce's connivance, Frank Budgen cites the *Book of the Dead* among the 'constantly recurring themes' (Budgen 1941, 364) of *Finnegans Wake*, as indeed it is, with frequent references to its gods and formulae.

We know that Joyce studied a lavishly produced facsimile of the best and fullest text of the *Book of the Dead*, the *Papyrus of Ani*, edited by E.A. Wallis Budge (1890), and also Budge's later (1895) translation of the text. Like the *Book of Kells*, the hieroglyphic *Book of the Dead* is pictorial—a book that cannot really be read. The famous 'Tunc' page of the Irish manuscript recalls the frequent appearance in the *Book of the Dead* of the *ankh*, or tau cross, an Egyptian symbol of life and so of rebirth, contained in Tutankhamen's name; Joyce continues the rebirth theme by using *tunc* as an anagram for *cunt*, and aptly conflates the Egyptian and Irish books into what he calls 'our book of kills' (*FW* 482.33).

The *Book of the Dead* is ancient Egypt's epic. Like *Finnegans Wake* it is an epic of which Everyman is the hero, and, again like *Finnegans Wake*, it is a manual of resurrection. For the Egyptians, the individual's adventures continued after death, in a journey through an underworld full of traps and perils, each to be surmounted only if one can honestly claim to have lived a virtuous life, can remember and pronounce the right formulae, and can address the various guardians and gate-keepers of the underworld by their proper names and titles. If Odysseus must outwit monsters and human enemies, and the seeker after the Grail must know the right questions to ask, each individual Egyptian, whether Pharaoh, priest, noble or peasant, must answer correctly to achieve salvation by becoming the resurrected god Osiris.

The *Book of the Dead* charts the journey through the underworld, and supplies the necessary formulae which allow the soul to perform that journey. It simultaneously narrates, guides, and predicts the soul's success-ful journey, its triumph over death and darkness. Though the hero is in a sense the god Osiris, at once dead and alive, each individual man or woman becomes the hero by becoming part of the epic text. A complete text was part of the burial furniture of kings, priests, and nobles, sometimes as papyrus scrolls, sometimes carved and painted on the walls of the tomb and on the coffins and sarcophagus. The poor had to make do with an abridged version, often very brief. But whether king or scavenger, the scribe who prepared the text filled in the name of the purchaser, so that he or she became the heroic traveller in realms of darkness. Each Egyptian became posthumously the hero of the national epic—a remarkable concept in a hierarchic society. The *Book of the Dead* is a truly democratic epic. As such, it became a model for Joyce's Everyman hero, HCE—Here Comes Everybody.

Death and sleep have traditionally been compared, and for Joyce the *Book of the Dead* and its journey through the dark underground of Amenti, the hidden place, offered a partial framework for a book about the dark place where we go when we sleep. In Amenti the soul of the deceased traversed a dark and dangerous terrain inhabited by ferocious beasts and monsters. To pass safety it was necessary to be a lord of language: to remember the correct spells and formulae, and to be able to mount a successful moral self-defence before Osiris, the resurrected god, who judged the dead.

The soul must be able to name things correctly. In the world of dream-ing that is *Finnegans Wake*, things refuse to be named. Words are fluid, as they shift by punning. The dreaming protagonist moves through a world that continually threatens not to mean. The reader does the same, but strug-gles to make sense, as the ancient Egyptian struggled to name the various obstacles correctly and so pass them by. The reader tries to understand the words in all their manifold multilingual meanings—to unwrap them.

Joyce's dreaming protagonist also suffers from guilt. His dreams are uneasy because certain embarrassing incidents and motions involving sex keep reappearing, clothed in different words, accusations that must be met. Dreams do dwell on such submerged anxieties, and the reader undergoes them vicariously by his/her own anxiety about understanding the text. If *Finnegans Wake* has a moral, it is to make the reader recognize his/her capacity for confusion, frustration, evasion, suppression. The trial of HCE, conducted at intervals, tries to bring his sins forward, as does the trial of the soul before Osiris, in Joyce's phrase 'Muster of the Hidden Life' (*FW* 499.15). *Finnegans Wake* is at once *Divina commedia* and Examination of Conscience.

Since *Finnegans Wake* is about resurrection, it is not surprising that Joyce drew on the *Book of the Dead*, more properly known as the *Book of Coming*

Forth by Day, or *Coming Forth into the Day*, a kind of do-it-yourself manual of resurrection. But he supplemented this with W. Masham Adams's *House of the Hidden Places*, an essential element in Joyce's localizing or Dublinizing the Egyptian resurrection doctrines and rituals. Adams argued that the arrangement of passageways and chambers inside the Great Pyramid reflected the stages of the soul's progress through the dark underworld as ordained in the *Book of the Dead*. In other words, the Pyramid was a kind of theatre for the re-enactment of the soul's ascent to Osiris, and eventual merger into his godhead. Later, as Joyce would have learned from Budge, the *Book of the Dead* formed the basis of a ritual drama performed in various Egyptian temples to re-enact the death, trial, and resurrection of Osiris himself (Budge 1895: cxiii–cxiv).

As we have seen, Joyce acquired his copy of *The House of the Hidden Places* in 1902. He may have been led to it by encountering Adams's article, 'The Mystery of Ancient Egypt', published in the *New Review* in December 1893. The article summarizes some of the main points of Adams's book, and emphasizes an important part of his thesis: that the *Book of the Dead* exists in two forms, in the written text and also in the physical structure of the Great Pyramid, the 'enigma in writing' paralleling 'the enigma in stone' (Adams 1893, 618). Joyce's habit of treating a cityscape, a house, a room as a text to be read owes much to his reading of Giambattista Vico, but his treatment of structure as text, especially as combined with the *Book of the Dead*, also draws heavily on Adams's theories.

'. . . The masonic symbolism of the Grand Pyramid affords a simple and practically indestructible means for perpetuating without betraying the doctrine of Egyptian wisdom', Adams declares;

> That expression, once formulated, was never repeated; the other tombs and Pyramids of Egypt claiming kinship only by subordinate and particular features with the work of the Grand Master. While then the written records of the Ritual . . . were liable to change and error, no lapse of time could impair, no variation could affect in the secret places, the masonry of the Pyramid of Light. This embodiment, at once secret and unalterable, forming literally a Masonic Ritual of the whole doctrine of light, accounts for the singularly piecemeal fashion in which the sacred words were committed to writing (Adams, *House* 36–7).

Adams's book collates the *Book of the Dead* with the pyramid's architecture. Not surprisingly, his emphasis on masonry leads him at times to echo terms and ideas from Freemasonry, though he does not claim to be exploring the origins of Masonic ritual. The pyramid is the setting for a ritual progress through darkness to light, as the 'Postulant' enters from the north through the 'Entrance Passage of the Pole Star' to move through chambers of 'Deep Water' and 'Central Fire', the great 'Double Hall of Truth', and finally enter the 'Chamber of the Grand Orient', to encounter Osiris, 'Grand Master of the Hidden Places'.

As a possible setting for a ritual passage through darkness into light, Adams's pyramid becomes a kind of gloss on the *Book of the Dead* and its rituals—rituals which, apparently, one need not die to perform. More boldly, Adams argued that both Pyramid and *Book of the Dead*, collated as they are, represent Egypt itself. The entire country was therefore a text, embodying the morally and literally regenerative doctrines of Egyptian religion. Landscape, map, Pyramid, *Book of the Dead*, and religious doctrine mirrored one another and could serve to correct or corroborate one another (Adams, *House* 62–6):

> . . . the chief localities on the material Nile represented the different stages on the Path of Light . . . In the masonic record therefore, the House of Osiris, we have a key to the whole politico-religious constitution of the country (Adams, *House* 97–100).

The Great Pyramid, and presumably the other texts, written and unwritten, served also as an exact Sothic calendar (*House* 140–1).

Adams describes the Pyramid as a stone image of the Delta, its Δ signifying the most sacred part of Egypt, where the divine Osiris died and was restored to life by Isis. The Nile Delta, phallic like the Pyramid, is created by the Nile, perhaps as Isis fashioned out of clay a phallus—the one missing part—for the re-assembled Osiris, and then lay with him to conceive Horus, Osiris's son and avenger: '*How to Pull a Good Horuscoup even when Oldsire is Dead to the World*' (*FW* 105.28). Adams remarks that 'the form of the Pyramid enters into the hieroglyph of the star Sothis, or Sirius', adding,

> the form used in the hieroglyph of Sothis consists of the masonic portion alone Δ, that is to say, the structure which represented to the Egyptian mind the Eternal Light . . . a Papyrus dating from the time of Khufu, the founder of the building, speaks of Isis as the ruler of the Pyramid; . . . a later inscription . . . identifies her with 'The Divine Sothis, the Star, the Queen of the Heaven' (Adams, *House* 7–8).

At once sister and wife of Osiris, mother and sister of Horus, Isis recalls the entangled genealogy of the dreamer's family in *Finnegans Wake*: Issy is herself, but also becomes her mother, Anna Livia, the Liffey, river of life. Joyce's siglum for Anna Livia is again that pyramidal hieroglyph: Δ (J to H.S. Weaver, 24 March 1924, *Letters* 1:213).

Adams calls the Nile 'the life-giving river', 'the stately river, the source of perennial life', which 'alone permits the very existence of an Egyptian people' (Adams, *House* 16, 45, 51). As the Nile is for Egypt, so the Liffey is for Dublin—'Nilbud' on one occasion (*FW* 24.01)—in Joyce's local mythic cosmogony, creating the city along its banks. Anna Livia wears the moon-crescent or cow's horn headdress of Isis, 'curlicornies for her headdress' (*FW* 102.11); she is associated with the star Sothis and Isis's sacred cow (*FW* 14.02). The identification of Anna Livia with the water of life and with the Liffey hardly needs commentary, so thoroughly has it been examined by Joyce critics. Joyce connects the nineteenth-century search for the source of the Nile with a search for the source of the Liffey in a passage combining the Dogstar (Sothis/Sirius), Horus ('horuscens'), 'the child of Nilfit's father', a tomb ('cubilibum'), 'our turfbrown mummy', and the Egyptian ritual of opening the mouth of the dead: 'He lifts the lifewand and the dumb speak' (*FW* 194–5). Anna Livia has a 'nil ensemble' (*FW* 493.05).

The dreamer in *Finnegans Wake* has among his anxieties a fear that Anna Livia will go off with a Norwegian sailor. This partly recalls that it was in fact the Vikings who founded Dublin as a port and emporium. But Joyce also manipulates Egypt, the Nile, and Nel, ancestor of the Irish, to provide a rich cluster of references.

Critics have seen Parnell as a constant but concealed presence in *Finnegans Wake* (Glasheen 223), and indeed in virtually all of Joyce's work. Nel provides the second syllable of his name, and is associated, like Parnell, with Moses and a Promised Land. I suggest that Nel is also a concealed presence, perhaps the secret protagonist of *Finnegans Wake*, especially as maker and breaker of language.

Bored and out of sorts at his aunts' party, Gabriel Conroy pictures to himself the Wellington Monument in Phoenix Park (*Dubliners* 202), an Egyptian obelisk; the phallic obelisk encodes his sexual eagerness which Gretta will later disappoint. Joyce hints at this when he mocks George Roberts's timidity about naming actual Dublin places in 'Gas from a Burner' (1909):

> Shite and onions! Do you think I'll print
> The name of the Wellington Monument,
> Sydney Parade and Sandymount tram,
> Downes's cakeshop and Williams's jam? (*CW* 244).

In *Finnegans Wake* the Wellington Monument is the phallus of the giant who sleep beside the Liffey, his head at Howth and his toes at Castleknock, and so of HCE sleeping beside Anna Livia.

The Duke of Wellington and Admiral Lord Nelson, the military and naval heroes of the Napoleonic Wars, existed in Dublin as two phalli, with Nelson's Pillar, which stood in front of the General Post Office in O'Connell Street until 1966, much closer to Anna Livia. With Parnell and Daniel O'Connell, Nelson made up the trio of adulterers who adorned Dublin's main thoroughfare. As if to prove Joyce's belief that a city's streets, squares, and buildings constitute a text to be read, Dublin's city fathers and mothers have replaced the phallic pillar commemorating the Victor of the Nile with the vaginal statue and fountain depicting a supine Anna Livia as an Irish Cleopatra, the irreverently named 'Floozy in the Jacuzzi'. A city is a text that can be revised.

Nelson was created Baron Nelson of the Nile for his 1798 victory off the Delta, and the date of the battle was carved on the Pillar's plinth. Joyce lists the Great Pyramid and the Pharos or lighthouse at Alexandria along with Dublin's prominent statues, from Parnell's in Parnell Square—pointing at the nearby maternity hospital and declaring, 'No man can set a boundary to the march of a nation'—to Thomas Moore's, above a public urinal. In the centre is 'Nielsen, rare admirable' (*FW* 553.13). Joyce associates Horatio Nelson and his daughter with Horus (*FW* 328–9); atop his Pillar he is a 'god at the top of the staircase' (131.17) like Osiris, 'the being who is on top of the steps' (Budge 1895: 274) or 'god at the top of the staircase' (Budge 1909, xxxv; Rose 4), and 'Lord of ladders' (*FW* 566.35; Budge 1909, lxxiv; Rose 8). Here he conflates with Parnell. Joyce puns on ladder and leader, and the pun recalls an embarrassing episode in Parnell's career, when he allegedly left Mrs O'Shea's house by the fire-escape—a rope ladder (Lyons 1977, 239–41). The Finnegan of the eponymous ballad also fell from a ladder, to rise again. Joyce knew that the Easter Rising began at Nelson's Pillar, when Pearse proclaimed the Irish Republic outside the Post Office and placed a copy of the Proclamation on the plinth. The phallic Pillar is associated with the resurrection of Ireland, and the resurrection imagery of Pearse's rhetoric.

As 'Onehandled adulterer', Nelson broods over central Dublin in *Ulysses* (*U* 123). Blazes Boylan passes 'Horatio onehandled Nelson' (*U* 226) en route to his adulterous visit with Molly. Earlier she has thrown a coin to a one-legged sailor who then turns from Eccles Street into Nelson Street (*U* 185, 204), growling Nelson's signal at Trafalgar: '*England expects* . . .' Here the Book of the City reinforces Joyce's text, to comment obliquely on the adultery taking place on 16 June 1904.

Given the ancestral role of Nel, all the Irish are Nelsons, O'Neills, until 1966 tacitly reminded of their ancestry by the phallic pillar in their capital. As for Nelson, he is associated with Egypt like Nel, and specifically with the Delta like Osiris. His body was dismembered like Osiris's, and like the god he was for a time concealed in a barrel: Nelson's body was brought back from Trafalgar in a barrel of rum. When the sailors discovered this, they drank the rum.

Given Joyce's sense of city as text, Bygmester/Master Builder Finnegan is at once the builder of Dublin, and therefore the encoder of the bricks and mortar text of *Finnegans Wake* which Joyce transcribes. He is conflated with Cheops/Khufu, builder of the great Pyramid and encoder of the

Book of the Dead in its masonry. His fall from the ladder, death, and resurrection ape the Postulant's descent into the darkness of the Great Pyramid. In the ballad, Finnegan comes back to life after being sprinkled with whiskey, the water of life; 'I give the waters of life to every mummy', says the goddess who 'presides' over the waters of the 'Well of Life' in the depths of the Pyramid (Adams 1893, 623). The Soul climbs a ladder to re-enter life.

Apart from its general outline of Egyptian resurrection doctrine, and its equation of a written text with a text embodied in architecture, Adams's *House of the Hidden Places* also helped to shape Joyce's effort to achieve a universal language, at once the method and a central theme in *Finnegans Wake*, and a return to Nel and the Tower of Babel. In an earlier book, *The Drama of Empire*, advertised and summarized in advertisements contained in *House of the Hidden Places*, Adams argued that the human race originated in Africa, spreading from Egypt throughout the world:

> From the Delta of the Nile, under the shadow of the Pyramids, the primaeval colonists radiated forth . . . Eastward to Phoenicia and to Persia, Northward to Asia Minor and the Black Sea, Westward to Greece and Italy; and then, in its turn, each fresh settlement, as it overflowed its boundaries, 'radiated' forth in ever new waves of conquest (Adams, *House*, extra page 2).

One evidence of this was the universal presence of the patriarchal family. Joyce invents such a family in *Finnegans Wake*, and gives it universal significance. As for universal language, Adams's 1892 lecture 'The Origin and Diffusion of Literary Symbols' claimed that the characters of the ancient Egyptian and the Runic alphabets were almost identical, though possessing different phonetic values (Adams, *House*, extra pages 2–3). In *The House of the Hidden Places*, he equates Egyptian and Chinese names of religious festivals (*House* 188), proving, at least to his own satisfaction, that many names are the same, and that therefore both languages and both religious systems have a single origin in Egypt.

Adams also connects European languages with ancient Egyptian. Viking means 'Angle-dweller, that is, an Englishman' in the language of the Pharaohs (*House* 76), and recalls the importance of pyramidal angles, triangles, and the Delta Δ. The Norse god Odin's name means 'Destroyer' in Egyptian, 'and his standard, the raven, was the Egyptian symbol of destruction . . . his followers were distinguished by the winged headdress . . . borne by the sacred scribe of Egypt, bestowed by Ra upon Thoth.' The Norse god Asar is Osiris (*House* 77). Pirate apparently derives from pyramid, '"Pir Aa" . . . "Great House"', as does Pharaoh (*House* 70).

The idea of resurrection was never far from Joyce's mind, partly because of his Catholic upbringing, partly because the resurrection of Ireland was a staple of Irish political oratory in his youth. Though he ceased to be a churchgoer as a young man, he sometimes attended Holy Week services because of the music and liturgy (Ellmann 1959, 320), among them *Tenebrae*, the Good Friday service, during which the church was gradually darkened while the choir sang funeral hymns. The ceremony aesthetically and symbolically created at once an awareness of Christ's death and an expectation of the Resurrection. The churchgoer accepted the finality of the death, but knew that on Easter Sunday death would give place to life— the Osirian hope, Finnegan rising from the dead. For Joyce, as for the Irish leaders of 1916, *Tenebrae* and Good Friday had the further symbolism of an Ireland dead until the Easter Rising, inevitably central to a book about resurrection and Dublin.

E.A. Wallis Budge's versions of the *Book of the Dead* provided Joyce with a framework for *Finnegans Wake*, paralleling the soul's journey through the dark underworld with the sleeping soul's sojourn in the dark of night. Adams's *The House of the Hidden Places* suggested ways of relating that journey to the actual topography of Dublin, and suggested also a language suitable to a book about Everyman. But the catalyst that enabled Joyce to combine these elements into *Finnegans Wake* was the juxtaposition of two events: Howard Carter's discovery of Tutankhamen's nearly intact tomb in November 1922, and the almost simultaneous inauguration of the Irish Free State, the partially dismembered and semi-animate corpse of the Ireland that had risen in 1916.

Arthur Power noted Joyce's immediate interest in the discovery of the tomb, especially its 'religious aspects' (Power 48). Noticing references to Tutankhamen 'scattered evenly through' *Finnegans Wake*, Atherton comments, 'The discovery of his mummy seems to have been counted by Joyce as a resurrection, so he is a type of H.C.E.' (Atherton 195). Tutankhamen's 1922 resurrection is probably the reason why the *Book of the Dead* figures so importantly among the books at the wake. But the coincidence by which Tutankhamen and Ireland rose together from the dead is a more compelling reason. The Liffey and the Nile are a single river, Issy and Isis are one.

On 4 November 1922, Howard Carter's workmen found a buried step under debris which had accumulated in ancient times in connection with making a tomb for Rameses VI, a Pharaoh who reigned some centuries after Tutankhamen. The next day they excavated the complete stairway, culminating in a door bearing the seals of the necropolis, and Carter wired his patron, Lord Carnarvon:

AT LAST HAVE MADE WONDERFUL DISCOVERY . . . A MAGNIFICENT TOMB WITH SEALS INTACT; RE-COVERED SAME FOR YOUR ARRIVAL; CONGRATULATIONS.

Carnarvon reached the tomb on 23 November, and the next day Carter found the cartouche of Tutankhamen on the door—and evidence that robbers had penetrated the tomb in ancient times. The first door was opened on 24 November, and a corridor cleared; on 26 November, Carter broke through a second door and looked into the antechamber of the tomb. In reply to Carnarvon's question, 'Can you see anything?' Carter replied, 'Yes, wonderful things' (Carter 1: 87–96): the heaped-up scattered treasures which had been buried for three thousand years. The tomb was officially opened on 29 November, with the press in attendance. Carnarvon had given the *The Times* exclusive rights (Carter 1:143). *The Times* carried news of the sensational discovery on 30 November 1922 (13f); on that day, or on 1 December, Tutankhamen was on the front page of virtually every European and American newspaper. *The Times* published stories, interviews, statements and leading articles about the tomb, sometimes with photographs, almost daily throughout December 1922 and the early months of 1923, even though work on the excavation was suspended in February. When the archaeologists resumed their work in April, stories again began to appear almost daily. Most of *The Times* stories were widely reprinted by the European and American papers. Tutankhamen was an inescapable presence in every newspaper, especially after Lord Carnarvon's sudden death on 6 April 1923 provoked legends about Pharaonic curses and occult influences.

Joyce was an avid newspaper reader, and various references to Tutankhamen in *Finnegans Wake* suggest that he kept abreast of the story as it developed. He may also have read all or part of Howard Carter's three volume *The Tomb of Tut-Ankh-Amen* (1923–33), though most of what Carter reports had already appeared in the daily press, and some of his discoveries confirmed information about Egyptian ideas of resurrection already available to Joyce from Budge's edition of the *Book of the Dead* and his *Osiris and the Egyptian Resurrection* (1891). Tutankhamen appears in *Finnegans Wake* at least fourteen times, in Atherton's phrase, 'scattered evenly through the book' (Atherton 195). The god Osiris had been murdered by his evil brother Seth or Set, who cut the body into fourteen parts and scattered them throughout Egypt; the sorrowing Isis searched for and found them, and reunited them.

As 'headboddylwatcher of the chempel of Isid', Tutankhamen makes his initial appearance in the *Wake* as 'Totumcalmum', performing one of the verbal rituals of the *Book of the Dead* (*FW* 26.18). There are references to 'Tuttut's cess' (*FW* 29.28) and 'The bane of Tut' (*FW* 102.22). He is 'Tate and Comyng' (*FW* 295.8), 'Tutty Comyn' (*FW* 367.10), and 'Two-tongue Common' (*FW* 385.4), or reversed into 'Nema Knatut' (*FW* 395.23). As 'lord of Tuttu' he places 'that initial T square of burial jade upright to your temple a moment' (*FW* 486.14)—a reference to the often pictured application of the *ankh* or tau cross of life to the forehead of a mummy. Later he is 'Toot and Come-Inn' (*FW* 512.34) or 'twotime hemhaltshealing' (*FW* 611.28). He is hidden like the fragmented Osiris in 'tutus . . . tutus   . . . kinkinkankan' (*FW* 113.8–9). A 'finalley' is 'flat as Tut's fut' (291.4). One hint that Joyce read at least part of Howard Carter's report is the juxtaposition of 'Old grand tuttut toucher up of young poetographies' (*FW* 242.18–19) and 'persona erecta' (*FW* 242.13); and of 'Tutty his tour in his Nowhare's yarcht' (*FW* 335.29)—a reference to the dead King's journey in the boat of Ra—with 'where obelisk rises when odalisks fall' (*FW* 335.33). In both cases we are in Phoenix Park, in the vicinity of the Wellington Monument. H.C.E. had an embarrassing sexual encounter nearby, and the phallic obelisk itself is the penis of the sleeping giant Finn, who seems also to be an Egyptian mummy (*FW* 25). Describing the body of Tutankhamen after the mummy had been unwrapped, Carter tells us that 'the phallus had been drawn forward, wrapped independently, and then retained in the ithyphallic position by the perineal bandages' (Carter 2:156)—another rising to suggest resurrection.

But Tutankhamen's was not the only resurrection to figure in the newspapers in December 1922, and Joyce's use of the risen Pharaoh is closely connected with political events in Ireland. Dáil Éireann voted to accept the Anglo-Irish Treaty, giving Ireland dominion status within the British Empire, on 7 January 1922, against the wishes of Eamon de Valera and his supporters, who then left the Dáil. The remaining members elected a provisional government, chaired by Michael Collins, on 14 January, which took power until a Free State constitution could be drafted, and approved by both the Dáil and the British Parliament. Despite the outbreak of civil war (28 June), the death of Arthur Griffith (12 August), and the assassination of Collins (22 August), the constitution was completed and approved by 5 December. The Irish Free State began its official existence on 6 December 1922, a few days after the discovery of Tutankhamen's tomb was announced. Tim Healy, whom Joyce despised because of his betrayal of Parnell at the famous meeting in Committee Room 15, became Governor-General. The date was inauspicious: Healy had led the attack on Parnell on 6 December 1890.

In early December 1922 Irish newspapers were full of stories about the new constitution, the new government, the new state, along with stories about Tutankhamen's tomb. Elsewhere, Irish news received less prominence, but nevertheless appeared in the same newspaper issues as the news of the tomb's discovery.

Tutankhamen and Ireland had risen together from the dead, Ireland to carry out that resurrection predicted and defined nearly twenty years

earlier by Arthur Griffith in his *The Resurrection of Hungary* (1904)—
which originated, according to Martin Cunningham, with Leopold Bloom
(*U* 276). Throughout *Finnegans Wake*, Joyce associates this resurrected
Ireland with ancient Egypt, and the *Book of the Dead*. Dublin becomes
Healiopolis (*FW* 24.18), Tim Healy's city but also Egyptian Heliopolis,
where the Phoenix rises from its own ashes, a city associated in the *Book
of the Dead* with the resurrection of Osiris. There Heliopolis is Annu
(Budge 1895, cxxxiii; Rose 22), and so becomes for Joyce Annapolis, the
city of Anna Livia Plurabelle. 'I have performed the law in truth for the
lord of the law, Taif Alif', runs a parody of the *Book of the Dead*; 'I have
held out my hand for the holder of my heart in Annapolis, my youthrib
city' (*FW* 318.22–5). In Healiopolis, the dead man is urged to stay dead
and buried, surrounded by his tomb furniture:

> Now be aisy, good Mr Finnimore, sir. And take your laysure like a god on pen-
> sion and don't be walking abroad. Sure you'd only lose yourself in Healiopolis
> now . . . You're better off, sir, where you are, primesigned in the full of your
> dress, bloodeagle waistcoat and all, remembering your shapes and sizes on the
> pillow of your babycurls under your sycamore by the keld water . . . and have all
> you want, pouch, gloves, flask, bricket, kerchief, ring and amberulla, the whole
> treasure of the pyre, in the land of souls . . . Not shabbty little imagettes . . . So
> may the priest of seven worms and scalding tayboil . . . come never anear you as
> your hair grows wheater beside the Liffey that's in Heaven! . . . The whole bag
> of kits, falconplumes and jackboots incloted, is where you flung them that time.
> Your heart is in the system of the Shewolf and your crested head is in the tropic
> of Copricaporn. Your feet are in the cloister of Virgo . . . Be not unrested! . . .
> Totumcalmum, saith: I know thee, metherjar, I know thee, salvation boat. For
> we have performed upon thee . . . all the things . . . ordered concerning thee in
> the matter of the work of thy tombing (*FW* 24–6).

The 'bloodeagle waistcoat' is presumably Tutankhamen's pectoral in 'the
form of a solar hawk of gold' (Carter 2:126) or his 'large pectoral-hawk-
collar in chased sheet gold' (121). The tomb also contained his head-rests
(Carter 3:116), gloves, shoes, head-coverings, and *Shawabti* figures,
images of workers and servants who will tend to the King's needs, as well
as celestial or solar boats. The heaped up profusion of the tomb's contents,
arbitrarily and hastily re-arranged after the initial break-in by tomb-
robbers, suggests the arrangement of *Finnegans Wake* itself.

Carter reminded his readers that, according to the *Book of the Dead*, 'the
palette, or the scribe's outfit, was essential for the deceased. They were the
implements of Thoth, the god of speech, writing and mathematics' (Carter
3:79). Tutankhamen's resurrection as Osiris depended on his ability to
read the *Book of the Dead*, and *Finnegans Wake* promises an analogous
resurrection. *Finnegans Wake* is pervaded with archaeology, especially
when Belinda the Hen digs up Shem's letter from the litter heap (*FW*

110–11; 420–1)—a letter that is in fact *Finnegans Wake* itself (Garvin 122). As a text that can be read in various ways, with each word potentially exfoliating into two, three, or more meanings and languages, it recalls the 'trifolium librotto' which is at once the Rosetta Stone and the 'Book of Lief' (*FW* 425.20).

Osiris was avenged by his brother-son, the god Horus, usually depicted as a hawk, and it is Horus who gives the dead man back a voice and guides him to salvation. As hawk, Horus connects with Dedalus, 'a hawklike man flying sunward above the sea' (*Portrait* 169), and with the nineteenth-century Fenian 'Head Center', James Stephens (1825–1901), who appears in police records under his alias, 'Mr Shook', in Irish 'an Seabhac', the Hawk. Stephen Dedalus is doubly named for the hawk, and performs Horus's function of opening the mouths of the dead so that they may speak. Ireland rising from the grave of history, Tutankhamen rising from the tomb, become each other:

> —Let Eivin bemember for Gates of Gold for their fadeless suns berayed her. Irise, Osirises! Be thy mouth given unto thee! . . . The overseer of the house of the oversire of the seas, Nu-Men, triumphant, sayeth: Fly as the hawk, cry as the corncrake, Ani Latch of the postern is thy name; shout! (*FW* 493.27–33).

Resurrection, either Ireland's or Tutankhamen's, is not Joyce's theme or motif. It is what *Finnegans Wake* is—a cryptic script. All the words in the book are simultaneously in a state of insurrection and resurrection, undergoing dismemberment or recombination like the dead Osiris. Words continually re-arise into new words. To pharaohphrase Samuel Beckett, *Finnegans Wake* is not *about* resurrection. It is resurrection. 'Phall if you but will, rise you must: and none so soon either shall the pharce for the nunce come to a setdown secular phoenish' (*FW* 4.15–17).

Delivered as a lecture at the James Joyce Summer School, University College Dublin, July 1993; a portion was earlier read at the XIIIth International James Joyce Symposium, Trinity College Dublin, June 1992.

14

The Burning Roof and Tower

Identity in Elizabeth Bowen's *The Last September*

> A shudder in the loins engenders there
> The broken wall, the burning roof and tower.
> > Yeats, 'Leda and the Swan'
>
> Whatever flames upon the night
> Man's own resinous heart has fed.
> > Yeats, *The Resurrection*

In a late autobiographical fragment, 'Pictures and Conversations', Elizabeth Bowen suggests that her transplantation from Ireland to England 'At any early though conscious age' may have been responsible for her becoming a novelist by making her acutely aware of 'a cleft between my heredity and my environment' (*PC* 23). Though she is emphasizing the differences between her Anglo-Irish background and her new English setting, Bowen's writings about Ireland often admit that the cleft was no less acutely felt in County Cork, where the Bowens shared the Anglo-Irish obsession with an identity defined in terms of their separation from the unhyphenated Irish. In her Irish novels and short stories, in *Bowen's Court* (1942)—her history of her family and their 'Big House'—and even in some of her novels and stories with non-Irish settings and characters, Bowen returns again and again to themes of transience, separation, isolation, and to the uneasiness associated with them. It is the same uneasiness that causes Maria Edgeworth's nervous manoeuvring around the explosive issue of inter-marriage and Le Fanu's Gothic fantasies of sexual possession. In Bowen's work, as in the work of so many of her predecessors, to write about the Anglo-Irish explicitly or implicitly is to create an atmosphere of social and sexual anxiety about that other race with which they shared Ireland. 'The

---

Frequently cited works by Elizabeth Bowen are cited parenthetically as follows: *BC*, *Bowen's Court*; *CI*, *Collected Impressions*; *CS*, *Collected Stories*; *HP*, *The House in Paris*; *LS*, *The Last September*; *PC*, *Pictures and Conversations*; *SWA*, *Seven Winters: Memories of a Dublin Childhood and Afterthoughts: Pieces on Writing*. I have usually employed page references alone in my extended discussion of *LS*.

relation between the two races remains a mixture of showing off and suspicion, nearly as bad as sex' (*HP* 89), muses the heroine of *The House in Paris* (1935), and Bowen herself, in her autobiographical *Seven Winters* (1942), recalls her own awareness, as a child, that 'the difference between the two religions . . . appeared to share a delicate, awkward aura with those two other differences—of sex, of class . . . I remember, even, an almost sexual shyness on the subject of Roman Catholics' (*SWA* 50).

But Bowen differs from her predecessors in her frequent willingness to confront that 'cleft' directly, and indeed to make it a central presence in her fiction, so that the social failure to cohere that she records and analyses becomes a principle of literary organization. Her Anglo-Irish have completely isolated themselves from the Irish, and made themselves irrelevant to Irish life. She shares none of Maria Edgeworth's optimism about mutual acceptance based on mutual interest, none of Yeats's optimism about the cultural leadership the Anglo-Irish could supply in lieu of their lost political and economic importance. It was she who described the Anglo-Irish as feeling at home nowhere but exactly in the middle of the Irish Sea, halfway between Ireland and England (Glendinning 13).

In *The Hidden Ireland* (1924) Daniel Corkery contrasts 'The unity that existed between Big House and cabin' in eighteenth-century Munster, when an old Irish family still lived in the Big House, with the mutual indifference and suspicion between Anglo-Irish or 'Planter' landlords and their Irish tenants, in terms that seem chauvinistic, but we find Bowen consciously or unconsciously endorsing them. 'The Gaels in the big houses were one with the cottiers in race, language, religion and, to some extent, culture . . . one, it may be maintained, with the very landscape itself,' Corkery declares;

> How different it was with the Planters . . . For them, all that Gaelic background of myth, literature and history had no existence. They differed from the people in race, language, religion, culture; while the landscape they looked upon was indeed but rocks and stones and trees . . . Gaelic houses . . . possessed . . . a closeness to the land, to the very pulse of it, that those Planter houses could not even dream of (*Hidden Ireland* 64–7).

Bowen describes the Anglo-Irish House as essentially

> an island . . . Each of these houses, with its intense, centripetal life, is isolated by something very much more lasting than the physical fact of space: the isolation is innate; it is an affair of origin. It is possible that Anglo-Irish people, like only children, do not know how much they miss. Their existences, like those of only children, are singular, independent and secretive . . . The land round Bowen's Court, even under its windows, has an unhumanized air the house does nothing to change. Here are, even, no natural features, view or valley, to which the house may be felt to relate itself. It has set, simply, its pattern of trees

and avenues on the virgin, anonymous countryside . . . The Irish and the English squire are very differently placed: the first is imposed and the second indigenous . . . Meanwhile the Gaelic culture ran underground, with its ceaseless poetry of lament. (Gaelic was spoken in the kitchens and fields and in untouched country the settlers did not know.) (*BC* 19–20, 125, 132).

Bowen's acute sense of Anglo-Ireland's isolation finds its most eloquent expression in her novel *The Last September* (1929)—a novel written, she tells us in a 1952 preface, to imagine—to confront—the burning of Bowen's Court by the IRA during the Troubles of 1919–22, when so many of the Anglo-Irish Big Houses went up in flames. 'In the same spring night in 1921, three Anglo-Irish houses in our immediate neighbourhood—Rockmills, Ballywalter, Convamore—were burnt by the Irish,' she tells us. 'The British riposted by burning, still nearer Bowen's Court, the farms of putative Sinn Feiners—some of whom had been our family's friends' (*BC* 439). Some houses were burned because they had entertained British officers, or supplied them with information and assistance, some were raided for guns and then destroyed, some were victims of local, intimate revenge. 'Castle Trent was raided for arms last night . . .' Laurence tells the rest of the family in *The Last September*. 'They think the thing was entirely amateur, nothing to do with the IRA at all . . . The Trents think one of the raiders was a gardener's cousin from Ballydarra who hates the family' (*LS* 127). All of them, ultimately, were victims of the Irish refusal to continue any longer under British rule, of their perceived English identity, and of their own all too successfully maintained apartness from Irish life.

Bowen's Court, as it happens, was not burned in the Troubles. It survived to suffer, like Lady Gregory's Coole Park, the more ignominious fate of demolition for the value of its materials after the class it had sheltered and represented had ceased to exist. But in *The Last September*, the novel originating out of Bowen's Court's imagined fate, Bowen was able to write a 'Big House' novel in which she at once portrays, examines, and rejects the social and literary traditions that the phrase 'Big House' implies. In doing so she reveals that 'proud solitude' which Yeats celebrated to be a dangerous, indeed fatal isolation.

As the elegiac title indicates, *The Last September* is set in autumn—September 1920; it begins at twilight. This twilit autumnal setting is that of Yeats's 'The Wild Swans at Coole' (1917), but Bowen imposes a finality rather than Yeats's expectation of cyclic recurrence. Coole Park's swans will return, but visits to Danielstown—the Big House in *The Last September*—are ended forever. Yet Bowen does not see the destruction of Danielstown as tragic. It is neither a social nor a personal catastrophe. The burning of the house frees her heroine from a kind of suspended animation—like Leopold in *The House in Paris*, she is 'like a young tree inside a tomb' who must 'crack the tomb and grown up to any height' (*HP* 202). In what is partially disguised as a comic novel of manners—manners that try to keep political reality at a distance—Elizabeth Bowen juxtaposes her favourite subject, a young woman beginning to awaken into sexual and psychological maturity, to a social order that has outlived whatever meaning it may once have had. Lois Farquar—Bowen's heroine—feels the irrelevance of Anglo-Irish life in 'this country that ought to be full of such violent realness . . . I might as well be in some kind of cocoon' (*LS* 56). Her cousin Laurence, the other young person in the book, is able to express more eloquently and precisely what is wrong. He characterizes Anglo-Ireland as 'our side—which is no side—rather scared, rather isolated, not expressing anything except tenacity to something that isn't there—that never was there . . . our sense of personality is a sense of outrage and we'll never get outside of it' (*LS* 100).

This is in effect a denial of Yeats's idealized Big House, a centre of social life, a focus for feudal loyalties, and a generator of literature and art. At Coole Yeats can still celebrate, in 1929, 'Great works constructed there in nature's spite/For scholars and for poets after us', and make the house, like the swan-frequented lake, a place of natural recurrent return for the writers and artists who have created a new Irish culture:

> They came like swallows and like swallows went,
> And yet a woman's powerful character
> Could keep a swallow to its first intent;
> And half a dozen in formation there,
> That seemed to whirl upon a compass point.
> ('Coole Park, 1929')

There are 'Beloved books that famous hands have bound,/Old marble heads, old pictures everywhere;/Great rooms where travelled men and children found/Content or joy' ('Coole Park and Ballylee, 1931'). But at Danielstown visitors are less frequent and less satisfying, and their return visits are thwarted or unpredictable. 'Visitors took form gradually . . . coming out of a haze of rumour, and seemed but lightly, pleasantly superimposed . . . till a departure tore great shreds from the season's texture.' The keys to the 'locked bookcases' have been lost, and photographs of 'Pale regimental groups, reunions a generation ago of the family or neighbourhood, gave out from the walls a vague depression . . . a troop of ebony elephants brought back from India by someone [Lois] did not remember paraded along the tops of the bookcases.' In the dining-room family and guests dine

under the crowd of portraits. Under that constant interchange from the high-up faces staring across—now fading each to a wedge of fawn-colour and each looking out from a square of darkness tunnelled into the wall—Sir Richard and Lady Naylor [the aging master and mistress of Danielstown], their nephew, niece and old friends had a thin, over-bright look, seemed in the air of the room unconvincingly painted, startled, transitory . . . each so enisled and distant that a remark at random, falling short of a neighbour, seemed a cry of appeal—the six, in spite of an emphasis in speech and gesture they unconsciously heightened, dwindled personally. While above, the immutable figures, shedding into the rush of dusk smiles, frowns, every vestige of personality, kept only attitude (*LS* 169; 6; 24–5).

We are far from Coole's invigorating 'scene well set and excellent company'. Nor does the IRA's destruction of Danielstown elicit the kind of angry denunciation that Yeats gives to the Old Man in *Purgatory* (1939). 'To kill a house/Where great men grew up, married, died,/I here declare a capital offence,' says Yeats's Old Man. Those who burn Danielstown are not murderers but 'executioners bland from accomplished duty' (*LS* 256), and the noun implies that there is a kind of lawful inevitability to their deed.

Bowen organizes her novel with great formal precision to bring us to that moment of execution and make us recognize its inevitability. The opening paragraph, when the Montmorencys arrive to pay a long promised and long deferred visit to Danielstown, is closely parodied in the penultimate paragraph, as Danielstown's last visitors—the IRA men who burn the house—depart. 'About six o'clock the sound of a motor, collected out of the wide country and narrowed under the trees of the avenue, brought the household out in excitement on to the steps', Elizabeth Bowen begins.

> Up among the beeches, a thin iron gate twanged; the car slid out of a net of shadows down the slope to the house. Behind the flashing windscreen Mr. and Mrs. Montmorency produced . . . an agitation of greeting . . . no one spoke yet. It was a moment of happiness, of perfection (*LS* 3).

Two hundred and fifty pages later,

> half way up the avenue under the beeches, the thin iron gate twanged (missed its latch, remained swinging aghast) as the last unlit car slid out with the executioners . . . The sound of the last car widened, gave itself to the open and empty country and was demolished. Then the first wave of a silence that was to be ultimate flowed back confidently to the steps. The door stood open hospitably upon a furnace (*LS* 256).

These two moments of hospitality, one conventional, the other ironic, and the pattern of arrivals and departures that pervades the book, emphasize the transiency of Danielstown and of the apparent stability it represents. Bowen divides her book into three sections to call our attention to this transiency. Part One is 'The Arrival of Mr. and Mrs. Montmorency.' The Montmorencys themselves are nomads, his ancestral home long since sold

(*LS* 12). Part Two, 'The Visit of Miss Norton', brings Marda Norton, whose occupation is being a house-guest, unsettled and unsettling. These arrivals, visits, and departures, these rootless and directionless characters, are reminiscent of Chekhov's plays, which had become popular in England and even Ireland in the 1920s, and perhaps of Shaw's Chekhovian 'Fantasia in the Russian Manner', *Heartbreak House* (1920). *The Last September* seems particularly close to *Uncle Vanya*, with Lois as a more fortunate Sonia, Marda as the sexually disturbing but indifferent Elena, Hugo Montmorency and Laurence as her fascinated victims Astrov and Vanya; it is worth remembering that some of Chekhov's plays have been performed with Irish settings as plays about the decline of the Anglo-Irish, notably Thomas Kilroy's 1981 version of *The Seagull*.

In Part Three, 'The Departure of Gerald', the young English officer in the 'army of occupation' (*LS* 42), with whom Lois has briefly believed herself to be in love, is killed in an IRA ambush. Lois, Laurence, and the visitors all depart, and the fire makes Sir Richard and Lady Naylor themselves transients and homeless. But from the very beginning, Bowen has emphasized the house's failure—or refusal—to be part of the landscape in which it stands, to be rooted. Above the greetings of the opening page, 'the large facade of the house stared coldly over its mounting lawns' (*LS* 3); Later, Lois and Hugo look down from a distance at the 'demesne trees of Danielstown' making

> a dark formal square like a rug on the green country . . . their isolation became apparent. The house seemed to be pressing down low in apprehension, hiding its face, as though it had Lois's vision of where it was. It seemed to huddle its trees close in fright and amazement at the wide light lovely unloving country, the unwilling bosom whereon it was set . . . Fields gave back light to the sky . . . Single trees . . . drew up light at their roots . . . Only the massed trees—spread like a rug to dull some keenness, break some contact between self and senses perilous to the routine of living—only the trees of the demesne were dark and exhaled darkness (*LS* 78–9).

Mount Isabel, another doomed house which will perish along with Danielstown on the last page, is 'a house without weight, an appearance, less actual than the begonias' scarlet and wax-pink flesh' (143). In her essay 'The Big House' (1940), written for Sean O'Faolain's Dublin magazine *The Bell*, Bowen tries to discover a role for the Big House in twentieth-century Ireland, but again concedes its traditional isolation:

> Unlike the low, warm, ruddy French and English manors, they have made no natural growth from the soil—the idea that begot them was a purely social one . . . That idea, although lofty, was at first rigid and narrow . . . the big house people were handicapped, shadowed and to an extent queered—by their pride, by their indignation at their decline and by their divorce from the countryside in whose heart their struggle was carried on (*CI* 196–9).

Even that opening paragraph in *The Last September*, describing 'the sound of a motor, collected out of the wide country and narrowed under the trees', suggests isolation and constriction, and contrasts with the sound of the IRA car at the end, which 'widened, gave itself to the open and empty country'. The Danielstown people see themselves as the centre of a network of feudal loyalties. Lady Naylor deplores the English addiction to country dancing ('if this is what you call getting in touch with the people give me what you call feudalism!'), Hugo broods over a weakness in 'The feudal system', the inefficiency of the Danielstown laundress, who holds her position because her 'father had helped to defend the house' against a Fenian uprising 'in the troubled "sixties"' (67, 228). But apart from Kathleen the Cook, who is confined to a single paragraph (209), the household servants play no part in the story, thus deepening the isolation of the family and guests; Bowen admits no one like the peasant nurse-confidant we find in Chekhov's *Uncle Vanya* and *Three Sisters*, who reminds us that some relationship with the peasantry is possible. When Lois takes Hugo Montmorency to visit one of the Danielstown tenants, the brief visit is a parody of sentimentally imagined feudal relationships. The tenant's children run and hide as they approach, the tenant is evasive about his sick wife and his IRA son, and clearly eager for them to depart. Lois describes the Connors as 'darling people', Hugo cannot 'remember if this was a man—Michael Connor—he ought to remember'. When they leave, Michael Connor watches them until they disappear, 'Looking longest after them, like an eye, a window glittered', and, though Connor's geese follow them briefly, they soon 'relinquished the chase abruptly . . . Their backs were more than oblivious; they made the trap, the couple in it, an illusion. And indeed Lois and Hugo both felt that their pause, their talk, their passing had been less than a shadow' (76–7). When Sean O'Faolain read *The Last September* in 1937, he wrote Elizabeth Bowen to praise it and to ask, 'is the wall between Danielstown and Peter Connor's farm as high as ever? I fear to think it is.' He recalled his own recent visit to a Big House, and his sense that he belonged with a tenant who came up with a petition, not on the steps among the gentry: 'It seemed that wall was just as high as ever. It made me feel like a spy inside it.' O'Faolain urged Bowen to write about a Danielstown 'that was at least aware of the Ireland outside . . . that, perhaps, regretted the division enough to admit it was there,' a request that 'The Big House' and *Bowen's Court* partially fulfil. He reminded her that Gogol and Chekhov had found ways to 'link up divided worlds . . . climb walls' (Glendinning 149–50).

Sean O'Faolain felt like a spy when visiting a Big House; in *The Last September*, Bowen continually reminds us that the countryside and its people are at once indifferent and watchful towards Danielstown and what happens there: 'Compassed about', thought Lois, 'by so great a cloud of witnesses' (38; Heb. 12.1). Visiting Mount Isabel, Laurence feels 'A sense of exposure, of being offered without resistance to some ironic uncuriosity', which makes him

> look up at the mountain over the roof of the house. In some gaze—of a man's up there hiding, watching among the clefts and ridges—they seemed held, included and to have their only being. The sense of a watcher, reserve of energy and intention, abashed Laurence . . . But the unavoidable and containing stare impinged to the point of a transformation upon the social figures with orderly, knitted shadows, the well-groomed grass and the beds in their formal pattern (*LS* 147).

Lois sees Danielstown as isolated and 'pressing down low in apprehension' (78) when for a moment she looks at the house as a spy on some vantage point might see it.

The reader too becomes in a special sense a kind of spy. Though we often share Lois's point of view and are privy to her thoughts, or those of other characters, we simultaneously watch her and events at Danielstown with that bleak awareness of their irrelevance that we share with the indifferent attentive countryside and country people. 'From the start, the reader must look—and more, must be aware of looking', Bowen declares in her 1952 preface, and though she goes on to define that looking as 'backward, down a perspective cut through the years' (ix), her command to 'look' places us in relation to the story. Sean O'Faolain, commenting on the novel's opening paragraph of arrival, remarks that 'we get, throughout, the sensation, are meant to get the sensation of being exterior spectators, unfused with the characters,' as if we were watching a film—a film, he adds, with the sound track gone silent (*Vanishing Hero* 174). The reader sees Danielstown as the countryside sees it, separate, aloof. We are placed amid that gallery of spectators for whom the Anglo-Irish, as Yeats and Elizabeth Bowen argued, performed what Yeats called, in his 1904 preface to Lady Gregory's *Gods and Fighting Men*, 'a play that had for spectators men and women that loved the high wasteful virtues' (*Explorations* 27). Bowen describes Bowen's Court as sustained 'by the inner force of its style' and returns to Yeats's notion of Anglo-Irish society as a kind of theatre: 'In raising a family house one is raising a theatre . . . but cannot tell what plays may be acted there . . . the builder could not do more than indicate that life ought to be lived in a certain way' (*BC* 21, 32). 'We are, or can become at any moment, the most undignified race on earth', she adds, noting the tendency of Irish and Anglo-Irish alike to satisfy English expectations that the gentry will be 'dashing', the 'lower classes . . . comic . . . while there is a gallery we must play to it' (*BC* 263). In her 1951 history of the Shelbourne Hotel, the Dublin centre for the Anglo-Irish gentry, she commends 'a brave acting-up' in troubled Dublin (*Shelbourne* 45). The unhyphenated Irish spectators may never have been as entertained as Yeats and at times Elizabeth Bowen declare them to have been; certainly in *The Last September* they are weary of the spectacle, ready for the show to end, and prepared to come on stage themselves to scatter the actors and strike the set. In *Bowen's Court* Bowen abandons the theatrical metaphor with its awareness of audience. 'If Ireland did not accept' the Anglo-Irish, she tells us, 'they did not know it—and it is in that unawareness of final rejection, unawareness of being looked out at from some secretive, opposed life, that the Anglo-Irish naive dignity and, even, tragedy, seems to me to stand' (*BC* 160).

If the unhyphenated Irish, and the reader with them, are spies rather than welcome guests at Danielstown, the English officers sent to Ireland to maintain British rule are equally out of place. The Danielstown people are staunch supporters of the Union with Great Britain, but they dislike the Army's aggressive tactics and loathe the Black and Tans—Sir Richard, on one occasion, dreams about riding 'round the country on a motor bicycle from which he could not detach himself. His friends cut him; he discovered he was a Black and Tan' (*LS* 133). The English officers seem vulgar, unimaginative, and ignorant; 'the Army isn't at all what it used to be', Sir Richard declares, 'They tell me there's a great deal of socialism now in the British Army' (26–7). The Army wives are vulgar, condescending, and ignorant: 'Oh, do you know,' cried Mrs Vermont, 'I never knew Tipperary was really a place till I came to Ireland?' (90). Encounters between the Anglo-Irish and their English defenders are as uneasy as the visit to Michael Connor's farm, or the 'bridge party' for Anglo-Indians and Indians in E.M. Forster's *A Passage to India* (1924). When one of the officers comes to Danielstown to tell Lois of Gerald's death, 'it seemed to him odd that there should be nothing to search for, nobody to interrogate', and the family 'felt instinctively that he had come here to search the house' (*LS* 249–51).

In the face of these threats from Irish rebellion and English vulgarity, Danielstown becomes an imposture, a pretence that Big House life can continue by ignoring the danger, by talking of other things. But, though the Naylors and their older visitors continue being 'careful not to notice' (50), the younger members of the household are less willing to pretend. 'Will there ever be anything we can all do except not notice?' asks Marda (100). Lois and her alter ego, Laurence, are more forthright. 'They both had a sense of detention, of a prologue being played out too lengthily, with unnecessary stresses, a wasteful attention to detail' (145). 'I should like something else to happen, some crude intrusion of the actual', Laurence announces. '. . . I should like to be here when this house burns' (49). Lois broodingly hopes 'that instead of bleaching to dust in summers of empty sunshine, the carpet would burn with the house in a scarlet night' (121). They eagerly await an inevitable catastrophe which will offer them the excitement of reality and a chance to escape the stifling and illusory rituals of Anglo-Ireland.

Even at the beginning of the novel Danielstown is a house and an estate with no future, a metaphor for the class it represents. There are no sons to inherit, and no direct heir—Lois is only Sir Richard's niece, his sister's child, and Laurence is Lady Naylor's nephew. There are no young Anglo-Irishmen in the novel, a reflection of the Anglo-Irish sense that their class had sacrificed all its promising young men on the battlefields of the Western Front; 'those poised, impeccable young officers who—hunting, shooting, fishing, dining and dancing . . . had long been the delight and resource of all Anglo-Ireland, almost all fell in the First World War' (xi), Bowen reminds us in her 1952 preface. To the Anglo-Irish their deaths were somehow responsible for their class's inability to retain its old power and position, though T.R. Henn, himself a son of the Big House—he was a 'Henn of Paradise' near Ennis in County Clare—and a student of its decline, suggests that 'By 1912' the Anglo-Irish 'Ascendancy . . . was growing a little tired, a little purposeless' (*Lonely Tower* 4). Among the visitors to Danielstown, the Montmorencys are childless—Hugo's wife is ten years his senior—and Marda still unmarried at twenty-nine. 'Talking of being virginal, do you ever notice this country? Doesn't sex seem irrelevant?' Laurence abruptly asks Hugo Montmorency, at the Danielstown tennis party.

> 'There certainly are a great many unmarried women,' said Mr Montmorency . . .
> 'It is: "Ah, why would we?" And indeed why should they? There is no reason why one should not so one never does. It applies to everything. And children seem in every sense of the word to be inconceivable.' (*LS* 48).

By centring her novel on one of those unmarried women, and emphasizing her isolation, her restless virginity, her confused simultaneous yearning for reality, excitement, sexual maturity, and safety, Bowen makes Lois herself into a metaphor for Anglo-Ireland without diminishing her believability as a character. Lois has no parents, no really close ties, and no purpose. She has a little of Emma Bovary about her—'she had cried for a whole afternoon before the War because she was not someone in a historical novel'—and something of that admiration for the desperate man which Yeats believed to be characteristic of Anglo-Ireland: 'There was a desperation about Mr Daventry she could have loved. But he apparently craved relaxation: she had found she did not relax Mr Daventry' (92, 181). Yet she remembers her wish to be in a historical novel 'with surprise' while feeling 'exposed and hunted' as she hides from a party of Black and Tans, and soon realizes that Daventry, a shell-shocked survivor of the Western Front, is 'like a ghost . . . she saw there was not a man here, hardly even a person' (*LS* 194–5).

Like Laurence, Lois yearns for 'violent realness' and change, but she is also afraid. 'Why do you stay here?' Marda asks her:

> 'I can't think,' said Lois, startled.
> 'You like to be the pleasant young person?'
> 'I like to be in a pattern.' She traced a pink frond [the pattern in the carpet] with her finger. 'I like to be related; to have to be what I am. Just to *be* is so intransitive, so lonely.'
> . . . She would like to feel real in London (*LS* 122–3).

'I want to begin on something', she tells Laurence. 'There must be some way for me to begin. You keep on looking into rooms where I am with silent contempt—what do you think I am for?' (199); later she impatiently exclaims, 'What they never see . . . is, that I must do something . . . If I learn German, they say, why not Italian? And when I learn Italian they take no interest (*LS* 232).

Lois decided to marry Gerald because he seems real and safe. He is 'At least . . . definite', though Lois can find this oppressive: 'I do wish you wouldn't, Gerald—I mean, be so *actual*' (232, 109). 'I thought you were a rock: I was safe with you,' she cries when she realizes she does not love him, that he is 'like a foreigner with whom by some failure in her vocabulary all communication was interrupted . . . "I didn't ask you to understand me: I was so happy. I was so safe"' (236–7). English Gerald's inability to understand her, his inability to provide the safety she believes she needs, makes their doomed love affair a little allegory of the imperfect union of Britain and Ireland. Bowen emphasizes the point by sending Marda into the safety of an English marriage with a man appropriately named Mr Lawe, who is '"Very worried and kind . . . Business-like, passionate and accurate" . . . So much of herself that was fluid must . . . be moulded by his idea of her. Essentials were fixed and localised by her being with him— to become as the bricks and wallpaper of a home' (*LS* 125, 159).

Lady Naylor rejects Gerald as a suitor for Lois because he is too young, too poor, and especially because he is socially too marginal. Lois rejects him because she realizes he can never understand her. By shooting Gerald from ambush—he has earlier been ambushed by Lady Naylor so she can tell him an engagement with Lois is impossible—the IRA confirms the political allegory of those rejections. Even Lady Naylor's domestic ambush has a faint political-military undercurrent: Gerald arrives too early, forcing her to 'manoeuvre more or less openly for position'. As their interview ends, 'two cushions covered with Union Jacks' are knocked off the sofa, and Gerald restores them so spiritlessly that he seems already dead (*LS* 221, 227–8). A love affair between men and women with different inherited loyalties/ identities is older than *Romeo and Juliet*. In Irish and Anglo-Irish literature it is almost invariably treated as political as well as personal, favourably and positively in the novels of Lady Morgan, tentatively by Maria Edgeworth, tragically by Trollope in *The Macdermots of Ballycloran* (1847), Brendan Behan in *The Hostage* (1959), Brian Friel in *Translations* (1980), and semi-allegorically by Seamus Heaney in such poems as 'Act of Union' and 'Ocean's Love to Ireland':

> Speaking broad Devonshire
> Ralegh has backed the maid to a tree
> As Ireland is backed to England
>
> And drives inland
> Till all her strands are breathless
> (*Poems 1965–1975* 201)

Bowen makes Lois hint at the political aspects of this theme and the allegorical forms in which they have traditionally been expressed, in a conversation with Gerald, which is characteristically frustrating to her because they cannot communicate. She has important things to say. He listens but is unable—does not try—to understand. 'But you never take in a word I say. You're not interested when I tell you about myself', she complains, after a sequence of unfinished sentences and vacuous replies to her questions, only to hear him say, 'You know I could listen all day to you talking'. In reply, she moves from their personal incompatibility to a generalization about England and Ireland in which she depicts Ireland as a woman and identifies herself with Ireland:

> '. . . When *we* do nothing it is out of politeness, but England is so moral, so dreadfully keen on not losing her temper, or being for half a moment not a great deal more noble than anyone else. Can you wonder this country gets irritated? It's as bad for it as being a woman. I never can see why women shouldn't be hit, or should be saved from wrecks when everybody is complaining they're so superfluous.'
> 'You don't understand: it would be ghastly if those things went.'
> 'Why? I don't see—and *I* am a woman' (*LS* 56).

Sean O'Faolain discerned 'an atmosphere of ancient fable behind all of Miss Bowen's fiction . . . Her characters are the modern, sophisticated, naturalistic novelist's versions of primitive urges' (*Vanishing Hero* 173). He identified Lois and Bowen's other 'dreaming but recusant girl[s]' with Proserpine. But Lois has mythic affinities nearer home, in that 'underground . . . Gaelic culture . . . with its ceaseless poetry of lament' (*BC* 132) which Bowen criticizes the Anglo-Irish for ignoring. In Gaelic laments of the seventeenth and eighteenth centuries, Ireland is portrayed as a woman—Kathleen ni Houlihan, Banba, Dark Rosaleen. Sometimes she is a poor old woman who has been robbed of her lands, the tradition Yeats adapts in his most popular play, *Cathleen ni Houlihan* (1902). More frequently she is young and beautiful, but, especially in the *aisling* or vision poems, she is also destitute, and needs a strong, brave husband to restore her to her rightful place. 'Young she is, and fair she is, and would be crowned a queen,/Were the king's son at home here with Kathaleen Ny-Houlahan!' as Mangan put it in the best known of his eight adaptations of *aisling* poems, in lines which Yeats used as an epigraph for his play. In the traditional *aisling*, the husband who is to restore Ireland and father strong sons upon her is initially James II or the Old Pretender; later he is Bonny Prince Charlie, and eventually Napoleon. Bowen would have been aware of this traditional figure by virtue of growing up in Ireland, where Kathleen was often the subject of patriotic songs and orations or of political cartoons. She may also have learned something of the poetic tradition from Daniel Corkery's study of the *aisling*, the lament, and related forms in *The Hidden Ireland* (1924), subtitled 'A Study of Gaelic Munster in the Eighteenth Century', or from Frank O'Connor's translations, which appeared in AE's *Irish Statesman* in the 1920s.

Lois's eagerness for sexual and emotional satisfaction, her eagerness to escape from a kind of captivity or spell, have therefore a political as well as a personal element, and echo a traditional Irish theme. But Bowen has deliberately adapted that theme to the altered circumstances of 1920–21. Lois represents Anglo-Ireland, not the Gaelic Ireland of the *aisling*; she is Lois Farquar, not Kathleen ni Houlihan, though her affinities with Kathleen are underlined when she wears a green dress to a dance at the British barracks where the dress is torn (205). The Kathleen of the Gaelic poets mourned the loss of her land, the destruction of her family, the absence of those who should be her defenders. Now the dispossessed Ireland that she symbolized is coming into its own after almost two centuries of Anglo-Irish usurpation. Lois too loses her home and her chance at an English marriage, and goes into exile, personifying the Anglo-Irish who are now being dispossessed as the Irish once were. 'It has taken the decline of the Anglo-Irish to open to them the poetry of regret' that formerly only the Irish had known and felt, Bowen remarks in *Bowen's Court*; 'only dispossessed people know their land in the dark' (*BC* 132).

The Last September also has affinities with another traditional Irish poetic form, the lament, which mourns the loss of a noble family and the destruction of their house. Just before she describes the burning of Danielstown, Bowen shows us the place where the house stood as it will be when the house is gone:

By next year light had possessed itself of the vacancy, still with surprise. Next Year, the chestnuts and acorns pattered unheard on the avenues, that, filmed over with green already, should have been dull to the footsteps—but there were no footsteps (*LS* 255).

Bowen describes a similar obliteration at Mitchelstown Castle, where she had been among the local Anglo-Irish who gathered there in August 1914, on the day war was declared. 'Ten years hence . . . the Castle itself would be a few bleached stumps on the plateau', she writes in *Bowen's Court*; 'To-day, the terraces are obliterated, and grass grows where the saloons were. Many of those guests . . . would be scattered, houseless, sonless, or themselves dead' (*BC* 436). But consciously or unconsciously, as she laments her own people's passing, she echoes one of the great Gaelic laments for the old Irish aristocracy, in which an unknown poet mourns the ruined Butler castle at Kilrush, in County Tipperary:

> My grief and my affliction
> Your gates are taken away,
> Your avenue needs attention,
> Goats in the garden stray.
> The courtyard's filled with water
> And the great earls where are they?
> The earls, the lady, the people
> Beaten into the clay (tr. O'Connor, *Kings* 100).

The new ruins will not be the castles of ancient Irish chieftains nor the cabins of evicted peasants, but the Big Houses of the Ascendancy. In *The Last September* Bowen suggests that the land itself never accepted them. Now it repudiates them. In *Bowen's Court* she makes the point more laconically, and more chillingly, when she records the disappearance of her own house: 'Today, so far as the eye can see, there might never have been a house there. One cannot say that the space is empty. More, it is as it was—with no house there' (*BC* 458). An illusory reality has ceased even to seem.

Bowen's imitation, parody, of traditional Irish themes and modes is particularly important in shaping one of the novel's most striking incidents, Lois's nocturnal encounter with a young IRA man trespassing in the woods of Danielstown demesne. The *aisling* frequently begins with the poet, usually a young man, taking a morning walk and meeting the mysterious young woman who embodies Ireland. He questions her about her identity and history, she explains or bewails her dispossession and prophesies her eventual restoration when the 'king's son' has come to marry her. Bowen reverses each of these characteristics. Lois walks out at night, her encounter is with a mysterious man, not a woman, and they do not converse—if Anglo-Irish Lois cannot talk with English

Gerald, she is equally incapable of communicating with this furtive Irish rebel. This time Ireland is not a helpless female looking for masculine assistance, but a resolute male clad in the trench-coat uniform of the IRA. He is not keening but silent and purposeful, not helplessly waiting but active:

> First, she did not hear footsteps, and as she began to notice the displaced darkness thought what she dreaded was coming, was there within her—she was indeed clairvoyant, exposed to horror, going to see a ghost. Then steps smooth on the smooth earth; branches slipping against a trench-coat. The trench-coat rustled across the path ahead to the swing of a steady walker. She stood by the holly immovable, blotted out in the black, and there passed within reach of her hand, with the rise and fall of a stride, some resolute profile powerful as a thought. In gratitude for its fleshliness she felt prompted to make some contact: not to be known of seemed like a doom of extinction.
>
> 'It's a fine night,' she would have liked to observe; or, to engage his sympathies: 'Up Dublin!' or even—since it was in her uncle's demesne she was trembling and straining under a holly—boldly—'What do you want?'
>
> It must be because of Ireland he was in such a hurry . . . Here was something else that she could not share. She could not conceive of her country emotionally: it was a way of living, abstract of several countrysides . . .
>
> Quite still, without even breathing, she let him go past in contemptuous unawareness. His intentness burnt on the dark an almost visible trail; he might have been a murderer, he seemed so inspired. The crowd of trees straining up from the passive disputed earth, each sucking up and exhaling the country's essence—swallowed him finally . . . A man in a trench-coat had gone on without seeing her: that was what it had amounted to . . . Conceivably she had surprised life at a significant angle in the shrubbery (*LS* 37–8).

The young IRA man is part of that 'violent realness' (56) Lois yearns for; he is clearly 'in a pattern' (122). Lois is excited rather than frightened by the encounter. She senses her own exclusion from the intense national feeling the man shares, the contempt in his unawareness, her own inability to feel intensely about anything or anyone she knows. But it is also a sensual experience, a moment of access to that 'life' for which she waits impatiently. It is as close as she comes to a sexual experience, as her trembling, the setting, and the purposeful menacing approaching man imply, and, like the promised marriage of Kathleen ni Houlihan, that sexual experience is at once sensual and political.

The episode's sensuality is continually emphasized. Lois walks in the woods after the family and their guests have sat through their mutually isolating dinner party under the family portraits, and Lois has tried to flirt with an indifferent Hugo Montmorency, once her mother's admirer. She has failed to interest the party in rumours of IRA guns buried in the woods, and, though she persuades them to take after-dinner coffee outside, on the steps, Francie Montmorency is afraid of being shot at (23). The elders are apprehensive when they hear 'A furtive . . . sinister' Army or Black and

Tan lorry patrolling (33), and the party retreat indoors to safety with the plea that the night is too chilly. Lois's own uncertain bravery and enterprise is her response to this stifling atmosphere, to their fear of excitement and sensuality:

> Laurels breathed coldly and close: on her bare arms the tips of the leaves were timid and dank, like tongues of dead animals. Her fear of the shrubberies tugged at its chain, fear behind reason, fear before her birth . . . She went forward eagerly, daring a snap of the chain, singing, with a hand to the thump of her heart: dramatic with terror. She thought of herself as forcing a pass. In her life—deprived as she saw it—there was no occasion for courage, which like an unused muscle slackened and slept . . . Now, on the path: grey patches worse than the dark: they slipped up her dress knee-high (*LS* 36).

This immediately precedes her meeting with the IRA man, and introduces that mixture of sensuality and terror which pervades the episode. Later, after she briefly engaged herself to Gerald, she is 'perplexed' and apprehensive when he kisses her among those same laurels:

> . . . her physical apprehension of him was confused by the slipping, cold leaves. Her little sighs elated then alarmed him.
> 'What's the matter?' he said, lips close to her face.
> 'I don't like the smell of laurels. Let's come out of here' . . . She wished that he were a woman (*LS* 213–14).

And later still, these two encounters in the wood underlie the metaphor in which she warns herself of Gerald's predictability, his imprisoning reliability: 'But when she looked for Gerald there seemed too much of him. He was a wood in which she counted from tree to tree—all hers—and knew the boundary wall right round. But how to measure this unaccountable darkness between the trees, this living silence?' (*LS* 218).

Lois has a second IRA encounter, which extends and underlines the sexual implications of her brief but deeply disturbing adventure in the woods. Walking with Marda and Hugo, she and Marda leave him to explore an old ruined mill. Lois has been fascinated by the mill. It has held for her the same promise of fearful but pleasurable excitement that she felt in the laurel woods: '. . . it frightened her. In fact she wouldn't for worlds go into it but liked going as near as she dared. It was a fear she didn't want to get over, a kind of deliciousness' (151–2). But Marda insists on going inside, and 'in an ecstasy at this compulsion' Lois enters, self-consciously dramatizing her own real fear, 'appealing, she felt quite certain, to a particular tenderness,' later making an 'unnatural gesture adequate to the drama' (153). Again Lois's yearning for 'violent realness' (56) is satisfied. There is an IRA man asleep in the mill, who wakes, covers them with a pistol, studies them 'with calculating intentness' (154), questions them, and warns them to give 'up walking . . . yez had better keep within the house while y'have it' (154). Then his pistol goes off by accident, wounding Marda on the back of her hand. The exploding pistol, the blood, and the sudden resulting frankness between the two women, suggest a kind of oblique sexual encounter. Lois's fright makes her resolve to marry Gerald, and makes her aware that Hugo is pursuing Marda; 'She thought how the very suggestion of death brought about this awful unprivacy' (157). Marda declares that in entering the mill they were not being 'girlish . . . we were being goatish', and a moment later says, 'inconsequent—"I hope I shall have some children; I should hate to be barren."' When Lois remarks, 'I'm glad [Hugo] wasn't my father', Marda sharply replies, 'He couldn't be anything's father' (157–8). Both women feel an intensity from which they exclude Hugo, and from the 'stronghold' of 'Their sex' (157) they jeer at his impotence, while each feels a need for a 'safe' English husband—Gerald, Leslie Lawe. Lois's sudden perception of the relationship between Marda and Hugo hints at a sexual initiation, as does her woman's scorn of Hugo.

Lois's skittishness about the ruins is linked with her simultaneous fear of and eagerness for sexual experience, and that in turn with the related political themes. Hugo has already defined the ruined mill politically as 'Another . . . of our national grievances. English law strangled the—' (152). He is half endorsing, half mocking the Irish nationalist doctrine that Irish trade and manufactures had continually been impeded by imperial policy in order to protect British prosperity from competition. But for Lois the ruined mill has even more serious implications. 'This was her nightmare: brittle, staring ruins' (152). It is a prophetic nightmare, looking forward to the destruction of Danielstown; the 'dead mill' has 'entered the democracy of ghostliness, equalled broken palaces in futility and sadness . . . showing not the decline of its meaning, simply decline; took on all of a past to which it had given nothing.' As the Big House is to do, the mill has confirmed its own irrelevance, an irrelevance which Lois has already sensed. When she enters the mill, she sees it in terms of Poe's House of Usher, at once a metaphor for family decay and for a morbid and terrifying sexuality: 'Cracks ran down; she expected, with detachment, to see them widen, to see the walls peel back from a cleft—like the House of Usher' (*LS* 152–3).

With that association, Bowen emphasizes the relationship between Lois's eagerness for sexual experience—even if it brings violation, pain, ruin—and her eagerness to see Danielstown burn (121); earlier, Livvy Thompson's flirtations with British officers could 'get the house burnt' over her father's head (137). Bowen links sexual desire and incendiary politics somewhat as Yeats does in his repeated identifications of Maud Gonne with Helen of Troy, of Helen's sexuality with the burning of the city. 'Was there another

Troy for her to burn?' he asks, thinking of Maud Gonne, in 'No Second Troy' (1910), and in 'A Man Young and Old' (1926) he tells us Helen 'had brought great Hector down/And put all Troy to wreck', while 'A shudder in the loins engenders' Helen and so causes Troy's 'broken wall, the burning roof and tower' in 'Leda and the Swan' (1924). Although Lois herself leaves the novel a few pages before it ends, the fire is the consummation she has been seeking, and the appropriate conclusion to this story of her restless craving for experience. Her only intense encounters have been with those who are to kindle that fire, and are set against her less exciting encounters with Gerald, who would prevent such fires from breaking out, and who cannot understand or arouse Lois.

By emphasizing the intensity of that encounter in the woods, with its overtones of sexual anxiety, Bowen once again enters that dangerous forbidden area of intermarriage between Anglo-Irish and Irish, which Lady Morgan endorses, which Le Fanu and Stoker turn into nightmare, which Yeats turns into a Beckettian act of endless repetition, at once penitential and pleasurable, punishing and satisfying. Lois's encounter is brief, but it is charged with her youth and excitement, and with the long history of mutual and self-conscious exclusion by Anglo-Irish and Irish, a mutual mixture of nervous disdain and prurient curiosity—in 'The Other Side' Seamus Heaney describes a Protestant neighbour at a Catholic funeral standing 'shyly, as if he were a party to/lovemaking or a stranger's weeping' (*Poems 1965–1975* 114). There is no possibility of any real sexual encounter between Lois and the IRA man, but the episode's brevity and inconclusiveness, appropriate in this novel of transiency, recall other situations of real or threatened miscegenation in Anglo-Irish novels.

Lois departs, or, more accurately, escapes from Danielstown and from the Anglo-Irish world it represents. As she does so, that world evaporates behind her, revealing its seeming solidity to have been an illusion. It was a gypsy encampment with the show of permanence, but its houses vanish in a night, and apparent feudal loyalties conceal at best indifference, at worst an eagerness for revenge. 'We shift about—all that great glory spent—/Like some poor Arab tribesman and his tent,' Yeats writes in 'Coole Park and Ballylee, 1931', imagining a time when Coole no longer stands. But Elizabeth Bowen declines to claim that 'that great glory' ever existed. In escaping from Danielstown, in being finally freed from its isolation and suspended life by the consummating fire, Lois also escapes the burden of Anglo-Irish history, that past encapsulated in Danielstown with its family portraits and family possessions. Like Bowen herself, Lois has 'resigned from history and turned to geography' (*SWA* 230).

It is a more modest flight than that of Stephen Dedalus, but perhaps it has the same ultimate destination. Stephen escapes in order to turn his experience into art. Lois tries to be an artist, and to find in her drawings, that 'illustrated the *Morte d'Arthur* and Omar Khayyám' and 'remembered Beardsley', a way of gaining 'the kind of surprised assurance one might expect from motherhood' (120–2). 'Go to a school of art', Lady Naylor suggests, when she is discouraging Lois's notion of marrying Gerald.

> 'Where?'
> 'It could be arranged.'
> 'But I don't think I really draw well.'
> 'That is no reason why you should marry' (*LS* 208–9).

When Marda examines Lois's drawings, she is not impressed. 'I think you're cleverer than you can draw,' she tells Lois; '. . . Why can't you write, or something?' (122). Though Lois demurs, her reply indicates the kind of book she would write, at once autobiographical and symbolic, the symbols at once revealing and concealing the book's confessional aspect: to write is '. . . so embarrassing. Even things like—like elephants' —she is thinking of those elephants, souvenirs of imperial adventure, which parade along the locked bookcases of Danielstown—'get so personal' (122). As for her alter ego, Laurence, he hopes to own a Picasso, the new art of fluid reality, and plans to write a novel (140, 148); in fact, he does, in a sense, write one during a sleepless night, in which he first longs for raiders and imagines how coolly he will deal with them, then imaginatively remakes the past to marry Hugo to Laura, Lois's mother, sends them to Canada, gives them four sons, marries Francie to Sir Richard, dies himself 'without having heard of Danielstown. Lois, naturally, was not born at all' (132). His creation of alternate destinies for all the novel's major characters reminds us of the novelist's power to alter or manipulate a seemingly fixed reality.

When Lois leaves Danielstown and Ireland—where art seems subversive, so that an Anglo-Irish visitor to Danielstown wants 'all the Irish art schools . . . to be searched . . . casts were hollow and you could keep a good deal inside the Venus of Milo' (214–15)—she goes, not to the vaguely projected art school in England, but to Tours, to learn French, after which she will learn Italian (253; some of Bowen's critics have misunderstood Lois's future as 'tours' or touring, but in context it is quite clear; see Heath 40; Blodgett 45). Earlier, Laurence has appropriately responded to her wish 'to begin on something' by handing her 'two grammars, a dictionary, and a novel of Mann's' (*LS* 199–200).

Lois is to be an artist, but her medium is to be language, and she will not illustrate, but narrate. Narrative is her true vocation and her true method of self-realization, as she senses when her immediate response to the thrill of her encounter with the IRA man in the woods is to narrate it to the other inhabitants of Danielstown, those who have gone indoors to be 'secure and bright like flowers in a paper-weight' inside 'the carpet-border' from which 'Fear curled back in defeat'. Lois runs 'back to tell, in excitement'. But Danielstown is not ready for her narrative; the house must fall before she can tell her story. At the moment of encounter the house and its furnishings oppose her wish to narrate:

> upstairs, the confidently waiting beds; mirrors vacant and startling; books read and forgotten, contributing no more to life, dinner-table certain of its regular compulsion; the procession of elephants that throughout peaceful years had not broken file.
> But as Lois went up the stairs breathlessly her adventure began to diminish . . . confidence disappeared in a waver of shadow among the furniture. Conceivably she had surprised life at a significant angle in the shrubbery. But it was impossible to speak of this . . . what seemed most probable was that they would not listen . . . (*LS* 36–8).

In a 1949 preface to a reissue of *Encounters* (1923), her first collection of stories, Elizabeth Bowen describes herself as turning to narrative fiction as 'a last hope. I was twenty; already I had failed to be a poet; I was in the course of failing to be a painter . . . I did not so much envisage glory as desire to known that I *had* made sense. I wanted proof that I was not prey to delusions' (*SWA* 183–4). She goes on to describe her life until then as very close to Lois's as we know it from *The Last September*: 'Motherless . . . in and out of the homes of my different relatives . . . constantly, shuttling between . . . Ireland and England', and to hint that the creation of fiction, like sexual initiation, was a way of achieving maturity: 'I lived with a submerged fear that I might fail to establish grown-up status. That fear, it may be, egged me on to writing: an author, a grown-up, must they not be synonymous . . . I must have been anxious to approximate to my elders, yet to demolish them' (*SWA* 187–8).

'Lois derives from, but is not, myself at nineteen' (xii), Bowen tells us in her 1952 preface to *The Last September*. Lois had yearned to be 'someone in a historical novel' (92); Bowen remembers that at twenty 'For me reality meant the books I had read' (*SWA* 185); to write was to create reality, and as a mature writer she was 'prepared to think . . . My writing . . . may be a substitute for something I have been born without—a so-called normal relation to society. My books *are* my relation to society' (*Why Do I Write?* 23). Is not Lois's escape an escape into art, to order in her imagination the last days of Anglo-Ireland juxtaposed with her own first days of womanhood? Bowen explains Lois's apparent indifference to the Troubles as 'partly because disorder in any form obstructed her own development . . . The growing nation left cold the growing girl' (xii). Lois has her own agenda, to gain a freedom from and therefore a perspective on those things that Bowen, in her 1947 preface to Le Fanu's *Uncle Silas*, listed as the characteristic elements in Anglo-Irish life: 'The hermetic solitude and the autocracy of the great country house, the demonic power of the family myth, fatalism, feudalism and the "ascendency" outlook', sexlessness and 'a sublimated infantilism' (*CI* 4).

Lois escapes in order to return in imagination; Bowen imaginatively recreates herself in Lois, to re-examine the class from which she herself came, their style and their failure, and to preserve in art her own approach to womanhood as that class declined; to preserve the setting, Danielstown/ Bowen's Court, conferring a permanence upon the house, as she did for Bowen's Court when, revisiting her account for republication in 1964, after the house had been demolished, she decided to leave her 'room to room description . . . in the present tense' (*BC* 459). Having often imagined the burning of Bowen's Court in her 'agonised mind's eye' she could call 'that terrible final page of *The Last September* . . . for me, also, something I have lived through' (xii); at the same time, she could burn the house itself by imagining, and so free herself from 'the family myth'.

'She wished she could freeze the moment and keep it always', Lois thinks, as she stands on the steps awaiting the Montmorencys on the novel's first page. Elizabeth Bowen has done precisely that, for Lois, for herself, for the houses and the class who inhabited them—freezing them all in a characteristic moment of transiency. 'I like to be in a pattern', Lois had said, tracing as she spoke the pattern of a frond in the carpet that had been 'to someone dead now . . . an idea of beauty' (121–2). She has already evoked a carpet as a simile for the house's alienation in the countryside—'a dark formal square like a rug on the green country' (78)—and as a metaphor for a stifling security (36), and this carpet with pink fronds is about to serve her as an image for the house's fiery end (121). She is in fact to create a pattern, not just 'be in' one. Perhaps, as Harriet Blodgett suggests (Blodgett 29), Lois's tracing the frond is a subtle reference to Henry James's short story 'The Figure in the Carpet' (1896). If so, Bowen is deftly hinting that we should examine her novel for what the novelist in James's story calls his 'general intention'. To James, in his preface, it is 'the intended sense of things' (*Art* 229)—that 'figure in the carpet' he has woven into 'the order, the form, the texture' of his tales, but which critics have failed to perceive, the novelist's perception of what his own life has meant, reordered into art. Lois is to build her 'house of fiction' (James, *Art* 46) out of the ruin of Danielstown; like Naomi in *The House in Paris*, 'putting away her aunt's home she began building her own' (*HP* 111). Like Bowen, she will travel to find 'somewhere nonchalant where politics bored them . . . perfect towns where shadows were strong like buildings, towns secret without coldness, unaware without indifference' (*LS* 123). Lois is to go to Italy, where Bowen found the setting and situation for her first novel, *The Hotel* (1927), itself a kind of 'Big House' novel about a small group of English guests isolated from the Italian world around them; much later, Bowen would match *Bowen's Court* with a second 'Big House' history, *The Shelbourne Hotel* (1951), celebrating the Anglo-Irish gentry's traditional Dublin home away from home and its ability to remain aloof from famine, rebellion, civil war, and the new Irish polity.

Describing the fire that destroys Danielstown and the way of life it embodies, Bowen notes the 'design of order and panic' that the night-time flames imprint upon the countryside, at last making the house conspicuous and real in a landscape that has denied its centrality and reality. The ordering illuminating fire is at once real, a political metaphor for rebellion, and a metaphor for that consummation towards which Lois seems headed, a consummation which is to be artistic rather than merely sexual. In a 1951 preface to some of her own reprinted early stories, Bowen recalled her limits when she began to write: 'I could spotlight, but not illumine steadily. I could expose or surprise people, but I had little sense of their continuity . . . The requisite for a novel is slow combustion; and I liked flashes . . . I wanted not so much to write a novel as to be able to write one if I wanted' (*SWA* 196). With *The Last September* she learned how to keep the fires—the home fires—burning or, to vary the metaphor, to combine the techniques of the time exposure and the flashbulb, to reveal and fix a way of life. The last words of *The Last September* are 'they saw too distinctly'.

Delivered in part at the national meeting of the American Conference for Irish Studies, Boston College, May 1986.

15

Elizabeth Bowen: Rebuilding the Big House

And may her bridegroom bring her to a house
Where all's accustomed, ceremonious;
For arrogance and hatred are the wares
Peddled in the thoroughfares.
How but in custom and in ceremony
Are innocence and beauty born?
Ceremony's a name for the rich horn,
And custom for the spreading laurel tree.

Yeats, 'A Prayer for my Daughter'

If *The Last September* freed Lois, and perhaps Bowen as well, from the constraints of 'the Anglo-Irish ambiguity' (*CI* 160), perhaps freed them into art, it also freed Bowen from a specific commitment to Anglo-Irish themes. In no other novel except *A World of Love* (1955), and in relatively few of her eighty short stories, does she return to an Irish setting to treat isolation, transiency, and a mixture of apprehension and eagerness about one's surroundings and those who inhabit those surroundings, the Anglo-Irish themes she defined in *The Last September*. Although these themes dominate Her presentations of human experience in many of her novels and short stories, their Anglo-Irish relevance is masked by English or European settings, as Le Fanu disguised his Irish themes in *Uncle Silas* with an English setting. Again and again a character fits uneasily and temporarily into the story's setting, while the setting contains hostile spies or other hidden dangers.

Frequently cited works by Elizabeth Bowen are cited parenthetically as follows: *BC, Bowen's Court*; *CI, Collected Impressions*; *CS, Collected Stories*; *HP, The House in Paris*; *SWA, Seven Winters: Memories of a Dublin Childhood and Afterthoughts: Pieces on Writing*; *TN, To the North*. I have usually employed page references alone in my extended discussion of *The Heat of the Day*.

The hotel guests who people her first novel, *The Hotel* (1927), are transients because they are guests. They are as isolated from the Italian population around them as the inhabitants of Danielstown were isolated from their Irish neighbours. Many beginning novelists, among them Bowen's contemporaries Virginia Woolf and E.M. Forster (Heath 23), have followed Henry James in using hotels and similar settings, which offer the novelist a chance to examine characters when they are separated from their usual circumstances. But most novelists are less consistently obsessed with transiency and isolation. If the hotel or tourist setting offers James a greater opportunity for psychological analysis by separating characters from their customary lives, for Bowen that setting isolates her characters from the mysterious foreign population around them, a distancing that even reappears in her 1951 history of Dublin's Shelbourne Hotel.

Bowen herself has recognized, a little defensively, that 'Someone remarked, Bowen characters are always in transit', adding that she portrays moments of transition because people are then more conscious, more alive (*Pictures* 41–2). Perhaps so, but the theme does coincide with the social anxieties she has portrayed in *The Last September*. Emmeline, the heroine of *To the North* (1932), is professionally involved with transients—she runs a travel agency. The story begins in a railway station, and she dies in a car crash. She is briefly in love with Markie, who 'lived in a flat, completely cut off, at the top of his sister's house . . . They made a point of not meeting . . . had separate telephone numbers' (*TN* 66). Nearing a break with Markie, Emmeline feels 'a sense of being swept strongly apart on a current from all she had held to' (*TN* 219). When she imagines the destruction of the house she shares with her sister-in-law, she imagines it in terms that deliberately recall the burning of Danielstown: 'Timber by timber [the house] fell to bits, as small houses are broken up daily to widen the roar of London. She saw the door open on emptiness: blanched walls as though after a fire (*TN* 218). *The House in Paris* (1935) also begins in a railway station, and is made up almost entirely of arrivals and departures, to end in another railway station. Portia is an awkward guest throughout *The Death of the Heart* (1938), and is spied upon by Anna. The subtitle of *Eva Trout* (1968) is *Changing Scenes*, and again the final scene takes place in a railway station. When she died, Bowen was at work on a novel to be called 'The Move-in', about unwelcome guests who invade a Big House in the West of Ireland.

Other elements that recall Bowen's Anglo-Irish themes appear in these novels. In *Bowen's Court* she describes a garden party at Mitchelstown Castle on 4 August 1914, the day Great Britain declared war on Germany. For her 'It was . . . a more final scene than we knew . . . That war—or call it now that first phase of war—was to go far before it had done with us.

After 1918 came the war in Ireland, with the burning down of many of the big houses' (*BC* 436). Given the particular significance of 1914 in Anglo-Ireland, we can understand when a character in *The House in Paris*, at a moment of crisis, is described as sitting 'nobly . . . behaving as she had behaved in August 1914' (*HP* 173). In *The Little Girls* (1964), the girls are separated from one another on 23 June 1914, the day Austria's ultimatum to Serbia began the series of mobilizations and declarations that led up to the War (Blodgett 70).

The House in Paris contains an important Irish episode which evokes some of Bowen's personal and class anxieties. When Karen, the heroine, visits her Anglo-Irish relatives in Cork, 'Country people transfixed them with sombre unseeing blue eyes' (*HP* 84). Her arrival by steamer is described in ways that emphasize her separation from Irish life on shore:

> The ship, checking, balanced uncertainly up the narrowing river . . . Houses asleep with their eyes open watched the vibrating ship pass . . . each turn of the river seemed to trap the ship more . . . A holy bell rang and a girl at a corner mounted her bicycle and rode out of sight . . . the tree-dark hill of Tivoli . . . looked like a hill in Italy faded; it stood in that flat clear light in which you think of the past and did not look like a country subject to racking change (*HP* 67–8).

The Anglo-Irish, as represented by Uncle Bill, whose 'house, Montebello, had been burnt in the troubles' (71), now live with their backs to the country they once ruled, looking endlessly out to sea. Bowen implicitly remembers Danielstown: 'Ghastly black staring photographs of the ruins of Montebello' hang in Uncle Bill's seaside villa 'outside the bathroom door' (71), an ironic ikon recalling *The Last September*. Karen's brief sojourn among the Anglo-Irish unsettles her, deflects her from her ordinary, orderly life and conventional expectations. Her dying aunt warns her that conventional life can be stifling, a nameless Irish girl she meets makes her think about making more daring choices. 'With Ray [her fiancé] I shall be so safe,' she tells her aunt; 'I wish the Revolution would come soon . . . I feel it's time something happened' (82). Back from Ireland, she turns to Max, foreign and purposeful like the IRA man Lois sees, and until now indifferent to her, despite her efforts to make him aware of her.

Bowen's short stories share these themes of transiency and isolation, as a sampling of their titles indicate: 'The Return' (1923); 'The New House' (1923); 'Coming Home' (1923); 'The Visitor' (1926); 'The Last Night in the Old Home' (1934); 'The Disinherited' (1934); 'Gone Away' (1946). The openings of many stories suggest the same themes:

> At the corner . . . a little man, hurrying back to his office after the lunch hour, was run over . . . ('The Evil that Men Do—', 1923)

The Contessina arrived at the hotel one Friday evening . . . ('The Contessina',
1924)

The train stopped every ten minutes after it left the junction . . . ('Aunt Tatty',
1926)

Herbert's feet, from dangling so long in the tram, had died of cold in his boots
. . . ('The Tommy Crans', 1930)

No sooner were the Watsons settled into their new home than Mrs Watson was
overcome by melancholy ('Attractive Modern Homes', 1936)

The car was sent to the train . . . to bring back Miss Fox, who was coming to
sew for a week ('The Needlecase', 1939)

Towards the end of her day in London Mrs Drover went round to her shut-up
house to look for several things she wanted to take away ('The Demon Lover',
1941)

Coming into Moher over the bridge, you may see a terrace of houses by the
river ('A Day in the Dark', 1955)

These themes are particularly prevalent in the comparatively small
number of short stories set in Ireland, which combine a sense of transiency
with an equally strong sense of tenacity, a combination particularly marked
in Bowen's supernatural stories. In 'The Back Drawing-Room' (1926), a
not very welcome guest at an intellectually pretentious party describes a
visit to Ireland just after the Troubles. Lost while bicycling, he enters a Big
House and encounters a weeping and obviously apprehensive lady: 'She
made me feel the end of the world was coming' (*CS* 208–9). Later he
learns that the Irish had burned the house two years before his visit. 'We
had expected it would have gone sooner, and the Barrans—the people
themselves—did too, though they never said a word,' he is told. 'Those
women went about looking green' (*CS* 209). The Barrans have left the
area, but cannot be any more alive 'than plants one's pulled up. They've
nothing to grow in, or hold on to' (*CS* 210). The story hints that the
Barrans' intense attachment to their house gives it a kind of imaginative
existence, makes it project itself onto the consciousness of a not very imaginative stranger; it is a version of the imaginative process by which Bowen
recreates Danielstown/Bowen's Court in her fiction. 'The Tommy Crans'
(1930)) is about an insubstantial but optimistic Anglo-Irish family; in 'Her
Table Spread' (1930), an Anglo-Irish castle, and the eager young woman
who owns it, are thrown into wild excitement at the social and sexual pos-
sibilities when a British destroyer enters the bay: 'These waters are very
lonely; the steamers have given up since the bad times; there is hardly a
pleasure boat' (*CS* 419).

Perhaps the most complex and revealing use of personal and political transiency is in a non-Irish story, 'Mysterious Kôr' (1944), in which wartime London seems 'like the moon's capital—shallow, cratered, extinct' (*CS* 728). The story is about personal transiency—two young lovers have no place to be private. But when the moon lights up London as clearly as the Danielstown fire lights up the Irish countryside, it too reveals 'too distinctly'. The girl sees London as Kôr, the lost ruined empty city in H. Rider Haggard's *She*. Her vision is of a larger transiency, as the besieged modern city becomes a desolate ancient city that suggests the transiency of all empires, dynasties, regimes, civilizations. Like the imaginatively recreated Big Houses in *The Last September* and *Bowen's Court*, only Kôr abides, because it is imaginary and therefore safe from destruction: 'By the time we've come to the end, Kôr may be the one city left' (*CS* 730).

The girl's vision draws on Bowen's own childhood response to reading *She*, which she recalled in a 1947 broadcast: 'I was inclined to see London as Kôr as London with the roofs still on. The idea that life in any capital city must be ephemeral, and with a doom ahead, remained with me—a curious obsession for an Edwardian child' (*SWA* 234). Bowen's own childhood experiences as she has described them in *Seven Winters* (1942) are marked by instability. Her father had a mental breakdown when she was about six, and her mother took her to live in England, where mother and daughter moved frequently. Her mother died when Elizabeth Bowen was thirteen; thereafter for a time she lived with one aunt or another. Given this personal experience of instability, and the fragility of the apparently stable Anglo-Irish society in which she grew up, Bowen's sense of the ephemeral is not such a 'curious obsession'. It is almost inevitable. Even in the late 1920s, she tells us, her father, visiting Dublin tea-shops, sat 'always, from some inherited landlord instinct, with his back placed firmly against a wall' (*BC* 445). Bowen's sense of personal and political insecurity uniquely qualified her to be a chronicler of life in wartime London. London's tension was familiar because it was Anglo-Ireland's tension on a larger scale. 'England became for me, when I was seven, the image of every kind of immunity', she tell us in *Bowen's Court*. 'The tradesmen's eyes, the houses themselves, looked *safe*. So much so that now, when I hear bombs fall on England, or see rubble that used to be a safe house, something inside me says "*Even here?*"' (*BC* 418). Now it is not an isolated Big House that is surrounded by hostile foreign forces, but an isolated England.

Bowen's response was to identify strongly with both England and Ireland during the War. She identified with England because the tense atmosphere of siege was already familiar to her, an Anglo-Irish habit. She identified with Ireland because neutral Ireland's 'abnormal isolation' from Britain, and unpopularity in Britain, also touched familiar moods of isolation and unpopularity. Writing in *The New Statesman and Nation* (12 April 1941), she defended Irish neutrality as 'Eire's first major independent act', and explained that 'the *positive* aspects of peace were newer, and seemed more essential, than Britain may realise' for a country 'now only just on the upgrade after internal strife . . . While the rights of Eire's neutrality may be questioned, the conviction behind it must be believed' (*New Statesman* 21:382–3). She also wrote reports on Irish public opinion for the Ministry of Information, stressing Ireland's commitment to neutrality and condemning Anglo-Ireland's continued British orientation and consequent aloofness from Irish affairs (Glendinning 202–4). She projects something of her own attitudes onto Francis Morris, an elderly Anglo-Irish landowner in *The Heat of the Day* (1949), who furiously defends Irish neutrality but also travels to England to offer his own services (*Heat* 69, 81).

Ireland's wartime enjoyment of that immunity which had once seemed characteristic of England became the theme of the several Irish short stories written during the War, and a major theme in *The Heat of the Day*. War overshadows 'A Love Story' (1940) and 'Unwelcome Idea' (1940), but these stories are about the War's comparative remoteness. The young girl in 'Sunday Afternoon' (1941) is, like Lois, stifling inside the dream that is Anglo-Ireland and its attachment to the past. She dreams of escaping to embattled London, and is eager for the anonymity she will achieve there, the loss of that special rooted identity her class has imposed upon her. In 'Summer Night' (1941), though war is still off stage, its tension pervades the language of the story and the moods of the characters. This tension is adequately explained by the story's events—a married woman drives through the night to visit her lover, the husband and children she has left behind are uneasy, her lover is trying to rid himself of unwanted guests. But the language suggests larger tensions and larger breakdowns of order. There are the apparently secure but threatened interiors familiar from *The Last September*. The house she has left is 'a fortress against the wakeful night' (*CS* 595), but in the rooms 'the human order seemed to have lapsed' and one child feels 'anarchy . . . all through the house tonight' (596–7). One of her lover's guests has come in order 'not to have to face the screen of his own mind, on which . . . the war-broken towers of Europe, constantly stood . . . In the heart of the neutral Irishman indirect suffering pulled like a crooked knife' (588). He too feels political and personal isolation. 'I say, this war's an awful illumination; it's destroyed our dark;' he observes, in terms that recall the illusion-banishing fires at the end of *The Last September*; 'we have to see where we are' (590).

In these stories, and in *The Heat of the Day*, Ireland is portrayed with a kind of nostalgia as a place where the order of the past still survives—or has been restored—and so as the embodiment of certain positive values.

Bowen's major non-fiction of the 1940s also focuses on Ireland as a place where order has been retained. 'I suppose that everyone, fighting or just enduring, carried within him one private image, one peaceful scene', she remarks in *Bowen's Court*. 'Mine was Bowen's Court. War made me that image out of a house built of anxious history' (*BC* 457). It is true that this mood partially reflects social reality. Those who were able to travel from England to Ireland during the Second World War did find themselves returning to pre-War comforts and abundance, if only comparatively. And the ending of Ireland's Civil War had removed any danger to Big Houses and their inhabitants. But it was clearly wartime experience that created for Bowen a more positive and welcoming Ireland, if only temporarily, and if only illusory: 'Like all pictures . . .' this 'picture of peace . . . did not quite correspond with any reality. Or, you might have called the country a magic mirror, reflecting something that could not really exist. That illusion—peace as its most ecstatic—I held to, to sustain me throughout war' (*BC* 457). This welcome atmosphere of peace, in contrast to the dangers of London, partially transformed Ireland in her imagination into a place where ancient enmities had been forgiven, perhaps forgotten.

But at the same time, 'The scene was a crystal in which, while one was looking, a shadow formed' (*BC* 457). Emotionally, perhaps, that shadow was the War waiting outside Ireland, but it is also the 'anxious history' of Bowen's Court and of Ireland, which obtrudes even in her celebrations and justifications of Anglo-Ireland. In *Bowen's Court* (1942), her essay 'The Big House' (1940), and her history of the Shelbourne Hotel (1951), while she is eager to affirm an Irish identity for herself, her family, and her class, and to place the tradition they represent near the centre of Irish life, she simultaneously undercuts these affirmations, either explicitly or implicitly. Her uneasiness with her assertions inevitably recalls her recognition of Anglo-Ireland's isolation and claustrophobia in *The Last September*. '. . . The preoccupations of war-time may have caused me to see Bowens in a peculiar or too much intensified light', she admits, at the end of *Bowen's Court*:

> They were in most ways . . . fairly ordinary Anglo-Irish country gentry . . . In the main, I do not feel that they require defence—you, on the other hand, may consider them indefensible. Having obtained their position through an injustice, they enjoyed that position through privilege. But, while they wasted no breath in deprecating an injustice it would not have been to their interest to set right, they did not abuse their privilege—on the whole . . . Isolation, egotism and, on the whole, lack of culture made in them for an independence one has to notice because it becomes, in these days, rare. Independence was the first quality of a class now, I am told, becoming extinct . . . I recognize that a class, like a breed of animals, *is* due to . . . become extinct should it fail to adapt . . . The gentry, as a class, may or may not prove able to make adaptations . . . To my mind, they are tougher than they appear. To live as though living gave them no trouble has

been the first imperative of their make-up: to do this has taken a virtuosity into which courage enters more than has been allowed. In the last issue, they have lived at their own expense (*BC* 456).

This passage is typical in its recognition of Anglo-Ireland's traditional isolation from Irish life, and echoes similar passages in *The Last September*, though the partial note of self-justification is new. Other passages in *Bowen's Court* are more confident in presenting the Bowens and the Anglo-Irish as accepted presences in Ireland. When she describes Henry Bowen III (1723–88), the fifth head of the Bowen family in Ireland and the builder of Bowen's Court, she remarks that 'In spite of his ancestry, he got from the country people the feeling they used to keep for their natural lords . . . In Ireland, one endears oneself by palpably having a good time. And Henry, for all his Protestant politics, by now *felt* as Irish as Lord Muskerry' (*BC* 125). In the Bowens' 'three or four generations of life in Ireland, something had worked on their temperaments: they were now Irish in being, if not in interest . . . They *were* the people, and others fell in with them' (*BC* 129–31). The Bowens 'did not let themselves be stampeded' (*BC* 276) into anti-Catholic hysteria in the 1820s. Thanks to the exertions of women like her great-grandmother, 'in the isolated big houses' during the Famine, 'natural ties were formed that have lasted since' (*BC* 311). She eagerly describes the crowd of tenants who turned out to unharness the horses and draw the carriage up the avenue when her father first brought his bride to Bowen's Court (*BC* 393). The crowd attending her father's funeral was 'A great sea of people, so many hundreds of people that it looked like a dream, people from all over the country, from the most remote mountainy places' (*BC* 446). She suggests that local acceptance of the Bowens kept Bowen's Court from being burned in 1920, so that 'the kind inherited tie between us and our country was not broken' (*BC* 440). More equivocally, Robert Cole Bowen (1830–88), perhaps the most serious landlord among the Bowens, was 'Among the country people . . . at once admired as a big handsome figure, "the Captain", a hard rider, and dreaded (not without relish) as a hard man' (*BC* 292). Because landlords were so widely blamed for the Famine, she suggests that 'Robert must, as an adolescent, have not only hated the Famine but hated his country for suffering. All this was the negation of his new cult, Success.' She describes his office, where 'rents were taken in, with a merciless punctuality, and wages scrupulously paid out . . . many remember trembling as they came this way' (*BC* 315–16).

Assertions that the Bowens were rooted in Ireland, and accepted, are swamped by passages in which they appear as alien and imposed rulers. She sees the landscape in which they settled as particularly lonely and inhospitable, and the family history itself is grim and full of rejections. 'The structure of the great Anglo-Irish society was raised over a country in martyrdom' (*BC* 248), she declares. She sees 'knockout home truths' (*BC* 223) in Lord Clare's speech advocating the Act of Union, which defines 'confiscation' as the only title to Anglo-Irish estates, and 'the old inhabitants of the island' as 'brooding over their discontents in sullen indignation' (*BC* 220). And, while recognizing the truth of Clare's speech, she deplores both its effect and the injustice it so accurately describes: '. . . the Union put the last seal on an injustice that had for centuries made the country unsound: that confiscation (or series of confiscations) Fitzgibbon [Clare] had named as being the English settlers' title was the first cause' of the 'landless distress' that agitated Ireland for much of the nineteenth century (*BC* 262–3).

The opening pages of *Bowen's Court* emphasize the emptiness and secretiveness of the landscape around the estate. 'The country conceals its pattern of life . . . it is not lack of people that makes the country seem empty. It is an inherent emptiness of its own' (*BC* 5). Nor did the 'unhappy family history' (*BC* 392) of the Bowens offer much evidence that they had rooted themselves in the lands they owned. The first Bowen in Ireland probably arrived in 1649 (*BC* 62), as a soldier with Cromwell, and so the Bowens owed their estate to the most savage of Ireland's conquerors, the cruellest villain—from an Irish nationalist point of view—in Ireland's sad history. The two ikons at Bowen's Court were portraits of Cromwell and William of Orange—unhyphenated Ireland's supreme anti-heroes—in matching frames, at the top of the main staircase (*BC* 105). Though Henry Bowen I received the Bowen's Court lands in 1653 (*BC* 73), neither he nor his three successors as heads of the family chose to live on those lands; there was no house there until Henry Bowen III built Bowen's Court in 1775. The next heir disliked Ireland, and moved to Bath, leaving an unhappy brother to cope with the estate, an onerous task briefly taken up by Henry Bowen V, whose romantic speculative nature was thwarted and contracted by his duties as landlord (*BC* 284–6). Henry V died in 1841, after ruling Bowen's Court for only four years, and compulsively wearing himself out in its service. His widow wasted money in a hopeless lawsuit, and struggled with the Famine. Their son Robert (1830–88) threw himself into managing the estate successfully, but 'cracked' (*BC* 364), partly from the strain of his exacting tyranny over his tenants, but chiefly from his bitter resentment at his heir, Henry Bowen VI, who preferred Dublin and the law to a squire's life in County Cork. In Robert Bowen's will, 'In fact, if not the destruction the headlong decline of Bowen's Court seems to have been implicit . . . he planned the destruction of his life's work . . . He determined Henry [VI] should not enjoy his trees, so wood after wood began to fall to the axe' (*BC* 376). Later, Henry VI's own mental breakdown sent his wife and daughter—Elizabeth Bowen—into English exile. Elizabeth Bowen herself inherited the estate in 1930, but spent only summers there until she tried to settle permanently in 1952. Even then her stays were intermittent. She sold the house and moved to England in 1959.

The Bowens' history, then, is one of uneasy relationships to Ireland, to their own estates, and to each other, victimized rather than sustained by the family myth. Several of them suffered from melancholia. Bowen's Court was attacked by the Irish in the 1798 Rising, and garrisoned against the Fenians in 1867. Though she sets out to celebrate and justify her family, their way of life, and their class, she is honest about the ambiguities of their position. The book is partly a plea for forgiveness, partly a bid for inclusion in Ireland even at this late hour. The Bowens were caught in the predicaments of Irish history. Their pattern related 'to the outside more definite pattern of history' (*BC* 452) even when they were unaware of that relationship. That history imposed upon them their equivocal identity.

Bowen asserts Anglo-Ireland's Irish identity more forcefully, but less convincingly, in a kind of coda to *Bowen's Court*, her 1940 essay 'The Big House', written for Sean O'Faolain's Dublin journal *The Bell*. 'I have stressed in my first chapter, and tried to make felt since, the unusual isolation of *Bowen's Court*', she tell us in *Bowen's Court* (*BC* 254), and Danielstown is also shown as isolated in *The Last September*. But in 'The Big House' she treats 'the isolation, or loneliness, of my own house' (*CI* 195) as something noticed by newly arrived travellers, but hardly perceptible to her: 'The loneliness of my house, as of many others, is more an effect than a reality . . . not so much isolation as mystery'. She concedes that Anglo-Irish Big Houses, 'Unlike the low, warm ruddy French and English manors, . . . have made no natural growth from the soil,' while 'the big house people were handicapped, shadowed and to an extent queered—by their pride, by their indignation at their decline and by their divorce from the countryside in whose heart their struggle was carried on' (*CI* 196–7). Not all Big Houses are really big, she points out, and many 'that had begun in glory were soon only maintained by struggle and sacrifice' (197) at great personal cost to their owners. She praises their inhabitants for a curious virtue: 'It is to their credit that, with grass almost up to their doors and hardly a sixpence to turn over, they continued to be resented by the rest of Ireland as being the heartless rich' (198). Bowen's central purpose is to plead that the Big House be accepted and even valued in Ireland:

> the idea from which these houses sprang was, before everything, a social one. That idea, although lofty, was at first rigid and narrow—but it could extend itself, and it must if the big house is to play an alive part in the alive Ireland of to-day. What is fine about the social idea is that it means the subjugation of the personal to the impersonal. In the interest of good manners and good behaviour

people learned to subdue their own feelings. The result was an easy and unsuspicious intercourse. 'Cannot we scrap the past, with its bitterness and barriers, and all meet, throwing in what we have?' . . . big, half empty rooms seem to ask . . . Symbolically . . . the doors of the big houses stand open all day; it is only regretfully that they are barred up at night . . . But who ever walks in? Is it suspicion, hostility, irony that keeps so much of Ireland away from the big house door? If this lasts, we impoverish life all round. The big house has much to learn—and it must learn if it is to survive at all. But it also has much to give . . . From inside many big houses (and these will be the survivors) barriers are being impatiently attacked. But it must be seen that a barrier has two sides (*CI* 199–200).

Ironically, when Bowen was interviewed for *The Bell* shortly after this piece appeared, the interviewer challenged her right to call herself an Irish writer. 'I regard myself as an Irish novelist', she replied:

As long as I can remember, I've been extremely conscious of being Irish—even when I was writing about very un-Irish things . . . All my life I've been going backwards and forwards . . . but that has never robbed me of the strong feeling of my nationality (Glendinning 207).

That interview took place in an appropriate setting, Dublin's Shelbourne Hotel, one-time Dublin headquarters for the Anglo-Irish gentry, and therefore, as a kind of ultimate and collective Big House, a congenial subject for Bowen's second work of Anglo-Irish social history. In *The Shelbourne Hotel* (1951) she once again examines her own class and its role in Irish life, to claim for the Anglo-Irish—not always with total confidence—a centrality and a share in Irish loyalty and love which she had denied in *The Last September* and only partially urged in *Bowen's Court*. The book's subtitle in its British edition—*A Centre in Dublin Life for more than a Century*—asserts the centrality, though hotels are usually centres only for a city's visitors, not for its inhabitants. Just as Yeats came to place the Anglo-Irish gentry at the centre of his definition of Irish virtue and heroism, so Bowen assigns to the Shelbourne and its regular clientele a national and social centrality:

For the Irishman in general it is a symbol, a legend—only not a myth because, happily, its existence in time and place is so exuberantly apparent. It stands for grandeur—which, in Ireland, we have not yet become ashamed to like. It stands for a certain social idea of life: It is the image of style and well-conductedness . . . We Irish . . . may also, because of our contrariety, have a respect for it because it is not wholly typical of our country. We have a reputation for distress, miscarried projects, evanescent dreams and romantic gloom: the Shelbourne is the antithesis of those things . . . The hotel's own past is related to that of Ireland; both its character and its place in the human pattern are important . . . this particular hotel . . . has carried on its own impassive, cheerful, wonderfully unchanged life throughout changing, sometimes distressful times . . . provided a social-domestic nexus for the country in which it has its being . . . it engages respect—most of all, perhaps, because of something dispassionate and impartial about its attitude when, all round it, feeling was running high (*Shelbourne* 10–12).

In praising the Shelbourne's social role and its impassivity, Bowen praises not only the headquarters but also the alleged virtues of her own class, using them to persuade her readers that that class constitutes the guardians and repositories of whatever is best in Irish tradition. It is a bold claim, advanced deftly and at times persuasively.

Given this bold claim that the history of Anglo-Ireland's favourite hotel can somehow represent the history of the Irish nation, what events emerge as important? Because the book is at once an institutional, a social and a national history, it is not surprising that institutional events should receive much attention. Negotiations about leases and building occupy many pages, while the Famine comes and goes in a sentence and a half. But Bowen tries to give such events as royal visits a national significance. When she describes them, she ignores the well-known protest demonstrations and other forms of nationalist resentment which they provoked. Joyce describes the Irish mockery of Prince Albert during Queen Victoria's 1849 visit, the Irish custom of making the performance of 'God Save the King' inaudible with 'a storm of hisses, shouts, and shushes', Queen Victoria's 1900 entry into Dublin 'in the midst of a silent people' (Joyce *CW* 163–5). On that occasion, Yeats and Maud Gonne had organized counter demonstrations. Nationalist attitudes toward Edward VII's 1903 visit appear in Joyce's 'Ivy Day in the Committee Room', which accurately reminds us that Irish public bodies were unanimous in refusing to greet the King with addresses of welcome. Incidentally, Bowen's description of Edwardian life in Dublin nowhere refers to Joyce, the most committed and meticulous recorder of citizen life during the period. Though she draws on George Moore's Shelbourne Hotel scenes in his *A Drama in Muslin* (1886), she ceases to quote Moore just as he moves into one of his most striking passages. Moore describes two young ladies departing from the Shelbourne to be presented at Dublin Castle. Hotel guests and servants admire them. Moore does not mention any admiring crowd of plebian onlookers, watching the spectacle from across the street. But Bowen has such a crowd. She calls them 'an audience of old timers, critical but well-mannered . . . connoisseurs'. The 'ceremony' is

satisfying to all . . . the pleasure-life of the Shelbourne . . . was a life conducted with the approval of the surrounding city . . . Ireland esteems pleasure and likes pomp; all she asks in return from those who enjoy is that they should comport themselves in a worthy manner (*Shelbourne* 133–4).

Instead of this loyal, adulatory crowd, Moore, in the passage Bowen does not quote, shows his ladies driving through the Dublin slums near the Castle, hungrily eyed by a sullen, tattered, sinister crowd, with every stain of misery . . . revealed to the silken exquisites who, a little frightened, strove to hide themselves within the scented shadows of their broughams: and in like manner, the bloom on every aristocratic cheek, the glitter of every diamond, the richness of every plume were visible to the avid eyes of those who stood without in the wet and the cold (Moore, *Drama* 171).

Bowen does at times recognize how the Shelbourne, like the Big House, was isolated from the main currents of nineteenth and twentieth century Ireland, and how anxious and isolated the Anglo-Irish were, even in their city refuge. 'On such . . . occasions' as Daniel O'Connell's funeral (1847), 'crowds and emotion tended to concentrate' north of the Liffey; 'The south side, wherein the Shelbourne stood, preserved a tense, ghostly, genteel quiet . . . more apprehensive guests could remain indoors, hurriedly draw their curtains, and close their eyes, only faintly hearing the distant uproar' (*Shelbourne* 70). She recognizes the importance of the great early years at the Abbey Theatre, but from the Shelbourne point of view the Abbey was 'a little suspect,' and to go there 'an escapade . . . one went, if at all, by stealth, or at least daringly . . . If one ventured to go, one generally wore an ulster, both as a protection against draughts and in order to conceal oneself from the notice, as far as might be, of what were thought to be "nationalistic" crowds' (*Shelbourne* 147–8). She commends the impassivity of an Easter Monday tea-time crowd attempting to ignore the 1916 Rising outside the windows.

As for Anglo-Irish anxiety and isolation, it is eloquently expressed when she remembers what the Shelbourne meant to people like herself: 'Oh, those first evenings when we have come to town—away from the leaks in our roofs, the ghosts on our stairs, the dark dripping woods, the silent mountains behind them!' (*Shelbourne* 32). Later, in a chapter entitled 'Gay Days', she praises the 'gaiety crackling through the Shelbourne' (148) in the 1880s, as the Anglo-Irish found themselves 'threatened by class war' under the double assault of agitation for tenants' rights and Home Rule:

Against this daunting background . . . how did the Shelbourne house party manage to carry on? Nonchalance, or even the air of it, does, all things considered, deserve esteem. The hotel . . . became a heartening fortress . . . Here one was in the company of one's fellows; one could foregather, talk unguardedly, let off steam, drink to better days . . . Those who so merrily coached . . . from the hotel went hunting . . . packed off their daughters to dance and themselves sallied out, resplendent . . . had demons of worry crouched on their Shelbourne bedposts . . . It may be said that just such survival worries had been inflicted by our friends themselves—or . . . by their progenitors, agents, kinsfolk—on helpless tenants, for generations past. The reply is, they did not see things that way. *Why* not? Because they did not—which, sufficient or not, is the answer I propose to give. If one does not excuse people, one need not explain them (*Shelbourne* 154–5).

Bowen's Irish fiction in the mid- and late 1940s extends her preoccupation with Ireland as an accessible, stable, and accepting past, anachronistically preserved in an anarchic world. She treats this theme ambiguously in 'The Happy Autumn Fields' (1944), with only slight ambiguity in *The Heat of the Day* (1949). In 'The Happy Autumn Fields', Mary, dozing in her bombed-out London flat, finds herself walking across the fields with an orderly Victorian family, led by 'Papa, who carried his Alpine stick' (*CS* 671). She is saddened to lose them when her lover awakens her, and her own life seems 'like a book once read [which] she remembered clearly but with indifference' (677); later, asleep again, she experiences part of the family's evening. William Trevor has insisted that the setting is Irish as well as Victorian: 'It is typical of the woman she was that nowhere in the story does Elizabeth Bowen say so. In her Anglo-Irish way she assumed all that must surely be obvious' (Trevor 131). In fact, the setting is Bowen's Court, and members of the Victorian family have names—Constance, Robert, Henrietta, Sarah, Fitzgeorge—found among Bowen's own paternal or maternal relatives (*BC* 381, 383–4, 460) in the nineteenth century. Papa with his Alpine stick and his drillmaster manner seems to be the formidable Robert Cole Bowen himself, on the August 11 walk the Bowen children of that time described in their jointly kept 1876 diary; in both story and diary, two of the boys are about to return to school (*BC* 334).

Bowen wrote the story in July–August 1944, just after her own London house had been bombed. It has been conventionally read as a kind of escapist dream, contrasting Victorian order and stability with wartime London and the literally tottering house in which Mary falls asleep: 'it is the blasted present that is fragmentary, impossible, and therefore illusory . . . the pre-1914 distant past, with its spaciousness and grace' is pitted 'against the crude war-torn present' (Glendinning 179); 'the lost idyllic world of Victorian Ireland' (Lee 159). The dream offers a kind of refreshing escape from the war in time, as Bowen's wartime visits to Ireland offered refreshment by a change of place—though she also reported on them to the British government. In a 1945 broadcast, Bowen suggests that reading Trollope's novels in wartime provided similar refreshment for many people (*CI* 231–45). But there are dark areas in Trollope's fiction, and the Victorian world Mary penetrates also has its shadows.

The family's walk through the fields is a rigid operation, with little Arthur's hand 'a twisting prisoner' (*CS* 671) in Papa's. The fields are autumnal, with 'the colour of valediction' (672), the boys oppressed by their imminent return to school and perhaps by the estate itself, unsuccessfully concealing 'the repugnance of victims, though . . . further from being heirs than Robert' (672). Papa's manner recalls the tension Robert Cole Bowen created in his own family, and 'The field and all these outlying fields in view knew as Sarah knew that they were Papa's' (671). During the walk, and later in the drawing-room, Sarah—in whose mind and body twentieth-century Mary finds herself—realizes that she is in love with Eugene, a neighbouring landowner, and that he loves her. But she also realizes that her younger sister, Henrietta, is fiercely possessive, and will work to thwart this love. Sarah feels 'dislocation . . . formless dread . . . apprehended that the seconds were numbered' as a result of 'what she must call her . . . bad dream' (681)—does Sarah visit war-torn London while Mary visits Victorian Cork? Henrietta makes explicit the threat that Sarah feels. 'Whatever tries to come between me and Sarah becomes nothing,' she tells Eugene; '. . . no one will ever be quite alone with Sarah. You do not even know what you are trying to do. It is *you* who are making something terrible happen' (683). Henrietta is quite right. As the story ends, Mary learns that both Sarah and Henrietta died young and unmarried, and that Eugene apparently died on the very evening he received this threat: 'Fitzgeorge wonders, and says he will always wonder, what made the horse shy in those empty fields' (685). Henrietta was a kind of witch, and her possessiveness led her to destroy Eugene.

Mary's visit to the past makes her impatient with the insecurities of 1944, and nostalgic for an apparently more stable world. 'The source, the sap must have dried up, or the pulse must have stopped, before you and I were conceived,' she exclaims to her lover. 'So much flowed through people; so little flows through us' (683–4). Her yearning for continuity prefigures a major theme of *The Heat of the Day*. But in fact, by finding—or by being found by—a box of old papers, Mary has been summoned—by her own yearning for stability, by Henrietta's answering determination that nothing change, by Sarah's apprehension of disaster—into a less than tranquil past. Henrietta's jealousy is as lethal as a bomb. Though Mary seems to find that past preferable, it is not. It is sinister, static, and stifling. Mary has a lover who cares about her, and apparently a future; Henrietta robs Sarah of both. Bowen's uneasiness about the idyllic myth of Anglo-Ireland before 1914 emerges clearly, and 'The Happy Autumn Fields', like 'The Demon Lover' (1941) and 'Hand in Glove' (1952) is one of several stories that anticipate the exorcism of that myth in *A World of Love*.

In *The Shelbourne Hotel*, Bowen briefly describes the tense period in which *The Last September* is set, with the burning of Big Houses and the consequent departure of many Anglo-Irish families into English exile. But 'Others', she tells us, 'more deeply rooted into their land, lived on in their stables or lodges, and, together with those who had somehow come through unscathed, waited to see what yet the future might bring. These chose well: they and their children were to become more closely and truly integrated into the Ireland that did at last emerge than, in the past, their ancestors could have thought possible' (*Shelbourne* 207–8). Bowen follows this with an assertion that the Hotel itself 'exemplifies not only this survival but this fusion—between veteran guests and veteran staff, with "the bad times" now safely behind them, there can be felt a link of unspoken things.' The choice of hotel guests and staff, masters and servants, to argue this integration and fusion suggests that for Bowen it must still be seen in feudal terms. A similar attitude shapes the Irish scenes in *The Heat of the Day* (1949), which present a Big House integrated into its landscape, and an Irish butler who rejoices at British victories and gladly sacrifices his own oil and candles to provide 'the mistress' with extravagant illumination (*Heat* 168).

The Heat of the Day is a dream of Anglo-Irish integration into Ireland by deliberately accepting and connecting with that myth of the Anglo-Irish past which elsewhere Bowen treats more negatively and describes as 'the demonic power of the family myth' (*CI* 4). Begun during the Second World War (Glendinning 187), the novel strongly reflects her eagerness to see Ireland as stable and welcoming during that period. The setting is wartime London, portrayed as partly destroyed, partly makeshift, and completely vulnerable. When an Irish kinsman unexpectedly leaves his estate to Stella Rodney's son, Roderick, she visits Ireland because Roderick's military duties prevent him from doing so. She finds the Big House, Mount Morris, a place of order, stability, traditional loyalties, and above all of continuity, in contrast to the transiency of wartime London. Stella is told that Mount Morris and all that it represents is 'a thing of the past' and urged 'to advise the boy to get rid of it—sell outright, before he ties himself up . . . he and his generation will have no use for that. All they will want is to travel light. After all, the future is in their hands' (*Heat* 82). But Roderick plans to settle there after the War, and attempt to fulfil his kinsman's testamentary 'hope that he may care in his own way to carry on the old tradition' (72).

Against the permanence of Mount Morris, Bowen sets the transiency of Stella herself, who lives in furnished flats, and the transiency of wartime London, where buildings and people can vanish overnight. Stella, long divorced, carries on an affair with Robert Kelway. She is haunted by the restlessly wandering Harrison, who rightly suspects that Robert is betraying secrets to the Germans. Robert's relatives live in a house that is permanently for sale, after a series of moves; 'everything was brought here from somewhere else, with the intention of being moved again,' he explains to Stella, 'like touring scenery from theatre to theatre' (121). Stella and Harrison have encounters with Louie, who wanders about seeking male companions. Louie, alone in London with her husband in North Africa, feels 'like a day tripper who has missed the last train home' (145). When

Stella visits Mount Morris, she recognizes her own acceptance of transiency as wrong. The visit empowers her to confront Robert with his treason, a confrontation that destroys him.

This emotional connection between Mount Morris as loyalty to the past and Robert's disloyalty ties the survival of Mount Morris to the survival of Britain, a point reinforced by repeatedly interrupting the story of Robert's treason, Harrison's enigmatic pursuit, and Stella's uncertainty about them both with news of important Allied victories. Stella learns of Montgomery's decisive victory at El Alamein (4–5 November 1942) during her visit to Mount Morris. The battle—to Churchill 'not even the beginning of the end. But . . . perhaps, the end of the beginning'—also marks a personal turning point. Roderick visits Mount Morris in February 1944, the year 'General Smuts called . . . the Year of Destiny' (308). Roderick's continuation of the Anglo-Irish tradition is to be a result of Allied victory.

Unlike Danielstown, and even Bowen's Court, Mount Morris belongs in its countryside: 'The river traced the boundary of the lands . . . This valley cleavage into a distance seemed like an offering to the front windows: in return, the house devoted the whole muted fervour of its being to a long gaze' (162). Its isolation is soothing and redemptive rather than threatening: 'assurance of being utterly out of reach added annullingness to [Stella's] deep sleep . . . Her place in time had been lost . . . Were these deep sleeps of hers periodic trances, her spirit's passing into another season? Were they the birth-sleeps, each time, of some profound change?' (*Heat* 168, 176).

In Mount Morris's atmosphere, Stella thinks of the house's continuity as a book, and realizes

> That her own life could be a chapter missing from this book need not mean that the story was at an end; at a pause it was, but perhaps a pause for the turning point? There was still to be seen what came of Cousin Francis's egotistic creative boldness with regard to the future, of his requisitioning for that purpose of Roderick. A man of faith has always a son somewhere . . . Roderick had . . . been fitted into a destiny; better, it seemed to her, than freedom in nothing (*Heat* 175).

Uncharacteristically, she thinks about the past and the future, of the generations of women who married into the house and of the bride Roderick will someday bring there, her 'eyes—unspent and fearless' (175). Stella herself even becomes for a moment, looking into a mirror, 'immortal as a portrait. Momentarily she was the lady of the house . . . She wore the look of everything she had lost the secret of being' (173–4). When Roderick is finally able to enter Mount Morris, he too sets 'himself to consider the idea of succession' and senses a confluence . . . nothing might *be* possible to finish—who would, indeed, aspire to be the final man? It was a matter of continuing—but what, what? As to that, there ought to be access to the mindless knowledge locked up in rocks, in the stayers-on . . . he ought to make a will . . . By a written will one made subject some other person—but he saw that what worked most on the world, on him, were the unapprehendable inner wills of the dead (*Heat* 312–13).

Bowen presents Roderick's eager acceptance of Mount Morris and his commitment to its tradition as a natural joining of past to present after a sharp but temporary and perhaps necessary rupture. Stella, thinking of Roderick's as yet unknown bride, asks herself

> Of how much, of what, or by whom, the entering smiling newcomer had been disembarrassed she never would know—the fatal connexion between the past and future having been broken before her time. It had been Stella, her generation, who had broken the link—what else could this be but its broken edges that she felt grating inside her soul? . . . this for the bride would be a room to be first marvelled at, then changed. Required to mean what they had not, old things would be pushed into a new position; those which could not comply, which could not be made to pick up the theme of the new song, would go (*Heat* 176).

As she meditates, Stella finds in a corner of the drawing-room a 'picture to banish', an old magazine illustration showing the sinking of the *Titanic*, and thinks 'The significance of this . . . picture . . . would never be known'. But perhaps it can. To many at the time, or looking back after the First World War, the sinking of the *Titanic* marked the end of the old idyllic pre-War world, with its traditional loyalties and comfortable assumptions about its own stability and permanence. To Bowen herself, the sinking had been 'the first black crack across the surface of *exterior* things' (*BC* 423). The picture reminds us that to connect with the past is possible, to recreate it is not.

Roderick himself has long sensed the deracination his mother's generation had created for themselves, and instinctively sought pattern and tradition. Even as a child, Stella recalls,

> In general, he was in favour of what was happening, but preferred what *had* happened as being more complete . . . *as* a child, preferring objects or myths to people he probably had resembled most other children . . . how if he came to set too much store by a world of which she, both as herself and as an instrument of her century, had deprived him? He would have esteemed, for instance, organic family life . . . Roderick was ready to entertain a high, if abstract, idea of society . . . what he liked about people was the order in which they could be arranged (*Heat* 60–1).
> Possessorship of Mount Morris affected Roderick strongly. It established for him, and was adding to day by day, what might be called an historic future. The house came out to meet his growing capacity for attachment . . . became the hub of his imaginary life . . . Whether he sought them out or they him; whether

they nourished him or he them, could not be said . . . They neither deceived him nor set up tension (*Heat* 50).

Roderick's commitment recalls Bowen's words about Henry Bowen III, who built Bowen's Court and established his family there: 'life flowed through him from the past on into the future and he resolved to make a worthy channel for it. He thought more of vocation and less of privilege' (*BC* 167).

Only here and there in *The Heat of the Day* does Bowen recognize, as she had so often in *The Last September*, the ways that the Anglo-Irish myth could be stifling. Like Lois, Stella had sought and obtained freedom from tradition. 'And to what did our fine feelings, our regard for the arts, our intimacies, our inspiring conversations, our wish to be free of the bonds of sex and class and nationality . . . bring us?' Bowen asks bitterly in *Bowen's Court*: 'To 1939' (*BC* 125). Roderick turns back to that 'Traditional sanctity and loveliness' that Yeats celebrated in 'Coole Park and Ballylee, 1931'. Yet even Mount Morris is shadowed by the Anglo-Irish sense of separation, though that sense is now something to be recognized and, if possible, overcome. Because Roderick is afraid he might be considered 'an usurper' (202) by his kinsman's widow, he visits her—in effect, visits the Anglo-Irish past—to make sure she does not resent his inheritance of the estate. But Cousin Nettie fled Mount Morris long ago, finding life there unendurable. 'There have been too many ancestors' (207), she tells Roderick. 'Nature hated us; that was a most dangerous position to build a house in—once the fields noticed me with him, the harvests began failing' (217). It was she who hung the picture of the sinking *Titanic* at Mount Morris as a kind of warning ikon. She has lived for years in an English rest home, but, as the picture suggests, she is not mad but clairvoyant. For her the 'illusion' of Anglo-Irish stability has been impossible. '. . . Was it not chiefly here . . . under this illusion that Cousin Nettie Morris—and who now knew how many more before her?—had been pressed back, hour by hour . . . into cloudland?' Stella muses;

> Ladies had gone not quite mad, not quite even that, from in vain listening for meaning in the loudening ticking of the clock . . . Virtue with nothing more to spend, honour saying nothing, but both present . . . knowledge was not to be kept from them; it sifted through to them, stole up behind them, reached them by intimations—they suspected what they refused to prove. That had been their decision. So, there had been the cases of the enactment of ignorance having become too much, insupportable (*Heat* 174).

The Heat of the Day therefore recognizes Anglo-Ireland's tense and illusory existence even as it endorses the importance of connecting with a revised version of that tradition, this time with a commitment to the land

itself rather than to a self-imposed aloofness. Roderick's task is not to re-
live the past but to fashion new channels which will connect it with the
future—a theme Bowen underlines with the analogous story of Louie, who
has a child by one of her casual partners, then learns of her husband's
death, and calmly, deliberately connects the child with him and her own
childhood home, rooting the future firmly in an ordered past.

16

A Ghost of Style

Exorcising the Anglo-Irish Past

'We cannot afford to have ghosts . . . I wish not to drag up the past but to help lay it.'

Elizabeth Bowen, 'Afterword' to *Bowen's Court*

Writing during the Second World War, Bowen was sufficiently attracted by the stability neutral Ireland seemed to represent to be eager to relate the Anglo-Irish tradition to the Irish tradition with which it had usually shared only a mutual sense of exclusion. She was also eager to present that Anglo-Irish tradition as viable and sustaining, while simultaneously recognizing its origin in conquest and its uneasiness about the unhyphenated Irish and their probable hostility, or at any rate their frequent refusal to love. But her own partially acknowledged uneasiness about both the reality and the myth of the Anglo-Irish past appears from time to time, even in *The Heat of the Day*. She had made that uneasiness a central theme in *The Last September*; it is central once again in *A World of Love* (1955), her last 'Big House' novel, a final closing of accounts with the myth of Anglo-Ireland. 'No age is golden', Bowen remarks, nearing the end of *The Shelbourne Hotel*; 'or not, at any rate, until it recedes a long way into the past'. The new post-Treaty Dublin 'offers the Shelbourne visitor something more than those ghostly, nostalgic beauties George Moore saw' (*Shelbourne* 221–2). In *A World of Love* Anglo-Ireland is present as a nostalgic ghost, for a brief time able to invade the world of the living, but too weak to remain there.

Bowen anticipates some of the key elements in *A World of Love* in several short stories written earlier. The collection of letters and photographs that send twentieth-century Mary into her visitation of nineteenth-century Anglo-Ireland in 'The Happy Autumn Fields' reappears in the novel, with

Frequently cited works by Elizabeth Bowen are cited parenthetically as follows: *CI*, *Collected Impressions*; *CS*, *Collected Stories*; *WL*, *A World of Love*. I have usually employed page references alone in my extended discussion of *WL*.

a similar uncanny power to evoke or recreate the past. In 'The Demon Lover' (1941) a woman is abducted into the world of the dead by the ghost of her soldier-lover, who died twenty-five years before in the 1914 War. 'I shall be with you . . . sooner or later', he had told her, leaving for the Front in August 1916; '. . . You need do nothing but wait' (*CS* 663). In *A World of Love* Guy makes a similar promise—or threat—on a similar occasion: "'*You'll* never see the last of me!'" (*World* 121). He too keeps his promise. 'Hand in Glove' (1952), which is perhaps partially indebted to Henry James's 'The Romance of Certain Old Clothes' (1868), centres on an episode which Bowen uses to initiate events in *A World of Love*, the removal of an old dress and some love-letters from an attic trunk; in 'Hand in Glove' the removal evokes a vengeful ghost. The dead can come back, the past can reach out—literally in 'Hand in Glove'—to destroy the living.

Taken together, these three stories suggest something potentially sinister about the allegedly idyllic pre-1914 Anglo-Irish past. That past has power to threaten the living. It can perhaps destroy them by enticing them into timelessness, away from their own lives, their own time. There is an echo here of that story so often told by Irish storytellers, and sometimes adapted by Anglo-Irish writers, about a young man or woman charmed away by the *sidhe*, to emerge long after from a fairy mound to discover that what seemed days were in fact years, that all friends have long since died:

> They stole little Bridget
> For seven years long;
> When she came down again
> Her friends were all gone.
> (William Allingham, 'The Fairies')

Le Fanu draws upon this tradition in 'The Child that went with the Fairies' (1870) and 'Laura Silver Bell' (1872), as does Yeats in 'The Wanderings of Oisin' (1889) and *The Land of Heart's Desire* (1894). In these tales the *sidhe* are both threatening and seductive. Often their victims hardly resist, or even assist the effort to coax them into the realms of the dead.

A World of Love is about Montefort, a Big House that was not burned in 1919–22, but has lingered on into post-Treaty Ireland to dwindle into shabby poverty:

> the small mansion had an air of having gone down . . . The door no longer knew hospitality; moss obliterated the sweep for the turning carriage; the avenue lived on as a rutted track . . . Had the façade not carried a ghost of style, Montefort would have looked, as it almost did, like nothing more than the annex of its farm buildings (*World* 11–12).

In a sense, *A World Of Love* is a sequel—a kind of alternate sequel—to *The Last September*, as the moss-grown drive and the door that 'no longer knew hospitality' remind us, by echoing the earlier novel's final pages. This is what happens to Big Houses that did not undergo the cleansing fires. And, though poor like the houses Bowen celebrates in her essay 'The Big House', Montefort does not seem to have anything to offer the new Ireland, least of all that hospitality she so earnestly advocates. 'Not since Montefort stood had there ceased to be vigilant measures against nightcomers', she comments, as the great front door of Montefort is barred for the night; 'all being part of the hostile watch kept by now eyeless towers and time-stunted castles along these rivers. For as land knows, everywhere is a frontier; and the outposted few (and few are the living) never must be off guard' (100).

There is only 'a ghost of style', of that nervous conspicuous assertiveness which Yeats and Bowen praised as the self-conscious drama that the Anglo-Irish performed before an Irish audience—that, and a literal ghost from Anglo-Ireland. Guy, once the owner of Montefort, died on the Western Front in the Great War, like so many of his class. Now he haunts Montefort, struggling to make his presence felt, either to act as a demon lover for young Jane, or to escape from the limbo in which he is imprisoned, kept there by obsessive memories of him among the living. Jane is twenty, one year older than Lois of *The Last September*, and like her moving into womanhood, waiting for something to happen, her 'face perfectly ready to be a woman's, but not yet so' (*WL* 13). Before his death, Guy was engaged to marry her mother.

Like the lovers on Keats's Grecian urn, and Arnold's Scholar Gypsy, Guy remains young and seems alive only because he is not. Though he has none of the menace of a Carmilla or a Dracula, he is nevertheless dangerous. He can seduce Jane into a love affair with the past, with what no longer exists, and so prevent her from living her own life in her own time. He is therefore a personal threat to Jane herself. But he also represents a gay lordly open-handed Anglo-Irish past, the idyllic pre-1914 world. His presence implies a kind of survival for Anglo-Ireland's myth of the past, and suggests how Anglo-Ireland's dreams about itself can at once be seductive, impotent, unreal, and dangerous. Guy is kept lingering in a world where he cannot belong by the obsessive nostalgia of those of his contemporaries who once loved him.

The opening sentence of *A World of Love* introduces the theme of survival from the past, a theme Bowen emphasizes by incorporating into the sentence the title of her previous Big House novel: 'The sun rose on a landscape still pale with the heat of the day before' (11). The action of the novel covers four June days in the early 1950s. Appropriately, in this novel about past invading present, Bowen begins the story on the second of those four days; the seminal events of the first day—that day whose vanished sun still makes the landscape seem pale—intrude into the novel later, in

Chapter Two, interrupting the progress of the narrative. The novel abounds with sentences that frustrate narrative and temporal progress by coiling back upon themselves: 'Mush for the chickens, if nothing else, was never not in the course of cooking' (26); 'Quite soon, what will the cattle do?' (107); 'Nothing now against [decay] maintained the place' (122); 'Hard was it not to tax him . . .' (123); 'Impossible is it for persons to be changed' (132). Nevertheless, that opening sentence is soon followed by a hint that this novel is to recognize that the past must inevitably be ousted by the present: 'This light at this hour, so unfamiliar, brought into being a new world—painted, expectant, empty, intense' (11). Jane is to escape from Guy and the spell of the past he represents. She will turn instead to present and future by falling in love with Richard Priam on the last page of the novel, as soon as he descends from the airplane which has brought him from Colorado, the 'new world'.

When Jane first appears, on the novel's second page, she has already entered her enthralled state, is at once part of the present and the past. She is 'Wearing a trailing Edwardian muslin dress'—is Bowen reminding us of George Moore's *A Drama in Muslin*?

> The cut of her easy golden hair was anachronistic over the dress she wore: this, her height, and some thing half naïve half studied about her management of the sleeves and skirts made her like a boy actor in woman's clothes, while what was classical in her grace made her appear to belong to some other time (*WL* 12).

Later the dress is specifically associated with the dead and the past. 'It must belong . . . to somebody dead', Jane opines, and Antonia agrees: '. . . it had had its funeral. Delicious hour for somebody, packing away her youth.' 'What egotists the dead seem to be', Jane comments. 'This summery lovely muslin not to be worn again because *she* could not? Why not imagine me?' (30). The dress symbolizes, the conversation encapsulates some of the novel's preoccupations: the egotism of the dead, their unwillingness to stay buried, their apparent ability to 'imagine' their possible victims among those living in the future.

Jane is reading a letter when we first see her, one from a bundle of old love letters written by Guy, which she has found with the dress, or rather, to which she has been summoned. On the previous day—that temporarily delayed first day of the story—she has attended her family's single annual social occasion, the Hunt Fête, with her parents, her sister Maud, and Cousin Antonia, Guy's heir and now the owner of Montefort. Like the Bowens, the family at Montefort have run out of male heirs.

For the family at Montefort, the Hunt Fête is their only chance to place themselves—somewhat precariously—among such Anglo-Irish gentry as still survive, and wealthy refugees from Socialist Britain's taxes, who have

leased some of the surviving Big Houses. Antonia, an absentee who has succeeded in London as an 'artist photographer', has enjoyed the occasion for
a time, then wearied of it. Jane, who usually lives in London with Antonia,
has assisted the organizers of the Fête. Jane's parents, Fred and Lilia, have
had a more ambiguous time. Fred is an illegitimate cousin of Guy and
Antonia, 'by-blow son of roving Montefort uncle . . . allowed to grow up in
the stable yards' (19); 'it was generally held' that his mother 'had foreign
blood', perhaps a hint that he is the product of miscegenation with the
unhyphenated Irish. At the Fête, Fred has immediately merged into the
crowd of Irish onlookers. Lilia, still dreaming of the local status she would
have enjoyed as Guy's wife, 'fashionably got up, stood apart, at bay, high
heels ground into the lawn. The lost lady suffered under wondering stares'
(35). When she finds herself left behind at the Fête and must ask a stranger
to drive her home, the man remarks, 'No idea there was anyone living here',
as he drops her at the gate to Montefort's 'extinct avenue' (37). Like dead
Guy, and the tradition it represents, Montefort itself is a kind of ghost, a
brief disturbance in the atmosphere, a half-noticed eddy in the current of
contemporary Irish life.

The Fête, by recalling almost dormant claims to gentle status, has itself
created a kind of disturbance: 'in the house itself residual pleasure-seeking
ghosts had been set astir' (34–5). Jane, remaining late at the Fête to dance
on the Castle lawn,

> left on an impulse. Music followed her . . . as she bicycled home . . . dust
> wraithlike rose from under her wheels . . . The air through which she was swiftly
> passing was mauve, and tense with suspended dew; her own beautiful restless-
> ness was everywhere.
>
> From somewhere out behind Montefort she at one time imagined she heard
> a call . . . still with that inexplicable feeling of being summoned, she looked into
> all the rooms . . . for her the house was great with something: she *had* been sent
> for, and in haste. Why? Only attics now remained to be searched; and how
> could they (she reflected, for she was practical) show anything? . . . She lighted
> a candle and went to look . . . The flame . . . consumed age in the air; toppling,
> the wreckage left by the past oppressed her . . . everything was derelict, done
> for, done with . . . she half thought a bat stirred . . . there *was* a stir, but within
> herself. Her halted shadow lay on a trunk . . . She . . . put the lid back, and
> began to draw out the inexhaustible muslin of the dress; out of it, having been
> wedged in somewhere, tumbled the packet of letters. They fell at her feet,
> having found her rather than she them (*WL* 33–4).

By summoning Jane to the letters, Guy's spirit has used her as a kind of
medium, so that he can manifest himself at Montefort, not only to Jane,
who senses him and responds to him as a ghostly lover, but also to Lilia
and Antonia. They were both in love with him, and have remained locked
together, at once rivals and sharers of their combined memories. Since his
death, both have lived lives they feel to be incomplete.

The three women are haunted by the letters, and by the faintly perceptible presence they evoke. They are watched by twelve-year-old Maud, who is a witch and traffics with 'her familiar' (60), a spirit she calls Gay David—in Irish, *aerach* suggests airy, gay, and eerie, *deamhan*, pronounced day-van, means demon. Gay David may be an indigenous spirit, older than Montefort—the nearby river features a haunted spot called 'Gay David's Hole' (58). The name Maud knows him by may be part translation, part anglicization. Or the Guy/Gay echo may suggest that Guy appears to Maud as familiar rather than demon-lover; David, like the Davy of Davy Jones, implies a conventional euphemism for devil.

Watching Jane in a retired spot where she has gone because the letters describe it and seem to summon her there, Maud sees her 'propitiatingly . . . rub' (62) the bark of a thorn tree—a tree traditionally sacred to the *sidhe* and therefore a dangerous place for a young maiden, as the girls in Sir Samuel Ferguson's 'The Fairy Thorn' (1834) discover:

> No scream can any raise, nor prayer can any say,
> But wild, wild the terror of the speechless three—
> For they feel fair Anna Grace drawn silently away,
> By whom they dare not look to see.

'What are you pretending about that tree?' Maud asks, then '"Just wondered what *you* were making up," explained the child, with the air of a connoisseur' (62) of supernatural activities. Maud herself has just been busy 'conspiratorially' (60) gabbling with Gay David, and clearly senses that Jane too has become involved with supernatural forces. A few minutes later, Maud unexpectedly asks her mother, 'How old would be Cousin Guy? . . . Getting on, like you all? . . . I wonder how long anyone lasts' (65–6).

After discovering the letters, Jane puts on the clothing of the dead so that she looks as girls looked when Guy was young. Seeing her walking out of doors in the muslin dress, Kathie, the Irish servant, wonders, '. . . could it ever have been a Vision?' (25), a hint at that *aisling* theme so lightly evoked in *The Last September*. Kathie is afraid of the attic, that repository of the dead or dormant past. So is Fred, who wants the rubbish of the past cleared away (50), and Lilia, who is afraid that what is stored in the attics will start a fire, to destroy Montefort from within as Danielstown was destroyed from without. Fred and Lilia are both right, he in wishing that the past be discarded, she in sensing that it is inflammable, and that Jane's invasion will start a fire. 'But if I'd started a fire, you'd know by now,' Jane points out, only to have Antonia accurately reply, 'We think we do . . . That's what's the matter. We think we can smell burning; or at any rate the beginning of burning, smouldering. What have you done? You have an igniting touch'— at which Fred advises Jane, 'Tell 'em to go to blazes' (51). Discovering the letters has ignited a blaze, none the less intense for being 'An agony of trance,/An agony of flame that cannot singe a sleeve.'

It is ultimately a purging fire. This unburned house must be freed from its past, cleansed of its ghostly presences. It must be clear that Guy, who has brought those living at Montefort together and held them together, is no longer master. Perhaps he is himself weary of his half life, earth-bound because he survives in the fading memories of those who loved him in life—evasive, elusive, as when he made several women believe he was in love with them, seeming rather than being. Guy's elusive quality in life hints that even before 1914 the Anglo-Irish myth was insubstantial; now it is the ghost of a pretence, but potentially a dangerous myth for those who still yearn for it to be true, or for those too young to remember it, but capable of infatuation with its shadow. In Guy, Anglo-Ireland survives as a myth of gaiety, power, and style, that 'demonic power of the family myth' (*CI* 4) Bowen recognizes at work in Le Fanu' *Uncle Silas*.

Jane's enchantment into this dream of the past is unexpected, and contrary to her character. She has spent much of her life away from Montefort's decaying grandeur, at school in England at Antonia's expense, and seems immune from the family myth:

> she had no particular attitude to the future, but she had an instinctive aversion from the past; it seemed to her a sort of pompous imposture; as an idea it bored her; it might not be too much to say that she disapproved of it. She enjoyed being: how could it not depress her to realize that the majority of people no longer were? Most of all she mistrusted the past's activity and its queeringness—she knew no one, apart from her own contemporaries, who did not speak of it either with falsifying piety or with bitterness; she sometimes had had the misfortune to live through hours positively contaminated by its breath . . . so far as she was against anything she was against the past; and she felt entitled to raid, despoil, rifle, balk, or cheat it in any possible way. She gloried in having set free the dress. But the letters—had they not insisted on forcing their own way out? (43)

Like Lois, and so many others among Bowen's young women, Jane is eager to break free into a future she cannot yet quite imagine.

Jane is enticed into the myth that Guy represents. Antonia, Lilia, and Fred have sustained that myth with their memories. Lilia has come to live in the house she would have ruled as Guy's wife, Fred has agreed to marry her because he 'Thought there ought to be something in Guy's girl' (131) and 'saw in her . . . What he once saw—I suppose. That *was* somewhere in her . . .' (103). Antonia's attitudes are more complex. 'You're far too quick to assume that people are dead' (47), she snaps, when Jane appropriates the muslin dress. Later she meditates on the tension between the living and the dead:

Life works to dispossess the dead, to dislodge and oust them. Their places fill themselves up; later people come in; all the room is wanted. Feeling alters its course, is drawn elsewhere, or seeks renewal from other sources. When of love there is not enough to go round, inevitably it is the dead who must go without . . . Their continuous dying while we live, their repeated deaths as each of us dies who knew them, are not in nature to be withstood. Obstinate rememberers of the dead seem to queer themselves or show some signs of a malady; in part they come to share the dead's isolation, which it is not in their power to break down—for the rest of us, so necessary is it to let the dead go that we expect   they may be glad to be gone. Greatest of our denials to them is a part to play: it appears that they now cannot touch or alter whatever may be the existent scene—not only are they not here to participate, but there would be disorder if they *were* here. Their being left behind in their own time caused estrangement between them and us, who must live in ours . . . for Antonia in the case of her cousin Guy . . . his death seemed . . . an invented story. Not that it was unlike him to be killed . . . but that it was unlike him to be dead . . . death, yes, why not?—but deadness, no . . . It would be long before Guy was done with life . . . he was a participator: how could he be expected to cease to act or agree to hold off? . . . these years she went on living belonged to him, his lease upon them not having run out yet. The living were living in his life-time; and of this his contemporaries—herself, Lilia, Fred—never were unaware. They were incomplete (*WL* 56–7).

Jane's discovery of the letters works to end this pervasive haunting.

Jane evokes Guy by reading the letters he has summoned her to find. In doing so she slips partly out of her own time, as the muslin dress suggests, and into the retroactively defined idyll of Anglo-Ireland before 1914. For Bowen, as a novelist, the dual power of writing and reading to make the unreal manifest is essential. In her notes for her unfinished *Pictures and Conversations*, which was to be a kind of 'free association' meditation about 'the relationship . . . between living and writing' (*Pictures* 61), in effect a discussion of the sources and development of her own imagination, she projects a book in five parts. Part five was 'Witchcraft: a Query. Is anything uncanny involved in the process of writing?' (63). She also speaks of the manifestation of fictional characters to her as 'visitations' (60). The letters Jane finds have the power to evoke Guy for Jane, as elsewhere Bowen evokes imaginary characters for her readers; Jane reads about Guy and he becomes real to her. The letters are love letters, but, like *Bowen's Court*, they are also writings about an Anglo-Irish house and estate, and Jane moves imaginatively into an earlier time as Bowen herself had done while writing *Bowen's Court*, as Mary does by reading old letters and documents in 'The Happy Autumn Fields'. Jane is a reluctant reader, but when she notices a reference to the obelisk that stands in front of Montefort, she is not only enticed into reading them—she dresses herself in the muslin dress and carries the letters to the obelisk to keep whatever tryst Guy had arranged with the woman in the past for whom the letters were originally written. She has begun to re-enact a written version of the past, to bring the past to life. The obelisk, we learn, represents an earlier attempt to evade oblivion. 'Chap put it up in memory of himself,' Fred explains:

> 'What, while he was still alive?' marvelled Lilia. 'Rather peculiar, surely? What was his name?'
> 'Couldn't tell you.'
> 'Oh, then he *is* forgotten!'
> During the pause, Antonia joined the group, was asked, looked bored, and supplied the name . . . 'Married the cook,' she went on, 'went queer in the head from drinking and thinking about himself, left no children—anyway, no legits. So this place went to his first cousin' (*WL* 173–4).

The letters also direct Jane to the thorn tree where Maud recognizes that some supernatural force is at work. The letters are about the estate, to which Guy, like Fred, Lilia, and Antonia, remains bound. Jane's reading of them temporarily makes her yearn for the ampler Anglo-Irish past as portrayed in *Bowen's Court* and *The Shelbourne Hotel*. When Jane is eager to hear of 'the former gay days . . . before it was 1914' (78), the phrase 'gay days' repeats the title Bowen used in *The Shelbourne Hotel* for her chapter describing the same period as the high point of the Ascendancy.

Antonia's brief biography of the forgotten builder of the obelisk— an Anglo-Irish novel in miniature—encapsulates important elements in *A World of Love*, for Guy's place too has gone 'to his first cousin' and there are no legitimate heirs to come—Fred and therefore Jane 'have the bar sinister' (31), as Jane points out. We are once again in that dangerous area of intermarriage so obsessively frequented by Anglo-Irish writers.

In that area sex and politics merge, sometimes in bizarre ways. The sexual politics at Montefort are particularly intricate, contrived and orches- trated by Antonia, who is, we should remember, an artist and a kind of novelist, Elizabeth Bowen's self-portrait (Glendinning 250–1). Antonia has arranged the marriage of Jane's parents and settled them at Montefort: 'Having escorted the couple home from the church, Antonia leaped back into the beribboned hackney and made her habitual dash to the boat train' (22). Like a novelist whose characters behave in discord with the contrived plot, she is 'aghast' when she finds that Fred and Lilia fall in love: 'they had passed beyond her—she had made the match, they the marriage' (22–3). Though the couple's mutual infatuation was short-lived, Antonia's jealousy later causes her to take Jane—product of that period of passionate infatuation—away from Montefort. She supports Jane in London, but there are incestuous and lesbian overtones to the relationship. Antonia is infatuated with Jane, partly, perhaps, because Jane is the daughter of her rival, the woman Guy planned to marry, and partly perhaps because Jane is the daughter of the only male left from the Montefort family: 'There are no more men . . .' Jane remarks late in the novel; 'No more to come, I mean' (183). Once again Bowen invokes that 'demonic power of the family myth' (*CI* 4) she had discerned in *Uncle Silas*. Fred, Antonia, and Guy are all cousins, Jane's 'affair' with Guy is with a cousin as well as a ghost. All the adults have some share in the engendering of Jane. Antonia's jealousy and possessiveness toward Lilia was behind her arranging the marriage of Lilia and Fred; both women loved Guy, and Fred worshipped him. Antonia 'had forced . . . Those two . . . to their bridal doom . . . Guy's death, even, had been contributory to Jane's birth. And so, what was Jane for? Beautiful, yes; but why?' (176). Jane is Fred's 'first and last, devouring, hopeless, and only love' (23); Guy becomes her demon lover. Antonia's sexual attraction to Jane is never made explicit, and Antonia herself does not recognize it as such. But when she senses that she is losing Jane to a rival, she thinks of seducing Fred, and instinctively writes, then destroys, a letter to her own former husband.

During the novel's four days, Jane is also taken up by the aging and sexually predatory Lady Latterly, whose name recalls Lawrence's heroine and also suggests the passing of time. Her bedroom is 'a replica . . . of a Mayfair *décor* back in the 1930's . . . The bedroom gained still more un-reality by now seeming trapped somewhere between day and night' (71). Lady Latterly's dinner party begins at twilight, when the dead are free to leave their tombs. Her guests are all elderly, Guy's contemporaries. They are indeed 'poor ghosts' (82) who can hardly stand the light. Jane has been invited because she is young, like the young men and women in so many Irish legends who are beguiled into the bright glitter of fairy mounds to give the bloodless *sidhe* an illusion of life. Initially the ghostly guests exclude her from their 'open-yet-closed half-circle', which she must 'invade . . . implacably making a place for herself among them' (78–9). Only at the round dining-table does she fully enter, and indeed dominate, their circle. Jane is kissed by Peregrine, Lady Latterly's current lover, and even drinks a 'potion' (77). Either kiss or potion could imprison her forever out of time among these shades, as the pomegranate seeds imprison Proserpina in the realm of the dead, and as eating or drinking anything offered imprisons those who visit the mounds of the *sidhe*. Bowen hints at the Proserpina aspect of this belief: Mamie, one of the guests, has 'pomegranate toenails', Peregrine, punning on 'making hay while the sun shines', plucks a hayseed from Jane's hair and places 'the seed on the cloth for Jane to study', and Antonia twice characterizes the dinner party as 'A seedy outing!' (82, 89, 92). Jane is rescued by Antonia, who jealously invades the dinner party to remove Jane prematurely, and accuses her of being drunk—the potion was several Martinis—and of 'nipping off the moment my back was turned . . . And you were seduced also, I daresay?'

'Oh, no; we sat in the drawingroom, then in the diningroom. Everyone she'd invited was quite old.'

'What d'you mean, "everyone she'd invited"?—Anyone crash the party?'

The girl was silent.

Antonia repeated: 'A seedy outing!' (*WL* 92–3).

Someone *has* crashed the party. Guy has made his presence felt at the dinner table, in the space set for an absent guest: 'Dominator of the margin of the vision, he was all the time the creature of extra sense. The face depended for being there upon there being no instant when it was looked straight at' (88). Everyone senses Guy's presence: the guests begin to speak of banshees and family curses, Irish Terence moves his chair away from the empty place 'uneasily', Mamie places a rose before the empty chair saying '*There*, darling! You're my ideal man,' and 'the Irish butler, moving about, gave the impression of harkening for something more' (83–4). Guy's presence vivifies this party of the dead. Although their contemporary, he is eternally young, and so rejuvenates them. Jane, wearing the muslin dress, is at once of his time and her own. Partnered by Guy, she assumes an 'odd bridal ascendancy over the dinner table . . . not a soul failed to feel the electric connection between Jane's paleness and the dark of the chair in which so far no one visibly sat. Between them, the two dominated the party' (84–5). Jane sees Guy as resembling Antonia; he vanishes, significantly, when Antonia arrives, heralded by the enigmatic phrase, 'the young lady's cousin has come for her' (89).

Like Dracula and Carmilla, Guy is a kind of vampire. He is kept alive, not by blood but by memory, by the inability of Antonia, Lilia, and Fred to accept his life and influence as ended. He contrives his own reappearance by using Jane as a medium. Her ability to function as such seems to be connected with the rare participation of members of the Montefort household in social events, the Fête and Lady Latterly's party, moments when a brief illusion of the old Anglo-Irish social life reappears.

Bowen treats Guy's role as demon lover both ambiguously and negatively. It is ambiguous because we are unsure about his motives, as perhaps we should be in a ghost story. Has he come to seduce Jane into the world of the dead, or has he come to use her as the instrument of his release from those earthly ties by which the Montefort adults hold him? Clearly he represents a threat to Jane's real life in the real world, if she vanishes into a dream of Anglo-Ireland before 1914, like Oisin's sojourn amid 'Vain gaiety' in Yeats's 'The Circus Animals' Desertion'. But Jane frees herself from the spell—from her infatuation with Guy and from the myth of Anglo-Ireland he seems to represent. And in freeing herself, she also frees the rest of the Montefort household from that spell.

Lady Latterly's house seems an enchanted castle. Montefort is also out-side of time. In the Montefort kitchen, 'routine abode in the air like an old spell'. The outdated calendar and the unreliable clock 'spoke of the almost total irrelevance of Time, in the abstract' (26–7), though 'outdoors, the farm ran by the watch strapped inexorably to Fred's wrist' (25–6). Maud, who traffics with Gay David and curses her father with phrases from the Old Testament for his willing enslavement to the past of Guy and Lilia, is alone in noting the passage of time. She regularly communes with another more temporal spirit of the air, Big Ben. She is devoted to those well-known chimes broadcast nightly by the BBC, though she has no interest in the news that follows.

In *The Heat of the Day*, the strength of Mount Morris is its ability to preserve the past, its freedom from time passing. At Montefort, these traits are isolating and life-denying. Bowen's final treatment of the Anglo-Irish myth negates that generally favourable version she presented in *The Heat of the Day*. Against Roderick's preference for 'what *had* happened' (*Heat* 64) she sets Jane's 'instinctive aversion from the past' (*World* 43), a trait that is temporarily suspended when she finds the letters, but reasserts itself when she destroys them.

Guy's manifestation supplements the uneasy memories of him which obsess Lilia, Fred, and Antonia with his disturbing but ultimately banish-able presence. His return frees them all. The letters, initially assumed to be his love letters to Lilia—but if so, why are they hidden in the Montefort attic, in the folds of someone else's dress?—may be to some other, unknown woman. They are found, read, and hidden by Jane, stolen by Maud, confiscated by Fred. He offers them to Lilia, who cannot identify them as hers, and does not want them. They are abandoned for Antonia to find, and finally, after Antonia and Kathie have failed to do so, burned by Jane. During their four day peregrinations, the letters disturb all the inhabitants of Montefort, who are already oppressed and apprehensive because of unseasonable hot weather. Jane has her infatuation and excitement; Lilia and Antonia confront their shared but rival memories; and Lilia, after Guy has 'come' to her in the walled garden, learns to accept Fred for himself, as her true husband and lover, rather than to see him as a poor substitute for the absent Guy. Antonia, perhaps now able to accept her inheritance of Montefort and the responsibilities towards past and future this implies, may be able to accept things as they are and settle there. Jane carefully re-inters the muslin dress in its resting place. She too senses that her provisional transient state is over. Like Tennyson's Lady of Shalott, evoked in the last chapter by the sight of Bunratty Castle, 'a castle like Shalott—willows whitened, aspens quivered' (184), Jane is 'half sick of shadows' and reflec-tions. Tennyson's own gloss on his poem can equally well summarize

Bowen's ending: 'The newborn love for something, for some one in the wide world from which she has been so long secluded, takes her out of the region of shadows into that of realities' (*Memoir* I:117; Hill, *Tennyson's Poetry* 15). Unlike her prototype, Jane's journey out of the shadows is not fatal; it is to life, not death. Like Gabriel Conroy, she travels westward, but to Shannon Airport rather than a graveyard.

Jane travels to Shannon with Maud and with Harris, Lady Latterly's chauffeur. They are to meet Richard Priam, one of Lady Latterly's discarded lovers. Jane leaves Montefort in 'a blind bridal rush . . . in white' with the enigmatic Harris. He is able to spot a four-leaf clover many feet away, and is bothered by Gay David's 'unnatural occupancy of his van' (181). His apparently random remarks have metaphysical overtones in the context of what has occurred: '"Harris", said Lilia, "says there's plenty of time". "Well, there's *time*, madam"'; 'Well, never say die' (174, 183).

Trapped in Limerick traffic, 'Jane studied the reflection of the van in the . . . window of an emporium—herself, in it, in town, in an impotent jam of halted traffic, caught; and she saw why she could not go back' (183) to her old waiting life. As she realizes this, 'the closure on Jane lightened and was gone'—a simple change of traffic lights, but also Jane's final repudiation of Shalottian shadows and mirror images. At the airport she confronts Priam as he leaves the plane. In the novel's final sentence 'They no sooner looked but they loved'.

Bowen perhaps learned from Le Fanu, in such stories as 'Schalken the Painter' (1839, rev. 1851) and 'Green Tea' (1869), the way to introduce a supernatural presence and simultaneously to suggest that it might be hallucinatory, leaving that little 'loophole for a natural explanation' which M.R. James recommends *(Ghosts and Marvels* vi) to writers of supernatural stories. Jane went to the attic in response to a ghostly summons—or because she remembered seeing there a hat like Lady Latterly's. When she saw Guy in the empty place at dinner, she had just drunk her first Martinis—three of them, in rapid succession. Lilia senses Guy's presence in the walled garden, but she has just had her hair cut short; perhaps, as Fred suggests, the sun has affected her. But despite these rational loopholes, and the oppressive heat which has made everyone nervous, there remains the dinner guests' uneasy awareness of Guy. Even Gay David makes his presence felt by Harris, and by Miss Francie, the local hairdresser (119).

Reading about the past, then, has briefly drawn Jane into infatuation with that past, and with its imagined gaieties—to her, 'any gay days' (78) ended before she was born. But her intrusion or seduction into the past ends that past. Guy has come back only—perhaps in order—to be banished forever, so that the living can escape from memory and get on with their lives. The family myth can be ended before Jane too becomes its captive, either by pining for a ghostly lover or as incestuous partner for Antonia. Jane's traffic with the past has freed her to move into the future; she has confronted the attractions of the past and rejected them.

In *A World of Love* Bowen tempts her heroine with the last enchantments of the vanished Anglo-Irish world, then frees her from them, and indeed frees all the book's captives, including Guy. If in *The Last September* she both recreated and then destroyed Bowen's Court, freeing Lois from the stifling atmosphere of the Big Houses so that she could rebuild it in art, in *A World of Love* she portrays her own recent enthralment to letters and journals recording the past of her own family and class as she wrote *Bowen's Court* and *The Shelbourne Hotel*, and her partially successful effort to present the Anglo-Irish favourably, as heroic and rooted in Ireland. In *A World of Love* the charm of pre-1914 Anglo-Ireland is real, but menacing. Even Guy himself, the ghostly representative of that past, seems eager to be released from his empty role, as a memory of something that perhaps once existed, but survives now only in written texts and in shifting memories. 'By now there are too many years ago, and I'm getting sick to death of the whole bang lot of them,' exclaims old Terence, when at Lady Latterly's Jane asks him about the 'gay days'. 'Rotten old romancing and story-telling: you make the half of it up, and who's the wiser? What does it matter, anyway? . . . you can't buy the past. What is it?—not even history. Goes to dust in your hand . . . I'm my own calendar' (80–1). Terence refuses to indulge in memory. In laying Guy's ghost, Bowen, having already killed Anglo-Ireland in *The Last September*, now kills its mythic memory as well. Like Le Fanu's Baron Vordenburg and Bram Stoker's Professor Van Helsing with their sharpened stakes, Bowen here kills that which is already dead. Her novel is not a requiem but an exorcism.

Delivered in part at the meeting of the Modern Language Association, New York, December 1988.

Bibliography

Aarne, Antti and Stith Thompson. *The Types of the Folktale*. Helsinki: Finnish Folklore Commission, 1973.

Abbott, Thomas Kingsmill. 'The Library'. *The Book of Trinity College, Dublin 1591–1891*. Dublin: Hodges Figgis, 1892, pp. 147–81.

Adams, W. Marsham. *The Drama of Empire*. London: Kegan Paul, 1891.

——. *The House of the Hidden Places: A Clue to the Creed of Early Egypt from Egyptian Sources*. London: John Murray, 1895.

——. 'The Mystery of Ancient Egypt'. *New Review* 9: 55 (December 1893): 618–28.

Albert, L. [L. Albert Herrmann]. *Six Thousand Years of Celtic Grandeur– Unearthed* (a republication of O'Connor's *Chronicles of Eri* to 1004 BC). London: W. and G. Foyle, [1936]. Albert also published a German translation of the *Chronicles*, Berlin, 1922.

Allingham, William. *The Poems of William Allingham*. Ed. John Hewitt. Dublin: Dolmen Press, 1967.

Arbois de Jubainville, Marie Henri d'. *The Irish Mythological Cycle and Celtic Mythology*. Trans. R.I. Best. Dublin: O'Donoghue/M.H. Gill & Son, 1903. This translation originally appeared in *The United Irishman* 1900–1902.

Archibald, Douglas N. 'Yeats's Encounters: Observations on Literary Influence and Literary History'. *New Literary History* 1:3 (Spring 1970): 439–70.

Atherton, James S. *The Books at the Wake: A Study of Literary Allusions in James Joyce's Finnegans Wake*. Carbondale: Southern Illinois University Press, 1959.

Auden, W.H. 'In Memory of W.B. Yeats'. *Collected Poems*. Ed. Edward Mendelson. New York: Random House, 1976.

Banim, John and Michael. *The Anglo-Irish of the Nineteenth Century*. 1828. 3 vols. Facsimile reprint New York: Garland, 1978.

——. *The Bit O' Writin' and Other Tales*. 1838. 3 vols. Facsimile reprint New York: Garland, 1979.

——. *The Boyne Water, a Tale*. 1826. 3 vols. Facsimile reprint New York: Garland, 1978.

———. *The Croppy; A Tale of 1798.* 1828. 3 vols. Facsimile reprint New York: Garland, 1978.

———. *The Denounced.* 1830. 3 vols. Facsimile reprint New York: Garland, 1979.

———. *The Ghost-Hunter and his Family.* 1833. 1 vol. Facsimile reprint New York: Garland, 1978.

———. *The Mayor of Wind-Gap* and *Canvassing.* 1835. 3 vols. Facsimile reprint New York: Garland, 1979.

———. *Tales by the O'Hara Family.* First series. 1825. 3 vols. Facsimile reprint New York: Garland, 1978.

———. *Tales by the O'Hara Family.* Second series. 1826. 3 vols. Facsimile reprint New York: Garland, 1978.

Barber, Paul. *Vampires, Burial, and Death: Folklore and Reality.* New Haven, Conn.: Yale University Press, 1988.

Beach, Sylvia. *Shakespeare and Company.* New York: Harcourt, Brace, 1959.

Benjamin, Walter. *Illuminations.* Ed. Hannah Arendt. Tr. Harry Zohn. New York: Schocken, 1969.

Berlin, Isaiah. *The Hedgehog and the Fox: An Essay on Tolstoy's View of History.* New York: Simon & Schuster, 1953.

Bishop, John. *Joyce's Book of the Dark, 'Finnegans Wake'.* Madison: University of Wisconsin Press, 1986.

Bjersby, Birgit. *The Interpretation of the Cuchulain Legend.* Upsala: A.-B. Lundequistska Bokhandeln, 1950.

Blavatsky, Helena P. *Isis Unveiled: A Master-key to the Mysteries of Ancient and Modern Science and Theology.* 1877. Point Loma, California: Theosophical Publishing Company, 1910.

Blodgett, Harriet. *Patterns of Reality: Elizabeth Bowen's Novels.* The Hague: Mouton, 1975.

Boland, Eavan. *A Kind of Scar: The Woman Poet in a National Tradition.* Dublin: Attic Press, 1989.

Bonheim, Helmut. *A Lexicon of the German in 'Finnegans Wake'.* Berkeley and Los Angeles: University of California Press, 1967.

Boswell, James. *Life of Johnson.* Ed. R.W. Chapman. New edition, corrected by J.D. Fleeman. 1953. London: Oxford University Press, 1976.

Bourgeois, Maurice. *John Millington Synge and the Irish Theatre.* 1913. Reprint New York: Benjamin Blom, 1965.

Bowen, Elizabeth. *Bowen's Court.* 1942. Second (revised) edition, 1964. New York: Ecco Press, 1979.

———. *Collected Impressions.* New York: Knopf, 1950.

———. *Collected Stories.* New York: Knopf, 1981.

———. *The Death of the Heart.* 1935. New York: Vintage, 1955.

———. 'Eire.' *New Statesman and Nation* 21 n.s. (12 April 1941): 382–3.

———. *Eva Trout, or, Changing Scenes.* 1968. New York: Avon, 1978.

———. *Friends and Relations.* 1931. New York: Avon, 1980.

———. *The Heat of the Day.* 1949. Harmondsworth: Penguin, 1985.

——. *The Hotel*. 1927. Harmondsworth: Penguin, 1943.

——. *The House in Paris*. 1935. New York: Avon, 1979.

——. Introduction to *Uncle Silas* by Sheridan Le Fanu (London: Cresset, 1947). Reprint, *The Mulberry Tree: Writings of Elizabeth Bowen*. Ed. Hermione Lee. London: Virago, 1986.

——. *The Last September*. 1929. New York: Avon, 1979.

——. *The Little Girls*. 1964. New York: Avon, 1978.

——. *Pictures and Conversations*. New York: Knopf, 1975.

——. *Seven Winters: Memories of a Dublin Childhood and Afterthoughts: Pieces on Writing*. New York: Knopf, 1962. *Seven Winters* was originally published in 1942 (Dublin: Dolmen Press).

——. *The Shelbourne Hotel*. New York: Knopf, 1951.

——. *To the North*. 1932. New York: Avon, 1979.

——. *Why Do I Write? An Exchange of Views Between Elizabeth Bowen, Graham Greene, and V.S. Pritchett*. London: Percival Marshall, 1948.

——. *A World of Love*. 1955. New York: Avon, 1978.

Bowen, Zack. *Musical Allusions in the Works of James Joyce*. Albany: State University of New York Press, 1974.

Bradford, Curtis. 'The Order of Yeats's *Last Poems*'. *Modern Language Notes* 76 (1961): 515–16. Reprinted in Stallworthy, pp. 96–7.

——. 'Yeats's Byzantium Poems: A Study of their Development'. 1960. Reprint in Unterecker, John, ed. *Yeats: A Collection of Critical Essays*. Englewood Cliffs, New Jersey: Prentice-Hall, 1963, pp. 93–130.

——. *Yeats's 'Last Poems' Again*. Dolmen Press Centenary Papers, VIII. Dublin: Dolmen Press, 1965. Reprinted in Stallworthy, pp. 75–96.

Brooke, Miss [Charlotte]. *Reliques of Irish Poetry*. 1789. Reprint Gainsville, Fla.: Scholars Facsimiles and Reprints, 1970.

Brown, Malcolm. *The Politics of Irish Literature from Thomas Davis to W.B. Yeats*. Seattle: University of Washington Press, 1972.

Brown, Terence. *Ireland: A Social and Cultural History 1922–79*. London: Fontana, 1981.

Budge, E.A. Wallis, ed. *The Book of the Dead, Facsimile of the Papyrus of Ani in the British Museum*. London: British Museum, 1890.

——. *The Book of the Dead, The Papyrus of Ani, the Egyptian Text with Interlinear Translation*. 1895. Reprint New York: Dover, 1967.

——. *The Book of the Dead. An English Translation of the Chapters Hymns, etc. of the Theban Recension*. 1899. Second edition London: Kegan Paul, Trench and Trübner, 1909.

——. *Osiris and the Egyptian Resurrection*. London: Medici Society, 1891.

Budgen, Frank. *Further Recollections of James Joyce*. London: Shenval Press, 1955.

——. 'Joyce's Chapters of Going Forth by Day'. *Horizon* (September 1941). In Givens, Seon, ed. *James Joyce: Two Decades of Criticism*. 1948. Revised edition New York: Vanguard, 1963, pp. 343–67.

Burgess, Anthony. *Joysprick: An Introduction to the Language of James Joyce*. London: Andre Deutsch, 1973.

Burke, Bernard. 'Conner.' *A Genealogical and Heraldic History of the Landed Gentry of Great Britain and Ireland.* Vol. 1. London: Harrison, Pall Mall, 1882.

Burke, Edmund. *Reflections on the Revolution in France.* 1790. Ed. Conor Cruise O'Brien. Harmondsworth: Penguin, 1982.

Butler, Marilyn. *Maria Edgeworth: A Literary Biography.* Oxford: Clarendon, 1972.

Canon Law Society of Great Britain and Ireland. *The Code of Canon Law.* London: Collins, 1983.

Carter, Howard, and A.C. Mace. *The Tomb of Tut-Ankh-Amen.* Vol. 1. London: Cassel, 1923.

Carter, Howard. *The Tomb of Tut-Ankh-Amen.* Vols. 2 and 3. London: Cassel, 1927, 1933.

Carter, Huntley. *The Theatre of Max Reinhardt.* New York: Michael Kennerley, 1914.

Caulfield, Max. *The Easter Rebellion.* London: Four Square, 1965.

Clark, David R., and James B. McGuire. *W.B. Yeats: The Writing of Sophocles' King Oedipus.* Philadelphia: American Philosophical Society, 1989.

Coffey, Diarmid. *Douglas Hyde.* Dublin: Talbot Press, 1938.

Cope, Jackson I. *Joyce's Cities: Archaeologies of the Soul.* Baltimore: Johns Hopkins University Press, 1981.

Corkery, Daniel. *The Hidden Ireland: A Study of Gaelic Munster in the Eighteenth Century.* 1924. Reprint Dublin: Gill & Macmillan, 1970.

——. *Synge and Anglo-Irish Literature.* 1931. Cork: Cork University Press, 1955.

Cross, Tom Peete and Charles Harris Slover. *Ancient Irish Tales.* 1936. Reprint New York: Barnes & Noble, 1969.

Curtis, Edmund. *A History of Ireland.* 6th edition, 1936. Reprint London: Methuen, 1950.

Curtis, L.P. *Apes and Angels: The Irishman in Victorian Caricature.* Washington, D.C.: Smithsonian Institution Press, 1971.

Davitt, Michael. *The Fall of Feudalism in Ireland.* London and New York: Harper and Brothers, 1904.

Deane, Seamus. *Heroic Styles: The Tradition of an Idea.* Field Day Pamphlet 4. Derry: Field Day, 1984.

Delargy, J.H. 'The Gaelic Story-Teller. With Some Notes on Gaelic Folktales'. *Proceedings of the British Academy* (1945): 177–221.

Deming, Robert. *James Joyce: The Critical Heritage.* 2 vols. London: Routledge & Kegan Paul, 1970.

Denieffe, Joseph. *A Personal Narrative of the Irish Revolutionary Brotherhood.* 1906. Shannon: Irish University Press, 1969.

Dickens, Charles. *A Christmas Carol* in *Christmas Books.* London: Oxford University Press, 1974.

Dillon, Myles, and Nora K. Chadwick. *The Celtic Realms.* London: Weidenfeld & Nicolson, 1967.

Dinneen, Rev. Patrick S. *An Irish-English Dictionary*. Dublin: Irish Texts Society, 1927.

Donoghue, Denis. *We Irish: Essays on Irish Literature and Society*. Berkeley: University of California Press, 1986.

——. *William Butler Yeats*. New York: Viking, 1971.

Dostoevsky, Feodor, *Crime and Punishment*. Tr. Jesse Coulson. Ed. George Gibian. New York: Norton, 1975.

Duggan, G.C. *The Stage Irishman: A History of the Irish Play and Stage Characters from the Earliest Times*. London: Longmans, 1937.

Edgeworth, Maria. *The Absentee*. Ed. W.J. McCormack and Kim Walker. Oxford: Oxford University Press, 1988.

——. *Castle Rackrent*. Ed. George Watson. London: Oxford University Press, 1964.

——. *Ennui* (in *Castle Rackrent* and *Ennui*). Ed. Marilyn Butler. London: Penguin, 1992.

——. *Ormond: A Tale*. Reprint of 1900 edition, Shannon, Ireland: Irish University Press, 1972.

Edgeworth, Richard Lovell and Maria Edgeworth. *Essay on Irish Bulls*. London, 1802. Facsimile reprint. Introduction by Robert Lee Wolff. New York: Garland, 1979.

——. *Memoirs . . . Begun by Himself and Concluded by his Daughter Maria Edgeworth*. 3rd ed. London: 1844.

Edwards, Ruth Dudley: *Patrick Pearse: The Triumph of Failure*. London: Victor Gollancz, 1977.

Eliot, T.S. *The Family Reunion* in *Complete Poems and Plays*. New York: Harcourt, Brace, 1952.

Ellmann, Richard. *The Identity of Yeats*. London: Macmillan, 1954.

——. *James Joyce*. New York: Oxford University Press, 1959.

——. *James Joyce*. 1959. Revised edition, London: Oxford University Press, 1982.

——. *Yeats: The Man and the Masks*. 1948. Reprint New York: E.P. Dutton, n.d.

Faulkner, Peter. *Yeats and the Irish Eighteenth Century*. Dolmen Press Yeats Centenary Papers 5. Dublin: Dolmen Press, 1965.

Ferguson, Samuel. *Poems of Sir Samuel Ferguson*. Dublin: Phoenix, n.d.

Finneran, Richard J., *Editing Yeats's Poems*. London: Macmillan, 1983.

Finneran, Richard J., George Mills Harper and William M. Murphy, eds. *Letters to W.B. Yeats*. 2 vols. New York: Columbia University Press, 1977.

FitzPatrick, William John. 'O'Connor, Roger'. *Dictionary of National Biography*. Vol. 14. Reprint, London: Oxford University Press, 1963–4.

——. *'The Sham Squire' and the Informers of 1798*. Dublin: M.H. Gill, 1895.

Flanagan, Thomas. *The Irish Novelists, 1800–1850*. New York: Columbia University Press, 1959.

Forster, E.M. *Pharos and Pharillon*. 1923. New York: Knopf, 1962.

Fortuna, Diane. 'The Labyrinth as Controlling Image in Joyce's *A Portrait of the Artist as a Young Man'*. *Bulletin of the New York Public Library* 76 (1972): 120–80.

Frank, Peter, ed. *Treasures of the Library, Trinity College Dublin.* Dublin: Royal Irish Academy, for Trinity College, Dublin, 1986.

Frazer, James. *The Golden Bough: A Study in Magic and Religion.* London: Macmillan, 1911–15.

Friel, Brian. *Translations.* London: Faber, 1981.

Garvin, John. *James Joyce's Disunited Kingdom and the Irish Dimension.* Dublin: Gill & Macmillan, 1976.

Gifford, Don. *Joyce Annotated.* Second edition. Berkeley: University of California Press, 1982.

Gifford, Don, with Robert J. Siedman. *Notes for Joyce.* New York: Dutton, 1974.

Gilbert, Sandra M. and Susan Gubar. *The Madwoman in the Attic: The Woman Writer and the Nineteenth Century Literary Imagination.* New Haven: Yale University Press, 1979.

Glasheen, Adaline. *Third Census of 'Finnegans Wake': An Index of the Characters and their Roles.* Berkeley: University of California Press, 1977.

Glendinning, Victoria. *Elizabeth Bowen.* New York: Knopf, 1978.

Grab, Frederic D. 'Yeats's *King Oedipus'*. *Journal of English and Germanic Philology* 71:3 (July 1972): 336–54.

Greene, David H. and Edward M. Stephens. *J.M. Synge 1871–1909.* New York: Macmillan, 1959.

Gregory, Lady. *Arabi and his Household.* London: Kegan Paul, Trench, 1882.

——. *Cuchulain of Muirthemne.* 1902. Reprint Gerrards Cross: Colin Smythe, 1976.

——. *Gods and Fighting Men.* 1904. Reprint Gerrards Cross: Colin Smythe, 1970.

——. *Our Irish Theatre.* 1913. Reprint New York: Capricorn, 1965.

——. *Seventy Years: Being the Autobiography of Lady Gregory.* Ed. Colin Smythe. Gerrards Cross: Colin Smythe, 1974.

Griffin, Gerald. *The Rivals* and *Tracy's Ambition.* Ed. John Cronin. C.E.R.I.U.L. Irish and Anglo-Irish Texts. Lille: Publications de l'Université de Lille, n.d.

Guthrie, Tyrone. Interview. Annaghmakerrig, County Monaghan, July 1958.

Harden, Elizabeth. *Maria Edgeworth.* Boston: Twayne, 1984.

Harris, Daniel A. *Yeats, Coole Park and Ballylee.* Baltimore: Johns Hopkins University Press, 1974.

Harrison, Jane Ellen. *Themis: A Study of the Social Origins of Greek Religion.* 1912. 2nd revised edition Cambridge: Cambridge University Press, 1927.

Hart, Clive. *A Concordance to 'Finnegans Wake'.* Minneapolis: University of Minnesota Press, 1963.

Heaney, Seamus. *Poems 1965–1975.* New York: Farrar, Straus & Giroux, 1980.

Heath, William. *Elizabeth Bowen: An Introduction to Her Novels.* Madison: University of Wisconsin Press, 1961.

Henn, T.R. *The Lonely Tower: Studies in the Poetry of W.B. Yeats.* 1950. Second edition, London: Methuen, 1965.

Hill, Robert W., Jr. ed. *Tennyson's Poetry.* New York: Norton, 1971.

Holloway, Joseph. *Joseph Holloway's Irish Theatre,* ed. Robert Hogan and Michael J. O'Neill. Volume III, 1938–1944. Dixon, California: 1970.

Hone, Joseph. *W.B. Yeats.* 1943. Reprint Harmondsworth: Penguin, 1971.

———. 'Yeats as Political Philosopher'. *London Mercury* 39:233 (March 1939): 492–6.

Howe, P.P. *J.M. Synge: A Critical Study.* 1912. Reprint New York: Haskell, 1968.

Hurst, Michael. *Maria Edgeworth and the Public Scene: Intellect, Fine Feeling and Landlordism in the Age of Reform.* London: Macmillan, 1969.

Hyde, Douglas. *A Literary History of Ireland.* 1899. London: Ernest Benn, 1967.

———. *Language, Lore and Lyrics: Essays and Lectures.* Ed. Breandán O'Conaire. Blackrock, Co. Dublin: Irish Academic Press, 1986.

Inglis, Brian. *Roger Casement.* London: Coronet Books, 1974.

The Irish Times, 14 June 1935.

James, Henry. *The Art of the Novel: Critical Prefaces.* Ed. R.P. Blackmuir New York: Charles Scribner's Sons, 1934.

———. 'The Lesson of the Master' (1888). *The Complete Tales of Henry James.* Ed. Leon Edel. Vol. 7 (1888–1891). Philadelphia: Lippincott, 1963.

———. 'The Romance of Certain Old Clothes' (1868). *The Complete Tales of Henry James.* Ed. Leon Edel. Vol. 1 (1864–1868). Philadelphia: Lippincott, 1962.

James, M.R. Introduction to *Ghosts and Marvels: A Selection of Uncanny Tales from Daniel Defoe to Algernon Blackwood.* Ed. V.H. Collins. Oxford: Oxford University Press, 1924.

Jebb, Richard C. *The Tragedies of Sophocles.* Cambridge: Cambridge University Press, 1917.

Jeffares, A. Norman. *A Commentary on the Collected Poems of W.B. Yeats.* Stanford, California: Stanford University Press, 1968.

———. *W.B. Yeats, Man and Poet.* New Haven: Yale University Press, 1949.

Jones, Ernest. *On the Nightmare.* 1931. Revised 1951. Reprint New York: Liveright, 1971.

Joyce, James. *The Critical Writings of James Joyce.* Ed. Ellsworth Mason and Richard Ellmann. New York: Viking Press, 1964.

———. *Dubliners.* 1916. Ed. Robert Scholes and A. Walton Litz. New York: Viking, 1969.

———. *Finnegans Wake.* 1939. New York: Viking Press, 1971.

———. *Letters.* Volume I, Ed. Stuart Gilbert. New York: Viking Press, 1957.

———. *Letters.* Volumes II and III, Ed. Richard Ellmann. New York: Viking Press, 1966.

———. *A Portrait of the Artist as a Young Man.* 1916. Ed. Chester G. Anderson. New York: Viking Press, 1968.

———. *Stephen Hero.* Ed. Theodore Spencer 1944, revised John J. Slocum and Herbert Cahoon. London: Paladin, 1991.

———. *Ulysses*. 1922. Ed. Hans Walter Gabler with Wolfhard Steppe and Clause Melchior. New York: Vintage, 1986.

Joyce, P.W. *English as We Speak it in Ireland*. Ed. Terence Dolan. 1910. Dublin: Wolfhound Press, 1979.

———. *The Origin and History of Irish Names of Places*. 3 vols. 1 and 2, Dublin: McGlashan & Gill, 1869–70. Vol. 3, Dublin: Gill, 1913.

Kearney, Richard, ed. *The Irish Mind: Exploring Intellectual Traditions*. Dublin: Wolfhound, 1985.

Keating, Geoffrey [Ceitinn, Seathrun]. *Foras Feasa ar Eirinn/The History of Ireland*. Ed. and trans. Patrick S. Dinneen. Vol. 2 (Irish Texts Society Vol. 8). London: Irish Texts Society, 1908.

Kee, Robert. *The Green Flag: Volume II, The Bold Fenian Men*. London: Quartet Books, 1976.

Kelleher, John V. 'Irish History and Mythology in James Joyce's "The Dead"'. *Review of Politics* 27 (1965): 414–33.

Kenney, Edwin J., Jr. *Elizabeth Bowen*. Lewisburg, Pennsylvania: Bucknell University Press, 1975.

Kermode, Frank. *Romantic Image*. London: Routledge & Kegan Paul, 1966.

Kinsella, Thomas. 'The Irish Writer'. *Davis, Mangan, Ferguson?: Tradition and the Irish Writer*. Writings by W.B. Yeats and Thomas Kinsella. Tower Series of Anglo-Irish Studies 2. Dublin: Dolmen, 1970.

Kohn, Leo. *The Constitution of the Irish Free State*. London: George Allen & Unwin, 1932.

Lawson, John Cuthbert. *Modern Greek Folklore and Ancient Greek Religion*. Cambridge: Cambridge University Press, 1910.

Leabhar Gabhála: The Book of Conquests of Ireland. Ed. and trans. R.A. Stewart Macalister and John Mac Neill. Part 1 (all published). Dublin: Hodges, Figgis, 1916.

Leavis, F.R. 'Joyce and "The Revolution of the Word"'. *Scrutiny* 2.2 (September 1933): 193–201.

Lebor Gabála Érenn. Ed. and trans. R.A.S. Macalister. 5 vols. Dublin: Irish Texts Society, 1938–56.

Lecky, W.E.H. *A History of Ireland in the Eighteenth Century*. 5 vols. 1892. Repr. New York: AMS Press, 1969.

Lee, Hermione. *Elizabeth Bowen: An Estimation*. London: Vision Press, 1981.

Le Fanu, Joseph Sheridan. *Ghost Stories and Mysteries*. Ed. E.F. Bleiler. New York: Dover, 1975.

———. *In a Glass Darkly*. Ed. Robert Tracy. Oxford: Oxford University Press, 1993.

———. *The Poems of Joseph Sheridan Le Fanu*. Ed. Alfred Perceval Graves. London: Downey and Co., 1896.

———. *The Purcell Papers*. Ed. Alfred Perceval Graves. 1880. 3 vols. Facsimile reprint New York: Garland, 1979.

———. *Uncle Silas.*, Ed. W.J. McCormack with Andrew Swarbrick. Oxford University Press, 1981.

Le Fanu, T.P. *Memoir of the Le Fanu Family*. Privately printed, 1924.

Le Fanu, W.R. *Seventy Years of Irish Life*. New York: Macmillan, 1894.

Lemesurier, Peter. *The Great Pyramid Decoded*. Shaftesbury: Longmead, 1977.

Lever, Charles. *Luttrell of Arran*. 1863–5. Reprint Boston: Little Brown, 1907.

Levin, Harry. *James Joyce: a Critical Introduction*. 1941. Revised edition Norfolk, Connecticut: New Directions, 1960.

Longford, The Earl of, and Thomas P. O'Neill. *Eamon de Valera*. Boston: Houghton, 1971.

Lover, Samuel. *Legends and Stories of Ireland, First Series*. 1832. Boston: Little, Brown, 1893.

——. *Second Series*. 1834. Boston: Little, Brown, 1893.

Lyons, F.S.L. *Charles Stewart Parnell*. New York: Oxford University Press, 1977.

——. *Culture and Anarchy in Ireland 1890–1939*. Oxford: Oxford University Press, 1982.

——. *Ireland Since the Famine*. London: Fontana, 1973.

Lysaght, Patricia. *The Banshee: The Irish Supernatural Death-Messenger*. Dublin: Glendale Press, 1986.

——. 'Fairylore from the Midlands of Ireland'. *The Good People: New Fairylore Essays*. Ed. Peter Narváez. New York: Garland, 1991 (1991a), pp. 22–46.

——. '"Is There Anyone Here to Serve My Mass?": the Legend of "The Dead Priest's Midnight Mass" in Ireland.' *Scandinavian Yearbook of Folklore* 47 (1991) (1991b): 193–207.

MacCabe, Colin. *James Joyce and the Revolution of the Word*. London: Macmillan, 1978.

Mac Cana, Proinsias. *Celtic Mythology*. New York: Peter Bedrick, 1983.

McCann, Sean, ed. *The Story of the Abbey Theatre*. London: New English Library.

McCormack, W.J. *Ascendancy and Tradition in Anglo-Irish Literary History from 1789 to 1939*. Oxford: Clarendon Press, 1985.

——. *Sheridan Le Fanu and Victorian Ireland*. Oxford: Clarendon Press, 1980.

MacDonagh, Oliver. *O'Connell: The Life of Daniel O'Connell 1775–1847*. London: Weidenfeld & Nicolson, 1991.

McHugh, Roland. *Annotations to 'Finnegans Wake'*. Baltimore: Johns Hopkins University Press, 1980.

——. *The Sigla of 'Finnegans Wake'*. Austin: University of Texas Press, 1976.

Mac Liammóir, Micheál. Introduction. *The Happy Prince and Other Stories*. By Oscar Wilde. Harmondsworth, Middlesex: Penguin/Puffin, 1965.

MacLysaght, Edward. *The Surnames of Ireland*. Shannon: Irish University Press, 1969.

Madden, Richard R. *The United Irishmen, Their Lives and Times*. Second Series, second edition. Dublin: James Duffy, 1858.

Maddox, Brenda. *Nora: the Real Life of Molly Bloom*. Boston: Houghton Mifflin, 1988.

Manganiello, Dominic. *Joyce's Politics*. London: Routledge & Kegan Paul, 1980.

Masefield, John. *John M. Synge: A Few Personal Recollections*. New York: Macmillan, 1915.

'Mass, Sacrifice of the'. *Catholic Encyclopedia* 10. New York, 1913.

Mercier, Vivian. *Beckett/Beckett*. New York: Oxford University Press, 1977.

——. *The Irish Comic Tradition*. Oxford: Clarendon Press, 1965.

Missale Romanum ex Decreto Sacrosancti Concilii Tridentini. Ratisbon/Rome/ New York 1898.

Montessori, Maria. *The Montessori Method*. Trans. Anne E. George. 1912. Reprint New York: Schocken, 1964.

Moore, George. *A Drama in Muslin*. 1886. Gerrards Cross: Colin Smythe, 1981.

——. *Hail and Farewell*. London: Heinemann, 1933.

Moore, John Rees. *Masks of Love and Death: Yeats as Dramatist*. Ithaca, New York: Cornell University Press, 1971.

Morgan, Lady [Sydney Owenson]. *Florence Macarthy: An Irish Tale*. 1818. 4 vols. Facsimile reprint New York: Garland, 1979.

——. *The O'Briens and the O'Flahertys; A National Tale*. 1827. 4 vols. Facsimile reprint New York: Garland, 1979.

——. *O'Donnel; A National Tale*. 1814. 3 vols. Facsimile reprint New York: Garland, 1979.

——. *The Wild Irish Girl; A National Tale*. 1806. 3 vols. Facsimile reprint New York: Garland, 1979.

Murphy, Richard. Interview. *The Irish Times*, 17 May 1973, p. 12.

Murray, Gilbert. *Oedipus, King of Thebes*. New York: Oxford University Press, 1911.

Murray, Patrick Joseph. *The Life of John Banim*. 1857. 1 vol. Facsimile reprint New York: Garland, 1978.

Newcomer, James. *Maria Edgeworth*. Lewisburg: Bucknell University Press, 1973.

——. *Maria Edgeworth the Novelist 1767–1849: A Bicentennial Study*. Fort Worth: Texas Christian University Press, 1967.

Nowlan, Kevin B., ed. *The Making of 1916: Studies in the History of the Rising*. Dublin: Stationery Office, 1969.

O'Callaghan, Margaret. 'Language, Nationality and Cultural Identity in the Irish Free State, 1922–7: the *Irish Statesman* and the *Catholic Bulletin* Reappraised'. *Irish Historical Studies* 24:94 (November 1984): 226–45.

O'Casey, Sean. *Autobiography, Book 4: Inishfallen, Fare Thee Well*. 1949. Reprint London: Pan, 1972.

——. *Blasts and Benedictions*. London: Macmillan, 1967.

O'Connor, Frank, tr. *Kings, Lords, and Commons: An Anthology from the Irish*. New York: Knopf, 1959.

O'Connor, [Roger]. *Chronicles of Eri; Being the History of the Gaal Sciot Iber: or, The Irish People.* 2 vols. London, 1822.

O'Conor, Charles [of Belanagare]. *Dissertations on the Antient History of Ireland.* Dublin, 1753.

Ó Cuív, Brian, ed. *A View of the Irish Language.* Dublin: Stationery Office, 1969.

[O'Donoghue, David James]. 'George Nugent Reynolds'. *Dictionary of National Biography.*

O'Donovan Rossa, Diarmuid. *Rossa's Recollections 1838–1898.* 1898. Shannon: Irish University Press, 1972.

O'Faolain, Sean. 'Almost Music'. *Hound and Horn* 2.2 (January-March 1929): 178–80.

———. *The Vanishing Hero: Studies in Novelists of the Twenties.* London: Eyre & Spottiswoode, 1956.

O Hehir, Brendan. 'The Christian Revision of *Eachtra Airt meic Cuind ocus Tochmarc Delbchaime Ingine Morgain*', *Celtic Folklore and Christianity: Studies in Memory of William W. Heist.* Ed. Patrick J. Ford. Santa Barbara, California: McNally & Loftin, 1983, pp. 159–79.

———. *A Gaelic Lexicon for 'Finnegans Wake'.* Berkeley and Los Angeles: University of California Press, 1967.

Ó Súilleabháin, Seán. *A Handbook of Irish Folklore.* Dublin, 1942. Reprint Hatboro, Pennsylvania: Folklore Associates, 1963.

———. and Reidar Th. Christiansen. *The Types of the Irish Folktale.* Helsinki: Finnish Folklore Commission, 1963.

O'Sullivan, Donal. *Carolan: The Life, Times, and Music of an Irish Harper.* London: Routledge & Kegan Paul, 1958.

———. *The Irish Free State and its Senate: A Study in Contemporary Politics.* London: Faber, 1940.

Owens, Cóilín. *Family Chronicles: Maria Edgeworth's 'Castle Rackrent'.* Dublin: Wolfhound, 1987.

Pakenham, Thomas. *The Year of Liberty: The Story of the Great Irish Rebellion of 1798.* 1969. Reprint London: Panther, 1972.

Parkinson, Thomas. *W.B. Yeats: The Later Poetry.* Berkeley: University of California Press, 1964.

Pearce, Donald R., Ed. *The Senate Speeches of W.B. Yeats.* Bloomington: Indiana University Press, 1960.

Pearse, Padraic H. *Collected Works: Plays, Stories, Poems.* Dublin: Maunsel and Company, 1918.

———. *Collected Works: Political Writings and Speeches.* Dublin: Maunsel and Roberts, 1922.

———. *Collected Works: Scríbhinní.* Dublin and Cork: Phoenix Publishing Co., n.d.

———. *The Letters of P.H. Pearse.* Ed. Séamas Ó Buachalla. Gerrards Cross: Colin Smythe, 1980.

———. *The Literary Writings of Patrick Pearse.* Ed. Séamas Ó Buachalla. Dublin and Cork: Mercier, 1979.

Porter, Raymond J. *P.H. Pearse*. New York: Twayne, 1973.
Power, Arthur. *Conversations with James Joyce*. Ed. Clive Hart. Chicago: University of Chicago Press, 1982.
Ransom, John Crowe. *The World's Body*. New York: Charles Scribner's Sons,1938.
Ridgeway, William. *The Origin of Tragedy*. 1910. Reprint New York: Benjamin Blom, 1966.
[Ridgeway, William]. *A Report of the Trial of Roger O'Connor, Esq., and Martin M'Keon at the Trim Summer Assizes, 1817*. Dublin, 1817.
Robinson, Lennox. *Selected Plays of Lennox Robinson*. Ed. Christopher Murray. Gerrards Cross: Colin Smythe, 1982.
Rose, Danis. *Chapters of Coming Forth by Day*. *Wake Newslitter* Monograph 6. Colchester: A Wake Newslitter Press, 1982.
Ryan, Desmond. *The Fenian Chief: A Biography of James Stephens*. Dublin and Sydney: Gill & Son, 1967.
Ryan, John, ed. *A Bash in the Tunnel: James Joyce by the Irish*. London: Clifton Books, 1970.
Sage, Victor. *Horror Fiction in the Protestant Tradition*. New York: St Martin's Press, 1988.
Scott, Sir Walter. *Waverley*. London: Oxford University Press, 1909.
Sellery, J'nan and William O. Harris. *Elizabeth Bowen: A Biblio- graphy*. Austin: Humanities Research Center, University of Texas, 1981.
Shaw, Bernard. 'Preface for Politicians' (1906) to *John Bull's Other Island*. *Complete Plays with Prefaces*. Vol. 2. New York: Dodd, Mead, 1963.
Sheehan, Canon P[atrick] A. *My New Curate*. 1898. Cork: Mercier Press, 1989.
Skene, Reg. *The Cuchulain Plays of W.B. Yeats: A Study*. New York: Columbia University Press, 1974.
Slocum, John J. and Herbert Cahoon. *A Bibliography of James Joyce [1882–1941]*. New Haven: Yale University Press, 1953.
Sophocles. *Sophoclis Fabulae*. Ed. Hugh Lloyd-Jones and N.G. Wilson. Oxford: Clarendon Press, 1990.
Stallworthy, Jon, ed. *Yeats's 'Last Poems': a Casebook*. London: Macmillan, 1968.
Stanford, W.B. 'Yeats in the Irish Senate'. *Review of English Literature* 4:3 (July 1963):71–80.
Stevenson, Lionel. *The Wild Irish Girl: The Life of Sydney Owenson, Lady Morgan*. London: Chapman & Hall, 1936.
Stoker, Bram. *Dracula's Guest and Other Weird Stories*. London: George Routledge, 1914.
Strong, L.A.G. *John Millington Synge*. London: George Allen & Unwin, 1941.
Sullivan, T.D., A.M., and D.B., eds. *Speeches from the Dock*. Revised edition. Dublin: Gill & Macmillan, 1968.
Sultan, Stanley. *Yeats at his Last*. New Yeats Papers XI. Dublin: Dolmen Press, 1975.

Swedenborg, Emanuel, *Arcana Caelestia*. 10 vols. New York: American Swedenborg Printing and Publishing Society, 1870.

Synge, John M. *The Aran Islands and Other Writings*. Ed. Robert Tracy. New York: Vintage, 1962.

——. *Collected Works*. IV. *Plays*, Book 2. Ed. Ann Saddlemyer. London: Oxford University Press, 1968.

Tennyson, Hallam. *Alfred Lord Tennyson: A Memoir*. 2 vols. New York: Macmillan, 1897.

Thompson, Stith. *Motif-Index of Folk Literature*. Revised edition. Bloomington: University of Indiana Press, 1957.

Thompson, William Irwin. *The Imagination of an Insurrection, Dublin, Easter 1916: A Study of an Ideological Movement*. 1967. New York: Harper, 1972.

The Times (London), 31 July 1911; 14 December 1911; 16 January 1912; 30 November 1922, 13f..

Torchiana, Donald T. '"Among School Children" and the Education of the Irish Spirit'. *In Excited Reverie: A Centenary Tribute to William Butler Yeats 1865–1939*. Ed. A. Norman Jeffares and K.G.W. Cross. New York: Macmillan, 1965, pp. 123–50.

——. *Backgrounds for Joyce's Dubliners*. Boston: Allen & Unwin, 1986.

——. *W.B Yeats and Georgian Ireland*. Evanston: Northwestern University Press, 1966.

Tracy, Robert. 'Joyce and Old Irish in *Ulysses*' (review of Tymoczko, *The Irish Ulysses*). *Irish Literary Supplement* 14:1 (Spring 1995): 26–7.

——. 'Leopold Bloom Fourfold: a Hellenic-Hibernian-Hungarian-Hebraic Hero'. *Massachusetts Review* 6 (1965): 523–38.

——. 'Loving You All Ways: Vamps, Vampires, Necrophiles and Necrofilles in Nineteenth-Century Fiction'. *Sex and Death in Victorian Literature*. Ed. Regina Barreca. London: Macmillan, 1990, pp. 32–59.

Trevor, William. 'Between Holyhead and Dun Laoghaire'. *Times Literary Supplement* (6 February 1981): 131.

Troy, Mark L. *Mummeries of Resurrection: The Cycle of Osiris in 'Finnegans Wake'*. Uppsala: Acta Universitatis Upsaliensis, *Studia Anglistica Upsaliensia* 26, 1976.

Tymoczko, Maria. *The Irish Ulysses*. Berkeley/Los Angeles: University of California Press, 1994.

Uí Ógáin, Ríonach and Anne O'Connor. '"*Spor ar an gCois is gan an Chos Ann*"': A Study of "The Dead Lover's Return" in Irish Tradition'. *Béaloideas* 51 (1983): 126–44.

Ure, Peter. *Towards a Mythology*. 1946. Reprint New York: Russell & Russell, 1967.

Vallancey, Charles. *Essay on the Antiquity of the Irish Language*. Dublin, 1772.

Wade, Allan. *A Bibliography of the Writings of W.B. Yeats*. London: Rupert Hart-Davis, 1958.

Webb, Alfred. *Compendium of Irish Biography*. Dublin, 1878.

Wilde, Oscar. *De Profundis*. New York: Vintage Books, 1964.
———. *The Picture of Dorian Gray*. Ed. Donald L. Lawler. New York: Norton, 1988.
Wilson, A.N. Introduction to *Dracula* by Bram Stoker. Oxford: Oxford University Press, 1983.
Wright, Doris T. 'Vladímir Propp and *Dubliners*'. *James Joyce Quarterly* 23:4 (Summer 1986): 415–33.
Yeats, W.B. *Autobiography*. New York: Collier Books, 1971.
———. *The Collected Letters of W.B. Yeats: Volume One, 1865–1894*. Ed. John Kelly. London: Oxford University Press, 1985.
———. *A Critical Edition of Yeats's 'A Vision' (1925)*. Ed. George Mills Harper and Walter Kelly Hood. London: Macmillan, 1978.
———. *The Death of Cuchulain: Manuscript Materials, Including the Author's Final Text*. Ed. Phillip L. Marcus. Ithaca: Cornell University Press, 1982.
———. *Essays and Introductions*. New York: Collier, 1968.
———. *Explorations*. Selected by Mrs W.B. Yeats. New York: Collier, 1973.
———. *Fairy and Folktales of Ireland*. Ed. W.B. Yeats. 1888–92. Reprint Gerrards Cross: Colin Smythe, 1973.
———. Introduction to *The Oxford Book of Modern Verse*. Chosen by W.B. Yeats. New York: Oxford University Press, 1937.
———. *John Sherman* and *Dhoya*. Ed. Richard J. Finneran. New York: Macmillan, 1991.
———. *Last Poems and Plays*. London: Macmillan, 1940.
———. *Last Poems and Two Plays*. Dublin: Cuala Press, 1939.
———. *The Letters of W.B. Yeats*. Ed. Allan Wade. London: Rupert Hart-Davis, 1954.
———. *Letters on Poetry from W.B. Yeats to Dorothy Wellesley*. 1940. Reprint London: Oxford University Press, 1964.
———. *Letters to the New Island*. Ed. George Bornstein and Hugh Witemeyer. London: Macmillan, 1989.
———. *Memoirs*. Ed. Denis Donoghue. New York: Macmillan, 1973.
———. 'Modern Ireland: An Address to American Audiences 1932–1933'. *Massachusetts Review* 5:2 (Winter 1964), 256–68.
———. *Mythologies*. New York: Collier Books, 1969.
———. *On the Boiler*. Dublin: Cuala Press, n.d. [1939].
———. Preface to *Cuchulain of Muirthemne* by Lady Gregory. 1902. Reprint Gerrards Cross: Colin Smythe, 1976.
———. Preface to *Gods and Fighting Men* by Lady Gregory. 1904. Reprint Gerrards Cross: Colin Smythe, 1976.
———. *Purgatory: Manuscript Material, Including the Author's Final Text*. Ed. Sandra F.Siegel. Ithaca: Cornell University Press, 1986.
———. *The Senate Speeches of W.B. Yeats*. Ed. Donald R. Pearce. Bloomington: Indiana University Press, 1960.
———. *Synge and the Ireland of his Time*. Dublin: Cuala Press, 1911. Reprinted in *Essays and Introductions*.

——. *Uncollected Prose by W.B. Yeats.* Ed. John P. Frayne. 2 vols. New York: Columbia University Press, 1970–76.

——. *The Variorum Edition of the Plays of W.B. Yeats.* Ed. Russell K. Alspach. New York: Macmillan, 1966.

——. *The Variorum Edition of the Poems of W.B. Yeats.* Ed. Peter Allt and Russell K. Alspach. New York: Macmillan,. 1957.

——. *A Vision.* 1937. Reprint. New York: Collier, 1966.

Young, David. *Troubled Mirror: A Study of Yeats's 'The Tower'.* Iowa City: University of Iowa Press, 1987.

Zimmermann, Georges-Denis. *Songs of Irish Rebellion: Political Street Ballads and Rebel Songs.* Dublin: Allen Figgis, 1967.

Index